Schumann's Music and E. T. A. Hoffmann's Fiction

Four of Schumann's great masterpieces of the 1830s – *Carnaval, Fantasiestücke, Kreisleriana* and *Nachtstücke* – are connected to the fiction of E. T. A. Hoffmann. In this book, John MacAuslan traces Schumann's stylistic shifts during this period to offer insights into the expressive musical patterns that give shape, energy and individuality to each work. MacAuslan also relates the works to Schumann's reception of Bach, Beethoven, Novalis and Jean Paul, and focuses on primary sources in his wide-ranging discussion of the broader intellectual and aesthetic contexts. Uncovering lines of influence from Schumann's reading to his writings, and reflecting on how the aesthetic concepts involved might be used today, this book transforms the way Schumann's music and its literary connections can be understood and will be essential reading for musicologists, performers and listeners with an interest in Schumann, early nineteenth-century music and German Romantic culture.

JOHN MACAUSLAN is an independent scholar who worked for many years in HM Treasury, at the National Gallery and as a Civil Service Commissioner, followed by ongoing work for the NGO 'War Child', concurrently with his PhD in music.

Schumann's Music and E. T. A. Hoffmann's Fiction

JOHN MACAUSLAN

CAMBRIDGE
UNIVERSITY PRESS

University Printing House, Cambridge CB2 8BS, United Kingdom

Cambridge University Press is part of the University of Cambridge.

It furthers the University's mission by disseminating knowledge in the pursuit of education, learning and research at the highest international levels of excellence.

www.cambridge.org
Information on this title: www.cambridge.org/9781107141230

© John MacAuslan 2016

This publication is in copyright. Subject to statutory exception and to the provisions of relevant collective licensing agreements, no reproduction of any part may take place without the written permission of Cambridge University Press.

First published 2016

Printed in the United Kingdom by TJ International Ltd. Padstow Cornwall

A catalogue record for this publication is available from the British Library

Library of Congress Cataloguing in Publication data
MacAuslan, John, 1953–
Schumann's music and E. T. A. Hoffmann's fiction / John MacAuslan.
Cambridge, United Kingdom : Cambridge University Press, 2016.
Includes bibliographical references and index.
LCCN 2015041125 | ISBN 9781107141230
LCSH: Schumann, Robert, 1810–1856 – Criticiam and interpretation.
Hoffmann, E. T. A. (Ernst Theodor Amadeus), 1776–1822 – Influence.
Music – Philosophy and aesthetics.
LCC ML410.S4 M178 2016 | DDC 780.92–dc23
LC record available at http://lccn.loc.gov/2015041125

ISBN 978-1-107-14123-0 Hardback

Cambridge University Press has no responsibility for the persistence or accuracy of URLs for external or third-party internet websites referred to in this publication, and does not guarantee that any content on such websites is, or will remain, accurate or appropriate.

Contents

List of figures [*page* vi]
List of music examples [vii]
Acknowledgments [x]

Introduction [1]
1 Chrysalis, 1827–1834: Schumann's emergence as a literary composer [9]
2 Notions of resonance and expression [27]
3 A musical carnival, 1834–1837: *Carnaval*, op. 9 [34]
4 Form, content and conception [70]
5 Dream images, 1837: *Fantasiestücke*, op. 12 [91]
6 'In possession of the secret', 1836–1838: Schumann's stylistic evolution [125]
7 New worlds, 1838: *Kreisleriana*, op. 16 [141]
8 Associations and expressiveness in Schumann's 'Hoffmann works' [174]
9 Antimatter, 1839–1840: *Nachtstücke*, op. 23 [194]
10 'The closed book': interpreting aesthetic entities [223]

Appendices [240]
  1 Concordance of citations from Novalis [240]
  2 Novalis and the Schumann of 1828 [244]
  3 Extracts from selected German original texts [244]
Bibliography [257]
Index [275]

Figures

3.1 'The Minuet', or 'Carnival Scene', G. D. Tiepolo, Musée du Louvre, with permission [*page* 36]
3.2 'The Charlatan', G. D. Tiepolo, fresco, 1757, Vicenza, Villa Valmarana, with permission [37]
3.3 'The Dance', after Callot (detail) [66]
3.4 'Undying Fealty', after Callot (detail) [67]
3.5 'She Knew How to Encircle Him', after Callot (detail) [68]
5.1 Goethe, 'Hexenszene', 1776–8, Klassik Stiftung Weimar, Inventar-Nr. GGz/0851, with permission [111]

Music examples

1.1 Schumann, *Papillons*, vi, bars 1–14   [*page* 18]
1.2 Schumann, *Intermezzi*, iv   [23]
1.3 Schumann, *Intermezzi*, i, bars 1–25   [24]
1.4 Schumann, *Intermezzi*, v, bars 132–6   [25]
3.1 Schumann, *Carnaval*, 'Préambule', bars 1–6   [41]
3.2 Schumann, *Carnaval*, 'Préambule', bars 7–18   [42]
3.3 Schumann, *Carnaval*, 'Préambule', bars 56–62   [44]
3.4 Schumann, *Carnaval*, 'Préambule', bars 71–6   [45]
3.5 Schumann, *Carnaval*, 'Préambule', bars 114–39   [46]
3.6 Schumann, *Carnaval*, 'Marche', bars 107–12   [47]
3.7 Schumann, *Carnaval*, 'Valse Noble', bars 27–40   [50]
3.8 Schumann, *Carnaval*, 'Promenade', bars 1–7   [61]
3.9 Schumann, *Carnaval*, 'Promenade', bars 68–93   [62]
5.1 Schumann, *Fantasiestücke*, i, bars 17–24   [95]
5.2 Schumann, *Fantasiestücke*, ii, bars 1–8   [97]
5.3 Schumann, *Fantasiestücke*, ii, bars 72–6   [97]
5.4 (a) Schumann, *Fantasiestücke*, ii, bars 94–116   [98]
     (b) Beethoven, Piano Sonata, op. 53 ('Waldstein'), i, retransition   [99]
5.5 Schumann, *Fantasiestücke*, iii, bars 1–8   [101]
5.6 Schumann, *Fantasiestücke*, iii, bars 26–42   [102]
5.7 Schumann, *Fantasiestücke*, iv, bars 61–75   [103]
5.8 Schumann, *Fantasiestücke*, v, bars 1–8   [106]
5.9 Schumann, *Fantasiestücke*, v, bars 77–84   [107]
5.10 Beethoven, Piano Sonata, op. 2.1, iv:
     (a) opening   [108]
     (b) retransition   [108]
     (c) end   [109]
5.11 Schumann, *Fantasiestücke*, vi, bars 60–7   [113]
5.12 Schumann, *Fantasiestücke*, vii, bars 1–31   [117]
5.13 Schumann, *Fantasiestücke*, vii, bars 63–94   [118]
5.14 Schumann, *Fantasiestücke*, viii, bars 1–16   [120]

5.15 Zumsteeg, *Lenore*, page 29   [121]
6.1 Schumann, *Davidsbündlertänze*, XVIII, bars 1–10   [132]
6.2 Schumann, *Davidsbündlertänze*, XVII, bars 30–50   [133]
6.3 Beethoven, Piano Sonata in A major, op. 101, iii, bars 9–18   [134]
7.1 'Ah vous dirai-je, maman'   [151]
7.2 Bach, 'Goldberg' Variations, 'Quodlibet', bars 1–4   [151]
7.3 Schumann, *Kreisleriana*, i, bars 1–4, from first edition   [154]
7.4 Schumann, *Kreisleriana*, i, bars 9–14   [154]
7.5 Mozart, Variations, K 265, VIII, bars 9–12   [155]
7.6 Schumann, *Kreisleriana*, i, bars 25–6   [155]
7.7 Bach, 'Goldberg' Variations, XXIX, bars 17–18   [155]
7.8 Schumann, *Kreisleriana*, ii, bars 1–8   [156]
7.9 Schumann, *Kreisleriana*, ii, bars 33–7   [158]
7.10 Schumann, *Kreisleriana*, ii, bars 158–65   [158]
7.11 Schumann, *Kreisleriana*, iii, bars 61–6   [159]
7.12 Schumann, *Kreisleriana*, iii, bars 77–82   [159]
7.13 Schumann, *Kreisleriana*, iv, bars 1–2   [160]
7.14 Schumann, *Kreisleriana*, iv, bars 18–23   [161]
7.15 Schumann, *Kreisleriana*, v, bars 28–36   [162]
7.16 Beethoven, Piano Sonata in A major, op. 101, Vivace alla Marcia, bars 30–3   [163]
7.17 Beethoven, Piano Sonata, op. 111, *Arietta*, bars 16–18   [164]
7.18 Schumann, *Kreisleriana*, vi, bars 21–30   [165]
7.19 Beethoven, Piano Sonata, op. 111, i, bars 17–26   [166]
7.20 Schumann, *Kreisleriana*, vii, bars 1–4   [166]
7.21 (a) Schumann, *Kreisleriana*, vii, bars 9–14   [167]
     (b) Mozart, Symphony, K 550, i, bars 1–3   [167]
7.22 Schumann, *Kreisleriana*, vii, bars 40–2   [168]
7.23 Schumann, *Kreisleriana*, vii, bars 89–116   [169]
7.24 Haydn, String Quartet, op. 76/6, i, bars 1–8   [169]
8.1 Beethoven, *An die ferne Geliebte*, op. 98, bars 266–7   [176]
8.2 Schumann, *Fantasy*, op. 17, i, end   [176]
9.1 Schumann, *Nachtstücke*
    (a) i, bars 1–4   [198]
    (b) ii, bars 1–4   [198]
    (c) iii, bars 1–8   [198]
9.2 Chopin, C minor Prelude, op. 28, bars 1–4   [202]
9.3 Schumann, *Nachtstücke*, i, bars 1–9   [202]

9.4 Schumann, *Nachtstücke*, i, bars 49–60   [203]
9.5 Schumann, *Nachtstücke*, i, bars 93–100   [205]
9.6 Schumann, *Nachtstücke*, ii, bars 1–4   [211]
9.7 Schumann, *Nachtstücke*, ii, bars 20–8   [211]
9.8 Schumann, *Nachtstücke*, ii, bars 71–7   [212]
9.9 Schumann, *Nachtstücke*, iii, bars 1–20   [216]
9.10 Schumann, *Nachtstücke*, iii, bars 165–72   [217]
9.11 Schumann, *Nachtstücke*, iv, bars 1–10   [219]
9.12 Schumann, *Nachtstücke*, iv, bars 21–8   [221]

Acknowledgments

Sources are listed in the bibliography. I am grateful to Henle for their generous permission to reproduce – in Chapters 3, 5, 7 and 9 – excerpts from their editions of the Schumann piano works; and to Dover for acknowledging my right to reproduce examples in Chapters 1, 6 and 8 from their version of the Clara Schumann edition. My thanks go to Edwin Hillier for the care and musical sensitivity he devoted to many of the other music examples.

For citations from the ancient authors, and from Shakespeare and Jean Paul, I have used the editions in the bibliography, but instead of page numbers in those particular editions the footnotes use traditional systems of reference, as they are both precise and indifferent as between editions. I lay weight on the versions of the works of Novalis known to Jean Paul, Hoffmann and Schumann, which differ from modern versions. For convenience, my references are to a modern reproduction of those early versions, but Appendix 1 gives a concordance allowing readers to find the passages in selected early or modern editions. Appendix 2 illustrates the influence of Novalis on the young Schumann, while Appendix 3 gives some key passages (from, for instance, Schumann, Goethe and Hoffmann) in their original German and their context. I give German in the text where translation is particularly difficult, contentious, or inadequate to the connotations of the original; unless otherwise noted, translations are my own, in several cases with invaluable help from Imogen Taylor.

Thomas Synofzik and the staff of the Robert-Schumann-Haus gave me a warm welcome in Zwickau, and were most helpful and courteous in finding material – despite my arriving at a time when work was getting under way on the impressive new edition of Robert and Clara Schumann's complete correspondence. I have used volumes of this that emerged in time; the complete set will be a landmark in Schumann scholarship. (Since it clearly marks the dates of letters, I have given those dates to ease comparison with my references to older editions.)

The staff of Senate House Library in London have been constantly willing to assist. Roger Harmon's generous help is described in Chapter 5. I have benefited from comments by Nicholas Marston and Thomas

Schmidt-Beste (as examiners) on the PhD from which this book is derived; Jeremy Adler kindly commented on the treatment of German writers in that PhD, Lawrence Kramer on a chapter, and Barry Cooper, Judith Chernaik and James Garratt on several drafts. I am most grateful to all of them.

My greatest professional debt is to Laura Tunbridge, my supervisor for the PhD, for her heroic patience, humorous detachment and above all acute but tactful insight.

My debt to my wife is of a different order altogether.

Introduction

This book is about four of Robert Schumann's works of the 1830s in which the writings of E. T. A. Hoffmann play a role. *Carnaval*, op. 9, composed in 1834–7, features contemporary artists and figures from the *commedia dell'arte*, and the combination may be one link to Hoffmann's carnival tale, *Prinzessin Brambilla*. In three other works, Schumann's title echoes that of a book by Hoffmann. His 1837 *Fantasiestücke*, op. 12, recalls Hoffmann's *Fantasiestücke in Callots Manier*; his *Kreisleriana*, op. 16, of 1838, borrows the title of Hoffmann's essays; and his *Nachtstücke*, op. 23, of 1839–40, shares the title of a collection of Hoffmann's stories. These four works, which I shall call Schumann's 'Hoffmann works', are (along with the rather different *Papillons*, op. 2, of 1832) the Schumann works of the time most obviously related to literature; and this book aims to make one sort of sense of each of the four as music, illustrating in new ways how music and literature can enhance one another.

Is another venture into this field needed? The proof of the pudding will be in the eating; but two aspects deserve a mention now. First, studies of Schumann's piano works sometimes assume that all that is at stake in their literary relationships is a marginal or decorative title echoing a work by Hoffmann, or very general similarities of character; others, more or less unreflectively, treat the music as programmatic in some sense; and recently it has become more fashionable to claim that Schumann adopted formal strategies parallel to those in literature. By contrast, studies of the aesthetic standpoints suggested by Schumann's criticism – for instance by Edward Lippman, Constantin Floros, Michael Struck, Ulrich Tadday and Holly Watkins – have explored alternatives to such approaches.[1] But when it comes to interpreting the individual works, Lippman and Tadday explore only the atypical cases of *Papillons* or 'In der Nacht' from the *Fantasiestücke*, which elicit from them (as from others) programmatic interpretations; Floros and Struck look at none of the four 'Hoffmann

---

[1] Lippman, 'Theory and Practice', 310–45; Floros, 'Schumanns musikalische Poetik', 90–104; Struck, 'Litterarischer Eindruck, poetischer Ausdruck'; Tadday, *Das schöne Unendliche*, 101–36; Watkins, *Metaphors of Depth*, chapter 3.

works'; and Watkins, while she interprets the music of two of Schumann's *Nachtstücke* as 'figurative', does not treat the literary connection to Hoffmann as having any more than tenuous significance. This book takes a new path.

Secondly, all four works have appeared difficult, and some have had relatively little attention as musical entities, even in modern times. They attracted only sparse critical comment when new: rarely played in public, and unappealing commercially to publishers.[2] Contemporaries sometimes asked for some words as guides through the music, and Schumann seemed to sympathise.[3] He wrote to a friend, Henriette Voigt, apparently in connection with the *Fantasiestücke*, that some of his music might be 'hard to read ... but once you are on the trail, it's as though it could be no other way'. In a letter to his colleague, Carl Koßmaly, Schumann described 'difficulties in form and content' of his works of the 1830s. They were 'reflections of my turbulent earlier life when man and musician always strove to express themselves simultaneously'. Koßmaly picked up some of these ideas in his 1844 review: Schumann 'loaded [his earlier works] with too much that was pithy, compacted and laden with meaning'. In 1846, Eduard Hanslick described Schumann's works as 'too interior and too strange ... too deep, too simple, too sharp, and too dry'; in 1861, Adolf Schubring judged that the difficulty of Schumann's work was due less to 'form' than to 'the closed book' ('verschlossenes Buch') of their 'content'.[4] By turning in 1840 to writing songs, whose text lies on the face of the score, Schumann in a sense opened the book. But for the 'Hoffmann works' the 'book of their content' remains largely closed, their literary and wider cultural connections scarcely elucidated.

Perhaps as a result, these compositions have had too little attention as musical wholes – two of them almost none. *Carnaval* has fared best of the

---

[2] *Jugendbriefe*, 189 (9 August 1832), 197 (17 December 1832) and 201; *Neue Folge*, 101 (22 September 1837), 109–10 (8 February 1838); *Briefwechsel*, I 146 (16 April 1838) and perhaps 126 (18 March 1838; *Briefedition*, I/4 266 has 'Etüden', not 'Stücken', narrowing the scope of the comment). Compare Brendel, 'Robert Schumann' (1845), 91–2; Kapp, 'Schumann in His Time', 224–5; Newcomb, 'Schumann and the Marketplace', 265–9 and Daverio, *Robert Schumann*, 137; Ferris, 'Public Performance', 381–406.

[3] For instance for *Papillons* (*Allgemeine musikalische Zeitung*, no. 37 (11 September 1833), transcribed in *Tagebücher*, I 432), *Carnaval* (*Zeitung für die Elegante Welt*, no. 185 (22 September 1837), 740, in Schumann *Tagebücher*, II 464–5, note 92, *Briefwechsel*, I 77 (18 January 1838) and II 353 (15 January 1839) and *Briefedition*, I/2 99–100 (11 April 1838)); *GSK*, I 213; *Briefwechsel*, I 75 (5 January 1838).

[4] *Neue Folge*, 121 (11 June 1838), 227, (5 May 1843); Koßmaly, 'Schumann's Claviercompositionen' (1844), 3, 18; Hanslick as translated in Botstein in 'History, Rhetoric and the Self', in Todd, ed., *Schumann and his World*, 4; Schubring, 'Schumanniana No. 4' (1861), 213.

four. This may be because its overall title suggests a familiar context for understanding the music, the relatively concrete titles to the individual pieces provide frequent reorientation, and no overt allusion to a little-known book mystifies audiences. Thus Hans Peter Simonett has written a full treatment of its music, ostensibly from a relatively narrow point of view, though less so in practice – but regrettably it seems scarcely known. Peter Kaminsky traces sources of tonal and motivic coherence across the work, and especially in the pieces between 'Pierrot' and 'Réplique', but does not ask what produces *Carnaval*'s idiosyncratically centrifugal form.[5] There are other partial analyses to which I am indebted: Charles Rosen offers insights into two pieces; and Lawrence Kramer's eclectic musical interpretations bring out cultural associations from the late nineteenth century and later.[6] As for literary connections, Erika Reiman's extended analysis focuses on various parallels of literary strategy with a range of works by Jean Paul, and there have been attempts (to my eye unconvincing) to find a programme from his novel, *Flegeljahre*.[7] An echo of Hoffmann's *Prinzessin Brambilla* has been suggested by at least five modern scholars, although not registered in print outside Italy and France, and not argued in detail even there.[8] Liszt implausibly attached the connection to *Faschingsschwank*, op. 26, perhaps misremembering what he had been told about *Carnaval* (whose title was once to be 'Fasching. Schwänke'); he was probably further confused by haziness about *Prinzessin Brambilla*.[9] He is not alone in that.

The character of the Kreisler of Hoffmann's fictions is familiar enough: in Schumann's words, 'eccentric, wild, inspired'. This opens a field for treatments of Schumann's *Kreisleriana*.[10] Rosen illuminates aesthetic aspects of the music of several pieces; Carey discusses the first two pieces; Münch explores some aspects of improvisation in Hoffmann and Schumann; von Adam-Schmidmeier briefly surveys the whole work.[11]

---

[5] Simonett, 'Taktgruppengliederung' (the only treatment of any of the four works comparable in ambition to Marston, *Schumann: Fantasie* or Appel, 'Schumanns Humoreske'); Kaminsky, 'Principles of Formal Structure', 210–16.
[6] Rosen, *Romantic Generation*, 12–13 and 98–100; Kramer, '*Carnaval*, Cross-Dressing', and 'Rethinking Schumann's *Carnaval*'.
[7] Reiman, *Schumann's Piano Cycles*, chapter 3; Chailley (*Carnaval de Schumann* and 'Zum Symbolismus'); Nattiez, 'Can One Speak of Narrativity in Music?' and Summer, 'Schumann's *Carnaval*'. Appel, 'Carnaval', 53, leaves the question open.
[8] See Chapter 3, footnote 2.   [9] Liszt, 'Robert Schumann', 240.
[10] *Neue Folge*, 148 (15 March 1839). Compare von Seyfried, 'Schumann, *Kreisleriana*', 113–14; Liszt, 'Robert Schumann', 236; Daverio, *Robert Schumann*, 167–9.
[11] Rosen, *Romantic Generation*, 669–83; Carey, 'An Improbable Intertwining', 19–50; Münch, 'Fantasiestücke in Kreislers Manier'; von Adam-Schmidmeier, 'Kreisleriana', 92–8.

Deahl draws out musical features linking the work as a whole, in order to develop a thesis about formal parallels with literature; like others, she relates the music more readily to a novel about Kreisler to which the title does not refer than to a set of essays to which it does.[12]

I know of no attempt to interpret the *Fantasiestücke* that is more than cursory. Rosen's musical analysis of 'Des Abends' is sensitive, but he does not discuss the other pieces in the set.[13] In the prevailing view, the work is an assemblage of pieces linked by shared style and character, and by paired keys; no thread connects the eight pieces' titles, which are more or less incidental, and offer images unrelated to one another; the literary connection is taken to be either very generally stylistic or insignificant, and critics have not tried to say whether the music relates to Hoffmann's *Fantasiestücke in Callots Manier*, or how, or what difference it might make.[14] This may reflect the fact that the overall title is less specific than that of *Carnaval*, providing little context for interpretation, and the titles to the individual pieces less concrete. For this work, however, Schumann provided one piece of guidance that was not too obscure so much as too specific. He suggested to Clara Wieck that the story of Hero and Leander seemed to fit 'In der Nacht';[15] and as a result what critical comment there is often resorts to that piece and that programme, neglecting the rest of the work.[16]

The one dedicated treatment of the *Nachtstücke*, by Moraal, views the work largely in terms of 'narrative strategies' paralleled in Hoffmann's works in general.[17] Otherwise, there was until 2011 very little reception history. Appel gives a few sentences on each piece, and affirms a link to Hoffmann's *Nachtstücke*, but finds it only in bizarre humour while denying any link of content.[18] Others say even less on the music, and offer by way of explanation of the link only very general parallels of spirit – described in terms like 'ghoulish', 'sombre, grotesque, threatening, and deathly', which are most plausible for Schumann's first piece.[19] I am not aware that anyone

---

[12] Deahl, 'Principles of Organisation' (including 97–8), and 'Robert Schumann's *Kreisleriana*', 131–45; Moraal, 'Life and Afterlife', 175–85; Crisp, '*Kreisleriana*', 3–18, who also sees 'some programmatic intent' (13). See also Arnsdorf, 'Schumann's *Kreisleriana*'.

[13] Rosen, *Romantic Generation*, 33–8.

[14] Heller, '*Fantasiestücke*', 68–9; Daverio, *Nineteenth-Century Music*, 49–50 and 67–8; *Robert Schumann*, 156–7. Moraal discusses only a few isolated passages: 'Life and Afterlife', 170–3.

[15] *Briefwechsel*, I 154 (21 April 1838).

[16] Tadday, *Das schöne Unendliche*, 141–2; Jensen, *Schumann*, 165–6 and Meier, *Robert Schumann*, 59–60.

[17] Moraal, 'Schumanns "Nachtstücke"'. [18] Appel, '*Nachtstücke*', 129–31.

[19] Jensen, *Schumann*, 171–2; Daverio, *Robert Schumann*, 180–1, and *Nineteenth-Century Music*, 59. Koßmaly had almost nothing to say: 'Schumanns Claviercompositionen' (1844), 36. Liszt,

has discussed whether the individual titles Schumann considered bear any relationship to Hoffmann. Watkins's 2011 interpretation of the first piece (and its relationship with the last), however, brings out one compelling way of looking at a trajectory in the work.[20] I do not hope to improve on that, but have come at those pieces from a different angle, and added interpretations of the second and third pieces and of the work as a whole. Watkins briefly suggests that the function of the overall title, and the link it creates to Hoffmann's stories, is to 'pay homage to [the] impulse' given to the work by 'the fecundity of Schumann's synesthetic imagination'; but I will go further, trying to clarify the link between these two works in ways that do not apply equally to multitudes of works of music and literature. I explore how Hoffmann's *Nachtstücke* resonate with the music, and how the individual titles Schumann considered for his four pieces relate to Hoffmann's book, in order to bring out what I take to be dense patterns of association between the music and the fiction.

Even in modern times, then, none of Schumann's 'Hoffmann' works has benefited from thorough debate of the sort that has flourished around the *Fantasy*, op. 17.[21] This book aims to show that each work rewards serious attention as a musical whole. It interprets aesthetic patterns giving each work shape, energy and individuality, examining how these are embodied in musical features resonating with aspects of musical and literary culture available to Schumann.[22] In looking at each work, I begin by highlighting musical patterns: selected musical features are described so as to bring out their contributions both to the patterns and to an expressiveness to which Schumann draws explicit attention, for instance in titles. I juxtapose musical interpretations with aspects of Schumann's musical and literary heritage, whether German, English or ancient, bringing to bear a wide range of examples – above all, from Bach, Beethoven, Mozart, Shakespeare, Goethe, Novalis and Jean Paul, as well as Hoffmann. These juxtapositions suggest cultural contexts in which musical features can be understood. The choice of contexts is prompted by and tested against the titles, the expressive nature of the music, and evidence as to Schumann's documented concerns at the time of composition. If then the book uses historical

---

'Robert Schumann' (1855), 237, found some gothic images. See also Herttrich in Schumann *Nachtstücke Opus 23*, Preface, III–IV.

[20] Watkins, *Metaphors of Depth*, 107–13.

[21] See Hoeckner, *Programming the Absolute*, 284 (note 121).

[22] I use the term 'culture' here and later in the book not as an exact concept, but as shorthand for the music, books, visual art, ideas, histories, and other intellectual inhabitants of the different, evolving and by no means solely German worlds at whose cross sections Schumann found himself through his life, and to which he contributed.

data about Schumann, it is to show how the cultural contexts may have mattered to Schumann at the relevant times – not to argue that the music presents autobiography, or that any persona imputed to the music is the historical Robert Schumann.

Each work emerges both in a new light and as it always was; and each is related to a fiction by Hoffmann: *Carnaval* only implicitly, *Kreisleriana* the most pointedly, none exclusively. *Carnaval* appears as a dizzying and exhilarating comedy, in the spirit of the German literary understanding of Italian carnival, and *Fantasiestücke* as a humorous, dreamlike sequence of images, resonating with literary tales of the artist's development, including in Hoffmann's *Fantasiestücke*. Tonal trajectories in *Kreisleriana* resonate with a central aspect of Hoffmann's *Kreisleriana* essays; its melodic patterns appear both in Bach's 'Goldberg' Variations and in trivial variation sets, which figure in the essays as emblems respectively of the profound and the philistine. *Nachtstücke* creates from plain rondos a paradoxically unsettled set, expressive of mental disturbances explored by Hoffmann's book of that name. Each of these four works uses Schumann's musical and literary culture as an echo-chamber in which its music can resonate, its expressive overtones brought out, amplified and given a larger cultural space in which to sound.

This book also reflects in more depth on interpretive concepts involved in its approach, dwelling on the question of how the music and the literature might possibly relate. This does not seem to me to admit of an obvious, definitive or universal answer. Ideally, this book would have expanded its focus to ask whether other works might have the same relationship, whether a general theory is possible, or whether any scholar has adopted concepts like those used here in discussing other works. I have not known how to conduct an exhaustive search, and if anyone has written such a work, my apologies are due. In what Schumann called 'poetic' music, I take form and content as ultimately inseparable, each subject to a musical conception; and I take the music as expressive, and as resonating with Schumann's musical and literary culture through dense webs of associations. Thus in 'poetic' music, 'content' is best treated as a way of talking about expressive aspects of the music – not as a separate schema, adequately specifiable independently, imposed on the music or shaping it (as talk of 'programmes' implies). Accordingly I reflect on how music may paradoxically be more richly associative the more its patterns are its own rather than the servant of something separate.

These reflections are consonant with but not dictated by a reading of Schumann's aesthetics. Schumann never presented a general aesthetic system, so I derive an overall picture from statements of different purposes and contexts; but I hope to avoid the temptation to treat each individual statement as a nugget of lapidary truth, by giving weight to the context of each, and to what he said often and in different ways. I deal largely in Schumann's statements from the period in which his 'Hoffmann works' were composed. This was a period over which his aesthetic presumptions evolved, I will suggest, with a core consistency shaded by changing nuances.

There are then stories to trace. The book takes a broadly chronological approach, aiming to bring out interrelated strands. Schumann's mastery of his compositional craft, his style, his aesthetic aims and his approach to combining literature and music evolved alongside one another over the years after he wrote *Papillons* and the *Intermezzi* in 1831–2. The four 'Hoffmann works' span only five years or so, from 1834–5 to 1839–40, but they show a remarkable ability to move on, never repeating a formula. Their differences may reflect not only the individuality of varied works of art: Schumann's command of musical means grew in power, and his aesthetic aims and compositional style evolved in partial codependence on that growth. The music gained ever greater independence from supporting words, and 'poetic' threads, as Schumann called them, came increasingly to coincide with core musical processes. This seems to have been stimulated at times by repeated absorption in the works of Bach and late Beethoven. A chronological approach brings out too how Schumann's deployment of aesthetic concepts in his criticism evolved in parallel with these developments.

In summary, I hope that practical interpretation of the works and reflection on relevant aesthetic concepts might cross-fertilise one another. Chapter 1 starts from Schumann's growth into becoming a literary composer in the years around 1832, noting some weaknesses in this respect of *Papillons* (despite its charm) and what the composer may have learnt from them. Chapter 2 introduces issues about musical and literary associations and expressiveness that lie close to the book's heart. Chapter 4 dwells on how the Schumann of around 1835 viewed form and content in music, used the term 'Geist', and understood the relationships between these aspects, and reflects on how far formal parallels and programmes might be primary, autonomous elements in the literary connections. The four 'Hoffmann works' of 1834–9 are each explored in Chapters 3, 5, 7 and 9 respectively, while Chapter 6 traces Schumann's stylistic evolutions around 1836–8, not least under the influence of late Beethoven, and Chapter 8 reviews how musical and literary associations and expressiveness have functioned in those interpretations.

A more subterranean stream rises to the surface in the concluding Chapter 10. The book's approach to the music is synoptic, focusing on each work as an aesthetic entity, rather than quarrying them for (for instance) exemplars in analytical, stylistic, musicological, documentary, scientific or sociological studies. It is also eclectic, deploying presumptions about, for instance, form, tonality, rhythm, metre, texture, style, genre and sonority, as well as gesture and expressiveness. These presumptions largely depend of course on others' explorations of theory, but there is no attempt to derive my interpretations from explicit theories in each area, or to deduce from theory which kinds of aesthetic pattern will be most significant in a given work; I know of no theory yielding such deductions. And as any work of art is open to indefinite numbers of alternative analyses, the book's aim is not to give 'the' interpretation of a work, but to stimulate alternative approaches. Since my concern is partly with expressive and associative qualities in the music, my treatments dwell more on characterising the foreground than some analysts would. Some may then question the relationship to professional musicology of the book's focus. All of this raises issues about analysis, theory, plurality of interpretation, aesthetics, history and culture, on which the concluding chapter dwells, hoping less to convince sceptics than to explain its stances.

1 | Chrysalis, 1827–1834
Schumann's emergence as a literary composer

For the young Robert Schumann, how music and literature might coexist, and enhance one another, was in part an issue about the direction of his life. In 1830, as a twenty-year old, he was studying law, infatuated with both literature and music, and nurturing an embryonic critical voice; and his future could have gone in any of these directions. The next year, he was studying piano with Friedrich Wieck, alongside Wieck's eleven-year-old daughter, Clara, in preparation for a career as a virtuoso pianist; he published his opus 1, the *Variations on the Name Abegg*, and his first music review, a prescient acclamation of Chopin's genius, and planned a novel, alongside artistic biographies of Hoffmann and Titian. In the early 1830s he often described himself as a cocooned artist not yet ready to burst out.[1] In the decade that followed, he maintained a voracious diet of musical, literary and other reading; he founded a new music journal, the *Neue Zeitschrift für Musik*, established its reputation and viability, and contributed hundreds of pages of reviews; and he had twenty-six of his own piano works published or on the way to publication, several of them with literary connections. He also found in Clara a sort of muse to his genius, and after a long, wearing struggle with Wieck, a wife as well. He had chosen from the possibilities before him to emerge above all as a professional composer; but the choice incorporated rather than banished his literary and critical enthusiasms. Music, literature and criticism – and to a greater or lesser extent commerce – remained in mutual dependence then and throughout his life.[2]

Schumann was the son of a publisher with wide literary interests, and his own reading was diverse and often intense. Its traces are visible in literary works, diaries and correspondence from his late teens onwards; they emerge too in the critical writings and letters of the adult, and in the collection of books he left behind.[3] Excerpts he made from his reading

---

[1] *Jugendbriefe*, 200 and 217 (10 January and 2 August 1833); compare *GSK*, I 23, 109, 128, 260.
[2] See for instance Daverio, *Robert Schumann*, chapter 2.
[3] Appel, ed., *Schumann und die Dichter*, especially Kruse, 'Robert Schumanns Lektüre', 123–34 and Nauhaus, 'Schumanns Lektürebüchlein', 50–87; Tadday, *Das schöne Unendliche*, 101–13 and Musgrave, *Life of Schumann*, 11–12.

throughout his life are preserved in surviving albums.[4] These form a record of ideas from a wider culture that struck him, and from them we can to an extent reconstruct what caught Schumann's eye, and when, and relate them to his compositions of the time. We should not presume that he endorsed or adopted each idea, but can at least trace threads of influence, not least from the five authors on whom I will concentrate: William Shakespeare (1564–1616), Johann Wolfgang Goethe (1749–1832), Jean Paul Richter (Jean Paul, 1763–1825), Friedrich von Hardenberg (Novalis, 1772–1801) and of course E. T. A. Hoffmann (1776–1822).

Schumann knew Shakespeare's work at least from 1827.[5] He probably read what we now accept in the canon, as well as other plays since evicted from it. He seems to have used mainly the translations by August Wilhelm Schlegel and Johann Joachim Eschenburg (published in Vienna in 1811–12). The first volume contained *The Tempest* and *Twelfth Night*, which Schumann studied intently, and which to a Romantic eye are tales of the recognition of the self, its twin, and its love, in a world which, while infested with puritans, thugs and schemers, is also illumined by the creative magic of the imagination. The plays were revered by Jean Paul, Novalis, and of course Goethe.

Schumann's appreciation of Goethe grew gradually as he matured through the 1830s. He read his way through the poems, plays, novels and letters. If the young Schumann did not 'yet understand Goethe', he found him a wholesome diet, judging in 1836 that he was 'always right'.[6] Schumann in his youth called *Wilhelm Meisters Lehrjahre* (1793–6) the '*non plus ultra* of Romanticism', and he read it three times, he said in 1847.[7] It is a novel of the formation of the self; its themes include self-recognition and self-development, doubled identities, madness, mediocrity and philistinism. Its hero is a young man destined for a mercantile career but infatuated by dreams of art, for whom Shakespeare 'opened a new world'. *Hamlet* is discussed and enacted and becomes a symbol in the book, which draws also on the Bible and myth.[8]

Wilhelm Meister both awed and repelled Novalis, who called it worldly and anti-poetic.[9] The reaction befitted an 'early Romantic', and Novalis

---

[4] Published in 1998 as the *Mottosammlung*: an invaluable work of meticulous scholarship.
[5] Draheim, 'Schumann und Shakespeare', 237–44. See also Finson, 'Schumann and Shakespeare'.
[6] *Jugendbriefe*, 17 (17 March 1828), 153 (21 September 1831) and 176 (8 May 1832); *Tagebücher*, I 372, 374 and 417; *GSK*, I 160.
[7] *Tagebücher*, I 96; Nauhaus, 'Schumanns Lektürebüchlein', 67 (Schumann claimed to have read *Hermann und Dorothea* ten times by 1845: 59).
[8] Goethe, *Wilhelm Meister*, IV/1, V/4 and 7–11 (*Werke*, IV (1973), 263–7, 275–89).
[9] Novalis, *Schriften*, V 1988, 233(fr. 263–4).

was indeed one of that remarkable circle of people born within a few years of 1770 – including the Schlegels (Friedrich and August Wilhelm), the Schellings (Friedrich Wilhelm and Dorothea), Friedrich Schleiermacher, Georg Wilhelm Friedrich Hegel, Friedrich Hölderlin, Ludwig Tieck and Wilhelm Heinrich Wackenroder. The version of Idealist philosophy propounded by Johann Gottlieb Fichte in his lectures at Jena University between 1793 and 1799 seemed to these young people epoch-making, and inspired variants of their own. Forms of Idealism, so different from English empiricism and commercialism, dominated German culture for decades thereafter.

Of all these 'early Romantics', however, few but Novalis (to whom I return below) leave many traces of an influence on the young Schumann. He does not seem to have engaged directly with Idealism's main philosophical texts by Fichte, Schelling or Hegel, and there is no evidence that he attended to the Schlegels' prose works beyond reading (in 1827) two essays by Friedrich, on old German literature and on 'Volksbildung'. It is not clear what he thought of Wackenroder, who played a seminal part in the development of early Romanticism, but barely features in Schumann's writings as published to date. As for Wackenroder's friend Tieck, in the 1830s Schumann cited his poems, and by 1840 he knew his stories as well as some at least of the prose, but his reading of Tieck is not well documented. Tieck was however a central figure in cultural life over decades. Hoffmann built both on the radical literary techniques of his 1790s dramas and on themes from his fictions – the concern with art and the artist in *Franz Sternbalds Wanderungen* (1798), and the engagement with the occult and psychotic in novellas such as 'Der Blonde Eckbert' and 'Der Pokal'.[10] Tieck's studies and translations helped to promote Shakespeare in Germany; and it was Tieck who with Friedrich Schlegel compiled and published two volumes of Novalis' work, in a posthumous tribute.[11]

Volume I of Tieck's Novalis contained the unfinished short novel *Heinrich von Ofterdingen*, which was in part a reaction to or against *Wilhelm Meister*, while Volume II contained a handful of poems, a philosophical colloquy in novelistic form (*Die Lehrlinge zu Sais*) and some

---

[10] GSK, II 235; Hoffmann quoted Tieck's *Phantasus* in his 1813 review of Beethoven's Mass in C (*Schriften zur Musik*, 155).

[11] Tieck's Novalis was published in Berlin in 1802 and reprinted four times up to 1837 (see Novalis, *Schriften*, V (1988), 191–5). Schumann's copy of the 1837 edition (*Schriften*, 1837) is still in Zwickau, with his markings in it. A separate 1827 Heidelberg edition called *Novalis Poesien*, which Schumann may have used in the 1830s, is substantially Tieck's version (*Mottosammlung*, 196–7).

sequences of prose thoughts. (A third volume, issued in 1846, contained some limpid, radical and ambitious statements of the analogous semiological status of mathematics, language and the arts, alongside pungent fragments on Schlegel's irony, on music's affinity with combinatorial analysis, and on arabesques as visible music; sadly, we have to assume that neither Hoffmann nor the Schumann of the 1830s had access to them.)

In Tieck's Novalis, the difficult Kantian concept of the 'transcendental' is minimised; but the volumes did not, as has been asserted, exclude the philosophy altogether.[12] Instead they conveyed philosophical ideas broadly, but compellingly and accessibly. Tieck's light editorial touch melded the fragments into something close to continuous prose, almost as coherent and accessible as the fictions. Taken together, the first two volumes bring out more clearly than modern versions the similarities of thought between the fragmentary aphorisms and the images and fables in the philosophical colloquy and unfinished novel *Heinrich von Ofterdingen*. Moreover they emphasise analogies Novalis found between different fields – music, poetry, aesthetics and metaphysics. Thus Tieck's compact version gives a rather different impression from the sprawling, disjointed, often radical fragments of modern editions. I use its first two volumes, in a way I have not seen in earlier studies, to re-create what Hoffmann and Schumann could have found in Novalis and to highlight recurring themes. Appendix 1, therefore, allows a reader to trace Novalis' aphorisms between different editions, and this is especially relevant in Chapter 8.

Schumann's interest in Novalis emerges in his diaries from 1828 onwards, and in his *Mottosammlung* in 1832–4 and again in 1837; his diaries reflect the impact on his style of Novalis' rhythms, vocabulary and key concepts and philosophy.[13] From Tieck's two pocket volumes, Schumann could absorb a version of Idealist thinking: we know he read a section which the 1837 edition called 'Philosophie und Physik', as there are excerpts both in his 1831–4 *Mottosammlung* and in his later *Dichtergarten*. More broadly, his letters, diaries and 1827 essay on aesthetic judgements suggest that in his teens he had taken in philosophical ideas from conversation and from reading.[14] He would have been able to recognise

---

[12] Tadday, *Das schöne Unendliche*, 106.
[13] Appendix 2 juxtaposes excerpts from Schumann and Novalis from 1828. Echoes can be heard in later years too: see for instance page 187 below.
[14] Krahe, 'Robert Schumanns Schulaufsatz'; *Jugendbriefe*, 5, using the Fichtean term 'Nicht-Ich' (July 1827), 23 on the study of philosophy (21 May 1828), 36 on the system of Idealism and 37 on a philosophical friend (2 October 1828; compare *Tagebücher*, I 106–7).

parodies of Idealist metaphysics in Hoffmann's stories, and versions of Idealist aesthetics in Hoffmann and in Jean Paul.

While there is no evidence that he engaged with the more radical aesthetic ideas of Friedrich Schlegel, he lavished attention on Jean Paul's assaults on them. In 1831–4 and again in 1836–8, Schumann read and excerpted Jean Paul's *Vorschule der Ästhetik* – which had been published in 1804, reissued in 1813, and distilled in 1825 into a *Nachschule*; central to it is the question of how poetry marries form and content. From his teens, Schumann had been infatuated with Jean Paul; he often imitated his words.[15] The great novels, from *Die unsichtbare Loge* (1793) to *Titan* (1803) and *Flegeljahre* (1804–5), exploit the scope of a capacious genre to include mystery, sentiment, disquisition, indulgent irony, authorial idiosyncrasy, and sheer digression. Context and narrative may be stretched at points to the borders of implausibility, but never beyond; apparent interventions of the supernatural are rarely wholly incomprehensible. There is a range of voices and perspectives, but a sense of (possibly erratic) authorial control, and some degree of resolution. For the novels – whose heroes may be rulers, lovers, scholars or bourgeois in eighteenth-century central Europe – concern the formation of the self and the quest for love, maturity and integration.

Jean Paul's characters often show complementary or dual identities, and such a plural self was a common expression of Romantic sensibility, and by no means always a negative one. In Novalis' unrealised plan for *Heinrich von Ofterdingen*, for instance, personalities were to merge creatively; elsewhere, Novalis opined that 'if someone only has a real inner "You", an elevated dialogue of mind and sense can take place. Genius is perhaps just the result of such an inner plurality'.[16]

In Hoffmann's stories, a plural personality is more likely to be fatally divided, and his fictions create a different world from those of Jean Paul. Both exploit irony, digressiveness, defamiliarisation, duality of character and multiplicity of perspective; but the two authors use these traits very differently. They apply them to different subjects, so as to create specific worlds, values and aesthetic standpoints that could not be confused one with the other. In Hoffmann, to oversimplify a complex *oeuvre*, fairy-tale elements and the supernatural intrude into the concrete, contemporary world of nineteenth-century towns like Dresden or Berlin; the intrusion

---

[15] See for example Otto, *Schumann als Jean Paul Leser*; Kruse, 'Robert Schumanns Lektüre', 125ff and Reiman, *Schumann's Piano Cycles*, 9–11. Imitations: see for instance *Tagebücher*, I 68, 74 and 78; and note 50 below.

[16] Novalis, *Schriften*, V 216(fr. 88); Blackall, *Novels of the German Romantics*, 110–12.

may remain beyond rational explanation, or may represent comic irony. His heroes are likely to be Romantic artists, appearing in many guises, exalted or bathetic; their personalities are often dangerously split, or frightening Doppelgänger.[17] Compared to Jean Paul, the multiplicity of voices can seem less under authorial or other control, less resolved, and with less integration of the narrating voice; dissonant genres are more sharply juxtaposed; narrative dislocations are deeper; and the irony may sometimes be more biting or agonised, the tone more obsessive, bitter or dark. The contrast reflects in part a difference between generations more striking than the thirteen-year difference in their ages would suggest. By the time Hoffmann was writing, Napoleon's long war had left the world harsher.

Equally, while Hoffmann affectionately praised Tieck's edition of Novalis, which provided iridescent images for some of his fictions, his more disillusioned, perhaps more experienced, turn of mind brought out not so much the astonishing coherence and ambition of the Idealist synthesis as its hazards.[18] The dreams of art or love that enthral some of his protagonists may lead them on to self-awareness and ironic humour, creatively nurturing love, life and growth – or they may isolate them from bourgeois society, becoming solipsistic, narcissistic, compulsive, regressive or destructive infatuations.

Schumann had read the fictions by 1828, and from 1831 they struck him with the force of a revelation, or perhaps a nightmare. He recorded then: 'In the evening read from that damned Hoffmann'; 'One scarcely dares to breathe when one reads Hoffmann', 'Read Hoffmann, ceaselessly. New worlds'. 'Read the one and only Datura Fluctuosa [sic] by Hoffmann. Lord God! What a mind!' An 1832 letter to Friedrich Wieck initially referred to Hoffmann as a 'lightning-bolt' on a par with Schubert, Chopin and Paganini, but Schumann crossed his name out. He celebrated 'Serapion-evenings' with friends in early 1833, in imitation of Hoffmann's *'Die Serapions-Brüder'*.[19] (In Germany more widely, Heine claimed in 1836, Hoffmann had gone out of fashion.)[20] Otherwise Schumann rarely mentioned Hoffmann's works.[21] He excerpted little from them for the

---

[17] Blackall, *Novels of the German Romantics*, chapter 10.
[18] Hoffmann, *Kreisleriana*, II/5, 313; *Fantasiestücke*, 136.
[19] *Tagebücher*, I 111, and 336–7, 349, 354 (5 and 6 June 1831, and 9 and 21 July 1831) (Hoffmann's tale is 'Datura Fastuosa'); *Briefedition*, I/2 53 (11 January 1832); *Neue Folge*, 66 (18 January 1836). He reread him in early 1854 to find material for *Dichtergarten: Tagebücher*, III/2 646.
[20] Heine, *Die romantische Schule* (1979), 193.
[21] He apparently did not know Hoffmann's music until he studied *Aurora* in late 1838: *Tagebücher*, II 83.

Mottosammlung or *Dichtergarten*. But their importance to him is clear from their appearances as titles to his musical works, as possible musical projects in the diaries, and as traces left in Schumann's own words; he was so steeped in Hoffmann's words that he could recognise stray echoes of them.[22] More disturbingly (and going beyond the callow imitation of Jean Paul that can be seen in Schumann's youth, or the biographical parallels between two writers and musicians struggling to make their way in difficult times), motifs from Hoffmann's stories of mad and suicidal artists seem to have haunted Schumann's last years. Of Hoffmann's fictions, *Kreisleriana* (1810–14), 'Der goldne Topf' (1814), the *Nachtstücke* (1814–17) and *Prinzessin Brambilla* (1820–1) are of central interest to this book, not least because they freely invoke musical styles, genres, works and composers.

The young Schumann toyed with writing his own musical fictions. In mid 1831, probably under the influence of his intensive reading of Hoffmann, he invented literary alter egos for himself and his colleagues – including 'Florestan', 'Eusebius', 'Raro' and 'Zilia' (or 'Caecilia', an avatar of Clara Wieck). He had it in mind to write a novel bringing those figures together with Paganini and Hummel, and in April 1832 he expressed the 'core' of his 'musical novel' as 'purity of art, the artist, mastery, and irony'.[23] He claimed in May 1832 that he 'had not yet read anything substantial and complete about the distractions and diversions of the artist before he reaches fulfilment'. It is an odd claim. A prominent theme in novels of the previous half-century had been the passage of a protagonist through hazards, ordeal or adversity to self-discovery or self-development, and perhaps to love. Goethe's *Wilhelm Meisters Lehrjahre* had become emblematic of the genre of the *Bildungsroman*, a term coined in the 1820s.[24] Novalis' *Heinrich von Ofterdingen* is a poetic specimen, and several of Jean Paul's novels fall into the genre, including *Titan* and *Flegeljahre*. Protagonists often had artistic traits, or were artists – as in Goethe's play *Torquato Tasso* (1780–90), the *Herzensergießungen eines kunstliebenden Klosterbruders* by Wackenroder and Tieck (1797), and Tieck's *Franz Sternbalds Wanderungen*. These works released a flood of artist-novels or 'Künstlerromane'.[25] Hoffmann frequently drew on this rich tradition. He subjected it to questioning in *Kreisleriana*, brought out the dark side in stories like 'Der Sandmann' (1815), and guyed it in the novel *Kater Murr*

---

[22] *GSK*, II 315; 418, note 349. [23] *Tagebücher*, I 339–44, 358, 359, 371, 379, 381 and 382.
[24] See Swales, *The German Bildungsroman*, especially 12ff.
[25] Paulin, *Ludwig Tieck*, 9; Ziolkowski, *German Romanticism*, 337–51; Wendt, ed., *Schumann und seine Dichter*, 7.

and in stories like 'Der goldne Topf' and *Prinzessin Brambilla*. Schumann's claim not to have seen such novels is then odd; but in any case, in 1832 he plotted a version of his own that he had been mulling:

Florestan soll der Künstler seyn; rein, leichtsinnig, empfänglich, genievoll; der Drang nach Gefallen des geliebtesten Wesens soll ihn weiter treiben. Krümelchen, das Prinzip der Mechanik, stößt ihm auf; Seraphine, als Bild des Geschmacks u. Mode verdunkelt fast Caecilia; Raro, als ironisches Princip, erscheint zuletzt, bis ihn endlich Caecilia zur Reinheit der Kunst zurückführt.

Florestan is to be that artist, pure, changeable, receptive, inspired; he is to be driven on by the urge to please his beloved. Krümelchen, the embodiment of the mechanical, gives him a jolt. Seraphine, as the image of taste and fashion, almost puts Caecilia in the shade. Raro as an ironic principle appears last, till in the end Caecilia leads him back to the purity of art.[26]

This novel came to nothing as a literary project, but it seems to have re-emerged in metamorphosed form, as a later chapter will suggest, in Schumann's musical compositions.

Hoffmann's fictions pointed to another way to combine music and literature, incorporating a kind of music criticism seen as a literary art form. He placed his criticism in a more conventional medium as well as in fiction: in journals such as the Leipzig *Allgemeine musikalische Zeitung*. That journal was readily available to Schumann, though we do not know how many of Hoffmann's reviews he actually read.[27] Schumann had himself published musical reviews from 1831, and in 1834 he set out to establish his own journal, the *Neue Zeitschrift für Musik*. Its mission was broadly conceived. The prospectus of 1834 promised not only theoretical and practical essays, critical reviews of new work and reports from abroad, but also 'musical material' from literature, and Schumann singled out literary authors including Shakespeare, Goethe, Jean Paul, Novalis and Hoffmann.[28] The very first issue came out under a motto from Shakespeare. Of course, Goethe's *Wilhelm Meisters Lehrjahre*, Jean Paul's novels, Novalis' *Heinrich von Ofterdingen* and Hoffmann's *Kreisleriana* and *Die Serapions-Brüder* all included discussions of art and music; but Schumann's interest in these

---

[26] *Mottosammlung*, IX 26. 'Krümelchen' is Hummel, for whose influence on Schumann see Lester, 'Schumann and Sonata Forms', 199–200.

[27] Bischoff, *Monument für Beethoven*, 243, raises the question. Burnham's review ('"Hoffmann's Musical Writings"') of Charlton's English version of Hoffmann's criticism gives an accessible summary of some main aspects.

[28] *GSK*, II 272. He added Johann Friedrich Rochlitz, playwright and music critic, and Wilhelm Heinse, whose novel *Ardinghello* (1785) is a guide to the thought of Greece and the art of Rome and the Renaissance, spiced with sun, sex, nudism, some buccaneering and a utopian end; its wide influence stretched from Hölderlin's elegiac *Hyperion* to Hoffmann's comic *Prinzessin Brambilla*.

writers was not restricted to aesthetics. A partly real and partly fictional League of David ('Davidsbund'), including 'Florestan', 'Eusebius' and 'Raro' alongside Schumann's colleagues under their own *alter egos*, collaborated in the journal. As befits a League of David, they championed 'poetic' music against the philistines, through dismissals of the mediocre and encomia of works of genius, not least those of Chopin and Berlioz; in the words of the renewed mission statement of 1839, the journal was to be 'a sea-wall against mediocrity'.[29] Schumann worked on the *Neue Zeitschrift* for ten years as editor and contributor, with prodigious energy and resourcefulness. His criticism at first luxuriated in poetic images, language, rhythms and forms, while also offering technical analyses; but over time the playful and extravagant literary style receded, and so did the 'Davidsbündler', including 'Florestan' and 'Eusebius'. Professionalisation set in. Schumann widened and deepened his musical reading.[30] His aesthetic views became more settled and his statements more lapidary, tending to the succinct, magisterial and sometimes academic.

Music criticism, like musical fiction-writing, was therefore a way in which Schumann was able to combine music and literature; but he gradually became clear that his destiny was instead as a literary composer. He knew that he had a lot to learn musically; but he remained adamant that a composer as 'whole person' must draw on a wide culture. He thought great literature part of the education of a composer and a person, as he said in 1838, and repeated in 1842: 'anyone who understands Shakespeare and Jean Paul will compose differently from one whose wisdom is drawn only from Marpurg, etc.'[31] Despite wrestling from the early 1830s with the issue of music's independence from other spheres, he persuaded himself that a composer may learn from and relate to a broad culture.[32]

Some of the tensions involved in simultaneously learning his craft as composer and exploiting a wider culture are evident in his *Papillons*, op. 2, of 1832. It is a poetic sequence of dances. But in letters to his family and to

---

[29] *GSK*, I 384.
[30] *Mottosammlung*, 87–8; Kruse, 'Robert Schumanns Lektüre', 128–9; Perry, 'Dissonance Treatment', 5–24.
[31] 'Und nun namentlich Künstler suche ich vergebens, d.h. Künstler, die nicht allein eines oder zwei Instrumente passabel spielen, sondern ganze Menschen, die den Shakespeare und Jean Paul verstehen': letter to Therese Schumann (18 December 1838), in *Erler*, 188 (in late 1838 Schumann excerpted a similar comment from Nissen's biography of Mozart at *Mottosammlung*, III 51: both may allude to Schiller's concept of 'der ganze Mensch' in *Sämtliche Werke*, V 358); *GSK*, II 115 (echoed in Brendel, 'Robert Schumann' (1845), 150).
[32] *GSK*, I 127 ('Das Anlehnen'), I 26 ('Raffaelschen'), 430 ('Lese doch'), II 73 (Goethe) and 265. Compare I 422 (Berlioz), 431 ('noch etwas im Spiele'), 440 ('Literatur').

Example 1.1: Schumann, *Papillons*, vi, bars 1–14

the critic Ludwig Rellstab, Schumann listed characters and narrative moments from the last scenes of Jean Paul's novel, *Flegeljahre*, that are in some sense in the music:

Masked ball – Walt – Vult – masks – Wina – Vult's dancing – exchange of masks – avowals – anger – revelations – hurrying away – final scene and departing brother.[33]

It looks like the imposition of a schema on music partly composed earlier.[34] Schumann marked relevant passages in his copy of the novel, apparently some time around the period of composition, and these markings seem to refer to the numbers of the pieces of *Papillons*, possibly in some sequence close to if not identical with the published order. But Schumann did not wholly succeed in fitting Jean Paul's narrative to pre-existing pieces: the relationship between music and novel is not always clear. The giant boot Schumann attributed to 'iii' clumps audibly enough in the music; the end of the ball and the disappearance of Vult surely figure in 'xii'. But if 'vi' represents Vult's description of Walt's dancing (though Schumann seems to have written, 'Vult's dancing'), are the opening six bars 'vertical' and the next eight 'horizontal', or vice versa (Example 1.1)?[35]

I find it hard to see the delicate touch of a lover's hand, despite Schumann's marking, in the 'straightforward dance' of 'viii'.[36] How is a listener to pick up an exchange of masks in 'vii' and 'ix', if indeed it is in those pieces? Few have tried to locate the 'anger' and 'revelations' that

---

[33] *Jugendbriefe*, 166–7 and 167–8 (17 and 19 April 1832); *Neue Folge*, 36 (28 April 1832), 46 (11 January 1834) and 54 (22 August 1834).
[34] Synofzik, 'Schumanns kompositorische Anfänge'.
[35] Chailley, 'Zum Symbolismus', 63, notes differing views; see also Beaufils, *La Musique*, 50.
[36] Jensen's phrase, 'Explicating Jean Paul', 141; he and Chailley, 64, nevertheless take Schumann's marking here as definitive.

Schumann mentioned; and in a published review the critic Rellstab objected, Schumann gathered, that it was not clear 'where and what Vult curses'.[37] In any case, as Rellstab pointed out:

If incidental, subjective aspects [rather than 'objective, necessary truths'] remain concealed, they leave a cipher to which the key is missing; once disclosed, they may be grasped or understood, but only externally ... A work of art should not make itself understood through an extraneous object [ein fremdes Etwas], but through itself, wholly and quite alone; its soul must dwell within it, not outside it; otherwise it is no more than a corpse on a bier.[38]

On the one hand, an 'extraneous' narrative can – unhelpfully – dictate expectations of what the music will do (Rellstab, Schumann noted, looked in vain for Jean Paul's character, Jakobine); on the other, both the musical features that produce an image, and the image itself, must work within the music as well as through an 'incidental' association with a book.

In response, one might seek a more abstract sequence than Schumann implied, boldly amending his list of items so that they can be understood in terms of *Flegeljahre*, but need not be, and are matched to each piece including the *Introduzione*:

Expectation – masked ball – bustle of masks – giant boot – an encounter – souls' gaze – angular dancing – butterfly wings – metamorphosis – into the hall – lovers' waltz – avowals, anger, revelations – final scene and parting.

But in that, as I think in any account, the logic of the sequence remains too obscure, especially in 'vi'–'ix', and too complex in 'x'–'xi', to be self-explanatory in and as music.[39] It is not clear that the final sequence makes psychological sense unless two male rivals can be distinguished in the music; but it does not help musical appreciation to worry about identities. Though Schumann hoped that *Papillons* worked as music in itself, the hope was vain, if academic commentaries are representative: critics have focused less on the work as a musically shaped whole than on how the programme fits.[40] The music only sustains a programmatic interpretation of the sort Schumann incautiously encouraged on terms vulnerable to Rellstab's critique. If *Papillons* are butterflies, they are not wholly free of the cocoon.

---

[37] *Tagebücher*, I 401. Mayeda, 'Papillons', 14, denies the presence of anger; Lippman, 'Theory and Practice', 317, finds it in 'xi'; I would point to bars 40–1.

[38] Schumann's transcription (*Tagebücher*, I 425) of Rellstab's review of 25 May 1832.

[39] Brendel, significantly, drops the thread after 'v' and does not pick it up again till 'x' ('Robert Schumann' (1845), 83). Knorr (*GSK*, II 456) skipped lightly over 'vi'–'viii'.

[40] *Neue Folge*, 54 (22 August 1834). See the modern commentaries noted above, and Daverio, *Robert Schumann*, 79–90. Kaminsky, 'Principles of Formal Structure', 209–10, Chernaik, 'Schumann's "Papillons"' and Neergaard, 'Sonority and Pedalling' are exceptions.

Schumann eventually gave heed: 'Rellstab was right about Jakobine'. In a subsequent exchange, however, while Rellstab insisted that the soul of a musical work must dwell within it, Schumann asked, 'what would ever be created, if the genius of an artist were not (consciously or unconsciously) an objective one?'[41] In effect, he pondered the nature of 'poetic' music; and over time, his criticism achieved a balance. At the same time, his music came back time and again to themes of human concern, and continued to find a role for literature. But his compositions at their best follow not an external 'schema' but musical trajectories of their own; he did not require music alone to create esoteric discriminations between identities; and he learnt, with rare lapses, the wisdom of not lending his authority as composer to detailed interpretations of his works, for fear of turning them into programmes. That development is one subject of this book.

There is, though, a separate question of how far the evolution of Schumann's musical style was influenced by literary models. Stylistic parallels between music and literature were often detected in Schumann's day and before. Theories of the sublime and of humour, developed largely in literary fields in the eighteenth century, were applied in the early Romantic era to instrumental music, in an evolution contemporary with the reception of Beethoven.[42] Broad aesthetic parallels had been seen between writers like Sterne or Jean Paul and composers like Haydn or C. P. E. Bach. Eighteenth-century fantasias could seem disrupted, subjective, open-ended, disconcertingly fragmented, digressive, and open to multiple readings and an ironic critique, with (in C. P. E. Bach's music, for instance) 'quick-changing effects', 'sudden changes of texture', an effect of 'requiring active listening', and the evasion of 'clear harmonic trajectories, period structure and formal design', and of regular metre or bar line.[43] Some Haydn works share such features, and similar strategies were identified in Beethoven. There was a small early nineteenth-century industry asserting or denying a likeness between Beethoven and Jean Paul, not least for some abstract formal strategies such as their abrupt transitions.[44]

Schumann knew of such comparisons, and knew that he himself was seen as Beethoven's successor. He testily rejected comparisons between himself

---

[41] *Tagebücher*, I 401; *Jugendbriefe*, 195 (7 December 1832). For Schumann's mature view of the distinction between objective and subjective in composition, see Brown, 'Higher Echoes', 513.
[42] Appel, 'Schumanns Humoreske', 87–103, 201–6.
[43] Richards, *Free Fantasia*, 15–22, 136–44, 152–5 and 176–8.
[44] Such features are not confined to Jean Paul, of course: they crop up also in Shakespeare and Cervantes, for instance, as well as Gozzi, Sterne, and Tieck. Two thousand years ago, Ovid's *Metamorphoses* delights in similar traits – at one point (I 302–3) defamiliarising dolphins by picturing them swimming up against the high branches of oaks.

and Jean Paul.⁴⁵ His youthful claim that painting, poetry and music share an aesthetic, though their material diverges, implies some confidence that aesthetic, and perhaps formal, features can be compared across different media; in 1829 he directly compared Schubert to Jean Paul, apparently referring to parallels of aesthetic strategy (and later mentioning the former's 'logical leaps'); and even in 1838–9 his reviews of Schubert's late works reveal sympathy for some unconventional stylistic traits which seemed to evoke comparable traits that Schumann admired in Jean Paul.⁴⁶ Literary aesthetics, inextricably entangled with the influence of Beethoven and with musical aesthetics and criticism, may indeed have played a role in the development of Schumann's style, and in his own and others' understanding of it; but Schumann did not say in these passages that his style was influenced by Schubert, let alone by Jean Paul, or how. Without such a statement – or even with it – it is not clear how literary influences on musical style could be confidently isolated, given the difference in medium.

The one statement from the mature Schumann that might imply any such specific influence emerges from a letter of 1839 in which he claimed to have learnt more counterpoint from Jean Paul than from his music teacher.⁴⁷ That comment is in part another of Schumann's many protests against academic musical doctrine; but though there can be no certainty what Schumann had in mind in making the claim, and many different ideas have been mooted, I am tempted to suggest one possibility.

Schumann noted in 1828 what music might learn from the 'combination of the ordered beat with a varying and lyrically supple bar-length' in Jean Paul's 'polymeters'.⁴⁸ These are prose-poems with a single extendable flow and multiple metres, without line-breaks or rhyme. Jean Paul gave an example in *Flegeljahre*, having first shown its metrical patterns:

⏑ – – ⏑ ⏑ – – ⏑ – – ⏑ – ⏑ – ⏑ –
– – – ⏑ – ⏑ ⏑ – – ⏑ – ⏑ – ⏑ – ⏑ – ⏑ ⏑ ⏑ –
– – – ⏑ – ⏑ ⏑ – ⏑ – ⏑ – ⏑ –

Gemein und dunkel wird oft die Seele verhüllt, die so rein und offen ist; so deckt graue Rinde das Eis, das zerschlagen innen licht und hell und blau wie Äther erscheint. Bleib' euch stets die Hülle fremd, bleib' es euch nur der Verhüllte nicht.

Jean Paul commented ironically: 'the unforgivingness of this verse (for instance the proceleusmatic: kĕl wĭrd ŏft dĭe – the second paeon: dĭe Hūllē

---

⁴⁵ *Briefwechsel*, II 368 (26 January 1839).
⁴⁶ *Jugendbriefe*, 82–3 (6 November 1829); *GSK*, I 26 (1834). See the balanced discussion in Brown, 'Higher Echoes', 538–42.
⁴⁷ *Neue Folge*, 149 (15 March 1839).   ⁴⁸ *Tagebücher*, I 113.

frĕmd – and the molossus: bleīb eūch stēts) will hardly elude a refined provincial ear, but might not the concision of the poet's ideas permit some metrical harshness?'[49] 'Polymeters' such as this can be analysed in terms of feet ('bars'), and phrases consisting of something like subject or countersubject, and entries marked by loose metrical similarity. Here, for instance, each 'entry' combines molossus and faster feet in the subject with a preponderance of trochees in the countersubject. Variations in the metrical phrase structure generate a sense of opening, development and closure. Schumann copied this and other polymeters out, and imitated them in words.[50] We know that he saw prosody as inherent in primal forms of speech as in music, noted analogies between speech and fugal structures in music, and excerpted Novalis' comment that 'music and poetry may probably be more or less the same'.[51] I would then compare some of Schumann's musical rhythms with those of polymeters, in order to cast one kind of light on his 1839 claim to have learnt counterpoint from Jean Paul; in particular I would point to Schumann's *Intermezzi*, op. 4, composed in summer 1832.[52]

The work's title suggests the invasion of the stage, in *entr'actes* of *opera seria*, by clowns from the *commedia dell'arte*; its pieces are studies, not least in rhythm, phrase lengths, motivic relationships, and contrapuntal strategies.[53] The fourth features asymmetrical rhythmic patterns, uneven but not random phrase lengths in a ternary structure with coda (1+4; 1+4; 4+1; 3, as marked in Example 1.2), and avoidance of expected closures – arguably the sort of music that might recall Jean Paul's polymeters.

The first piece features a variety of descending dotted rhythm motifs, strongly marked but of disparate characters (with a whiff of parody), abrupt shifts between successive motifs, and irregular phrase groupings.

---

[49] Jean Paul, *Flegeljahre* §8; §15.

[50] *Tagebücher*, I 37, 40–1 ('iv', 'v' and 'viii'), 90–1, and perhaps 69, 77 and 81 (compare 55 and 82); *Jugendbriefe*, 95ff (11 November 1829) and *GSK*, II 196–8 ('Polyrhythmen').

[51] *GSK*, I 74 (1835, on Berlioz's phrase structure) and II 261 ('fugenartig'); Novalis, *Schriften*, I 211 (*Mottosammlung*, I 78). Others before him, including Beethoven, may have used poetic prosody in music: Solomon, *Late Beethoven*, 102–34. Compare Watkins, *Metaphors of Depth*, 96.

[52] This argument, admittedly, neglects the vertical aspects of counterpoint, but it is not clear how those aspects can be reflected in Jean Paul's prose or polymeters, or therefore in what Schumann learnt from them. Appel, *Schumann und die Dichter*, 13, thinks polymeters may have influenced Schumann's style, adducing their rhythmic mystification, asymmetrical syntax, and resistance to the tyranny of the bar line, but (like Otto, *Robert Schumann als Jean Paul Leser*, 10) understating their potential for metrical patterning.

[53] *Neue Folge*, 40 (5 April 1833); *Tagebücher*, I 394; compare Daverio, *Robert Schumann*, 92. The influence of Jean Paul on his *Intermezzi* may have been in Schumann's mind in 1839 because of his recent work on his comparable op. 32.

Example 1.2: Schumann, *Intermezzi*, iv

Example 1.3: Schumann, *Intermezzi*, i, bars 1–25

The first fourteen bars are grouped as 3 + 6 + 6, but with an elision so that the 6 + 6 forms only eleven bars. After a three-bar passage, like an incipient sarabande, comes what turns into a sort of stretto, and the motif's position relative to the bar line shifts unpredictably (Example 1.3).

These pieces experiment not only with counterpoint but also with textures, and with harmony. For instance, the extraordinary transition back from the B flat major *Alternativo* of number 5 to the F major of the reprise proceeds, ordinarily enough, via a decorated German augmented

Example 1.4: Schumann, *Intermezzi*, v, bars 132–6

sixth chord of D minor; but it is written so that over three bars the left hand appears to play in B flat major and the right in A major (Example 1.4).

Of course, that transition is hardly literary in influence. More generally, the counterpoint in these pieces might also be thought to owe something to Bach, whom Schumann had been studying with admiration in early summer 1832. The 'prose' rhythms and phrase structures could have come from any of myriad musical influences.[54] Even with a clue from Schumann himself about Jean Paul and counterpoint, I do not see how in the absence of some compelling evidence we can disentangle literary from musical influences in the evolution of his style.

But in any case, in these pieces we can see the young Schumann venturing into musical territory new to him, and expanding his mastery of his craft. And that evolving craft fed into all of his compositions, not just those he marked out as literary. What he learnt from his critical study of other composers, past and present, his experience with *Papillons*, and his continued fascination with literature, was all becoming focused in a 'single point', as he had hoped in 1830.[55]

But questions remained. *Papillons* raised the issue as to the sense in which music might be literary (beyond merely showing general stylistic characteristics common to much music and much literature), and indeed how instrumental music can relate to something outside itself – literature or anything else – without falling foul of the trap to which Rellstab had pointed. And like *Papillons*, the *Intermezzi* showed Schumann incorporating the mercurial, antithetical and idiosyncratic within his music, but perhaps neither fusing them into a convincing whole, nor varying the basic formal pattern sufficiently. Over the years, Schumann addressed

---

[54] Compare, as one example from many, what Schoenberg ('Brahms the Progressive', 415–16) called the 'freedom of rhythm' and 'independence from formal symmetry' of the 'prose-like' bars 9–24 of Mozart's String Quartet in D minor, K 421.
[55] *Jugendbriefe*, 136 (15 December 1830).

these issues in the development of his style: from the *Impromptus*, op. 5, of 1833,[56] through *Carnaval* of 1834–7, a masterpiece of humour that capitalises precisely on an absence of fusion, to the *Nachtstücke*, op. 23, of 1839–40, with *Kreisleriana* of 1838 as one culmination. In 1840, the turn to song yielded another convincing answer; but his attempt to relate instrumental music to literature raised above all the spectre of music's expressiveness and associations; and that issue is broached in the next chapter.

[56] Rosen, *Romantic Generation*, 658–69 discusses the original version.

2 | Notions of resonance and expression

This book treats Schumann's music as capable of expressiveness, and as capable of creating in the minds of listeners resonant associations with other music and with a wider culture. All my interpretations of his 'Hoffmann works' hang on whether, how far and in what senses his music can (in his own words) 'connect with remote interests'.[1] The question is therefore close to this book's heart; but how it is put is contentious enough, let alone how it is answered. This book does not articulate a cut-and-dried theory. Instead, odd-numbered chapters illustrate an approach in practical interpretations, while the even-numbered series that begins here offers more abstract reflections.

For people familiar with cultural worlds close enough to those of the music, literary and musical associations may enhance aesthetic appreciation, and I often use the metaphor of resonance to describe that. In acoustic resonance, given effective coupling between a source and a resonator, a driving frequency that matches a resonator's natural frequencies will be amplified, and its overtones drawn out; the more degrees of freedom possessed by the source and resonator, each as a system in itself, the more frequencies can thus resonate in sympathetic vibration. My use of this metaphor has no pretensions to rigour: it does not imply, for instance, that an aesthetic resonance is independent of a perceiver as its physical counterpart is. Nor is it novel. But I have not seen an exploration of how such 'resonance' works.[2]

In the aesthetic case too, resonance between a work of Schumann's and something from the culture depends on 'coupling' and 'matching'. Though some will impose more demanding standards than others, 'coupling' will generally be more convincing where Schumann knew the literature (or music) in question, and ideally left evidence that it touched on his concerns of the time; expected an audience, however small or putative, to know it too

---

[1] *Briefwechsel*, I 146 (16 April 1838): 'an entfernte Interessen anknüpfen'.
[2] Knapp, 'Brahms and the Anxiety of Allusion', 9, 14 and 16, uses 'resonance' and 'embedded resonator' to talk about meaning in musical reminiscences 'deeper than the denotative, referential surface'. Schumann, *Tagebücher*, I 304 (1832), wrote that 'the future should be the higher echo of the past', though he did not say in what sense.

and be ready to engage with it and gave some indication, perhaps through a title, of its relevance. (Schumann's expectations of his audience's cultural understanding were often disappointed, of course; and the evidence for his concerns is less abundant before 1838–9, when his correspondence with Clara Wieck became voluminous and revealing.) Musical and literary features need to 'match' well under descriptions convincing in their own terms; descriptions that seem contrived to manufacture a match will yield no resonance. And the more the music and literature, as systems in their own right, are each rich in their own independent features ('degrees of freedom') with a wealth of potential internal relationships ('overtones'), the larger resonances their juxtaposition will yield. A literary connection is *more* resonant when it is not necessary for understanding musical patterns and processes – for which there are ideally musical explanations.

Reference points away from the music, to something particular, and at a fully conscious level. Literary resonance, by contrast, does not refer to, represent, depict or 'say something' about anything in a book. Instead, where there is convincing enough coupling and good matching between music and literature that are each poetic in their own right, it emphasises and enriches what the music already is. The echo chamber of the wider culture amplifies musical features in their own nature.

A hearing sensitive to such literary or musical resonances is of course only one way to hear any piece of music or its cultural associations; and it only functions if the listener has internalised aspects of the cultural tradition that were second nature to the composer. Otherwise, 'coupling' is ineffective, and literary resonance will probably seem like dead reference. But ideally associations repeatedly enrich interpretation anew, as on fresh hearings their persisting, perhaps subconscious, action highlights different musical threads or details.[3]

Associations operating in ways like this may be an aspect of expressiveness in music. This raises thorny issues, and at this preliminary stage, I will let Schumann himself introduce them. In his 1835 review of Berlioz's *Symphonie Fantastique*,[4] he wrote:

Was überhaupt die schwierige Frage, wieweit die Instrumentalmusik in Darstellung von Gedanken und Begebenheiten gehen dürfe, anlangt, so sehen

---

[3] Compare Burkholder, 'A Simple Model for Associative Musical Meaning'; Newcomb, 'Schumann and the Marketplace', 279 and Kramer, *Classical Music and Postmodern Knowledge*, 68–71.

[4] Republished at *GSK*, II 212–17 and I 69–85, and discussed in Bent, *Music Analysis*, II 161–5; Maus, 'Intersubjectivity and Analysis' and Plantinga, *Schumann as Critic*, 235–45. See Appendix 3–2(a).

hier viele zu ängstlich. Man irrt sich gewiß, wenn man glaubt, die Komponisten legten sich Feder und Papier in der elenden Absicht zurecht, dies oder jenes auszudrücken, zu schildern, zu malen. Doch schlage man zufällige Einflüsse und Eindrücke von außen nicht zu gering an. Unbewußt neben der musikalischen Phantasie wirkt oft eine Idee fort, neben dem Ohre das Auge, und dieses, das immer tätige Organ, hält dann mitten unter den Klängen und Tönen gewisse Umrisse fest, die sich mit der vorrückenden Musik zu deutlichen Gestalten verdichten und ausbilden können. Je mehr nun der Musik verwandte Elemente die mit den Tönen erzeugten Gedanken oder Gebilde in sich tragen, von je poetischerem oder plastischerem Ausdrucke wird die Komposition sein, – und je phantastischer oder schärfer der Musiker überhaupt auffaßt, um so mehr wird sein Werk erheben oder ergreifen. Warum könnte nicht einen Beethoven inmitten seiner Phantasien der Gedanke an Unsterblichkeit überfallen? Warum nicht das Andenken einer großen gefallenen Helden ihn zu einem Werke begeistern?

As for the difficult question of how far instrumental music may go in representing thoughts and events, many people take too anxious a view. It is certainly wrong to believe that composers take up paper and pen with the paltry aim of expressing, describing or painting this or that. One should not though underestimate the role of incidental influences and impressions from outside. Often an idea continues to operate subconsciously alongside the musical imagination, the eye alongside the ear, and within the sounds and notes, the eye, that ever-active organ, grasps certain sketchy outlines that can thicken up and grow into distinct shapes as the music rolls on. The more that elements related to music then carry within themselves the thoughts or images produced with the notes, the more the composition will be poetic or plastic in expression – and the sharper or more imaginative the composer's concept, the more his work will uplift or move us. Why should the imagination of a Beethoven not be seized in the midst of his creative work by a thought about immortality? Why should he not be inspired to compose by the remembrance of a great, fallen hero?[5]

This passage not only says that instrumental music may 'represent thoughts and events'; it can also be read, and filled out from Schumann's other comments, to suggest how that can happen. 'Eye' and 'ear' seem here, as often, to represent mental as well as sensory functions. 'The eye' was for Jean Paul the organ of clear, definite, objective perception, suited to a

---

[5] *GSK*, I 84. My translation connects 'Idee' with Schumann's use of the term earlier in the review. It interprets 'sounds and tones' as musical, as did Tadday, 'Life and Literature', 43; Bent, in *Music Analysis*, II 193, treats them as ambient noises. I take 'der Musik' as 'music' in preference to 'the music', 'Elemente' rather than 'Gedanken' as subject of 'tragen', and 'mehr' as qualifying 'tragen' rather than 'Elemente'. Each choice is debatable. Watkins (*Metaphors of Depth*, 97) takes 'mehr' to refer not to the degree with which thoughts or images are carried in truly musical elements, but to 'the profusion of non-musical ideas involved in its conception'; and whatever the particular phrase means, the passage as a whole implies both meanings.

plastic art like sculpture; the ear was suited to music, and in it 'both extension and intension are inherent': it perceives both the objective sound and the indefinite, poetic or 'Romantic' realm of idea, symbol or subjective feeling.[6] Schumann had already in 1829 echoed the idea that the eye is the organ of objective perception, but added the qualification that a 'poetic eye ... grasps the objective subjectively'. In the Berlioz review he speaks of 'the eye' as the organ of relatively 'distinct' 'outlines' – not necessarily strictly visual, but including also for instance a state that may arise from whatever 'particular idea the composer wished to present'. These 'outlines' operate 'alongside the musical imagination', which with its more fluid, less definite and more subjective elements is the realm of 'the ear'.[7] Where 'the eye' is guided by a 'programme', 'the ear' may not hear the music independently; but the more that 'outlines' of thought or image are carried forward in features that are intrinsically musical (the realm of 'the ear'), the better – the more 'poetic' or 'plastic' – the work; in poetic music, therefore, even if it suggests images, 'the ear need borrow nothing from the eye'.[8]

Thus, musical features may sometimes suggest to 'the eye' an 'outline' – a sense of figure, movement, sound, gesture, action, character, personal state or feeling. This may be, for instance, something angular and awkward, or with a broad undulating swell, or bird-like, or floating, or anxious, or funereal. In 1833–4, Schumann listed kinds of musical features that may contribute to the 'expression' of 'thought, feeling or passion'. Keys may bring connotations of character or state, though no rule-book can fix the relationship. In the right context, he later wrote, a particular chord can summon a compelling image and feeling; and 'deeper penetration into the secrets of harmony enables the expression of finer shades of feeling' (as Hoffmann said too).[9] Form can align the music's character with a subject indicated in a title; rhythm and instrumentation too may contribute. In 1837, Schumann criticised a composer's 'common harmonies, ordinary

---

[6] Jean Paul, *Vorschule*, §27: 'Bei dem Ohre ist Extension und Intension zugleich vonnöten'. Watkins, *Metaphors of Depth*, 30–2, adduces similar views in Herder, J. W. Ritter and Hoffmann. Jean Paul drew a distinction between the 'plastic art' of the ancients and the music of the moderns (*Vorschule*, §§17, 22, 25, 31 and 23, which Schumann excerpted in the early 1830s: *Mottosammlung*, IX 28). Hoffmann followed suit: 'Alte und neue Kirchenmusik', *Die Serapions-Brüder*, 409.

[7] *Jugendbriefe*, 71 (31 August 1829); *GSK*, I 69, 84.

[8] *GSK*, I 91. By 'poetic music', I take Schumann to mean roughly works that constitute compelling aesthetic entities, while also being expressive (and perhaps resonant).

[9] *GSK*, II 205, 207, I 105–6 (keys), 285 (chord), 27; Hoffmann, *Kreisleriana*, I/4, 48; compare II/6, 314–15, on a modulation in Mozart's *Don Giovanni*.

rhythms and melodies': it was a neglect of the sort of 'material means' through which, in the hands of a composer like Schubert, music can become 'material', or 'more sensual or painterly'.[10]

'As the music rolls on', the Berlioz review continued, sequences of these 'sketchy outlines' 'can thicken up and grow into distinct shapes'. A musical sequence can convey, for instance, 'the memory of happiness experienced', 'the image of the sea, or a Spring twilight', or something of a Shakespeare play.[11] A theme can suggest the same persona every time it appears, albeit in different moods or conditions: in the Berlioz Symphony, to think of its main theme is precisely to think of the woman it suggests, 'pale, slender as a lily, veiled, still, almost cold'.[12] A composer like Schubert may, Schumann wrote, 'have music for any feelings, thoughts, events or scenes: what he sees with his eye ... he transmutes into music'. He was equally explicit in 1842: 'Who would deny that our art can express a great deal, and even in its own way trace the development of an event?'[13] He only sometimes acknowledged that listeners are more likely to perceive the same 'distinct' shape only if guided by some verbal signal.

This passage is broadly representative, I think, of Schumann's views on expression in the 1830s. But he came to doubt how far a composer intended to use 'poetic music' to express or translate something he already had in mind in another medium, verbal or visual: 'a thought about immortality', rather than being a verbal thought which Beethoven then deliberately translated into music, would have come to him *as* a musical funeral march in a work such as the *Eroica*. In 1843, he gave vent to his irritation with 'academic types', who 'often have peculiar presumptions about composing, and always cite Mozart, who is supposed not to have had a thought in his head when writing his music':

The battle of 'Supposedly not-a-thought-in-his-head-when-composing' and its opposite is flaring up once again. The philosophers surely exaggerate the evils here; they are certainly wrong when they think that a composer who is working from an idea sits down like a preacher on Saturday afternoon, schematises his topic in the usual three sections and then dutifully writes it up; they are certainly wrong. The creative process of a composer is something quite different, and if some picture, some idea, hovers before him, he won't be satisfied with his work until it

---

[10] *GSK*, I 361 (form), 73 (march; compare Hoffmann on the military connotations of certain rhythms: *Schriften zur Musik*, 283); 78 ('In der Vision'); 269–70 (material means).
[11] *GSK*, I 84 (sequence); compare II 361 ('a plastic shape').
[12] *GSK*, I 78, 82; II 213. Compare I 432 on 'den Harfenspieler'.   [13] *GSK*, I 125; II 112 (1842).

comes towards him in lovely melodies, brought by those same unseen hands as the golden vessels of which Goethe somewhere speaks.[14]

What counts is that in the completed work the idea comes as good music; but in Goethe's image of the divinely-sustained unity of all things, resonating in harmony through the universe, the vessels are brought by *unseen* hands: there is no point hoping to catch them at their mysterious work.

How a listener senses wider significance in the flow of sounds is equally mysterious. Of the two mysteries, this book's concern is not the compositional process but the aesthetic impact. Schumann often wrote as though he did not distinguish the two very clearly, talking about ideas hovering before the mind of the composer as though that also addressed aesthetic impact.[15] But sometimes he concentrated on the distinction. In 1838, he described how the sensitive ear of a 'true poet' (here Sterndale Bennett) could pick up ('ablauschen') half-hidden musical possibilities in nature – the sounds of sea, millstream and fountain:

Auf welche Weise die Skizzen übrigens entstanden seien, ob von innen nach außen, oder umgekehrt, macht nichts zur Sache und vermag niemand zu entscheiden. Die Komponisten wissen das meist selbst nicht, eins wird so, das andere so; oft leitet ein äußeres Bild weiter, oft ruft eine Tonfolge wieder jenes hervor. Bleibt nur Musik und selbstständige Melodie übrig, grüble man da nicht und geniesse.

Whether the compositional process flowed from inner [musical impulse] towards outer [circumstance], or the other way round, is of no account and cannot be determined. Composers normally do not know that themselves: sometimes it is one way, sometimes another; often an outer image leads the music on, often again a musical sequence elicits an image. As long as music and melody remain sufficient in themselves, let us not agonise but simply enjoy it.[16]

He certainly thought of his own music as expressive. In 1838, he wrote:

Es afficirt mich Alles, was in der Welt vorgeht, Politik, Literatur, Menschen – über Alles denke ich nach meiner Weise nach, was sich dann durch die Musik Luft machen, einen Ausweg suchen will. Deshalb sind auch viele meiner Compositionen so schwer zu verstehen, weil sie sich an entfernte Interessen anknüpfen, oft auch bedeutend, weil

---

[14] *GSK*, II 129–30: Appendix 3–2(b); Goethe, *Faust*, Part I, 'Nacht', 449–50 (*Werke*, II 25). In 1605, William Byrd had written (*Gradualia*, 'Dedication') of the relationship between words and music in religious works: 'In the very sentences ... there is such a hidden and concealed power that to a man thinking about divine things and turning them over attentively and earnestly in his mind, the most expressive measures come, I know not how, as if by their own free will, and freely offer themselves to his mind.'

[15] Compare Lippman, 'Theory and Practice', 324–5.   [16] *GSK*, I 368 (1838).

mich alles Merkwürdige der Zeit ergreift und ich es dann musikalisch aussprechen muß.

Everything that goes on in the world affects me – politics, literature, people – and in my own way I think about everything, and then it vents itself or seeks an outlet through music. That's why many of my compositions are so difficult to understand, because they connect with remote interests, often to a significant degree, because I am gripped by all the remarkable things of the time and then have to express them musically.[17]

He went on to describe his music as an 'intellectual poem', or 'a product of poetic consciousness'; elsewhere he noted the impact on his music of 'literature, surroundings, inner and outer experiences', and of 'his turbulent life'.[18]

Over the years around 1835, then, Schumann touched on hard questions about musical expressiveness. Is musical expressiveness transitive or intransitive, expressing something in particular, or simply expressive, but not of any entity other than itself, visual, verbal or otherwise?[19] How far is it in the mind of the listener only, rather than also in the music? And what, finally, of paradoxes apparently built into the basic terms of the Berlioz review – that Schumann briskly dismisses the notion that a composer picks up his pen with the aim of 'expressing, describing or painting this or that', while also speaking of the 'particular idea the composer wished to present'; and that he claims that a composition will be more expressive, the more that images or thoughts arise, take shape and develop in 'elements related to music'?

Such questions about associations 'with remote interests' and expressiveness haunt this book. My aim is not to exorcise those spectres from the start by reductive explanation, but to let them loose among Schumann's 'Hoffmann works' before confronting them again thereafter. It is now time, then, to turn to the first of those works, *Carnaval*, which Schumann was composing as he wrote the Berlioz review.

---

[17] *Briefwechsel*, I 146 (16 April 1838).
[18] *Neue Folge*, 157 (14 June 1839) and 227 (5 May 1843).
[19] Compare Scruton, 'Expression', in *New Grove*, VIII 466–71.

3 | A musical carnival, 1834–1837
Carnaval, *op. 9*

Schumann described *Carnaval*'s origins in 1834–5, juxtaposing strands of love and art, and featuring his fiancée, Ernestine von Fricken, alongside Clara Wieck and Chopin:

Ernestine and Clara ... September – union with Ernestine ... Increasing depression – exchanged letters with Ernestine.
   1835 ... continued working on *Carnaval* ... Release from Ernestine in summer and autumn – oh! – With Clara every day...
   Chopin – Clara's eyes and her love ... The first kiss in November – broke with Ernestine.[1]

These themes and characters, some lightly disguised, are among those suggested in *Carnaval* as published in summer 1837. Its pieces' titles (Table 3.1) are far from self-explanatory, but evoke, in a confection of fact and fiction, a cast from the *commedia dell'arte* and from Schumann's circle of artists ('Florestan', 'Eusebius', 'Chiarina', 'Chopin', 'Estrella'), along with a magician of the violin ('Paganini'), disparate images (Sphinxes, butterflies, dancing letters), dances, and some vestigial events ('Réplique', 'Reconnaissance', 'Aveu', 'Promenade').

Such elements make richer sense to me against a background like that of the Italian carnival than that of a social ball or a dance sequence. Schumann's work suggests carnival settings, including theatre, street and masked dances; its titles name carnival characters including clowns and artists; its vestigial plot, sometimes dizzying features and exhilarating comedy are at home in a carnival.

The work takes its place in a German tradition of the Italian carnival alongside Gozzi, Goethe, Tieck and Hoffmann's story, *Prinzessin Brambilla* (henceforward abbreviated to *Brambilla*).[2]

---

[1] *Tagebücher*, I 420–1.
[2] To my knowledge, Schumann made no reference to *Brambilla*, and its relevance has never registered in print in German, American or British work; but it has been mooted in French and Italian publications: Brion, *Schumann*, 170–6; Chailley, *Carnaval de Schumann*; Rastelli, '"Carnaval" e "La principessa Brambilla"' and Giani, 'L'Italia di Robert Schumann'; and Thomas Synofzik has said that *Brambilla* 'inspired *Carnaval*' (*The Fantastical World of Robert Schumann*, BBC Radio 3, 12.15 p.m., 29 May 2010).

A musical carnival, 1834–1837: Carnaval, op. 9   35

Table 3.1: *Carnaval*'s titles, keys and Sphinxes

Title	Main keys (Sub-dominant / Tonic / Dominant areas)			Sphinx
'Préambule'		A♭ major		2
'Pierrot'		E♭ major		3
'Arlequin'		B♭ major		(3)
'Valse Noble'		B♭ major		3
'Eusebius'		E♭ major		(3)
'Florestan'		G minor		3
'Coquette'		B♭ major		3
'Réplique'		G minor		-
'Sphinxes'		[None]		
'Papillons'		B♭ major		3
'Lettres Dansantes'		E♭ major		2
'Chiarina'		C minor		2
'Chopin'	A♭ major			-
'Estrella'	F minor			2
'Reconnaissance'		A♭ major / C♭ major		2
'Pantalon et Colombine'		F minor / F major		2
'Valse Allemande'		A♭ major		2
'Paganini'		F minor		(2)
'Aveu'		A♭ major		2
'Promenade'	D♭ major / B♭ minor			2
'Pause'		A♭ major		2
'Marche des Davidsbündler'		A♭ major / E♭ major etc. / A♭ major		1

Key areas include related minor keys
The dotted line below 'Promenade' marks the resolution of thematic patterns

Goethe described the carnival he saw in Rome in 1788, and much of his description re-emerged in *Brambilla*: promenades, dances and theatre; the *commedia dell'arte*; suspended social norms, cross-dressing ('alluring hermaphroditic shapes') and flirting; and a cast including masked lovers, magicians, a strutting Capitano, and

Figure 3.1: 'The Minuet', or 'Carnival Scene', G. D. Tiepolo

German artists.[3] Most of these features are prominent too in the plays of the Venetian Carlo Gozzi (1720–1806). His drama was aristocratic but popular, conservative in philosophy but cavalier in mixing genres. Aesthetic criticism sits alongside dramatic metamorphoses; there are love stories and dances (both emblematic of carnival: Figure 3.1). City streets jostle courts and fairyland, mixing kings, nobles, celebrities, clowns, wizards and the familiar carnival character of the charlatan (Figure 3.2). The plays revel in stock motifs, including confusion of identity and ultimate recognition, and adopt a traditional theatrical plot structure, with trials and quarrels resolved in a triumphant concluding assembly or dance. Gozzi's plays became popular in Germany, admired by Mozart, Schiller, Jean Paul and Hoffmann; though it is not certain whether Schumann read them, he must have known they were admired.[4]

---

[3] Goethe, *Italienische Reise* (*Werke*, VI), 500–4, 511–12. Excerpts are at Appendix 3-3.

[4] Schiller translated Gozzi's *Turandot*; Jean Paul, *Vorschule*, §§25, 32, 36, 39; Hoffmann, *Fantasiestücke*, 135 and 698–704. Schumann's 1840 review of an opera (*GSK*, I 487–9) gives no clue that the libretto's source was a play by Gozzi, even though he presumably at least read Hoffmann's summary of it ('Der Dichter und der Komponist', *Die Serapions-Brüder*, 84–7).

Figure 3.2: 'The Charlatan', G. D. Tiepolo, fresco, 1757

The spirit of Gozzi entered German literature in part through Tieck's early plays. Like Gozzi, Tieck reaffirmed the tradition of the *commedia dell'arte*, with its improvised comedy, which earnest spirits in the eighteenth century had sought to banish; his *Die verkehrte Welt* (1796–7), true to its title, shows a world turned upside down in carnivalesque fashion. His plays were also spectacular examples of aspects of early Romantic aesthetics, such as irony, alienation, self-reflexiveness, and defamiliarisation.

Two decades later, Hoffmann's *Brambilla* echoes Gozzi in myriad ways, acknowledging his significance in a 'Preface', itself modelled on Gozzi; but it also leans on Goethe and on Idealist thought. The Roman Carnival shapes its images, ideas, narrative and characters, its shifting, uncertain identities, the lacunae that it flaunts, and its dislocations of narrative level, form and genre. The book makes the reader question how far it resolves these confusions, and if there is an answer, it lies in humorous self-recognition, irony and love, which laugh off dislocations, aesthetic and personal. It frequently calls itself 'a capriccio', and of it Heine remarked that if it 'does not make your head spin, you have no head'.[5]

---

[5] Gozzi: *Brambilla*, 211; dislocations: 229, 298, 311, 326. 'Capriccio': *Brambilla*, 209, 211, 229–30, 261, 296, 298, 310 and 317. Heine: 'Wem diese durch ihre Wunderlichkeit den Kopf nicht schwindlig macht, der hat gar keinen Kopf', cited in Hoffmann, *Späte Werke*, 870.

Schumann's *Carnaval* seems to me equally capricious, an exhilarating comedy of gesture and character with a dizzyingly humorous shape. This chapter explores what produces that sense, looking at its dislocations of structure and genre, motivic mystifications and metrical extravagances, and its carnivalesque associations, labile identities, divergent images and resolution in recognition and humour.

Structure

Carnaval's pieces make up a succession of fleeting scenes, too many to convey a clear shape or structure, and what gives the work an idiosyncratic shape and energy, paradoxically and aptly, is the unruly spirit of carnival. Aside from the clear divisions between the first piece and what follows, different aspects suggest other divisions at different points, and if Table 3.1 is complicated by conflicting ordering principles, it may in that respect reflect the work. The titles suggest divisions at 'Sphinxes' and 'Reconnaissance', and shifts between the three Sphinxes suggest divisions at 'Lettres Dansantes' and 'Marche'.[6] More powerfully, as discussed below, the main motivic patterns resolve at the end of 'Promenade'. But the tonal pattern (which moves from A flat major into dominant areas at 'Pierrot' and back at 'Chopin', with a leap to C flat major in 'Reconnaissance') resolves near the end of 'Marche' – only to be followed by a coda that restores an expressive imbalance, especially through its metre. A multiplicity of structural divisions and a divergence between structural markers contribute – in the context of a work that is carnivalesque in other ways – to a centrifugal nature.

Genre

As befits a carnival tale, *Brambilla* contains elements of lyrical love story, fairy tale, comedy, parody, aesthetic treatise and philosophical spoof; and *Carnaval* too is a whirligig of genre and style – the fantastical, the witty, the humorous, the sentimental, the mock-portentous and the incongruous.[7] It is in part a 'Maskentanz', a dance of masks, as 'Valse Noble' and 'Valse

---

[6] Compare Kaminsky, 'Principles of Formal Structure', 210–16, which downplays divergences in favour of coherence.

[7] Otherwise opposed reviews of 1837 noted that 'some dances break through, then all is once again swirling confusion', in what seems 'a potpourri': quoted in *Tagebücher*, II 464 and 467. Compare Appel, 'Carnaval', 50–1; Reiman, *Schumann's Piano Cycles*, 77.

Allemande' suggest and as Schumann described it.⁸ But Schumann also downplayed the notion that it is a dance sequence, characterising it (in a draft letter of 1837) as 'much rather showing the whole crazy business of the carnival of the imagination, in many interwoven scenes, right down to some little sketches of love-sport', with 'something humorous about the whole idea'.⁹ Even if this description was a protest against the worries of a potential publisher in France about the work's appeal there, and even if under-counting the pieces that could be waltzes ('at the most three, as you can check from the varied metres of the other pieces'), it carries both weight and plausibility as suggesting that the work embeds its dances in larger contexts.

Carnaval was also described in the *Leipziger Tageblatt* of 29 March 1840 – probably by the composer himself – as a 'humorous novel of masks', with characters appearing in 'fleeting musical sketches, between which an escapade seems to unfold' ('sich ein Abenteuer zu entwickeln scheint'). The novel which Schumann had projected in 1831–2, featuring among others Florestan, Paganini and Clara, was never written.¹⁰ If some of its motifs re-emerged instead in *Carnaval*, they have in the process jettisoned well-defined events and causal sequences – and unlike in *Papillons*, the resulting uncertainties are, I think, essential to the conception with its mesmerising instabilities of meaning.

As well as masked dances and novel, *Carnaval* is a critical manifesto. This is reinforced by an essay Schumann released on 19 May 1837.¹¹ It is a review of recent music, and its postscript exclaims that, 'as I had foreseen', a review of *Carnaval* had said that 'composers should not imagine that by hanging a little tail on thought worth 0 they can turn it into a 9'.¹² Presumably the 'tail' is an ironically derogatory term for verbal elements attached to a work – including this essay, which by implication is relevant to *Carnaval*, whose opus number was to be '9'. In fact the review of *Carnaval* was a fiction, and *Carnaval* had not yet appeared. This may then have been Schumann appropriating a device famously used by Tieck in *Der gestiefelte Kater*, which begins comically with fictional criticism of a work that has not yet appeared. Tieck's drama contributed to the

---

⁸ *Neue Folge*, 92 (23 August 1837).
⁹ *Briefedition*, III/8, 376–7 (12 February 1837): 'Erstens besteht der Carnaval nicht aus lauter Walzern, deren höchstens drei darin sind was Sie schon aus den verschiedenen Taktarten der anderen Stücke überprüfen können; vielmehr soll es das ganze tolle Treiben eines Faschings der Fantasie in vielen verschlungenen Bildern bis auf die kleinen Liebesspiele abschildern . . . Es dünkt mir etwas Humoristisches in meiner ganzen Idee zu sein.'
¹⁰ *GSK*, II 436, note 440; for the novel, see Chapter 1.   ¹¹ *GSK*, I 256–61.
¹² Schumann borrowed the image from Abrantes: *Mottosammlung*, IX 66 (1831–4).

German revival of Gozzi (whose plays were also prefaced by answers to criticism), and Schumann's essay aligns *Carnaval* with this tradition.

In the essay Florestan reports on 'the latest art-historical ball at the house of the critic', attended by the Davidsbündler, at which he falls in love with one of the host's two daughters, Beda. But she is in love with the absent Chopin, whose portrait she shows Florestan. Florestan comments: 'Chopin, you beautiful robber of hearts, if I had never been jealous of you, I was in that moment'. Beda mistakes Eusebius for Florestan; Florestan does not accept a proposal of marriage to Beda's prosaic sister; and there is a stand-off with the officious de Knapp, whose musicianship is denigrated by contrast with that of Paganini. In one postscript, de Knapp is routed; in another B-E-D-A is transcribed into musical notes. The essay thus flags the possibility that *Carnaval* intermingles dance, music criticism and a rectangle of love, throwing in jealousy of Chopin, confusion of identity, the rout of pompous philistines by true artists, and musical rebuses.

Finally, *Carnaval* is a sequence of comic vignettes, gestures and characters. Its subtitle, 'scènes mignonnes', might suggest a magic lantern show of the sort Schumann described in an essay of 1836 as a detailed retrospective poetic *mise-en-scène* for Schubert's *German Dances* – featuring carnival and masked ball encounters.[13] Or the 'scènes' could be imagined as *tableaux vivants*, or the phantasmagoria operated in towns all over Europe (including Hoffmann's Berlin).[14] And into this mix come theatrical overtones. For theatre was a carnival tradition, for which 'the Romans' passion', Goethe said, 'was once even greater at carnival time as that was the only time in which it could be satisfied'.[15] Theatre is central to *Brambilla*, which begins with a scene in a theatrical costumier's, leading into the equivalent of the opening of a comic opera: a crowd fills the Corso, accompanied by cymbals, pipes and drums, for the start of carnival. The plot features the conflict in Rome's theatres between the *commedia dell'arte* and the earnest verse of alexandrines.[16] And in a refraction of its own story, *Brambilla* summarises a theatrical pantomime of Colombina and Arlecchino – the initial helplessness of the lovers, their avowal of love, the routing of Pantalon, the magical transformation of the scene and the final triumphal procession.[17] Like carnival and *Brambilla*, *Carnaval* too has overtones of theatre, and 'scènes mignonnes' may also suggest dramatic

---

[13] *GSK*, I 203. [14] Hoffmann, *Fantasiestücke*, 263; Warner, *Phantasmagoria*, 147–56.
[15] Goethe, *Werke*, VI 518; *Brambilla*, 292–4.
[16] *Brambilla*, 212; Goethe's *Wilhelm Meister* also pits these styles against one another, and they were matched by warring operatic fashions in Joseph II's Vienna: Goethe, *Werke*, IV 242; Gutman, *Mozart*, chapter 10.
[17] *Brambilla*, 237–8.

sketches. In April 1836, Schumann had in mind 'a dozen Faschingsschwänke', and advertised the work as 'Fasching. Schwänke' – which latter, though often translated in English as 'pranks' or 'jests', has connotations rather of comic acts featuring stock characters and motifs.[18]

'Préambule' and motivic mystification

'Préambule' gives many signs of a theatrical opening ensemble or overture. The fanfare of bars 1–6, with its rising melody, and harmonic ascent from IV through I to V, is a call for attention, like a rising curtain (Example 3.1). But it is immediately repeated, as though ignored the first time, and countermanded by a depressive closing down in bars 7–10: it has to be reasserted even more emphatically in 10–24, as though in a comic altercation, like that in Tieck's *Der gestiefelte Kater*, as to whether the show is ready to start (Example 3.2). In the following eighteen bars (25–35), a busy motif occurs over twenty times, with scarcely any harmonic movement: the repetitions jostle one another, perhaps, like acts treading on each other's toes. The episodes in bars 25–109 often show features of transitions, and might be heard as those acts each hurried on and then off by the crush, in a wealth of gestural comedy. After a precipitate vivo in the dominant, a presto conclusion (Example 3.5) reaffirms the tonic and ratchets up expectations of action to come.

But 'Préambule''s tonal vector – clear and conventional as it is – is comically contradicted by a waywardness of form. It might be heard as an overture in 'pot-pourri' form, with its maestoso opening fanfares, dance rhythms, 'low' musical style, and suggestions of medley. Or it might be heard as a sonata without development, another normal form for such an overture; but it is only in retrospect and with doubts that one can ask if bars

Example 3.1: Schumann, *Carnaval*, 'Préambule', bars 1–6

[18] *Neue Folge*, 419 (13 April 1836) and 537, note 505.

Example 3.2: Schumann, *Carnaval*, 'Préambule', bars 7–18

25–35 (and 67–70) represented a tonic first group, recurring in dominant key areas from bar 79, and recapitulated in 102ff.

Moreover, though 'Préambule' introduces the work's main motivic material, that material plays an oddly understated role. Its various patterns – fugitive rather than salient, and forming only a loose web – are of a sort which in Mozart, for instance, would have been mere opening gestures or the simple fare of closing sections. But here, in a carnivalesque (or perhaps Schumannesque) inversion of convention, they acquire greater significance: they are the material of 'Préambule', largely repeated in the closing 'Marche', and in between enrich the individual character of groups of pieces. They give the work a dilute, subliminal sense of continuity and a loose shape – albeit one that does not match the tonal shape – not least through their partial resolution in the subdominant 'Promenade' and the comic reassertion of metrical imbalance in the tonic 'Marche'.[19]

'Préambule' opens with a repeated anacrusis, stepping up from $\hat{5}$ to $\hat{6}$ (Example 3.1). The anacrusis recurs in the key of C flat major (bars 10–13) and in the home major again (14–17); but first there is a contrasting step up in the minor (bars 7–10) (Example 3.2). This anacrusis evolves in various directions in 'Préambule' and the rest of the work.

---

[19] Kaminsky, 'Principles of Formal Structure', 213–16, looking primarily at pieces from 'Pierrot' to 'Papillons', finds different strands with different roles.

First, there is play between steps up and steps down. A step up, derived perhaps from the anacrusis, opens the second strain in 'Pierrot' (bars 8–9, etc.), and 'Réplique', while steps up close 'Estrella', 'Pantalon et Colombine' and 'Promenade', with varied gestural implications. Such steps up are missing from the concluding 'Marche'. Meanwhile a *sforzando* step down closes the minor strain of 'Préambule' (Example 3.2, bar 10), while the equivalent step down in the major (23–4) ends the first section of the piece. Something comparable occurs in 'Coquette' (bars 5, 9, etc.), and similar steps down mark closes particularly in the second half of the work.[20] The main theme of 'Marche' ends with a step down. Secondly, the più moto section of 'Préambule' (bars 24–6) opens with fourfold repeated octaves, and these recur (35–6, 41–2, 55–6) to set its episodes in motion, along with variants (39, 45, 59–60). They are repeated in 'Marche'; but there a dotted variant with a descending sixth forms a contrasting gesture: it becomes a closing motif, interrupting music that had been continuous in 'Préambule', and then becoming the linear descent and cadence that represents a conclusion to the work.[21] These subtle shifts of weight from opening to closing motifs may help to shape the work.

A third, more thematic transformation of the opening anacrusis, contrasting $\hat{6}$ in bar 1 of 'Préambule' and $\flat\hat{6}$ in bar 7, looms large in the first half of the work. Since the $\flat\hat{6}$, highlighting dissonance or incompletion, leads towards A flat minor, and then C flat major, it is implicated not only in a central thematic contrast, and an expressive opposition, but also in what turns out to be a tonal extreme of the work in 'Reconnaissance'. A variant characterises 'Pierrot', with $\flat\hat{6}$ and then $\hat{5}$ in the tenor, *piano*, followed in the next bar by the major version, *forte* (bars 2–4, etc.). In 'Valse Noble', the bass opens by hitting the dissonant $\flat\hat{6}$, and waits a bar before resolving on $\hat{6}$. The contrasting step from $\hat{6}$ to $\hat{5}$ is withheld in the melody in bars 4–5, and only granted at the very end (38–9: Example 3.7). A similar contrast marks 'Florestan', is replayed in 'Coquette' in a different spirit, and develops further in 'Réplique'.[22] The contrast

---

[20] For instance in 'Lettres Dansantes' (bars 12 and 16), 'Chiarina' (end), 'Estrella' (4, 12, etc.), 'Valse Allemande' (end) and 'Aveu' (end); all except the last are emphasised or *forte*.

[21] Bars 102, 106, 108, 198, 202, 204–25; compare 'Estrella', 3, 7, 11, 31, 35.

[22] In 'Florestan' $\hat{6}$ (G in B$\flat$ flat major) falls to $\hat{5}$ in bars 8 and 18, while in bars 2, 4, 12, 14, 56, etc. (in G minor), G falls to F♯. In 'Coquette', see bars 5, 13 and 15. In 'Réplique', the opening minor anacrusis contrasts with major steps at 1–2 and 3–4. 'Lettres Dansantes' brings back the pitch of the contrasted opening anacruses of 'Préambule', but reversed and in different tonal contexts (bars 11–12 and 15–16).

Example 3.3: Schumann, *Carnaval*, 'Préambule', bars 56–62

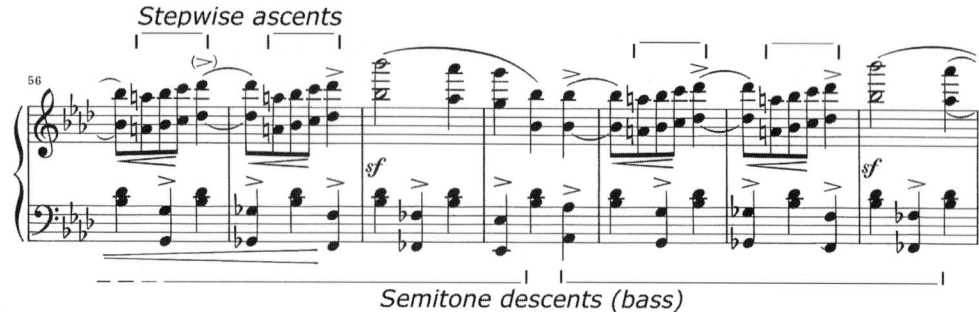

between $\hat{6}$ and $\flat\hat{6}$ seems to suggest continuities of personality or state of mind in the characters of the first half; it disappears in the sequence from 'Chiarina' to 'Promenade'.

Another thematic strand involves ascents and descents, again generally from $\hat{5}$, $\hat{6}$ or $\flat\hat{6}$. Beneath the rising opening theme of 'Préambule' lies a gapped descent in the left hand (bars 3–6: Example 3.1); meanwhile a scalar descent runs from F♭ to C♭ in the minor (9–10: Example 3.2). Later, an ascending quaver figure tries to get off the ground (Example 3.3).

Only in the *presto* conclusion (bars 114ff) does such an ascent achieve lift-off, echoing the opening fanfare's move from $\hat{5}$ to $\hat{6}$ (E♭ to F), and turbocharged by metrical dislocation (Example 3.5). Meanwhile, the ascents of bars 56–62 have an answering scalar descent in a conflicting metre (62–7), and this seems a source of a flowing scalar ascent and descent in 'Florestan' (8–10 and 18–22), setting major against minor with different metres. Other stepwise ascents or more often descents from $\hat{5}$ (sometimes $\hat{6}$ or $\flat\hat{6}$) are a staple of 'Marche', having been salient in many pieces in both halves of the work.[23]

Meanwhile, 'Préambule' also introduces descents and ascents by semitones. The former is accented in the bass in bars 55–62 (Example 3.3); the latter occurs in 87–90 (bass) and in 71–8 (Example 3.4).

---

[23] Stepwise ascents or descents occur for instance in:

First half	*Second half*
'Arlequin' 7–8, etc.	'Chiarina' 1–6, etc.
'Valse Noble' 1–8, etc. (bass), 9–14, etc.	'Chopin' 10
'Eusebius' 3–4, 7–8	'Reconnaissance' 12–14
'Florestan' 30–6	'Pantalon et Colombine' 5–8
'Réplique' 9–14	'Valse Allemande' 5–8, 10
	'Aveu' 5–8

Example 3.4: Schumann, *Carnaval*, 'Préambule', bars 71–6

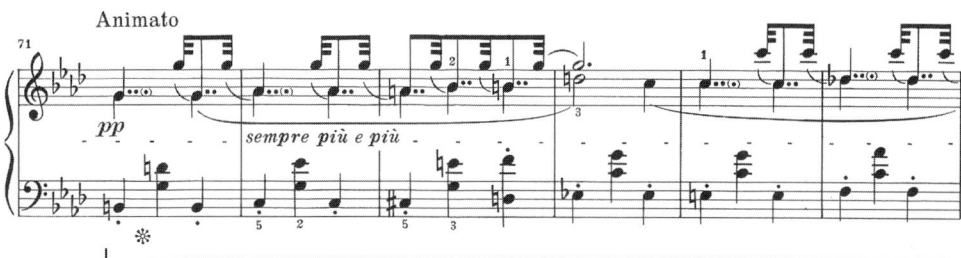

Semitone ascent (treble and bass)

These recur throughout the work and in 'Marche'.[24] This strand, like the others, is ordinary enough to remain largely below the level of consciousness. But sometimes a passage seems coloured by the semitone ascent ('Papillons' bars 17–20, or the middle of 'Estrella'), or a stepwise descent ('Chiarina'); and something like a dialectic emerges between ascent and descent. This may occur between pieces, as in 'Chiarina' and 'Estrella'; sometimes it appears within a piece, as in 'Eusebius' (bars 1–3 versus 3–4), the middle of 'Valse allemande' (10, 12 & 14 versus 13–16), or 'Aveu' (5–8, upper versus lower voices). This dialectic finds fulfilment and resolution in the conclusion of 'Promenade', whose significance as the first extended conclusion in the work will emerge.

It is characteristic that Schumann lays weight on other kinds of strand, and in particular a comedy of metrical conflict.[25] Thus 'Préambule', in $\frac{3}{4}$, sometimes suggests $\frac{3}{2}$: in bars 62–6 and especially 114–35, the left hand suggests $\frac{2}{4}$ and the right $\frac{3}{2}$, one beat out of sync.[26] Three anomalous bars contain four beats each (101, 120 and 128); and in 120 and 128, the extra beat is what brings the metre back into brief $\frac{3}{4}$ consonance before it flies apart once more (Example 3.5).

---

[24] Descents and ascents by semitones occur for instance in:

'Arlequin' 25–8 (tenor)	'Estrella' 5–11, 13–16
'Eusebius' 1–3, 9–13, 17–21 (bass)	'Valse Allemande' 13–16
'Florestan' 31, etc.	'Aveu' 2–3
'Papillons' 17–20, 25–6	'Pause' 1–4
	'Marche' 81–9, 103–4, 178–87, 195–6

[25] Another kind of strand might involve a sharp dissonance, accented and *forte*, often on a downbeat, and used for a range of gestural purposes: farcical for instance in 'Préambule' (bars 37, 39) or disruptive (88, 90, recapitulated in 'Marche'); awkwardly or sadly clowning in 'Pierrot' (1, 5, 15); absurd in 'Pantalon et Colombine' (5, 7); *passionato* in 'Chiarina' (2, 3) and perhaps pained in 'Estrella' (6, 12). (I owe this suggestion to a conversation with Judith Chernaik.)

[26] Compare Krebs, *Fantasy Pieces*, 87.

Example 3.5: Schumann, *Carnaval*, 'Préambule', bars 114–39

'Arlequin' may echo this metrical imbalance. So may 'Florestan', whose change of pace in bars 18–22 appears more or less to double the length of each bar (with a thematic pattern related to that of the end of 'Préambule'); it too has in its last four bars the wrong number of beats for the time signature. 'Promenade', having systematically set $\frac{3}{2}$ in bars 1–4 against $\frac{3}{4}$ in 5–8, etc., then resolves their opposition (Example 3.9). But 'Marche' opens in a $\frac{3}{4}$ that nonetheless sounds like a march, and ends by recharging the metrical centrifuge of 'Préambule'.

The patterns are not unconnected with the more famous 'Sphinxes' – each a sequence of notes, appearing mysteriously in archaic notation half-way through the score, with nothing settling whether they are to be played.[27] The Sphinxes may seem to portend personal and musical

---

[27] They are discussed by most commentators on the work, for instance in Rosen, *Romantic Generation*, 221–2. It is in the spirit of the work that it is in fact composed on five notes, though the title page declares 'four', as noted by Giani, 'L'Italia di Robert Schumann', 29, note 67.

Example 3.6: Schumann, *Carnaval*, 'Marche', bars 107–12

enigmas, but are in truth mock-runes, mystification and masks. The first (E♭, C, B, A) contains in German notation the musical letters of Schumann's own name, S-C-H-A. In the event, this Sphinx initiates none of the pieces in the set. But it is not quite inaudible: it can be heard in the 'Marche', in the bass in the first beats of bars 108–10 and – after a rest – of 111 (Example 3.6).

Perhaps the Sphinx, appearing evasively here, but nowhere openly (not even in a piece called 'A.S.C.H. – S.C.H.A.'), shows Schumann casting himself as akin to Hoffmann's Celionati.[28] For Celionati is presented both as a character in the tale and as the master puppeteer who invisibly controls its action: its author, Hoffmann, in another guise. In an ironic self-image for an artist, Celionati is often called a charlatan ('Scharlatan', which Schumann's S-C-H-A might possibly also suggest).[29]

The second and third Sphinxes are spelled in German As-C-H and A-Es-C-H respectively. Since Asch was Ernestine's birthplace, Schumann seems to invite us to see them as keys to an autobiographical love element in the work. But either the second or third Sphinx occurs in almost every piece, whatever the character presented in the title – in 'Florestan' and in 'Chiarina' as much as in 'Estrella'. So these two Sphinxes are not exclusively associated with 'Estrella', let alone with Ernestine. *Carnaval* is more a work of art with suggestions of autobiography than a work that encodes a detailed personal history.[30]

---

[28] One might conceivably hear the Sphinx in 'Florestan' (bars 49–50, and again in 53–4), taking the alto A with the soprano H, or in 'Eusebius' (1–2), finding the final A in the bass. Daverio, *Robert Schumann*, 140 aptly describes Schumann as 'an unseen presence, a master puppeteer regulating the motions of his creations from behind the scenes'.

[29] *Brambilla*, 220, 224, 257, 292, 323 and frequently at 308–13 (compare 'Doge und Dogaressa', *Die Serapions-Brüder*, 376). Compare Jean Paul, *Vorschule*, §34: 'the humourist is his own quartet from the *commedia dell'arte*, and the director as well'.

[30] Might the Sphinxes even have begun life in late summer 1834 suggesting other characters too? Schumann spoke then of 'three names', meaning Henriette Voigt, Ernestine and Ludwig

Nor are the Sphinxes musically profound. The structural implications of their alternation diverge from those of the motifs and titles; and they support rather than generate *Carnaval*'s tonal trajectory. The first three notes of the third Sphinx (which contains A, E♭, C and B), all fit a harmony of V^7 in B flat major, and A and C fit that of V^7 in G minor; and so it appears in most of the pieces of the first half, 'Pierrot' to 'Papillons'. In the second Sphinx (which is A♭, C and B), A♭ and C are part of I in A flat major and F minor, and of V of D flat major; so it appears, its first two notes harmonised accordingly, in 'Préambule' in A flat major (in the bass at bars 92–4 and 96–8), and in most of the pieces of the second half, which from 'Chopin' onwards are largely in A flat major and its relative minor, F minor, or in one case in D flat major. But the Sphinxes do not drive this tonal trajectory or the main shifts of tonality. The first piece that the third Sphinx opens, 'Pierrot', is in E flat major, which can scarcely be generated by that Sphinx, because it contains the A♮ of B flat major, not the A♭ of E flat major. The second Sphinx does not restore A flat major with its arrival in 'Lettres Dansantes', which is instead in E flat major again, and the only piece whose tonality is related to its 'H', or B, is 'Chiarina', in C minor; but there the accompaniment introduces the B (bar 1) before the Sphinx does. The Sphinxes do no more than support an emphasis on C flat major dramatised in 'Préambule' long before any Sphinx appears.

Sometimes a Sphinx introduces one of the motivic patterns; sometimes there is a contrapuntal relationship;[31] and in the first piece to start with a Sphinx, the E flat major 'Pierrot', both Sphinx and patterns emphasise ♭$\hat{6}$. But the Sphinxes show no progressive thematic transformation or development; they do not reveal deeper unity in surface diversity. Instead they sit on varied themes, parading a relatively static surface unity on top of the themes' underlying diversity in harmonic function, pitch shape, rhythmic shape, and accents.[32] Musically, it is a carnivalesque inversion of the procedures of thematic development traditional in the decades before Schumann; poetically, it suggests static masks, beneath which lie individual, mobile faces – as in *Brambilla* fixed and recognisable pantomime masks sit upon the labile identities of the main characters.[33]

Schunke, as 'musical names, which I will call "Scenes"', and referred to Henriette as an 'A flat major soul' ('As dur Seele'). 'As' could then represent 'Aspasia', H Henriette (both Henriette), S-C-H Ludwig Schunke, C perhaps Clara and Chopin. The Sphinxes also occur in the words 'Fasching' and 'Schwänke'. (*Neue Folge*, 54 of 22 August ('Aspasia') and 56 of 4 September).

[31] Literally so in 'Valse Noble' 1–8, 'Eusebius' 1–3, 'Papillons' 25–8, 'Chiarina' 1ff.
[32] Compare Kramer, *Classical Music and Postmodern Knowledge*, 103.   [33] *Brambilla*, 298.

Schumann talked on 23 August 1837 of 'deciphering' the work; a letter of 3 July 1836 used the same concept of the Sphinxes.[34] The latter implies only two Sphinxes at that stage (presumably omitting the first), and with one printed in each of two volumes the enigma would be all too easy. Indeed his mock-portentous Sphinxes are almost always audible and visible, appearing in most pieces in the first few notes of the melody, and in only a few later or not at all – assuming, as I do, that the notes of a Sphinx normally appear sequentially (with other notes intervening only in 'Eusebius'), in the given order (out of order only in 'Valse Noble'), and in one voice. (Admittedly, no two critics agree exactly on all the appearances of Sphinxes, or what constitutes an appearance, though since this is Schumann, and carnival, one should not insist on rules.) If Schumann's Sphinxes are a cipher-script, the key is on the surface; like Oedipus' perhaps, they are not the locus of the true enigma, which is the nature of the musical process; instead they operate as a conjuror's patter, distracting us from other motivic patterns.

Labile identities, divergent images and conflicts

Equally carnivalesque are the work's characters, images and situations. What appears first after the tour de force of 'Préambule' is the solitary figure of 'Pierrot', the first of two clowns from the *commedia dell'arte*. The *piano* opening phrase introduces a tenor version of the third Sphinx (which Schumann described, in one manifestation, as 'very pained', 'sehr schmerzvoll'),[35] with $\flat\hat{6}$ in bar 2; a contrasting *forte* motif (possibly echoing 'Préambule' bars 119–20, etc.) reinstates $\hat{6}$ in place of $\flat\hat{6}$, and clownishly disrupts the metre.[36] 'Arlequin', another clown from the *commedia dell'arte*, opens with dominant 7th harmonies suggesting an arrival in mid-act. His two-bar routine is repeated in four different positions in bars 1–8; the staccato octaves in 7–8 seem more mechanical each time they too are repeated.[37] But bars 1–24 evoke an agile, not to say double-jointed, creature: do they begin with the upbeat to twelve bars of $\frac{3}{2}$, or to alternate bars of $\frac{4}{4}$ and $\frac{2}{4}$, or

---

[34] *Neue Folge*, 92 and 419. As a marketing ploy, Schumann's Sphinxes paid fewer dividends at the time than they have since.
[35] *Neue Folge*, 57 (23 September 1834).
[36] It closes 'Marche' (bars 255–61) equally assertively (compare Kaminsky, 'Principles of Formal Structure', 213–16).
[37] 'Arlequin' may sound like a mechanical puppet, as Giglio, the protagonist in *Brambilla*, sometimes was (*Brambilla*, 225, 235–6 and 307).

Example 3.7: Schumann, *Carnaval*, 'Valse Noble', bars 27–40

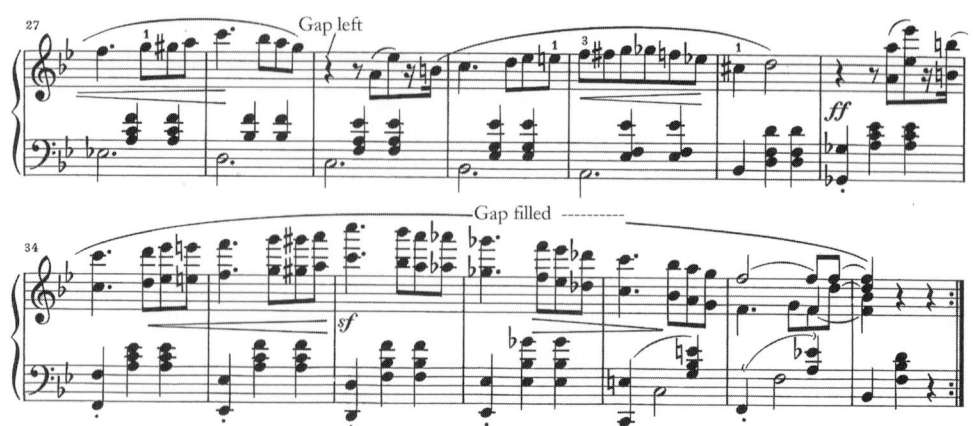

to twenty-four bars of $\frac{3}{4}$ as marked, but displaced by a beat? Both 'Pierrot' and 'Arlequin' – with their limited repertoire, thematically and harmonically, and mechanical repetitions – are artificial by contrast with the 'real' characters that follow. But in each there is also a moment when an actor appears from behind the mask: in bars 40–9 of 'Pierrot', the melancholy act gives way to gestures suggesting applause, its acknowledgment, and a bow; in bars 25–9 of 'Arlequin', the act softens into more intimate uncertainty as the metre relaxes into $\frac{3}{4}$.[38]

For Goethe, dance was central to carnival, 'generally expressing something characteristic of pantomime';[39] *Brambilla* too features several carnival dances, and the prints on which it is professedly based – made after the etchings of the seventeenth-century artist Jacques Callot, which it calls 'capriccios' – show carnival scenes that are often dances (Figure 3.3, page 66). So now Schumann has a dance, a 'Valse Noble'. It leads from his clowns to 'Eusebius'. Its opening is marked by comic jolts, but these are softened in a reprise: the second-beat accent that upset bar 8 is missing in 32, and the sudden gap in the treble on the first beat of bar 5 (and indeed 29) is filled in by the continuous melody of 37–9 (Example 3.7).

The inward, sensitive character of the middle section had prepared for this softening, with a molto teneramente marking, G minor orientation, poignant discords, and tenor voice brought out by staccato marks.[40] Thus as nobles and clowns alternate on Gozzi's stage or in carnival settings, so

---

[38] Simonett, 'Taktgruppengliederung', 75–95; Giani, 'L'Italia di Robert Schumann', 29–32.
[39] Goethe, *Werke*, VI 519.
[40] Clara once wrote of Schumann's waltzing: 'How beautifully you danced, so calmly, so nobly – exactly as you are': *Briefwechsel*, I 107 (2 March 1838).

after Schumann's clowns, his 'Valse Noble' leads into two pieces boasting 'knightly' names and complex characters.[41]

'Eusebius' has a delicate and irregular interplay between the voices, with intricate metrical superpositions.[42] Soft lower notes fall through the tracery of the treble. The absence of pedal and sotto voce marking make for a reserved tone; by contrast, bars 17–24 introduce warmer sonorities as the pedal is held down and bass chords – in 17–20 mainly resonant tenths – are spread.[43] 'Florestan' on the other hand is thematically fragmented, metrically disrupted, and conflicted between a passionato G minor that is never firmly established and the leggiero B flat major of bars 8–10 and 18–20. Those major passages develop a motif which on its second appearance is marked '(Papillon?)', as though Florestan stumbled upon a memory of love (represented here by Schumann's earlier *Papillons*, op. 2). Its unification of the ascending and descending scalar patterns remains only fragmentary, however, until fulfilment in 'Promenade'. From bar 30 an upper voice descends from $\hat{5}$, highlighting by its rests the pitches E♭, D, C and B♭. These may seem to echo the *forte* motif from 'Pierrot', as though it were shared by the clown and the noble.[44]

Just from the point where there is a suggestion of the first Sphinx, the piece hurtles towards melodic and harmonic disintegration, and breaks off, out of metre, with resolution in neither harmony nor melody. Closure is only provided by the opening three bars of 'Coquette', which bring back a consonant $\frac{3}{4}$ metre, and a satisfactory B flat major cadence (bars 2–3).[45] That opening, repeated at the close of the piece, develops into the opening of 'Réplique'. But there the cadence is progressively weakened, with more extended and inconclusive cadential phrases. Lower and upper voices engage in a tonally unsettled dialogue before ending on G minor, a key which is not home. The soprano alternates the (laughing?) motif of bars 1–3 of 'Coquette' with their tenor theme, which the lower voice adopts. The piece can then be seen as a duet, courteous but fruitless, between the 'Coquette' and a mask, presumably 'Florestan'. Its absence of

---

[41] Compare 'Ritter' in *Zeitung für die Elegante Welt*, no. 185 (22 September 1837), 740 (reproduced in *Tagebücher*, II 464, note 92).
[42] For instance, bars of 7 on 2 (bars 1–3, etc.), and 5+3 on 3 (bars 11–12, etc.).
[43] As brought out by Rosen, *Romantic Generation*, 12–13.
[44] As pointed out by Kaminsky, *Principles of Formal Structure*, 213 and 216.
[45] Its fluttering waltz motif (especially bars 17ff), suggestive perhaps of theatrical dancers, may recall those of 'Préambule' (bars 26–52, 80–5, 102–9) and 'Florestan' (5–6, etc.).

tonal closure and slowing pace leaves the first half of *Carnaval* incomplete, with no delivery on the expectations aroused in 'Préambule'.[46]

Though the titles in that first half suggest five different characters, none has a firm identity. The first two clowns briefly allow their masks to slip to reveal a human face beneath; 'Eusebius' and 'Florestan' are familiar as alter egos of Schumann, and as *Doppelgänger*; and the latter shares something with the clowns, and is flagrantly incomplete, closing only in the piece that follows. Behind these four male characters lies a hint of psychological development in a single subject, and even a vestigial story of confused identity and loneliness that could give rise to that development. Such stories are familiar in the German tradition. In *Brambilla*, for instance, the protagonist Giglio is an overblown tragic actor, in love with the poor seamstress Giacinta. He is depressed, unstable and incomplete without his love; he suffers from a split personality ('chronic dualism'), having adopted, or had foisted on him, the 'noble' character of the (presumably fictive) Assyrian Prince Cornelio Chiapperi. The Prince, in search of the (equally fictive?) Princess Brambilla, adopts the pantomime disguise of the strutting Captain Pantalon to join the carnival – unless it is Pulcinella behind Pantalon's mask, or even Giglio himself.[47] But Giglio, who sometimes believes himself the Prince's rival for Brambilla's love, also intuits an affinity or even identity between himself and the clown Arlecchino. Both the Princess and Giacinta are confused with Arlecchino's girl, Colombina; and whether the Princess and Giacinta are jealous rivals in love or alter egos remains long in doubt. These three pairs of identities – the 'real', 'noble' and *commedia dell'arte* lovers – intertwine in mutually tangled stories, and the head spins. In the light of Hoffmann's constellation of personae, Schumann's 'Pierrot', 'Arlequin', 'Eusebius' and 'Florestan' can be seen as varied characters sharing an underlying bond of identity; but the music only works if its characters are seen as Schumann's, not Hoffmann's.[48]

---

[46] Compare Wadsworth, 'Directional Tonality'. (Chailley, *Carnaval*, 16–22, recalls how Giglio searched for Brambilla along the Corso, 'checking every female mask, paying no attention to coquetry'.)

[47] Pulcinella's standard prop, adopted by Giglio to woo Brambilla and kill rivals was a wooden dagger (*Brambilla*, 227, 246, 259, 262, 293, 298–9, 317; see Figure 3.3). On 15 July 1835 (Robert-Schumann-Haus Zwickau, 280A-2), Schumann congratulated his brother's widow Emilie on her engagement, teasingly picturing himself as her 'oldest bridegroom', with his 'Italian jealousy' and a 'wooden dagger': traces, conceivably, of Schumann's reading of *Brambilla*.

[48] Brion, *Schumann*, 170–7, relates *Brambilla*'s themes of identity, duality, masks and love to *Carnaval*.

After this sequence, 'Sphinxes' marks a break. Its title has nothing in common with anything that has come before. It is an intrusion in the score, as archaic, portentous and mysterious as a rune. If it is a non sequitur, the title of the following piece, 'Papillons', is another (unless 'Sphinxes' punningly suggests night-moths before the daytime butterflies of 'Papillons'). Worse, it opens with a repeated horn call in the left hand marked *Quasi Corni*, as though to summon an audience back after an interval: what have horn calls to do with butterflies? But the phrases gradually lengthen, from two bars in 1–8, to four in 9–24, and then eight in 25–32;[49] the melody, encased in an inner part in 1–8, begins from bar 17 to climb; and in 25–6 the third Sphinx escapes into the upper register as a fluttering melody, in fleeting independence from the metre of the bass, like a butterfly into the light.

The butterfly had varied associations, deriving from a rich tradition in mythology, the visual and literary arts and science – including love, or the soul, or art, emerging from the grub and flying vulnerably into the light.[50] In 1833, after *Papillons* but before *Carnaval*, Schumann copied into his *Mottosammlung* a scientific description of butterflies as the highest insects, living in light and air, only for love.[51] In *Brambilla* the image expresses exactly that sort of metamorphosis:

When ... the Prince kisses me on both shoulders, you'll see of course how the loveliest, brightest, most lustrous butterfly wings will sprout in a moment and how I'll float up high – high in the sky. Ah! That is real joy, to sail through the azure sky with the Prince.[52]

At the art-historical ball, Florestan dreams likewise of soaring through the blue sky with Beda. The fragile iridescence of butterflies could also be an emblem of artistic self-fulfilment in a final stage of exuberant beauty. Schumann wrote that 'a tranquil Psyche with wings folded together has only half her beauty; she must soar into the sky!'; he had described himself as a cocooned artist not yet ready to burst out.[53]

---

[49] Simonett, 'Taktgruppengliederung', 116–23.
[50] See for instance Jean Paul, *Die unsichtbare Loge*, 7th, 37th, 38th, 48th, 49th, and 52nd Sektors; compare *Flegeljahre*, nos. 36, 47, 63.
[51] *Mottosammlung*, IX 233, from Menzel's *Naturwissenschaften*, citing Lorenz Oken's scientific work. Compare Schelling, *Erster Entwurf eines Systems der Naturphilosophie* (1799), quoted by Pfau, 'From Autonomous Subjects', 112: sexual maturity is attained only 'at the peak of individuation'; but the butterfly apparently assumes 'this ultimate developmental stage solely for the purpose of propagating its species': 'nature aims at the annihilation of the individual'.
[52] *Brambilla*, 302: compare Schumann's fantasy of early 1836 (*Briefwechsel*, II 367 (25 January 1839)).
[53] *GSK*, I 260, 23; *Jugendbriefe*, 200 and 217 (10 January and 2 August 1833); compare *GSK*, I 109, 122 and 128. Schubert's setting of Friedrich Schlegel's 'Der Schmetterling', D 633, has some

The title, 'A.S.C.H. – S.C.H.A. (Lettres Dansantes)', is a third non sequitur. The presence of the composer is implicated through the title, though the sequence S-C-H-A is nowhere visible. The music is so dazzlingly static and repetitive as to seem shapeless. The underlying harmony repeats a single progression without strong harmonic movement, and apart from bars 13–16, continuous dominant pedals and chromatic decorations cloud each individual harmony, with relatively few pure chords, and not a single root position tonic chord. The metre and the often dissonant appoggiaturas (bars 1, 5, 9, 13 etc.) give a flickering overlay to this essentially static harmony: the downbeat is constantly unsettled, and the accents or *sforzandos* on the third beats of seven of the first eight bars set up a cross-current of metrical displacement; later (bars 25–32) the right hand, with accents on diminished chords, is displaced from the left by two beats. The material of bars 1–4 is repeated so often that it becomes difficult to find a shape in the piece; the final chord of bar 32 is not a conclusion, but only sets the entire piece going again. There is no reason for it ever to end; instead it dissolves into the image of 'Chiarina'. Similarly, in *Brambilla*, for the lovesick Giglio, reading the script of a bombastic drama, 'every letter on every page dissolved into an image of the pure and lovely Giacinta'.[54]

Accordingly, perhaps, female protagonists now at last appear: 'Chiarina' and 'Estrella'. They bring conflicts which will demand resolution; and between them comes 'Chopin', which integrates muted dissonances of metre, phrase length and harmony with a mildness better fitting the stereotype of the feminine than the masculine. One could see it as 'Chiarina''s portrait of 'Chopin', like Beda's in Schumann's essay. Thinking of Chopin's role in that essay, one may read into the sequence both a composer's and a lover's admiring jealousy of him; and listening to Clara's works of this period (for instance the *Soirées Musicales*, op. 6) one might feel in them the gravitational attraction for her of Chopin's music, which she played from age 11 or so, giving it, Schumann thought, 'almost

---

similarities to 'Papillons' in shape and accompaniment: the image there is of the adolescent urged to taste all the beauties of sex.

[54] *Brambilla*, 269. It is a spoof, perhaps, of Novalis' Idealist image of a magical solvent thrown over our post-lapsarian eyes, so that letters swim, and sign and signified remain apart: Novalis, *Die Lehrlinge zu Sais*, in *Schriften*, I 79. The image of confused letters and words is in Goethe's *Wilhelm Meister* (III 12, *Werke*, IV 177). Schumann wrote in 1840 of Liszt that in his playing 'sounds and emotions rustled like the letters and concepts in a dictionary whose pages one raffles': *GSK*, I 479 (compare 122: 'The letters flicker into one another'). Wackenroder contrasted 'the sounding sea of music in which doubt and pain is lost' with 'the dizzying flicker of words and hieroglyphs': 'Die Wunder der Tonkunst', 131.

more meaning than [Chopin] himself'.[55] The style of her compositions, and even their titles – the Nocturne, two Mazurkas, Ballade and Polonaise in her op. 6, for instance – suggest a stronger influence from Chopin's music than from Schumann's.

'Chiarina' wilfully insists on a stress on both the first and third beats of the bar to the very end; its character might recall the 'moody', 'self-willed' and 'irresistible' 'smorfia' that Hoffmann attributes to Giacinta.[56] 'Estrella' mirrors those conflicts, with awkward intervals in the melody, harsh discords (e.g. bars 6, 15, 23), dynamic contrasts (12–13 and 28–9), and abrupt transitions (28–9); in bars 13–28 the metre is conflicted, with every weak beat accented, and treble and bass out of sync. It has ascending phrases in each hand as opposed to 'Chiarina''s descents, but both pieces employ the assertive repeated octaves. If 'Estrella' expresses anything about Ernestine von Fricken, it is perhaps not so much her character, which was 'pure, childlike . . . tender and thoughtful', as Schumann's tortured, 'feverishly conflicted' feelings about her as rival to Clara.[57] 'Chiarina', 'Chopin' and 'Estrella' might then form a group showing a tangle of conflicts and tensions for the persona of Schumann's music not unlike that between Giacinta, the Prince and Brambilla for Giglio.[58] In the shape of *Carnaval* as a whole, these two assertive minor pieces reinforce a sense of modal and metrical conflict in contrast to the milder major 'Chopin'.

Recognition and resolution

As 'Réplique' had followed the first, largely male group of characters, so 'Reconnaissance' now follows the second, largely female group. 'Reconnaissance' makes an instant contrast to what has gone before. After mainly triple time pieces, it is in duple time; after harmonic and metrical tensions, the bubbling gaiety of its A flat major polka opening suggests a half-ironic enjoyment on the part of the music's implied persona of a potentially sentimental style. Bar 9 adapts the Sphinx's 'H' (B or C♭) to turn to A flat minor, whence a middle section (17–44) shifts to the relative

---

[55] *GSK*, II 287; *Neue Folge*, 78–9 (14 September 1836).   [56] *Brambilla*, 219–20.
[57] *Jugendbriefe*, 243 and 259 (2 July and 2 November 1834), and *Briefwechsel*, I 96, 129, 200 (11 February, 19 March and 13 July 1838).
[58] Each features ♭II or its relatives (♭II in bar 12 of 'Chopin', V^6 of ♭V (or ♭II^6) in bar 34 of 'Estrella', ♭ii in bar 22 of 'Chiarina'), as no other pieces in *Carnaval* do except 'Lettres Dansantes', where ♭V appears near the end. This peculiar tonal feature may link 'Lettres Dansantes' to the other three pieces, suggesting continuity between the pieces, or an affinity between the personae involved.

major, C flat (notated as B major). It is the first notated key change within a piece in the entire work, and to the most remote key in the work. The introduction to 'Préambule' adumbrated a similar move from A flat major through the tonic minor to replay the opening in C flat major in bars 11–14; and at a similar stage (bars 15–16) of the concluding A flat major 'Marche' there are also striking chords of C flat major.

The move to B major opens a view into a distant world in which recognition ('Reconnaissance') may occur. The texture clears, after the frothier opening: treble and bass mirror one another in a two-part imitation that develops the polka motif, with syncopated triads transparently in the middle: first the soprano leads (bars 17–22), then the bass (28–9), and then they move together (35). Despite the sheen of metrical dissonance, the metre shows no conflict or complexity; instead there is a steady gaze, in contrast with the iridescence of 'Papillons' and the dazzle of 'Lettres Dansantes'. Syncopations, acting like diminutions, with consonant triads, motivic imitations and mirror-inversions in descending sequences give a sense of brimming fulfilment. It is like a duet, with suggestions of reflection in a surface clarified so as to become a mirror.[59]

In *Brambilla*, mutual recognition in the mirror of a magic spring brings about the union of Giglio and Giacinta. For the gloomy King and glassily cheerful Queen of the fabled land of Urdargarten, who might also somehow be projections of Giglio and Giacinta, had seen themselves and each other in the spring's water. In that mutual recognition ('Erkenntnis') they found a humorous union and a new world of life and pleasure, or so we are told, and conferred it on their people. But thereafter the King and Queen had declined, and the pool had turned murky and later swampy. Only when Prince Chiapperi and Princess Brambilla merge back into Giglio and Giacinta, through mutual recognition, abetted by love and humour, and Giglio's 'chronic dualism' is healed, was the pool magically purified, 'its spring gleaming clear as a mirror'. By then we have to suppose that Giglio and Giacinta were also the King and Queen, as they

> looked into the clear, mirror-bright water ... and *recognised* ['erkannten'] themselves, gazed at one another, broke into laughter ... and fell into one another's arms in delight.[60]

---

[59] Compare Hatten, *Interpreting Musical Gestures*, 249, on 'plenitude'. Kramer ('*Carnaval*, Cross-Dressing', 318–19; *Musical Meaning*, 119–26) sees mirrors here (as also elsewhere: he claims that 'the cycle is a musical hall of mirrors').

[60] *Brambilla*, 256, 289, 320–1 (Hoffmann italicises 'erkennen' and repeats it at 323, 324, 326; compare 256). Hoffmann echoes a lyrical image in Goethe of Dorothea leaving a muddied village spring to find a purer source in which she and Hermann 'saw their images trembling in

As the German artists in Rome suggest in a dialogue with the charlatan, 'the spring of Urdar ... is nothing other than what we Germans call Humor'; and at the end the spring is equated with the theatre of the *commedia dell'arte*.⁶¹ For in Urdargarten as in Rome, what brings about reintegration of personality, union of lovers and a thriving theatre is 'Erkenntnis', or recognition, of the self, an alter ego, or the beloved, in the mirror of art or of lyrical humour. Thus Giacinta and Giglio become a pair of comic actors 'whose deepest essence was true imagination, a true humour ... who were also in a position to recognise [erkennen] this state of mind and feeling objectively, as if in a mirror, and so to have it step out into the real world'.

The German word, 'erkennen', conveys knowing, recognising, acknowledging, identifying and realising as no English word can. Hoffmann's book plays with its multiple roles in Idealism, as a revelation of self, relatedness, love, destiny and even cosmic harmony. Mirrors, as instruments and images of recognition, contain reflection and self-reflection, and potentially infinite self-reflexiveness; they show to the subjective self both an objective self and the external world. They thus encapsulate concerns of variants of Idealism with knowledge, creation, art and the restoration of wholeness, and *Brambilla*, in which they are prominent, makes fun of these imposing connections.⁶²

The grand connections had grand ancestry. Luther's Bible used 'Erkenntnis' for the Tree of Knowledge, and for Paul's first Letter to the Corinthians, XIII.12, 'Then shall I know even as I am known'. In Shakespeare's *Twelfth Night*, as in *The Comedy of Errors*, twins are separated by life's storms, and forced to alter identity and even gender; only recognition, as if in a mirror, can untangle crossed loves and bring unity. Novalis' Hyacinth dreams that in lifting the veil of the statue of Isis he recognises himself behind it, but sees that the figure is also the higher essence of the girl he has always loved: 'Every fixed point established in the infinite fluidity [der unendlichen Flüssigkeit] becomes for him a new revelation of the spirit of love [des Genius der Liebe], a new tie between the You and the I.'⁶³ More portentously, Novalis had a voice declare, 'We

---

the blue of the sky, and ... exchanged friendly greetings in the mirror': *Hermann und Dorothea*, 7th Canto, *Werke*, I 613.

⁶¹ *Brambilla*, 258, 324–5.

⁶² Mirrors are used to describe the spring at Urdar (256, 284, 289, 321), humour (324), the windows of Brambilla's coach and Colombina's triumphal carriage (221–2, 238), how Giglio sees himself (280), and a lover's eyes (219, 274, 304).

⁶³ Shakespeare, *Twelfth Night*, V.i.275, *Comedy of Errors*, V.i.420; Novalis, *Die Lehrlinge zu Sais*, in Novalis, *Schriften*, I 101.

sit at the spring of freedom [Quell der Freiheit] and gaze; it is the great magic mirror [Zauberspiegel], in which the whole of creation reveals itself in purity and clarity.' That 'contemplation, that creative dimension of real satisfaction, deep self-recognition' ('jenem schöpferischen Moment des eigentlichen Genusses, des inneren Selbstempfängnisses'), is 'the original purpose of ... existence', and the artist in his creative contemplation of himself and the world is emblematic of humanity, which sees itself 'actively reflected in the theatre'; for Novalis saw 'almost everyone' as 'to some degree an artist'. Goethe similarly had had a character say of a poet, 'How charming it is to reflect oneself to oneself in the mirror of a beautiful mind!'; and Wackenroder said, 'the human heart learns to recognise itself in the mirror of music'.[64]

More cosmically, in Fichte's monist version of Idealism, the objective world only comes into being through the absolute mind's free activity of self-recognition, as 'Das Ich', observing itself, appears to itself as an object ('Nicht-Ich'); in positing an absolute, unitary and indeterminate self, Fichte leaned on ancient accounts of the way in which an absolute, infinite divinity created a contingent, finite world. In Schelling's version, a dualism of objective and subjective is also an identity, the 'World-Soul' ('Weltseele'), whose self-recognition is a creative act, both free and necessary; and the process is reflected in artistic creation. Jean Paul and A. B. Marx expressed similar analogies between artistic and cosmic creation, the latter with a similarly prominent role for 'Erkenntnis' in his musical aesthetics.[65]

Recognition might also heal mythic fractures. Romantic culture exploited a triadic archetype of primal union, alienation, and the quest for restoration of harmony. In the pristine state, for Novalis, every being was, and was named as, itself; signs and beings were one. Since then, sign and signified have become separated, languages mutually incomprehensible, and poetry and science opposed; 'an alkahest seems to have been poured over men's senses ... everything swims in their gaze'. We have had to deal through 'intimations' of a 'cipher-script' that 'will not settle in any fixed shapes' of an understandable language; but in Novalis' 'creative Idealism', true philosophy,

---

[64] Novalis, *Die Lehrlinge zu Sais*, in *Schriften*, I 89, 101; V 266(fr. 476), 229(fr. 228); compare V 249(fr. 336), and 'poetry is the proper mode of action of the human mind': Novalis, *Heinrich von Ofterdingen*, in *Schriften*, I 287; Goethe, *Torquato Tasso* III/3 (Werke, II 759); Wackenroder, 'Das eigentümliche innere Wesen der Tonkunst', 148. Hence the resonance in the tradition of the loss of one's mirror image: Hoffmann, *Fantasiestücke*, 262–83.

[65] Blackall, *The Novels of the German Romantics*, 137–42; Marx, *Musical Form*, 32–3 (1841) and 36 (1868).

science, poetry, fable and dream converge to give glimpses of a restored primal union of instinct, 'Anschauung' and self-reflection.[66]

It was a grand vision, ripe for parody. The *Nachtwachen von Bonaventura* (IX) satirically puts a counterpart of Fichte, in the shape of a 'demented Creator', in the madhouse, mocking his Idealism of the Ego and the monomaniac Romantic assimilation of metaphysics, theology and aesthetics. Hoffmann, who had read and critiqued the Idealism of Schelling, joined in. In his *Brambilla*, a chorus intones: 'Who is the Ich that can from itself beget a Nicht-Ich?', and magi deliver mock-portentous oracles:

Der Gedanke zerstört die Anschauung und . . . in blinder Betäubtheit [wankt] der Mensch heimatlos umher, bis des Gedankens Spiegelbild dem Gedanken selbst die Erkenntnis schafft, daß er *ist*.

Thought destroys Intuition, and . . . man will wander homeless, blind and dazed until Thought's mirror-image creates for Thought itself the Recognition that he *is*.

But these oracles, whose deciphering is thus given out to be the precondition for restoration of Urdargarten's well-being, are incomprehensible to the philistine ministers in the tale, who clearly have not read their Fichte or Schelling, and show themselves 'donkeys'.[67] Nevertheless, at the end a magus declares 'the world, the Ich' to be found, as a pair of lovers in Rome have recognised each other. Apparently the oracles did not after all need to be deciphered; the true enigma lies elsewhere; and Hoffmann both spoofs and endorses the speculations of Idealism.[68] Schumann's Sphinxes, though purporting to be runic, are similarly more a distraction than a key to the true musical process.

But 'Reconnaissance' does lead to a turning point in *Carnaval*, as it should. For recognition featured in the poetics of the German Enlightenment, and in particular in theatre and comic opera, as a descendant of Aristotle's ἀναγνώρισις, which in his analysis leads on to περιπέτεια, the turning point in a theatrical drama.[69] And as recognition traditionally brings fulfilment in love and art, so in *Carnaval* 'Reconnaissance', the pivot of the second half, brings on the resolution – or at least its beginning.

---

[66] Novalis, *Die Lehrlinge zu Sais*, in *Schriften*, I 79 (an alkahest is an alchemist's universal solvent); *Schriften*, V 205(fr. 15) ('Anschauung' and reflection), 209(fr. 43), 210(fr. 52) (union of all fields); 217(fr. 92) (instinct); 211(fr. 61) (signs); 264(fr. 451) and 269(fr. 494, fr. 496) (fable and dream). See Dickson, 'E. T. A. Hoffmann', 252, 259–60.

[67] *Brambilla*, 283, 286. Brion, *Schumann*, cites the chorus' ode (170ff; not in the English edition), and connects 'Reconnaissance' to the spring of Urdar.

[68] *Brambilla*, 288, 253, 257, 320; O'Brien, 'E. T. A. Hoffmann's Critique of Idealism', 390–406. The oracles are redolent of the doctrine of θεωρία in Plotinus (for example, *Enneads*, III.8); Plotinus influenced Novalis and Schelling (compare Novalis, *Schriften*, IV 269).

[69] Aristotle, *Poetics*. It had cousins in Sanskrit drama, including for instance *The Recognition of Sakuntala*, admired by Herder and Goethe.

The concluding series of pieces speeds the pace of dramatic movement and contrast. There are continuing conflicts between different keys, modes and metres, picking up those emphasised in 'Chiarina' and 'Estrella', but these are progressively softened and eventually resolved. In 'Pantalon et Colombine', a cantankerous opening in F minor and a metrically conflicted C minor are opposed to a subtler D flat major middle section, and soften into F major at the end: perhaps Colombine pleads with her father for her lover, as in the pantomime in Hoffmann's *Brambilla* – and ultimately, it seems, 'Colombine' thumbs her nose at 'Pantalon' in the final gesture, in a carnivalesque usurpation of a male clown's role.[70] (Or perhaps we can hear the rout of de Knapp from Schumann's essay?) An A flat major 'Valse Allemande' juxtaposes a delicately twisting opening with the comic energy, repeated octaves, dramatic leaps and weak-beat *sforzandos* of its middle section (bars 9–16).[71] It is interrupted by a largely F minor *Intermezzo* called 'Paganini'. In this conjuror's illusion, an appearance of virtuosity results largely from the displacement of the left hand by a semiquaver (with the bass beamed unconventionally), perhaps as if to suggest double stopping.[72] And after a wrenching reversal of the metrical roles of the voices in bars 33–4, there is a further conjuring trick, this time with the pedal. Out of the overtones of what had been an F minor chord (bars 35–6), 'Paganini' creates a chord that has not been struck, solely through the sympathetic vibration of undamped strings, and demands a crescendo and decrescendo that cannot be executed but only suggested by the performer's body-language. The effect is magical, and such conjuring can be a metaphor, in *Carnaval* as in the traditions of carnival and Idealism, for the experience of both art and love.

In 1832, Schumann described the famous caricature of 'Paganini in the magic circle'; for Paganini was, for him as for others, a magician of humour, an embodiment of Italian comedy in music, and associated with the idea of the Charlatan.[73] In *Brambilla*, the 'Charlatan' Celionati, who is often called a sorcerer, pulls off a conjuring trick to bring on the

---

[70] Compare Hatten, *Interpreting Musical Gestures*, 151–2, for a similar gesture in Beethoven.

[71] The masculine theme and leaping bass it adopts from Clara Wieck's *Valses Romantiques*, op. 4 (1835–6) suggests some cross-dressing; contradictory gender signals had occurred also in 'Coquette', 'Chopin', and 'Estrella'. Kramer, '*Carnaval*, Cross-Dressing', 306, 313–15 sees cross-dressing in several pieces. Compare Messing (*Schubert in the European Imagination*, chapter 1) on gender uncertainties in Schumann's writings.

[72] 'The artist as mesmeriser': Kramer, '*Carnaval*, Cross-Dressing', 321. Compare Reiman, *Schumann's Piano Cycles*, 113, on the piece's 'smoke and mirrors'.

[73] *Tagebücher*, I 404 (4 June 1832), 363, 437; *GSK*, I 15 and 468. On Paganini in German culture from 1828 onwards, see Gooley, 'La Commedia del Violino', especially 410–12 for his musical influence on *Carnaval*.

Example 3.8: Schumann, *Carnaval*, 'Promenade', bars 1–7

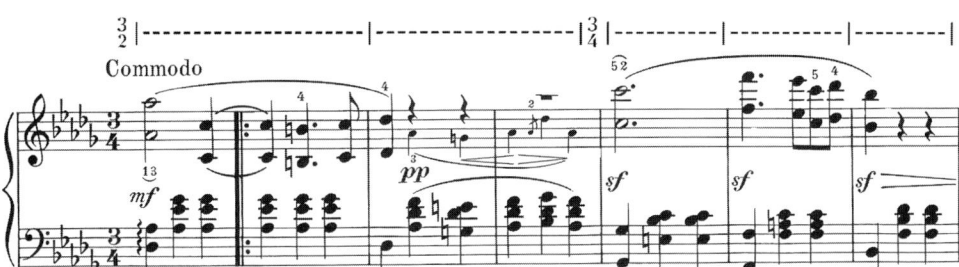

resolution.[74] The conjuring trick in 'Paganini', in the midst of a 'Valse Allemande' featuring Clara's own theme, and at a moment analogous to that of Celionati's conjuring trick in *Brambilla*, may pick up an idea Schumann had expressed before: in his projected novel, Paganini was to 'work magic on Zilia' (Clara).[75]

'Aveu' resolves F minor into A flat major, the two modes no longer in conflict, and there are only mild syncopations between its voices, rather than metrical dissonance; and 'Promenade' ends the resolution sequence as 'Reconnaissance' began it, as an island of stability. It opens with a theme (bars 1–4) which sounds as if its true, $\frac{3}{2}$, bars are twice as long as the notated $\frac{3}{4}$ bars; the melody's second half is notated entirely in grace notes, not so much a signal of an ornament, perhaps, as a visual representation of distance.[76] The B♮ of the Sphinx is less harsh here in D flat major than harmonised as a tritone in F minor in 'Estrella', and the mild harmonies, with the major mode, lilting rhythm, and *pp* ending, create a broad sweep of graceful movement. By contrast, the B flat minor motif in bars 5–8, with its dissonant opening tritone, insistent $\frac{3}{4}$ rhythm, and *sforzando* on the first beat of each bar, struts rather than sweeps (Example 3.8).

---

[74] *Brambilla*, 232, 248–9, 258, 236, 318.

[75] *Tagebücher*, I 342. In life, Clara's compositions attracted Paganini's notice, and she was often in his company as a 9-year-old; Schumann thought Paganini's influence on Clara unmistakable: *GSK*, II 287, 351, 271–2 and 353 (Florestan dreamed of playing the violin in a wine bar when Paganini entered, and of playing a Paganini caprice to attract the maestro's attention. It may however be coincidental that Schumann once described the violinist Lipinski, the dedicatee of *Carnaval*, as Paganini).

[76] Bars 3–4, 11–12, 19–20, 27–8, 51–2. The grace notes have durational value and melodic function; Schumann even inserts a real grace note to the highest of these 'grace notes' (bar 4, 2nd beat, etc.). What the smaller font adds to the *pianissimo* marking in aural terms is perhaps that the treble is a little quieter in relation to the bass than one might expect: thus we may hear the treble notes as further away than the bass as well as than the preceding ones: visual and aural signals of distance coincide.

Example 3.9: Schumann, *Carnaval*, 'Promenade', bars 68–93

The minor theme holds the field at the end of the first half (bar 32); but thereafter, and especially from bar 56, the major motif supplants it, in a more prolonged conclusion than in any other piece. The flowing ascending steps of bars 46–7 are complemented by descending steps, forming something like the cadential phrases in a classical work. The conflicting pair, $\frac{3}{2}$ and $\frac{3}{4}$, are reconciled. The ♭6̂ of the relative minor theme disappears after a last spasm (bars 38–55). A residue (bars 62–3, 69–70) of what in bars 1–2 had been a Sphinx vanishes, and is eventually recalled only by accented C♭s (73 and 81) resolving to B♭. Over a D♭ pedal dissonant Cs fade and eventually resolve (86–93) into a D♭ chord (Example 3.9).

The ending thus resolves both the major / minor conflict, and thematic and metrical tensions; but it cannot be the last word. It is already subdominant in relation to the A flat major of the work as a whole; the C♭s lean further towards G flat major; and the final D♭ chord is made a little strange by the harmonic and voice-leading progression from the preceding bar.

Conclusion and humour

What is required classically is a finale in the home tonic; and 'Pause', returning to the vivo of 'Préambule', appears indeed as a summons to a concluding ensemble. But only in carnival would a 'Pause' be precipitandosi; and it brings back accented dissonances (bars 2 and 4) and a Sphinx with its sore C♭ marked *sforzando* (bars 8 and 12). Its emphatic dominant preparation leads into a concluding 'Marche des Davidsbündler contre les Philistins' which balances the scale of 'Préambule', and brings back its key and much of its material, but also reaffirms an exhilarating imbalance. Its opening material stems from nothing but the Sphinx, ascents and descents (scalar and semitone) and in bar 15 accented repeated octaves; but its $\frac{3}{4}$ metre is in itself disruptive of march time, its first bar involves sharp dissonance, and it has significant F minor colouring. To the mix of march and waltz, some elements of sonata are added, in a humorous medley. An acceleration and dominant pedal (bars 25ff) are a lit fuse of laughter. With a move to C major, a sudden change of dynamic and register (bars 40–1) ratchets up excitement anew for the entry of the E flat major 'Grossvatertanz' (50ff), combining parody with a sense of the end of a social ball. The repeated octave gesture that set acts going in 'Préambule' is replaced by a dotted and increasingly frenzied variant which in bars 106, etc. interrupts them and shuts them off; but the music is still in the dominant. On a second attempt, now in the tonic, in bars 201–12, this variant, over an emphatic dominant pedal, leads to a descent (217–25) from $e\flat^3$ to $a\flat^2$ and a resounding perfect authentic cadence – more conclusive than anything in 'Préambule'. The two pieces, and the work as a whole, are united by this cadence, especially if it is heard as resolving the $e\flat^3$ so prominent in bars 6, 25 and 102 of 'Préambule'. The opening motifs of 'Préambule' have been converted into closing motifs, and the coda that follows links the work's end back to its beginning. But in that coda the metre flies apart once again, despite the metrical resolution in 'Promenade', so that the work ends with imbalance repeated and further unbalanced by acceleration. Carnival, Goethe said, 'goes by like a dream, like a fairy tale': after suspending social norms it allows the existing order to resume.[77] Likewise, *Carnaval*'s confusions are ultimately affirmative and integrative; but a laughing imbalance remains, and for so long as the music lasts, hilarity trumps order.

Here, as in the conclusion to *Brambilla*, sentimentality, pomposity and theatrical artifice are transformed into the triumph of humour over philistinism. 'Marche' suggests snooks cocked, forms destabilised, and dizzying humour. It may share the spirit of Schumann's 1842 contrast between true humour and the old-fashioned rococo spirit of the philistine, who 'calls Romantic anything that is not clear to him, while what he does understand gives him hope of the return of the old times'.[78] *Carnaval* thus has elements of a critical manifesto, championing a new poetic age, turning stuffy norms inside out, and raising 'trivial' genres to higher levels through subtlety, parody and wit. Like *Brambilla*, it adopts the self-reflexiveness dear to the Idealist tradition – as though it embodied in music the view of Schumann's successor at the *Neue Zeitschrift für Musik*, Franz Brendel, that in modern times reflection on music had separated itself from musical practice, splitting the subjective from the objective mind, and so required and made possible a new kind of music in which music and music criticism were reunified.[79]

The laughter of 'Marche' crowns a humour that is melancholy in 'Pierrot', clownish in 'Arlequin', pantomime in 'Pantalon et Colombine' and self-ironic and indulgent in 'Reconnaissance'. These are all variants of a humane humour akin to *Brambilla*'s. Hoffmann's 'Humor' sits easily with an 'Erkenntnis' resting on ancient traditions of thought and given new significance by Idealism: 'Humour [is] the power of the mind to create its own ironic double . . . in which it recognizes its own follies . . . and those of all creation, and takes delight in them.'[80] At the end of the story, Giacinta and Giglio as wife and husband congratulate one another on the success of the comedy they have just performed together: 'We carried on improvising

---

[77] Goethe, *Werke*, VI 523. Compare Kramer, *Classical Music and Postmodern Knowledge*, 104 and Reiman, *Schumann's Piano Cycles*, 77.

[78] GSK, II 72, on the Romantic humour of Beethoven's last quartets.

[79] Schumann probably heard Brendel articulate such a view before *Carnaval* was published, as he spent considerable time with him in 1833–4 and in summer 1837 (*Briefedition*, II/5 211–12). In summer 1837 Friedrich Wieck mocked Brendel's article for confusing subjective and objective (*Briefedition*, I/2 85–6), which as published it did not mention: probably the mockery worked as caricature because Brendel typically went on about them. In any case, it was a view characteristic of the age: Dahlhaus, *Klassische und Romantische Musikästhetik*, 264–7.

[80] *Brambilla*, 258; compare Jean Paul's description of the 'Besonnenheit' of the artist as 'seeing the self, turned both away and to the image at the same time, in two mirrors simultaneously': *Vorschule*, §12.

our main scene for over half an hour while the spectators kept up their warm-hearted genial laughter' ('gemütlichen Lachen').[81] Their word echoes Hoffmann's German artist's claim that 'even for the farcical' ('dem Possenhaften'), there must be an injection of 'Gemütlichkeit' of a sort 'intrinsic to our German nature'; he doubts that 'in Italy one could find men endowed with that profound humour'.[82] Schumann expressed similar thoughts. In a letter to Simonin de Sire about his 'Humoreske', op. 20, he regretted that the French would not understand his title, as they had no word for 'concepts like warm-hearted geniality ['das Gemütliche (Schwärmerische)'], and 'humour', which is the successful fusion of warm-hearted geniality and wit' ('die glückliche Verschmelzung von gemütlich und witzig').[83] These, he thought, were ideas 'deeply rooted in the German nationality', in contrast to the French. In 1834, Schumann defined 'Capriccio' – a term Hoffman used for *Brambilla*, and apt for *Carnaval* – as 'the genre of music that distinguishes itself from the lower form of comedy that is burlesque through its fusion of sentiment and wit' ('Verschmelzung des Sentimentalen mit dem Witzigen').[84]

It has been said that Schumann was here adopting Jean Paul's concept of 'Romantic comedy'.[85] Jean Paul indeed claims that humour's 'mildness and indulgence ['Duldung'] of individual follies is explained through its universality ... as the humourist cannot abjure his own kinship with humanity', and 'that universal mockery of the humourist ... warms the soul'; and he talks of the 'good-heartedness' ('Gutmütigkeit') of German humour. His notion was probably an influence on many writers, including Hoffmann, and one source of Schumann's view of 'Humor'.[86] Certainly in 1828 Schumann associated 'a combination of the sentimental and the humorous' with Jean Paul.[87] But in two respects, Schumann's 1839 letter is closer to Hoffmann's *Brambilla* than to Jean Paul.[88] It is Hoffmann, not Jean Paul, who highlights Schumann's word 'gemütlich', a concept that became

---

[81] *Brambilla*, 323. Perhaps Schumann's appreciation of the spirit of humour with which the young Clara Wieck played reflected in part his wish that she and he might become a loving couple of humorous artists: *GSK*, II 207.

[82] *Brambilla*, 247–8. Giani, 'L'Italia di Robert Schumann', 29–32, compares Hoffmann's statement with the mixture of farce and inwardness in 'Arlequin'.

[83] *Neue Folge*, 148–9 (15 March 1839).   [84] *GSK*, II 207.

[85] Daverio, *Nineteenth-Century Music*, 64.

[86] Jean Paul, *Vorschule* 32 and 34, which to some extent theorise a view already expressed in Tieck and others, long associated with 'Verschmelzung': Appel, 'Schumanns Humoreske', 110, 140 and 171–2.

[87] 'Verbindung des Sentimentalen u. Humoristischen': *Über Genial- Knill- Original- und andre Itäten*, in Otto, *Schumann als Jean Paul-Leser*, 112.

[88] *Pace* Appel, 'Schumanns Humoreske', 167.

Figure 3.3: 'The Dance', after Callot (detail)

associated with Germany after the long war of liberation from Napoleon. And for Hoffmann, true to that more nationalist time, 'Humor' is specifically German, and incomprehensible to foreigners, as it is for Schumann. Hoffmann, that is, borrows a nationalism of humour from Gozzi ('No other nation can carry it off. The Italians are the only brave wits who … have been able to manage this genre of improvised theatre') while changing the nationality, and indeed echoing Goethe's initial dislike of the humour of the Roman Carnival.[89] Jean Paul's 1804 statement, by contrast, was internationalist – noting examples of 'Humor' from England, France, Italy and Spain, the influence of Sterne's 'Humor' on Diderot, and the 'Welt-Humor' of Voltaire and Rabelais, while talking of a 'German deficiency in poets of "Humor"'.

Carnaval, in sum, evokes an Italian carnival, a world where everything is also something else. Its comedy of character and gesture, its images, dances and sense of theatre, its cast of clowns, nobles and artists, and its vestigial narrative of disguise, recognition, conflict and love resonate with the

---

[89] Gozzi, *Five Tales for the Theatre*, 4; Goethe, *Werke*, VI 208.

Figure 3.4: 'Undying Fealty', after Callot (detail)

carnivals of Goethe, Gozzi, Tieck and Hoffmann. Its kaleidoscopic humour, evanescent meanings and disruptive details make the head spin, its loose shape complicated by divergent formal signals and obscured by the dissembling Sphinxes; and it is in an equally carnivalesque context that *Brambilla* achieves a similar exhilarating spirit, through the humorous verve of the style, dizzying confusions between different worlds and characters, play with levels of reality, and mixture of genres.[90] Likewise, any narrative analogies to *Brambilla* or word-painting that may be detectable in *Carnaval* can be taken in the same broader context.[91] Detailed, almost narrative parallels could indeed be seen between the resolution sequences. 'Valse Allemande' could be compared to Giglio's wild dance with Brambilla: '"See how I circle round you, and elude you just as you think you've caught me, held me fast. And again!"' and '"Hey what steps, what

---

[90] Reiman, *Schumann's Piano Cycles*, chapter 3, focuses on formal and stylistic parallels, but with a diverse range of Jean Paul's novels, not with Hoffmann.

[91] Chailley (*Carnaval de Schumann* and 'Zum Symbolismus') finds programmatic echoes of Jean Paul.

Figure 3.5: 'She Knew How to Encircle Him', after Callot (detail)

leaps!"' (Figure 3.3).[92] 'Paganini' could be compared to Celionati's conjuring tricks, 'Aveu' with the Prince's avowal of love to the Princess (Figure 3.4), and 'Promenade' with the promenade of the strutting Pantalon and the sweeping Brambilla: as Pantalon 'paraded up the Corso and down again', 'his boundless solemnity gave him an almost comic air', while Brambilla 'moved majestically around the Corso in her splendid opulent costume', and 'deployed her skill to circle him' (Figure 3.5).[93] And 'Pause' and 'Marche' could be compared to Celionati's summons to the final assembly, and the final procession and performance that crowns the triumph of the *commedia dell'arte*'s love and humour over tragedy and bombast.[94] Once you are on the hunt for narrative and pictorial echoes, they may begin to dominate interpretation. But they need not be taken programmatically. They may be no more than fanciful. Or some of the pictures by Callot that Hoffmann incorporated in *Brambilla* may have inspired Schumann. Or perhaps in the year or two before *Carnaval*'s publication *Brambilla* influenced how the idea of carnival gave shape to

---

[92] *Brambilla*, 293–4.
[93] *Brambilla*, 318–19, 315–16. The 'Spaziergang' comes earlier in Hoffmann's sequence than in Schumann's.
[94] *Brambilla*, 318–19, 322–5.

music which could even have been largely pre-existing: for instance how a resolution sequence was fashioned to reconcile modal and metrical conflicts, softening self-assertion into humour, irony and consonance, as conflicts of character are resolved in *Brambilla*. At any rate, Schumann made no connection between *Carnaval* and *Brambilla*, and the music would appear much the same if *Brambilla* had never been written: the German literary tradition of the Italian carnival would still exist, if in impoverished form, and *Carnaval* could still be interpreted in its light.

I prefer, in short, a wider interpretation of the music's associations, and the next chapter steps back to reflect on these different approaches.

4 | Form, content and conception

Papillons and *Carnaval*, in their different ways, raised issues about the aesthetic functioning of similarities of form and content as between musical and literary works. This chapter begins to explore the possibility that Schumann's music can be seen as relating to literature not through either programmatic connections or parallels of formal or stylistic strategy taken in separation, but in a fusion of the two. The suggestion is not novel, but has not, I think, been related to musical analyses of Schumann's 'Hoffmann works', traced back to Novalis, Jean Paul and Hoffmann or supported by rebalanced interpretations of terms central to the argument, 'Geist' and 'unendlich'.

I start from Schumann's views as expressed in his criticism. He admired 'poetic' works whose form and content arise in musical processes shaped by a conception rather than constituting autonomous schemata imposed on the music – to develop formulations appearing not least in his 1835 review of Berlioz's *Symphonie Fantastique*.[1] Schumann in turn seems to have been influenced by the Idealist tradition;[2] and I will draw out in particular notions from Jean Paul's *Vorschule der Ästhetik*, which Schumann read and excerpted both in 1831–34 and again in 1837. Schumann's views, though, evolved throughout the 1830s, so that by the end of the decade his Berlioz review – of which he was still proud in 1840 – might have seemed a shade too cut-and-dried.[3] In it, he wrote:

> The manifold material that this symphony offers for us to ponder could easily become too entangled, and so I prefer to go through it under separate headings, even though they often overlap with each other – that is, under the four aspects under which a musical work can be considered: the form (of the whole, of the separate movements, of the periods and of the phrases), the musical composition (harmony, melody, articulation, working, style), the particular idea that the composer wished to present, and the conception [Geist] that holds sway over form, material and idea.[4]

---

[1] *GSK*, I 69–70, 72–3, 106; II 208. Appendix 3-2(a) reproduces some passages from the review.
[2] Bonds, 'Idealism', 387–420, sketches the tradition.   [3] *Neue Folge*, 183 (19 February 1840).
[4] *GSK*, I 69.

These 'aspects' no doubt reflect comparable lists in the musical and wider aesthetic thought of preceding generations. I suppose a resemblance to Aristotle's four kinds of 'causes', or explanations, which one could put as form, material, originating idea and final aim, may be due to the influence of Aristotelian thinking on aestheticians including Jean Paul; I would not claim that Schumann himself studied Aristotle carefully. Jean Paul's own list of aspects of 'poetic character' begins like Schumann's, with form, material and origin, but ends with 'technical presentation'; Schumann's last 'aspect', 'Geist', is more ambitious, more Idealist and perhaps more Aristotelian (surprisingly) than Jean Paul's.[5]

Aristotle did not believe it possible to isolate pure matter or pure form in this sublunary world, where both are projections, encountered only as fused in phenomena;[6] but as in his metaphysics, so in musical aesthetics, it is hard to dispense with some such concepts. I will use Schumann's 'four aspects' to help structure the argument of this chapter – but under three headings, as I will take form and 'musical composition' together, before looking at 'the idea' (or content) and at 'Geist'.

Form and formal parallels

This book distances itself from a view that the aesthetic significance of literary connections in Schumann's 'Hoffmann works' lies primarily in formal parallels. Schumann's own comments do not support such a view. Form was very important to him, and he discussed it often (not least in the Berlioz review). Formal features can contribute significantly to appreciation of a work as an aesthetic entity; from about 1838 onwards in particular we often find him talking about mastery of forms, his own and others'; he stipulated in 1850 that 'only when the form is completely clear to you will the "Geist" be clear too': form is an expression of a conception or 'Geist'. But he also declared to Clara Wieck in 1839 that 'there are ancient and eternal states and moods that govern us; it is not figures and forms that make up the Romantic, though it will show up in them of its own accord if

---

[5] Barnes, *Aristotle*, 121–2; Bonds, *Wordless Rhetoric*, 68ff; Jean Paul, *Vorschule*, §57 ('Form', 'Materie', 'Entstehung' and 'technische Darstellung'). The last is close to the 'Ausarbeitung' of Forkel's eighteenth-century division of musical stages on rhetorical lines. Might Aristotelian influence explain Schumann's reformulation, later in the sentence, of 'musical composition' (close to 'Ausarbeitung') as 'material' ('Stoff')?

[6] Barnes, *Aristotle*, 119 note 12, and 171–2.

only the composer is a poet'.[7] Accordingly, Schumann did not use abstract formal terms like 'Fragment' or 'Half-torn pages' as the titles of his 'Hoffmann works' (as he did for his very different opp. 99 and 124); instead he used emblems of the individual expressive conception of each work. Writing to an admirer about his *Kreisleriana*, Schumann talked about an 'eccentric, wild, inspired Kapellmeister'; he did not explain that Hoffmann's fictions were based on a formal principle of 'interleaving'.[8] I will later suggest that a way of describing the music of one of Schumann's works of 1838 (not one of the 'Hoffmann works') is through interleaving – but as just one aspect of a musical process with rich aesthetic and expressive qualities and associations, all shaped by a powerful musical conception similar to Hoffmann's.

In arguments about 'formal parallels', however, form can sometimes seem to be detached as a separately specifiable schema to be carried across from a book. In this narrow sense, musical form is a static, abstract or standard template imposed by composer or listener (ternary form, perhaps, or variation). This sense can be useful, and seems reassuringly technical and objective; but the idea that literary relationships in Schumann are primarily parallels of formal strategy in this narrow sense yields a relatively thin and arid approach, excluding all other expressive and aesthetic aspects. One could go to the other end of the spectrum, stretching 'form' beyond a mere template, accommodating extra dimensions, incorporating both static 'Form' and dynamic, temporal 'Formung', and covering any emergent aspects of musical processes, or almost all that an individual work is and does – including all that falls within Schumann's 'composition' or the Aristotelian 'material'. Schiller and A. B. Marx followed this line; more recently, Newcomb claims that 'form' is 'the seat of musical expression'.[9] I have some sympathy for this as one, perhaps extreme, formulation of a paradox about musical expressiveness; but here I will carp. In a narrow, reassuringly technical sense of 'form', the slogan is invalid, as in that sense form constitutes only one seat of musical expression. In a stretched sense, on the other hand, in which 'formal' means something like 'musical' or 'aesthetic', the term is almost redundant, leaving only a truism, 'music is the seat of musical expression'; if the thesis

---

[7] *Briefwechsel*, I 100 (11 February 1838); *GSK*, II 170 (1850); *Briefwechsel*, II 368 (26 January 1839).
[8] *Neue Folge*, 148 (15 March 1839).
[9] For instance, Schiller, *Sämtliche Werke*, V 696–8 (*Über Matthissons Gedichte*, 1794); Marx, *Musical Form*, 56, 63; Langer, *Feeling and Form*, 24–31; Newcomb, '"Those Images"', 227; compare 232: 'formal processes themselves create expressive meaning'. Compare Bonds, *Wordless Rhetoric*, 13–52.

about formal parallels with literature becomes more convincing as a result, it is only as a truism. (The thesis sometimes exploits a tacit slide between narrower and broader senses in order to eat its expressive cake and have its technical 'objectivity'.)

There is another question here: how far abstract formal or stylistic strategies typically invoked in such arguments plausibly occur in the book or the musical work, and how far they are persuasively described as parallel.[10] It is often unclear what counts as a parallel between strategies in different media: what counts in music as refocalisation, for instance, or defamiliarisation, and what in literature, and what makes either a marked feature, rather than part of the ordinary language of the art form. It is not obvious for example that cases of defamiliarisation in literature should be equated with use of tonal variety in musical works.[11] Similarly, if irony in literature is a strategy that distances the reader from what is being told, or creates an unresolved juxtaposition of finite and infinite, there may be only a very remote parallel with musical techniques such as interruption, digression, and playing with the apparent function of an event.[12] Claims of parallels become more plausible when literary 'form' or 'style' is stretched, as it often tacitly is, to cover what is more naturally described as content.

Yet another question is why claims about formal parallels single out any particular work. Such parallels have been found in all of Schumann's opp. 2, 4, 6, 9, 12, 16, 18, 19, 20, 21 and 23, and traced apparently interchangeably to both Hoffmann and Jean Paul.[13] They appear in so many works that they no more compellingly connect any particular Schumann work to Hoffmann or Jean Paul than they do several other compositions to any of a host of writers. Emphasis on such abstract parallels leaves one work looking much like another, individuality bleached away. Indeed, some of the formal strategies described in recent musicology are so abstract that they were associated in Schumann's day with both the sublime and the comic, as analysed by Michaelis in 1805–6 and Keferstein in 1833 respectively; and as Schütze pointed out at the time, the formal means thus abstracted do not suffice to account for the individual nature of a work's music.[14] For form and style function differently in the different ecologies of

---

[10] A question raised fifty years ago: Taylor, 'Formal Parallels', 14–16.
[11] As implied in Reiman, *Schumann's Piano Cycles*, 37–9.
[12] As in Moraal, 'Life and Afterlife', 55–8, 170.
[13] Daverio, *Nineteenth-Century Music*, 58–75; Reiman, *Schumann's Piano Cycles* (Jean Paul); Moraal, 'Life and Afterlife' (Hoffmann).
[14] Michaelis, 'Über das Erhabene', 1805, 179–80; 'K. Stein', 'Versuch über das Komische', 1833, 243–61; Schütze, 'Über das Verhältnis der Komik zur Musik' (1834), 200.

different media, genres and artists – in Ovid, Jean Paul and Hoffmann, for instance, or in C. P. E. Bach, late Beethoven quartets, or Schumann – and in the different landscapes of different works with their varying aesthetic and expressive qualities. It is not clear, finally, whether or how a parallel with a literary form might in itself affect appreciation of a work – unless through a pleasure like that of discovering a likeness between two friends.

Content and programme

In the 1830s, Schumann often discussed imagery, mental states and drama in music, but came over the decade to see content not as something external imitated or translated by music, or dictating its course, but as transmuted ('verwandelt') into it: like form, content becomes inseparable from expressive musical processes shaped by a work's 'Geist'.

Hoffmann had defended Haydn's *The Seasons* against criticism of its image-painting: it is a picture 'of the whole of human life' and 'the world's gaudy shapes'. 'The true composer', however, while able to summon 'before the mind's eye a particular scene from life', attends to the effect of the whole and ensures that 'melody, instrumentation, harmonic structure all work together'; and like Beethoven, Hoffmann thought that 'true musical painting must not make botched copies [nachpfuschen] of individual sounds of nature, but strive to arouse in the listener's mind the feeling that would in reality take hold of it'.[15] Purely pictorial music is 'ridiculous', and 'condemned to justifiable oblivion': a fashionable vice, through which instrumental composers betray 'the true essence of their art', trying to 'represent defined feelings or even events . . . and to handle as plastic the art that is the very antithesis of the plastic'.[16] The qualifier 'defined' should not be downplayed.

The young Schumann protested, perhaps naively, against the denigration of pictorial music: 'after all, in Haydn's *Creation* you can hear the grass grow!' The notion that 'masters like Beethoven and Schubert could translate any object into the language of music' recurs so often in Schumann's writings in the years before about 1835 that it can be taken as a constant of his aesthetic at that time. He uses 'translate' ('übersetzen') and 'transmute' ('verwandeln') almost interchangeably, suggesting that he was not at this

---

[15] *Schriften zur Musik*, 228, 115, 335.
[16] Hoffmann, *Kreisleriana*, I/4, 41: Appendix 3–4(a). A fuller version (*Schriften zur Musik*, 34–51) was first published in 1810.

stage as sensitive to the drawbacks in the idea of 'translation' as he gradually became.[17] He asked whether music had not told us of 'Italy, the Alps, the image of the sea, a Spring twilight'; indeed music might suggest almost any object, scene or event.[18] Even when a work only suggests generic types of images, a listener's imagination may supply images of the type in question, whether gothic terrors, or the pleasures of the Rhine.[19]

The balance between purely pictorial elements, the evocation of human states and the musical shape, which Hoffmann stressed, was a factor for Schumann too. In 1828 he noted that 'music in itself cannot paint what the emotions had not first painted'; in 1833 he saw music as often both reflecting states of mind ('Seelenzustände') and evoking things or situations ('Lebenszustände'); and in 1834 he said that a composer is often tempted to neglect the quality of either the picture or the music.[20] Even before 1836, he noted Novalis' claim that music uses natural sounds but transmutes them into poetry:

It is nowhere more striking than in music that it is only the mind which makes poetry out of objects ... and that the beautiful, which is the object of art ... does not sit ready made in what we perceive. All the sounds that Nature produces are raw and inanimate. Only a musical spirit feels that the rustling of the trees, the whistling of the wind, the song of the nightingale, the plashing of the stream are melodious and significant. A musician draws the essence of his art from himself.[21]

Schumann will also have read how Hoffmann echoed Novalis:

Our kingdom is not of this world, say the musicians, for where in nature do we find, as ... plastic artists do, the prototype of our art?... Melody lies only in human hearts ... Only to the musician are the audible sounds of Nature, the sighing of the wind, the burbling of springs ... chords and then melodies.[22]

And as the years passed, Schumann came to downplay literal scene-painting in music in favour of painting that was steeped in feeling, or as romantic or poetic as a landscape by Claude Lorraine.[23] The music must be good enough to live, so that 'the ear need borrow nothing from the eye',

---

[17] GSK, I 19, 112, 125.   [18] GSK, I 84–5.
[19] GSK, I 51, 223, 191. This shades into cases where Schumann imputes images as a hermeneutic tool: GSK, I 85, 121–2, 179 ('interessanter Bilder'), 202–3, 250 ('durch ein Bild'), 333 (Najaden).
[20] Tagebücher, I 112 (1828), GSK, II 207 (1833), 209 (1834).
[21] Novalis, Schriften, V 228–9(fr. 228); Mottosammlung, IX 185.   [22] Kreisleriana, II/7, 325–6.
[23] GSK, I 65, 247; II 265. This view of Claude was shared by Schiller (Sämtliche Werke, V 691), A. W. Schlegel (Die Gemähdle) and Jean Paul (Vorschule, §22).

images 'match the sense of the music', and each listener can follow their own imagination.[24]

Hoffmann thought music 'capable of thousands and thousands of nuances'; it 'releases an inexhaustible spring of expressive means precisely where paltry speech dries up'; for instance, he characterises passages in Beethoven's Fifth Symphony variously as ominous, anxious or ingratiating.[25] Schumann too thought a work of art could convey personal states, or states of mind. He started from the view that music is 'the language of the soul', and copied some of Jean Paul's frequent remarks to that effect.[26] He rebuked 'musical puritans: if music had only sounds and no language or signs for states of mind it would be a paltry art form'. He saw no reason why music should not convey a memory of happiness experienced, or indeed any state of mind. He laid emphasis on the finer shadings and rarer states that art should convey, such as anger or remorse; in 1839, describing Chopin as 'the boldest and proudest poetic spirit of the time', he claimed that his Preludes, op. 28, 'contain even the sickly, the feverish and the repellent'.[27] He perhaps underestimated, at least in the 1830s, how often listeners might disagree on states of mind conveyed in music – though he conceded that there might be a question about the clarity with which they are conveyed, or the objectivity with which they can be identified by the listener. He even imagined tests of this, rather as Hoffmann imagined hearing Beethoven's *Coriolanus* Overture without the 'playbill'.[28]

Hoffmann thought music could convey drama too. An instrumental work such as a symphony can, he said, be its own single 'drama'.[29] Or it can reflect a literary drama, catching its quality, character and mood, and suggesting relevant images. In a review of Beethoven's *Coriolanus* overture, Hoffmann shows how the music is specifically suited to grand, tragic events, in which heroes appear and fall. Beethoven's *Egmont* music matches states of mind portrayed in the drama: at one point the 'citizens' alarmed state' matches its 'short, fragmented phrases'. But Hoffmann

---

[24] *GSK*, I 235 ('lebt nicht'); 91 ('borrow nothing'); II 243 (Marschner: 'match the sense'); I 143 ('Jugendphantasie'); 146 ('das ihrige') and 333 (Najaden) (listeners' imaginations). By 1842, he preferred too to suggest the character of imputed hermeneutic images rather than give detail (II 108).

[25] Hoffmann, 'Der Dichter und der Komponist', in *Die Serapions-Brüder*, 93; *Schriften zur Musik*, 37, 39–41, 44.

[26] *Neue Folge*, 110 (8 February 1838), *Jugendbriefe*, 189 (9 August 1832).

[27] *GSK*, I 22 (puritans and states of mind), 84 (happiness), 27, 112, 125, 179, 343 (rarer states), 418 (Chopin).

[28] *GSK*, I 285 (1837), 65, 98 (clarity); Hoffmann, *Schriften zur Musik*, 98.

[29] Hoffmann, *Schriften zur Musik*, 19–20, 24. For Wackenroder, a symphony could be 'a whole world, a whole drama of human emotions': 'Wesen der Tonkunst', in *Herzensergießungen*, 150–1.

carefully preserves the autonomy of instrumental music by claiming not that the music evokes the drama of the play but that a playgoer familiar with the music will at particular points recall passages of the music: as though the play were an interpretation of prior music rather than vice versa.[30]

Schumann agreed. A dramatic trajectory could be the composer's own idea – 'sequences from the life of the artist', for instance; or the musical drama could chime with a pre-existing literary work, with mutual gain: 'Shakespeare could conjure a work worthy of himself' from a composer.[31] Schumann often described the wealth of association that may thus be awakened in the imagination of a listener adequately furnished with images and ideas from the culture; conversely, failure to recognise 'the dramatic thread' may spoil appreciation. He knew that music might track a literary work 'from start to finish' but that it might more probably catch 'the spirit of the whole', or dwell on particular passages.[32] By 1836–9, he thought that what music echoes from an associated literary work is typically the outline of imagistic scenes, or a configuration of psychological or emotional states or the protagonists' characters. A listener to Mendelssohn's *Melusine* Overture, based on a work by Tieck, need only be aware of the broad sweep of the story, not the detail: the music does not follow 'a coarse narrative thread', but sketches the nature of the protagonists and their watery embrace. Moscheles' overture to Schiller's *The Maid of Orleans* suggests the humble heroine and the knightly Talbot, and a particular scene; and though each listener's imagination 'follows its own track', there could be no other subject than Joan of Arc, because the music is so saturated in the spirit or 'Geist' of the play. Berlioz's *Waverley* Overture suggests how 'dreams of love and a lady's charms give place to honour and to arms'. The literary work must of course be susceptible of musical treatment – of being transmuted into music.[33] If it deals with music, so much the better; but other literary works too 'contain obviously musical elements', Schumann said in 1837, referring to 'the ruler's arrogance, the oppressed people', and the conflict, pain and sacrifice described in a poem by Goethe.[34]

---

[30] Hoffmann, *Schriften zur Musik*, 98 (*Coriolanus*), 176, 172–3 (*Egmont*); compare 238 ('Der Komponist ... selbst Dichter des Liedes werde') and *Kreisleriana* II/2, 292.
[31] *GSK*, I 82, 454 (sequences), 84.   [32] *GSK*, II 221; I 100.
[33] *GSK*, I 143 (Mendelssohn), 145–6 (Moscheles), 422 (Berlioz).
[34] *GSK*, I 66 and 268. The latter resembles Goethe's comment of 1832 to Zelter about another story from Jewish history, which Schumann copied out between 1836 and 1838 (*Mottosammlung*, I 216): 'The old fable: the defeated, oppressed, first suffering, then resisting and after varying fortunes achieving liberation, is a very promising theme, particularly responsive to music.'

provided that this amounts to associations supervening on musical features subject to their own musical logic, not to a controlling external schema. Hence, I suppose, his approving remarks about the Mendelssohn, Moscheles and Berlioz overtures. Music that does not follow its own autonomous and compelling patterns is likely to have no life; and an external schema will not enliven lifeless music, as Rellstab pointed out about *Papillons*.

Conception and transubstantiation

One way in which Schumann talked about what gives each work musical logic and life is through the metaphor of 'Geist'. 'Geist' is untranslatable: 'spirit' may undervalue the intellectual aspect, while 'mind' is scarcely applicable to a work; neither captures the sense of a work's essential, animating and individuating principle. A. B. Marx in 1841 included within 'Geist' 'perception, intellect, higher feeling and the conception', and related it to inspiration.[45] I treat it as conveying whatever gives a work its distinctive shape, energy and individuality.

The 'Geist' 'holds sway', Schumann said of the Berlioz symphony, over the 'idea that the composer wished to present', the material, and the form, which is its 'vessel'. The 'Geist', then, cannot be the same as any such 'particular idea' connected to the wider world. That idea might be a schema which the composer can set down in words; but for Schumann, a work's 'Geist' is not a schema (literary, narrative, imagistic or other) translated into music, and can scarcely be articulated in words. It 'is intrinsic' to the music ['inwohnt'].[46] Even if the composer adds words to the work, the key is whether the 'Geist' inheres in music without the added words.[47]

Even where a composer's intentions for a work are stated in words, that is relevant information about the 'Geist', but not a touchstone; a stated intention is only a starting point, and the 'Geist' is primarily discernible, even for the composer, not in separate words, but in the work as it emerges from the compositional process.[48] Indeed, as Schumann said, 'an "intention" often sends the creative process astray'.[49] In his youth Schumann had copied from the *Kunstblatt*:

---

[45] Marx, *Musical Form*, 27. [46] GSK, I 69–70, 85. [47] GSK, I 91.
[48] Often crucially including the very latest stages: as we will see with *Fantasiestücke* and *Nachtstücke*, and possibly as with *Carnaval*, where Schumann on 13 April 1836 offered a publisher not the twenty-odd pieces published the next year but only a dozen: Erler, 83.
[49] *Neue Folge*, 60 (28 November 1834).

What has been taken really deeply out of nature is more deep and universal than the artist himself knows; for it awakens responses even in such spheres as were beyond his ken: it opens for everyone different perspectives on life.

His claim that 'the poetry of the imagination lies in its darkness or its unconsciousness', though a youthful protest against learning music theory, may rest on a similar view. Of the way his own works expressed remote interests, he said, several years later, 'I am not aware of all of this while I'm composing; it only emerges later'.[50] This was a common view in Schumann's culture. For Jean Paul, 'genius is in more senses than one a sleepwalker', and 'the most powerful element in the poet is exactly the unconscious ... An ineradicable feeling imbues us with something obscure, not so much our creation as our creator'; and 'associations from life would be better reflected in images than in lifeless abstractions – but different images for each person, as nothing shows up people's idiosyncrasy as much as the effect of poetry on us'. Novalis put it another way: 'the true reader must be an extended author', as the author is to an extent only one reader.[51] None of this, of course, is to deny the role in composition of the conscious mind, or of authorial intention – that would be insane. It is instead to give primacy not to a composer's stated intention for the work, but to the work itself.

Schumann claimed that 'a genuinely artistic piece of music will have a centre of gravity, towards which everything tends, and from which all its conceptual rays [Geistesradien] emanate'. Some such conception shapes the music even across a multi-movement work, and gives the work a poetic unity and coherence deeper than simple regularity or symmetry.[52] Such views were widespread. As Schumann noted, Heinse had written in the 1780s: 'No one can wholly understand a part, without first having a grasp of the whole, and vice versa'; and 'one cannot judge anything of which one has no essential concept' ('kein Ideal'). Goethe wrote that 'in every art work, large or small, everything down to the smallest detail hangs on the conception' ('Konzeption').[53] Schumann noted Jean Paul's comment that many appreciate a work's limbs, and their charm, but not the 'Geist' and beauty with which only genius can infuse the whole; elsewhere Jean Paul

---

[50] *Tagebücher*, I 390 (compare *GSK*, I 462–3); I 350; *Briefwechsel*, I 146 (16 April 1838).
[51] Jean Paul, *Vorschule*, §§12–13, 1; Novalis, *Schriften*, V 232–3(fr. 260) (in Hoffmann, *Die Serapions-Brüder*, 644, a performance may enlighten an author about his own play).
[52] *GSK*, I 162 ('Geistesradien'), 179 ('Geist'), 52, 59, 71 ('Ganzes'), 72–3, 224 and II 72 ('Zusammenhang').
[53] Heinse, *Ardinghello*, in *Mottosammlung*, X 3 and 4; Goethe, 'Maximen und Reflexionen' (*Werke*, III 480(fr. 224)).

claimed that 'without an inner necessity, poetry is merely feverish dreams'.[54] Novalis' aphorisms contain a similar message: Schumann noted statements that 'every work of art has an ideal essence a priori, and carries within it the necessity of its own existence' ('ein Ideal a priori, eine Notwendigkeit bei sich da zu seyn'); and that composers could learn from poetry 'the poetic self-sufficiency and inner conception [Geist] of every real work of art'.[55] And great composers had indeed learnt the lesson, in the view of Hoffmann: each 'conceived and brought forth his work as a whole' ('in einem Gusse'). For Hoffmann, the material ('Stoff') of music or literature should 'serve the higher conception' ('Geist'); equally, 'imitation of form' can 'never create the conception which alone shapes form'. Likewise, A. B. Marx in the 1820s saw in Beethoven's works the primacy of what he there called the 'Idee', of which form is the realisation.[56]

This reflected Idealist thinking. Fichte had taught that the objective universe appears through the self-recognition as Other ('Das Nicht-Ich') of absolute mind ('Das Ich'), or what Schelling called the 'world-soul'. Jean Paul said that the 'Geist' that genius brings should animate a work in every limb, as the world-spirit does nature.[57] Similarly, Marx in 1856 wrote that 'impulses of inner life' are 'to the spirit what cosmic material is to the universe'; 'shapeless and indeterminate' matter 'becomes everything when it determines itself'. Again, 'the spirit sets its musical content in musical form', and 'by so doing comes to itself . . . and its consciousness'. Form then is not 'imposed from without, and is not something arbitrary', but is 'the unmediated expression of the spirit'.[58]

'Geist', as whatever gives a work individuality, shape and energy, can be seen as its DNA; and Schumann and his contemporaries often described a work in related ways, speaking of a work as 'organic', as though it were a natural kind. For Goethe, *Hamlet* is not to be artificially dismembered: it is a tree whose trunk, branches, leaves, flowers and fruit are all organically related. Similarly, Jean Paul contrasted the 'anatomical demonstration' performed by Goethe the critic with the living creation of character by Goethe the novelist; and Hoffmann juxtaposed organic life and the

---

[54] Jean Paul, *Vorschule*, §9 (*Mottosammlung*, IX 13) and §62.
[55] Novalis, *Schriften*, V 229(fr. 230) (*Mottosammlung*, IX 186), I 286 (*Mottosammlung*, I 60).
[56] Hoffmann, *Schriften zur Musik*, 313; *Kreisleriana*, II/6, 316–7; A. B. Marx quoted in Burnham, 'Criticism, Faith and the "Idee"' (1990), 184–6. Compare Brendel, 'Robert Schumann' (1845), 150: familiarity with the forms of the old masters should 'only serve the expression of a new conception'.
[57] Jean Paul, *Vorschule*, §14.
[58] Marx, *Musical Form*, 60–2. Today, of course, an analysis of 'Geist' avoiding vicious kinds of essentialism would require care.

composer's aversion to anatomical dissection.[59] Schumann too described the best music as 'organic', 'breathing one life': different aspects participate in and enliven others, and may lose their meaning if isolated, for what counts is the way they hang together as a whole. He wondered whether his 'dismembering critique' of the Berlioz symphony served the reader, remarking that the composer, who had studied medicine in his youth, 'could scarcely have dissected the head of a handsome murderer with more reluctance than I have his first movement'.[60] But a work is not a natural kind, even where the analogy is illuminating up to a point; and a Schumann work is not necessarily organic in the sense of stemming from the implications of its basic material, stated at the outset, worked out through the form, and driving to a logical and resolving conclusion, as proposed for other music by A. B. Marx.[61]

Schumann used other ways too to emphasise wholeness. He often adopted more static images, including the traditional image of 'threads'.[62] He talked of 'conceptual rays' ('Geistesradien'), 'roundedness', 'wholes' and 'hanging together', for 'in music the coherence, the whole, is everything'; he wrote that 'in a masterpiece every note can be accounted for', and there is 'a poetic depth and originality throughout, in the whole and every detail'.[63] Some diversity of images and frameworks seems necessary in this book too, given the diversity of ways in which Schumann's 'Hoffmann works' hang together. There can be no finite set of kinds of characterisation of the sorts of properties that contribute to aesthetic impact, or what Hoffmann called 'this indivisible whole in the total impact on a listener'.[64]

Schumann will have found such notions in the aesthetics of Jean Paul, who insisted that 'poetic' art is neither pure formal patterning nor the reproduction of external material, but instead takes external content and transmutes it into art. Jean Paul dwelt on the debate about form and content in art in the opening sections of his *Vorschule*, in passages to which Schumann returned over a number of years in the 1830s, repeatedly making new excerpts.[65] Jean Paul describes the widespread eighteenth-century view that art imitates nature, and that visual and plastic arts represent the concrete, objective and

---

[59] Goethe, *Wilhelm Meister*, V/4 (*Werke*, IV 263–4); Jean Paul, *Vorschule*, §57; Hoffmann, *Schriften zur Musik*, 343–4.
[60] GSK, I 124, 52, 423 and 72. Compare Bent, *Music Analysis*, I 7–14 and 21–3.
[61] Marx, *Musical Form*, 92–101.
[62] GSK, I 186, 233, 251, 400, 424 and II 221 ('Band'); see also I 59, 155, 210, 284, 335 ('gezogenen Linien'), Kranefeld, *Der nachschaffende Hörer*, 160–71, and Grey, '"Wie ein rother Faden"', 196–207.
[63] GSK, II 8, 9, 10 ('Rundung', 'abgerundetes'); 297, I 343 (accounted); see also note 52 above.
[64] Hoffmann, *Kreisleriana*, II/6, 314.   [65] *Mottosammlung*, I 25–35 and IX 11–17.

delimited in nature; he opposes to it the doctrine that art is a reflection only of the creative self, or pure formal patterning empty of all representation of the objective world. He even-handedly mocks both schools, the old-fashioned 'unpoetic materialists', and the modern 'poetic nihilists', preferring what he calls 'the old Aristotelian formulation', that 'locates the essence of poetry in the beautiful or inspired imitation of nature', because 'it excludes these two extremes'.[66] Thus he claims that 'for the materialists, the material has no life, and the form is lacking'; despite their claims, the import of poetry is not just the representation of the objective world. By contrast, for the 'nihilists' – above all, the young, inexperienced Jena Romantics including Friedrich Schlegel – 'the material is lacking, and thus there is no life in the form' ('Dem Nihilisten mangelt der Stoff und daher die belebte Form').[67] For them, in Jean Paul's 1825 caricature, 'form is everything, even the true import'; it is as though the vessel is taken as the substance, or 'a Chinese teacup is also Chinese Caravan Tea'.[68]

But in true poetry, material taken from the outer world is metamorphosed:

Wenn in dieser [der poetischen Nachahmung] das Abbild mehr als das Urbild enthält, ja sogar das Widerspiel gewährt – z.B. ein gedichtetes Leiden Lust – : so entsteht dies, weil eine doppelte Natur zugleich nachgeahmt wird, die äußere and die innere, beide ihre Wechselpiegel . . . Die äußere Natur wird in jeder innern eine andere, und diese Brotverwandlung ins Göttliche ist die geistige poetische Stoff.

If in poetic re-creation, the image contains more than the original, or even vouchsafes its contrary – as the suffering expressed in a poem gives pleasure – then that occurs because two aspects of a double nature are being re-created at once, outer nature and inner nature, each the mirror image of the other. . . . Outer nature is transformed in each inner nature, and this transubstantiation of bread into the divine is the mind's poetic material.[69]

---

[66] Jean Paul, *Vorschule*, §1: 'welche das Wesen der Poesie in einer schönen (geistigen) Nachahmung der Natur bestehen lässet'. Interpreting Jean Paul's antithesis as between external material and the poet's individual feeling (as perhaps in Watkins, *Metaphors of Depth*, 102–3) is a narrower reading.

[67] Jean Paul, *Vorschule*, §4. Novalis may have been inexperienced through youth, but he stressed the value of experience for a poet, and the hazards of writing from intense feeling uninformed by real experience: in one passage, he develops an argument (from which Schumann made two excerpts: *Mottosammlung*, I 60 and I 80) that concludes: 'poetry rests wholly on experience' (*Heinrich von Ofterdingen*, chapter 8, in *Schriften*, I 285–6). Compare *Mottosammlung*, I 27, from Jean Paul, *Vorschule*, §2, and Tadday, *Das schöne Unendliche*, 107–9.

[68] Jean Paul, *Nachschule*, §20.

[69] Jean Paul, *Vorschule*, §4. I wonder if the 'two aspects' (such that suffering in a poem gives pleasure) might reflect a reading of Aristotle, *Poetics*, 14, 1453b12: 'the pleasure which the poet should afford is that which comes from pity or fear through imitation'.

For Aristotle, a food when consumed is transmuted, no longer bread but a person's flesh; in medieval Christian Eucharistic theology, with its sub-Aristotelian concepts, it is transubstantiated into God. So for Jean Paul, external content ('the original') is transubstantiated in art as 'poetic material', its qualities transfigured (suffering becoming also pleasure).[70]

The debate whether 'poetry needs material, or reigns only through form, is easy to resolve'. 'Form' and 'content' are interdependent: 'there is of course an outer mechanical material of no concern to poetry unless ennobled through form'. That ennobled stuff is the 'inner material – which is ... intrinsically poetic, around which the form is ... just the container'. 'The poet creates in the excitement of the moment only the outer form; he carries the 'Geist' and the material with him through half a lifetime'. 'This material is what marks the originality of genius', whose 'trademark' is 'a novel view of the world or of life'.[71] 'The play of poetry, for it and for us,' he wrote, 'is only a means, never an end in itself'; but nor does the true poet ape nature, but marries art and nature so as to give finite, objective matter the limitless suggestiveness of ideas: 'eine begrenzte Natur mit der Unendlichkeit der Idee umgeben'. In a ringing phrase, which Schumann copied out, Jean Paul said: 'the Romantic is the beautiful without limits, or the beautiful "Unendliche"'. He was talking not only of spatial and temporal infinity, but of the indeterminate, undifferentiated, indefinite and indefinable, in contrast to what is susceptible of verbal definition.[72]

Hoffmann too sees the poetic or 'Romantic' as 'consuming' 'definite' everyday material (scenes or emotions) to transmute it into the 'unendlich', into itself. A true master starts from 'the liveliest awareness of a definitely delineated region', hearing 'how love and hate, ecstasy and despair sound'; and 'from deep within the artist's mind, the objective, the rounded takes shape'.[73] This is what became Hoffmann's 'Serapiontic Principle', that art requires first the close observation of images from life's gaudy flux, and then an aesthetic firing of those images by the poet's 'Geist' as if in a crucible ('auf die Kapelle'), so that artistic shapes ('Gestalten') emerge from that chemical process. In opera, music 'steps into life', dealing with its phenomena, and with 'definite feelings and actions', 'all of which sink

---

[70] Jean Paul, *Vorschule*, §4.
[71] Jean Paul, *Vorschule*, §14. He said elsewhere (§2, excerpted by Schumann in *Mottosammlung*, IX 11) that genius 'sees nature more richly and more completely' than talent, and 'is able to create something new'.
[72] Jean Paul, *Vorschule*, 'III. Kantate-Vorlesung' ('das Spielen der Poesie kann ihr und uns nur Werkzeug, niemals Endzweck sein'), §4 and §22 (*Mottosammlung*, IX 29). 'Unendlich' is untranslatable. Recent academic work focuses on spatial and temporal infinity.
[73] Hoffmann, *Schriften zur Musik*, 285; see also *Kreisleriana*, II/6, 316–17.

away' as music 'fills us with ineffable yearning'. 'Each passion – love – hatred – anger – despair . . . is clothed by music in the purple shimmer of the romantic'; even the material of life 'leads us out of life into the realm of the infinite'; each passion appears, but 'transfigured' ('verklärt') into the indeterminate. In Beethoven's instrumental works, where there is no libretto to define 'specific things' as the subject, the music nevertheless starts from emotions such as 'love, hope, joy', but 'the pain of indefinable yearning . . . consumes [them] within itself without destroying them' ('in sich verzehrend, aber nicht zerstörend').[74]

The process Hoffmann describes is akin to Jean Paul's transubstantiation, or Wackenroder's notion of the 'poeticisation of everyday emotions' in music that 'does not know how its feelings connect with the real world'.[75] It is in this sense, I believe, that we should read Hoffmann's renowned statement that instrumental music, as 'the most Romantic of all art forms', is a transport to 'an unknown land that has nothing in common with the external world of the senses' ('dem äußern Sinnenwelt'), its 'subject the indefinite' ('das Unendliche').[76]

Hoffmann's 'unendliche Sehnsucht' (or 'unnennbare' or 'unaussprechliche') can perhaps be taken as objectless longing – a fittingly paradoxical concept whose application to music is comprehensible – and this may be part of the sense in which it is for Hoffmann the essence of Romantic instrumental music. Beethoven's symphonies all 'speak of that far Romantic land in which we live succumbing to ineffable yearning'.[77] He finds it in much of Beethoven and Mozart, including in Beethoven's Fifth Symphony (which was so striking an emblem of the kind of Romantic music he championed). But 'unnameable yearning' is a vague and weak unifying factor for a particular work, comparatively unsuited to the Fifth

---

[74] Hoffmann, *Die Serapions-Brüder*, 404 and 83; *Kreisleriana*, I/4, 42–3 and *Schriften zur Musik*, 343. See Brown, *Hoffmann and the Serapiontic Principle*, 47–9, 84–5.

[75] Wackenroder, 'Wesen der Tonkunst', in *Herzensergießungen*, 149. If my argument is right, Hoffmann's 'ineffable yearning' expresses a concept less like the one for which Jean Paul used *that* phrase (as in his rhapsody, noted and regurgitated by the young Schumann: *Mottosammlung*, V 250, *Tagebücher*, I 80) than it is like 'transubstantiation'.

[76] Hoffmann, *Kreisleriana*, I/4, 41 (Appendix 3–4(a)). On the contemporary debate, see for instance Dahlhaus, *Klassische und Romantische Musikästhetik*, 144–8 and 375ff, with Tadday's corrective, *Das schöne Unendliche*, 71–2 and 122–36. In a short-lived *Berlinische musikalische Zeitung*, C. F. Michaelis ('Vermischte Bemerkungen' (1805), 21–2 and 'Nachtrag' (1805), 137–8: Appendix 3–4(b)) made claims characteristic of his time: that the power or sublimity of music arises because it does not reproduce or imitate actual, defined, limited objects, or what words can express, but 'has a certain self-sufficiency' ('eine gewiße Selbständigkeit') and 'creates its own invisible, conceptual world' ('unsichtbare geistige Welt'), which a listener tries in vain to capture in words, concepts or images.

[77] Hoffmann, *Die Serapions-Brüder*, 76–7 ('Der Dichter und der Komponist').

Symphony (and especially to its first movement), and certainly not distinctive of it. So when Hoffmann concludes that 'jene unnennbare ahnungsvolle Sehnsucht' unifies the symphony, as what a sensitive listener will feel throughout, perhaps we should take 'objectless longing' as marking the Symphony as 'Romantic', but 'ahnungsvoll' – picking up the 'Ahnung', 'Angst' and 'Drohung' (foreboding, anxiety and threat) that he finds throughout – as distinguishing it as an individual work. *This* symphony can be taken as suggestive of 'the Sublime'; but 'Romantic' works in general transmute determinate emotions into indefinable feeling.[78]

Schumann's thinking may have reflected similar notions. The young Schumann described mature creativity in words reminiscent, perhaps, of Hoffmann's 'Serapiontic Principle' as 'the confluence of "Geist" and form, technique and imagination'. He wrote that 'despising material means is far from the ideals of art; the task is to transform the content so far into 'Geist' that what is material is forgotten'.[79] In 1835 he described Beethoven's *Pastoral* Symphony as about not a single day in springtime, 'but the obscure confluence of lofty songs about humanity … the whole infinite creation'; and he talked of a composer like Schubert transmuting anything into music – using 'verwandeln' as Jean Paul had in his 'Brotverwandlung'.[80]

And over the 1830s, Schumann came increasingly to affirm that images, feelings and drama, once transmuted into music, become less distinguishable from one another and from music, leaving the listener unconstrained by specific external references; he came to talk less of music conveying definite things (events, scenes, objects), more of firm shapes receding in 'a seductive twilight' that words cannot nail down; so that, in one case, where the music of an overture at first appeared an opaque curtain, it may become on repeated hearing a 'veil, behind which a host of joyful and sorrowful shapes become perceptible to the unsuspecting eye'.[81] His description in 1837 of one piece of music as 'anxiety softened by pure enjoyment of art' seems to recognise something like Jean Paul's view that 'the suffering expressed in a poem gives pleasure'. He wrote in 1838 that a work might convey a poetic image to one person, but to another only an associated feeling. In 1839, he expressed still greater caution about defining what

---

[78] Hoffmann, *Kreisleriana*, I/4, 41–5. Bonds, *Music as Thought*, chapters 1–3, describes the background of Idealism and 'the Sublime'; in my view Hoffmann both exploited Idealism's concepts and extended them. See also Rumph's political interpretation ('A Kingdom Not of This World').
[79] *Tagebücher*, I 354; *GSK*, II 265 and 276.   [80] *GSK*, I 66 (*Pastoral*), 125 (Schubert).
[81] *GSK*, I 250, 310.

might lie behind a piece of instrumental music, whether a 'poem, image or experience'; but the next year, discussing a Schubert symphony, he affirmed 'that the external world ... reaches deep down within the poet and composer', and that there could be 'more than mere lovely song', 'more than simple pain and joy': 'there is life in every fibre', 'import throughout' ('Bedeutung überall').[82] And in 1842 he insisted that 'if you want to check the value of the music, try deleting any appended words and see if it still works'; for as he said the next year, if 'some picture, some idea, hovers before a composer, he won't be satisfied with his work until it comes towards him in lovely melodies'.[83] By 1844, he was warning young composers to make music above all, rather than hoping 'to use music <u>merely</u> as a servant, to translate something' – a far cry from his insistence ten years before that music could translate any specific thing.[84]

Jean Paul, Hoffmann and Schumann did not wholly escape the view they inherited of music as 'the language of sentiment'; but they arrived at a more profound truth. Poetic music is not the *creature* of external material; it is, Schumann said, 'the orphan whose father and mother none can name', and 'perhaps it is precisely in the mystery of her origin that the charm of her beauty lies'. Jean Paul had used the same image to express his notion of the relation between 'the notes themselves, those offspring of the gods, which suddenly appear before us, motherless and armed like Minerva', and the 'shapes' which gradually present themselves in it to the 'inner eye'. And in 1856 A. B. Marx likewise differentiated music from other arts: 'Only music appears as that solitary maiden, not of this world', of whom the poet said, '"one knew not whence she came"'.[85]

In 1837, Schumann's friend Keferstein said similarly that while some music, like tapestry, may consist only of 'pure musical form' or patterns, other music contains 'artistic thoughts'.[86] These 'artistic thoughts' are not verbal propositions, but clusters of images and feelings understood by listeners with whatever broad contextual understanding of the relevant culture they can bring to bear. Two years before, Schumann's acquaintance, August Kahlert, wrote in the *Neue Zeitschrift* that presenting concepts in music does not yield a work of art, and an instrumental composer must 'think purely in music'; but to claim that music is pure formal patterning, has no content, and gives nothing to think about, is to

---

[82] *GSK*, I 285 (1837), I 333 (1838), 431 (1839), 462 (1840: Appendix 3-4(c); compare 274–5).
[83] *GSK*, II 112–13 (1842); 129–30 (1843: Appendix 3-2(b)).   [84] *GSK*, II 469 note 558 (1844).
[85] *GSK*, I 44; Jean Paul, *Vorschule*, §77; A. B. Marx, *Musical Form*, 61.
[86] 'K. Stein', 'Bemerkungen eines irrenden Theoretikers' (1837), 14–44, *passim* and at 19–22, 25–6.

destroy its essence; in music, beauty, he affirmed, is 'both form and content'.[87] In 1851 Schumann said that each work has its own thought or content bringing with it its individual form.[88] He gravitated, that is, towards a view that poetic music fuses musical ideas and wider concerns, rather as in Jean Paul's 'transubstantiation', or Hoffmann's firing 'in the crucible', and distanced himself from crasser versions of 'materialism' without resorting to 'formalism'.[89]

Similar ideas can be applied to Schumann's works. Before the 1850s, understanding of them had tended to the poetic rather than the narrowly programmatic or formalist. Thus von Seyfried in 1840, calling Schumann's *Kreisleriana* 'a genuinely poetic conception', asked 'Who does not know the Capellmeister Johannes Kreisler?', and went on to draw out accordingly the import of each piece, including the ambivalent disappearance in the last; but he felt no need to track Hoffmann's events or sequence.[90] In 1839 Brendel cited Julius Becker's view that 'In der Nacht' does not paint or imitate night, and 'works not indirectly through the image but directly through the inherently musical idea'; and in 1845 he suggested that Schumann's works developed the musical tradition where Beethoven had left off, each based on a content that shapes form.[91] The early works are 'narratives or cycles of interconnected lyrical poems'. They may seem to contain sequences of images suggestive of 'narratives', but do not, he said, normally 'paint events': 'occasionally externalities are signified, but in the whole the subjective and objective swim indistinguishably as one, in a creatively imaginative way'. 'The poetic idea is predominant, and the parts are linked ... by poetic threads'. In such 'poetic' interpretations, programmes (in either Schumann's or the modern sense) were not at issue. In 1839 Brendel denied that 'In der Nacht' 'follows a schema'; in 1845, he claimed that Schumann's titles 'often serve to give final definition to a piece', not a 'pre-existent schema after which the composition was modelled'.

The understanding of Schumann's music seems to have altered as the meaning of 'programme' evolved and ideology moved on. In 1837, Liszt had taken a 'poetic' line on Schumann, saying that 'the objective is turned, so to speak, into the subjective' as something 'intimately associated with the music'. It would sometimes have helped, he said, if 'the poetic drift had

---

[87] Kahlert, 'Die Genrebilder in der Modernen Musik' (1835), 189 ff; 'Recensionen' (1835), 109.
[88] *Neue Folge*, 347 (22 September 1851). Compare *GSK*, I 106, II 208.
[89] *GSK*, I 249–50, 269–70. [90] Von Seyfried, 'Schumann, *Kreisleriana*' (1840), 113–14.
[91] Brendel, 'Der Neuromantiker' (1839), 191; 'Robert Schumann' (1845), 67, 82–3; 91: Appendix 3–4(d).

been intimated through some words' – which he seems a few lines later to term a 'programme', implying Schumann's sense of the term.[92] The absence of 'some words' means that the works are not programmatic in that sense. In 1855, however, Liszt said that Schumann 'often gave a work a programme in the form of a title', which might be 'borrowed from literature only if the music was saturated in the conception ['Geist'] of the literary work'; 'no one before Schumann had issued a series of works whose content aligned so perfectly with their programme'.[93] This seems to be a shift in the meaning of the word away from Schumann's sense. If so, Liszt was not wholly wrong about Schumann's music; but his new terminology tendentiously co-opted it under the banner of 'programme music', where it had previously not belonged. Thereafter, to oversimplify the story, Liszt and others seized territory in the name of 'programme music'; Johannes Brahms, Eduard Hanslick and others counter-attacked; and a polarisation between 'programme' and 'absolute music' developed. Schumann's 'poetic' music soon became stranded in a no-man's land between battle-lines, or was dragooned into either the 'absolute' or the programme camp.[94] Schumann's own comments on *Papillons* and 'In der Nacht' have encouraged many critics up to today to understand the 'Hoffmann works' as programmatic – even critics sensitive to the implications of Schumann's own aesthetics.[95]

This book explores an approach in which each 'Hoffmann work' is taken as, ideally, setting its own course; neither 'form' nor 'content' is treated as a schema separable from or dictating musical process; and if the music brings matter or content with it, it is as transmuted into expressive, resonant music. Interpretation, then, ideally integrates discussion of the aspects Schumann called 'Geist', 'form', 'composition', and 'idea' or content. In the light of these reflections, I now turn to the work from which 'In der Nacht' comes, the *Fantasiestücke* of 1837.

---

[92] Liszt's 1837 article, translated into German in 'Franz Liszt über Robert Schumann' (1840), 67.
[93] Liszt, 'Robert Schumann' (1855), 236 and 240 (compare Altenburg, 'Robert Schumann und Franz Liszt', 136).
[94] Thym, 'Schumann in Brendel's *Neue Zeitschrift für Musik*', 35, quotes Theodor Uhlig's 1851 claim that Schumann was an 'absolute musician' (compare Pederson, 'Defining "Absolute Music"', 246; Newcomb, '"Those Images"', 227–31).
[95] Floros, 'Schumanns musikalische Poetik', 104 ('esoteric programme music'); Tadday, *Das schöne Unendliche*, 40, 134–6 and 141–2 (but contrast 38, and 'Life and Literature', 42–3).

5 | Dream images, 1837
Fantasiestücke, *op. 12*

Schumann's *Fantasiestücke*, op. 12, was begun in summer 1837 – just before *Carnaval* finally appeared – and published in February 1838. The word Schumann adopted for his title had particular connotations from visual art.[1] But it also echoes the title of the book that made Hoffmann's name, *Fantasiestücke in Callots Manier*.

In Schumann's work, vivid images succeed one another like dreams, without the solidity of objects or the clarity of logical connections.[2] Thus the first half evokes an evening of chiming bells and serpentine intertwining ('Des Abends'), lifting into flight ('Aufschwung'), 'why?' ('Warum?'), and comic clumsiness ('Grillen'); the second half then offers a stormy drama at night with a distorted duet ('In der Nacht'), awakening into fable ('FABEL'), conflict and frozen immobility in the confusion of dreams ('Traumes Wirren'), and finally the loose-limbed strength, galloping hooves and submarine elegy of the concluding 'Ende vom Lied'. (I will try to suggest the range of connotations of each German title through varied English versions, none of which should be taken as definitive translations.)

At the same time, however, the work suggests that there may be threads of continuity between these disparate elements. The title of the last piece, 'End of the Song', suggests some single entity behind the different pieces; and at its end, Schumann gratuitously wrote *Fine*, having put no comparable marking at the end of any of his other early piano pieces: presumably it marks not just the obvious end of one piece, but of something that began with 'Des Abends'.

The work begins with what in retrospect is the submediant, D flat major. It then traces a basic tonal movement from F minor, through that contrasting D flat and the dominant C major to a concluding F major.

---

[1] Schumann in 1834 promised 'Phantasiestücke' among the articles in the *Neue Zeitschrift*, and in 1839 suggested the title for pieces by Clara Wieck: *GSK*, II 272; *Briefwechsel*, II 629 (10 July 1839). I am not aware that it had been used for a musical work before 1837.

[2] As was understood by Brendel at the time: 'Robert Schumann' (1845), 89 (Appendix 3–4(d)): 'an anxious dream', 'contrary states of mind', 'a landscape veiled in mist out of which here and there something steps out in sunlight'.

Supporting this tonal trajectory, the A♭ prominent in the keys of the first five pieces (D flat major in three of them, and F minor in two) yields in the second half of the work to the A♮ of F major, C major and A minor, before a descent through G (as $\hat{5}$ of C major and $\hat{2}$ of F, for instance) to F as $\hat{1}$. A motif f^1-g^1-$a♭^1$ features in the opening phrase of 'In der Nacht', and is eventually resolved by $a♮^1$-g^1-f^1 in the last piece. A cluster of minor mode motifs (associated with a dark or threatening character) often includes f^1-$e♭^1$, sometimes pitted against f^1-e^1. But this also sounds, in minor or major versions, through much of the first five pieces, and recurs in the sixth, set within a frame emphasising a continuing descent E-D-C; and in the final piece that motivic descent returns from c^2 down to f^1, linking thematic and tonal resolution. At the same time, a family of major mode themes exploits a rise, up a triad, or to $\hat{5}$, followed by a stepwise descent, often in uniform crotchet motion, or with dense chords in a low register, sometimes treated sequentially: in the opening theme of 'Grillen' (and its relative in the middle section of 'Traumes Wirren'), the cantilena section of 'In der Nacht', and the final piece.

The energy and shape of the work, however, seem to come also from contrasts of form, sonority, texture and metre loosely associated with those tonal and thematic relationships. The second and fifth pieces, in F minor, show some of the dynamism of sonata form while the third and fourth, in D flat major, are more purely static, the sixth and seventh only feint at such dynamism, and the last brings a relaxed resolution. The ring of rhythmically driven percussive *forte* discords powers the F minor 'Aufschwung'; similar discords maintain the tension in 'In der Nacht' (29, 33) and are markers of impending return to darker minor music in 'In der Nacht' and 'FABEL'. These sonorities contrast with the crystalline chimes of 'Des Abends' and delicately ornamented textures of 'Warum?', both in D flat major; so too the final accented F minor discord of 'In der Nacht' relaxes into the delicate and subtle play of the C major 'FABEL'. Percussive *forte* discords recur in 'Traumes Wirren' in B flat minor, but are dissolved in its concluding F major spray. Meanwhile, other contrasts of sonority appear, between the chiming of 'Des Abends' and the acid chromaticism of the cantilena in 'In der Nacht', for instance, or between a rhythmic immobility in bars 63–94 of 'Traumes Wirren' and a passage of gross metrical conflict in 'Grillen'. The humour of 'Ende vom Lied' resolves and assimilates all these contrasts within a freely moving if cacophonous F major theme, and dissolves disparate sonorities in the submarine bells of the coda.

This chapter explores how these features all resonate with images and associations from Schumann's literary culture, and in particular from Hoffmann's *Fantasiestücke*. I concentrate on one item from that book, the *Bildungsroman*, or tale of an artist's development, 'Der goldne Topf' (1814); but resonances with that tale need not exclude or compete with other items in the collection, through which images ramify with the vivid inconsequence of dreams. 'Der goldne Topf' features images evoked by Schumann's pieces; like his music, it embraces melodrama, comedy, irony and elegy, confounds dream and waking, and is filled with contrasting sonorities, especially of crystal and metal. These bring rich but ambivalent connotations: crystal is associated with art and fable, but also with an old hag's curse;[3] metals (which appear surprisingly often) with witchcraft and the banausic, but also with the authority of the Archivarius, the master, magus, and champion of art.[4] Elsewhere, crystal could be an image of the longed-for soul, of Eden or of art, while metals had more dire connotations. In Novalis' *Heinrich von Ofterdingen*, 'Iron' is a mythic symbol of a primeval curse, and in the fable featuring the character Fabel, the sound of ringing metal is contrasted with crystal. In Tieck's 'Der Runenberg' (1802), the thrall of 'this accursed metal' ('dieses verfluchte Metall') alienates a man from life. In Hoffmann's 'Der Magnetiseur', magnetic metals are tools of a psychic power both therapeutic and sinister; in his 'Bergwerke zu Falun', the protagonist descends into an underworld of metals, which seem in a vision to metamorphose into pure crystal, but then bury him.[5]

Thus when Schumann's *Fantasiestücke* suggests an evening vision, for example, contrasts dreaming and waking, or creates patterns of contrasting sonorities, it may evoke cultural backgrounds on which Hoffmann also played. The character and images of the music are brought into focus by the titles, and enriched by associations with Hoffmann's tale and those general resonances.

---

[3] Hoffmann, *Fantasiestücke*, 179, 201, 239–40, 253. In the footnotes to this chapter, references to 'Hoffmann, *Fantasiestücke*' relate to 'Der goldne Topf' unless otherwise stated.

[4] Hoffmann, *Fantasiestücke*, 193, 195, 207, 220, 222–3, 233, 237, 248–9, 251 (a 'polished metal mirror' is held up to the author by malicious spirits to show him his melancholy sleepless face). Witchcraft: 179, 195, 222, 231, 242, 243, 248, 249; the Archivarius' metallic voice and coins: 195 and 226; 'Speziestaler': 190 (twice), 241 (he is compared to Satan, as is Anselm: 179, 185, 246). Of course the golden pot itself is metallic.

[5] Crystal: Hoffmann, *Die Serapions-Brüder*, 335–6, 352 ('Die Automate'), 492–3 ('Das Fremde Kind'). Metals: Ziolkowski, *German Romanticism*, chapter 2; Hoffmann, *Fantasiestücke*, 168; *Die Serapions-Brüder*, 190–1. Schumann also called poetry 'bright crystal', and saw metals as capable of psychic power, describing the 'Psychometer' as 'an as yet inexplicable invention resting on the magnetic interaction of metals with physical forces': *GSK*, II 184; *Jugendbriefe*, 204–5 (9 April 1833).

i: 'Des Abends' ('Of an Evening')

The music creates a sonority of chiming triads and intertwining sinuous lines. Metre and harmony have a shimmering fixity: the right hand suggests three in a bar, while the notated duple pulse is probably heard as a cross-rhythm, and a tonic D flat major triad, overlain with other harmonies, sounds in each of the first six bars.[6] The left thumb strikes a♭^{1} (as so often in 'Warum') to chime with D♭ in the bass; an inner voice features f^1, e^1 and later e♭^{1}. A theme descends the scale from G♭ (bar 1) to a chromatic G♮ and winds up again (3–4); delicate dissonance shades into consonance and back, in a *piano* and legato texture, with a pedal unifying the registers.

Throughout the piece, eye and ear both find – in the tones and on the page – a seemingly endless curve of undulating melody. It is however but one of three upper lines that run through the piece. They intertwine for hand as well as for ear and eye, as left and right thumbs are crossed almost throughout. The intertwining takes on a new shape in the middle section (bars 17–38). In bar 21 the melody continues on the even-numbered semiquavers rather than the odd, slipping in that syncopated form beneath what had been the lower line. The effect is that for a while the lower line slithers past the soprano (in metrical terms) and above it (in pitch terms), sliding the more freely for its adoption in bar 22 of the grace notes from the soprano line in 20 (Example 5.1).

Repeated harmonies of V of E major from bar 25 do not break the spell. The melody slips back up above the accompaniment, reverting to the original odd-numbered semiquavers, and the process repeats. The music thus gives a sense of a continuous undulation without forward movement. Only in the coda, when the texture is varied, and the tenor sings in harmony with the soprano, does sufficient movement occur for closure to ensue; the hands, previously entwined, separate widely for the final chord, breaking the unified texture and the trance.

The title, 'Des Abends', suggests not 'Evening' but what occurred 'of an evening'; and the music, with its shimmering fixity, tonic chimes and intertwining sinuous lines, resonates with what happened one evening at the start of 'Der goldne Topf': a vision of three entwined, slim, serpentine bodies slithering in an elderflower bush by the water – full of erotic yearning, and accompanied by crystal chimes and tonic triads – entranced

---

[6] I am indebted to Rosen, *Romantic Generation*, 33–8.

Example 5.1: Schumann, *Fantasiestücke*, i, bars 17–24

the young would-be poet Anselm.⁷ It was Ascension Day, and Ascension was Jean Paul's image for artistic transport from the concrete to the 'unendlich';⁸ and a dream-vision traditionally launched a young artist on his course, as in Novalis' *Heinrich von Ofterdingen*. But Hoffmann's serpents are an idiosyncratic version. In ancient mythologies, the serpent was a primal power, undifferentiated and protean, remorseless but potentially healing; and it was a commonplace of contemporary aesthetics that beauty lay in the serpentine line, even for music.⁹ But for Anselm, like Adam, the snake that slithers and twines so seductively in the tree may offer the knowledge of art or love, or only perdition. In the golden age, Goethe says, when a bush entwined the lovers in its tender branches, the serpent was harmless, but now it is an instrument of the enemy: 'It slithers up, the little snake, hissing its enchanting sounds with flickering tongue. How lovely it seemed!' For Wackenroder's Berglinger, art is a 'goddess' but also 'a seductive, forbidden fruit', a taste of which leaves one 'irretrievably

---

⁷ Hoffmann, *Fantasiestücke*, 180 and 184 ('Dämmerung'), 182–4 ('Abendsonne' thrice, 'Abendwind' four times, 'Abendwolken'); 183, 198, 201, 214, 227–8 (serpents); crystal chimes and triads: 182, 183, 184 (twice), 189 (twice), 198, 201, 216, 226, 227, 245. Perhaps Schumann's image of 'music that calls one of an evening over to the far side of the water' (*GSK*, I 368, of 1838) suggests some associations 'des Abends' could carry for him.

⁸ Jean Paul, *Vorschule*, §§4 and 18.

⁹ 'Romantic melody consisted of a single unbroken, shaped curviline, and was invested with the ability to evoke the ideal, maternal feminine': Cramer, 'Of Serpentina and Stenography', 165 (Abstract).

lost to the world of life and activity'. The hero of Hoffmann's *Meister Floh* is seduced by an other-worldly figure with a voice like silver bells, whom he comes to see as 'the serpent of Paradise' and rejects in favour of true love.[10] Such images amplify the associations of Schumann's serpentine lines, crystal chimes and sense of enchantment – after which the next piece is a violent contrast.

ii: 'Aufschwung' ('Taking Wing')

In 'Aufschwung' something lifts into flight. Its opening two-bar motif is marked by brevity, a rushing tempo, F minor tonality, and an accompaniment of repeated staccato chords; bars 2 and 4 open with a step f-e. When the opening motif is repeated, a low octave on C in bar 3 rings against the repeated high D♭. The magisterial, dark sonority that results from the association of this deep C with the metallic ring of the repeated *forte* percussive chords contrasts with the crystalline chimes of 'Des Abends', and comes to seem progressively an engine of the piece, if not the work.

In bar 4 the low C is propelled up four octaves, from where a now airborne melody floats to a cadence in A flat major in bars 7–8. A sort of tonal up-draught, from the apparent B flat minor of the opening bar, through F minor to A flat major, might itself suggest lifting into flight. And in bars 4–8, the eye too might find such an image in the score (Example 5.2).

The image persists through the following D flat major episode, as a melody lifts up by semitones (bars 16–20) over a rippling figuration, and floats gently down to a plagal cadence (23–4). While this suggests rondo form, from bar 40 a restatement of the first four-bar motif introduces some of the conventional signs of classical development: stretto (bars 44–8), imitative writing (53–5), a sequence (71–82), changes of texture (61ff), a move to a related key (52) and brief forays towards more distant keys. From bar 71, the upper voices scurry up in eight staccato steps, one step back for every two up, leap an octave, and tumble down again (73–4) (Example 5.3).

The scherzando marking suggests some humour. Perhaps the music mimics the shape of the main theme, a chick's attempts to learn from the magisterial flight of the opening. It is a bathetic centrepiece for a development section, all the more so by contrast with the slowly building tension of a 'retransition' (Example 5.4a).

---

[10] Goethe, *Torquato Tasso*, II/1 and IV/3 (*Werke*, II 735, 774); Wackenroder, *Herzensergießungen*, 153; Hoffmann, *Späte Werke*, 793 and 795.

Example 5.2: Schumann, *Fantasiestücke*, ii, bars 1–8

Example 5.3: Schumann, *Fantasiestücke*, ii, bars 72–6

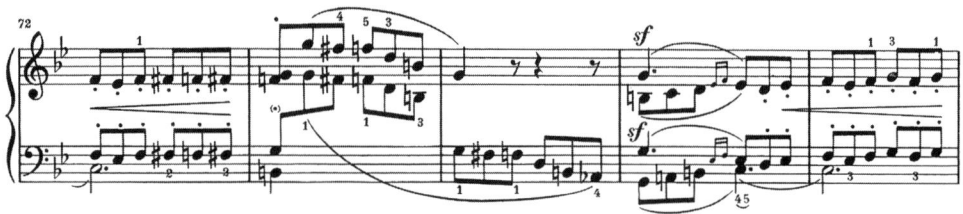

This is reminiscent of Beethoven: compare for instance the retransition of the *Waldstein* sonata, with its swirling deep bass accompaniment, dominant pedals, gradual *crescendo*, rising register and coalescing melodic fragments (Example 5.4b). Schumann's 'recapitulation' (from bar 115) folds the quaver movement of the bass into its surge of energy, as though folding callow flapping into mature flight. A concise eight-bar coda has a cadence (on e^1 and f^1) in F minor: the first in the piece. It is not a float into an indefinite distance, as in bars 7–8, but an abrupt halt.

Taking wing and soaring were long-standing metaphors for artistic maturity and poetic rapture. The image dates back at least to Pindar in the fifth century BC, and was widespread in the eighteenth and nineteenth centuries. For Wackenroder's Berglinger when hearing church music, 'it was as though great wings stretched out from his soul and he wafted up to the lucid heavens'; and Hoffmann's inspired 'poet' of music 'stirs himself for bold flight into the distant land of Romanticism', and 'on his wings we soar over the abyss'. 'The true artist's inner voice constantly challenges

Example 5.4a: Schumann, *Fantasiestücke*, ii, bars 94–116

him: "Why is your flight so lowly, so crippled by earthly powers – shake out your wings afresh and soar aloft to the gleaming stars!"[11] Schumann frequently used 'taking wing' (often with the word 'Aufschwung') as a metaphor of artistic maturity: the great artists, not least eagles like Beethoven, had a broad steady wing-beat; weakness, lameness, clipping or overloading of wings made for ineffectual flapping.[12]

---

[11] Wackenroder, *Herzensergießungen*, 91; Hoffmann, *Die Serapions-Brüder*, 83–4; compare 293; *Kreisleriana*, I/5, 54 and II/7, 327.

[12] *GSK*, I 290, 385, II 67, 220 ('Aufschwung', in one case owing to Beethoven), I 11, 32 ('Federn'), 193 ('Adler'), 23, 93, 95, 123, 307, 170, II 184, 348 ('Geniusflügel', 'Schwung', 'Fluge', etc.).

Example 5.4b: Beethoven, Piano Sonata, op. 53 ('Waldstein'), i, retransition

In a fable in Hoffmann's 'Der goldne Topf', there is a prophecy that a young man, hearing the crystal voices of the three serpents, will feel intimations of that distant land of wonder to which he can soar away ('emporschwingen'); and Anselm, after being apprenticed as a callow youth to the snake Serpentina's father, came to exercise his craft without blotting the manuscripts, and eventually 'spread his wings confidently' as a poet in Atlantis. But the tale's dominant image of soaring is the dark, almost sinister way in which his master (whose voice had been described as 'ringing like metal') disappears in the deepening dusk:[13]

> he seemed more to glide than to walk away down the valley . . . the wind got into his huge coat and lifted the flaps so that they beat the air like a pair of great wings . . . and it seemed to Anselm . . . as if a large bird were spreading its wings for rapid flight . . . As Anselm stared into the twilight, a white-grey vulture rose high in the sky.

'Aufschwung' or 'soaring' is an image for magisterial achievement. Suitably, then, the urgent energy of Schumann's piece evokes aspects of Beethoven's style and in places the dynamism of sonata form, contrasting with the more static forms of the adjacent pieces. But the opening theme, though suggesting F minor, closes in A flat major, and an A flat major recapitulation of the second group seems at odds with the F minor close to the coda, whose abrupt end, moreover, shows no relaxation of phrase structure.[14] This may leave scope for some further resolution in the work as a whole. By contrast, the first movement of Beethoven's first published sonata, also in F minor, only moves to A flat major with the second group, and that is then recapitulated in the tonic minor before the full tonic resolution. Given the nature of Schumann's music, the implications of his title, and his views on musical history, one could see in his ambivalent evocation of classical sonata elements and of Beethovenian energy an image of the authority of the musical tradition: magisterial but constantly demanding rethinking, as Schumann often pointed out.[15]

---

[13] Hoffmann, *Fantasiestücke*, 195 and 226, 230, 254, 202.

[14] The abruptness was introduced only at proof stage: for the excised earlier ending, see Boetticher, *Robert Schumanns Klavierwerke*, II 210.

[15] For instance, *GSK*, I 394–5; II 10. Of course Beethoven experimented: compare Hepokoski and Webster (in Bergé, ed., *Musical Form*, 71–120) on his F minor Egmont Overture, with its A flat major second group recapitulated in D flat major, preparing for an eventual F major coda. Hoffmann described that structure without remarking on anything non-classical: *Schriften zur Musik*, 172–3.

Example 5.5: Schumann, *Fantasiestücke*, iii, bars 1–8

iii and iv: 'Warum?' ('Why?'), and 'Grillen' ('Brooding')

These two D flat major pieces portray a characteristic from opposite sides. 'Warum?', in contrast with 'Aufschwung', is marked 'langsam und zart', with a texture whose delicacy is enhanced by ornaments. Its opening is a question stretched out over 4 bars – interrogative in melody (the downbeats of bars 1–3 rising $\hat{1}$–$\hat{2}$–$\hat{3}$), harmony (suggesting A flat major in bars 1–2 and D flat major in 2–3), and metre (dynamic markings in bars 1–2 throwing into question whether the downbeat comes on the first or second crotchet). The rhythm of the accompaniment, initially independent of that of the melody, turns in bars 3–5 into a vamp, undercutting the bar line (its f^1 will fall in 5 to e^1) (Example 5.5).

Bars 1–4 are thus an opening that is also an expectation of something new to follow. The expectation remains baffled: the piece is a maze, repeatedly circling back to the same place. The dotted rhythm recurs six times in bars 5–13. In bars 17–25 the opening motif is echoed in the bass, and stretched to rise up a triad and add a seventh (21–3), tracing the notes of V^7 of ii. Though accented chords in the alto in bars 20 and 24 promise $\hat{3}$–$\hat{2}$–$\hat{1}$ to answer the opening question, the final $\hat{1}$ does not materialise, and the harmony is instead diverted towards ii. From bars 25 to 30 the motif comes every other bar in repeated overlapping demands, leaving no room for an answer, while repeated chords of V^7 of ii (21–9) never reach their conclusion. Instead they lead (bar 31) into the same spread V^7 of V chord as in bar 13, suggesting the return of the opening music. The music indeed now enters a new loop, itself a tangle of loops (Example 5.6).

The soprano suggests, by restarting the opening theme in bars 31, 35 and 39, that it consists of three four-bar phrases. At the same time, the soprano

Example 5.6: Schumann, *Fantasiestücke*, iii, bars 26–42

Db of bar 38 is tied into 39, and a slur covers 35–7, suggesting a grouping of 4+3+4+1. But the opening f¹ in bars 33 and 37 comes a quaver later than in 3 and 15, and so functions also as the upbeat of its answer, and the harmony in bar 38 matches 34: thus the twelve bars could be grouped as 2½+4+4+1½. The loops are inextricable.

In the last bar, the melody remains inconclusively on $\hat{3}$, the harmony on $^6_4$, and the rhythm on an offbeat; the vamping accompaniment, as in bars 3–4, sounds more like a preparation than an ending. On the repeat, the music simply stops on that interrogative note. The piece neither came in with a proper beginning, nor reaches a firm conclusion; it lacks clear structure; it leaves the listener expectant, circling, lost.

'Grillen' seems very different. It is a clear-cut rondo, marked *Mit Humor*. Dense chords in bars 1–3, a minor inflection in bar 1, and a subdominant leaning in 3–4 suggest brooding. The robust harmonic structure, low register and strong accents convey a latent but clumsy strength. The melody ends with an ungainly staccato lurch up an octave at the cadence in bars 7–8, and metrical complexity here offers neither shimmer nor expectation (as in the previous pieces) but awkward jolts. The repetition in bar 1 of the first two chords creates a duple time at odds with the $^3_4$ time signature; the bass in bar 2 tends to undercut the downbeat; the third-beat accent of bar 3 clashes with the bar line; and second-beat accents in bars 5

Example 5.7: Schumann, *Fantasiestücke*, iv, bars 61–75

and 6 render the bass theme awkward.[16] An F minor episode (bars 16–24) gives the movement a swing, but still with awkward accents on the upbeats in bars 16 and 20. The simplicity of the theme and harmonies suggests the gaucherie of a rustic dance; and the repeated thick bass chords in bars 17 and 21 hint at the drone of a peasant *musette* (as if in a Trio movement by Haydn or Beethoven). An A flat major variant (bars 24–32) retains the drone in a tonic pedal, but exaggerates the gaucherie: *forte* where the F minor dance was *piano*, with accented upbeats as a feature of each bar.

That is nothing to the tour de force of metrical jolts and stumbles that follows in bars 60 to 95.[17] This largely retains the low register and thick texture of the opening; bar lines are undermined by chords tied across them (Example 5.7). The metre appears to change more often than marked, sometimes at odds with the marking. Accents in bars 66 and 67 undercut both the implied and the notated bar line, implying a cross-rhythm of $\frac{3}{4}$, while in a climactic succession of violent jolts, those in 67–70 crash against both the previous metre and the notation. Metrical conflict persists as bars

---

[16] Compare *Myrthen*, op. 25.6, setting the clumsy waiter of Goethe's text: 'Setze mir nicht, du Grobian, / Mir den Krug so derb vor die Nase!'

[17] Compare the analyses in Daverio, *Nineteenth-Century Music*, 67–8 and Krebs, *Fantasy Pieces*, 49 and 148.

72–6 can be heard as $\frac{3}{2}$ again, and 76–80 likewise; the last two beats in each case feel supernumerary.

'Warum?' and 'Grillen' form a pair of character studies. Though simple, with but one theme, repeated and varied, 'Warum?' is also endlessly involved, with tiny inflections to confuse the sense of direction. It is a picture of childlike innocence, asking questions without finding answers – the way the brooder feels from the inside. 'Grillen' then shows how the person asking 'Warum?' looks from the outside: the clumsy moodiness of self-absorption is observed with amusement.

The pairing reflects a complex of concerns in the literary tradition. Absent-minded, childlike self-absorption or dreaming was an image, for the early Romantics, for both the creation and the appreciation of art. Wackenroder has a composer say: 'Is not the whole of life a beautiful dream? A lovely soap-bubble? My composition likewise'; escaping from 'Grillen' (here of worldly troubles), 'like children we view the world as if through the glimmering of a lovely dream'. Joseph Berglinger in the *Herzensergießungen* 'lived in heavenly dreams' and was suspected to be 'simple'. For one character in Novalis, poets 'simply play with the imagination, just as a child plays with its father's magic staff.'[18] In a passage excerpted by Schumann in the 1850s, Hoffmann described the artist as 'devoting himself with childish simplicity to what the spirit conjures in him ... like the apprentice who reads out loud from the Sorcerer's book'.[19] Childish infatuation, however, may displace the maturity, self-possession and craft needed for creation. The literary tradition is replete with those who failed to maintain such sobriety, including Goethe's Tasso, Werther and Wilhelm Meister, Wackenroder's Berglinger, and Hoffmann's Kreisler.[20] The failure may be associated with 'Grillen'. Normally translated as 'daydreams' or 'whims', the word, now largely out of use, is perhaps closer to brooding or moping; in Goethe's *Young Werther* it is used of almost adolescent 'moods'; in *Wilhelm Meister* it obstructs art; in *Faust* it trivialises what for Faust are

---

[18] Wackenroder, 'Die Wunder der Tonkunst', 131, 134 and 90; Novalis, *Die Lehrlinge zu Sais* (*Schriften*, I 100).

[19] Hoffmann, *Kreisleriana*, I/2, 33; *Dichtergarten*, 304.

[20] Compare Jean Paul on 'Besonnenheit', *Vorschule*, §12. Schumann copied out his remark: 'No hand can hold steady and control the poetic paintbrush if the feverish pulse of passion beats in it': *Vorschule*, §3, *Mottosammlung*, I 30. Compare *Tagebücher*, I 378 and Paulin, *Ludwig Tieck*, 73–5.

moments of vision in which he dreams of soaring like an eagle.[21] Schumann adopted this complex of ideas. He wrote to his brother that he 'prayed continually to his guardian angel to sustain him in the childishness of the artist', copied into his *Mottosammlung* the epitaph for Mozart comparing him to a child, and excerpted Jean Paul's remark: 'For whom amongst us does music not conjure up our childhood?' He was seen by others as one who 'is forever turned inwards to brood away [hinbrütet], and in the twilight opens his piano'; and in November 1837 and early 1839 he used the term 'hinbrüten' of himself.[22]

Hoffmann's Anselm too is described as 'childlike'. He falls victim to otherworldly traits: self-absorbed dreaming, absence of mind, brooding ('hinbrüten'). He repeatedly asks questions to which there is no answer. He complains that his 'foolish brooding' ('Grillen') and clumsiness unsuit him for social interaction and bourgeois respectability; he crashes into tables, scattering cups and plates and inkwells. Serpentina explains that she is permitted to marry only

a childlike poetical spirit – and such a spirit is usually found in young men who are mocked by ordinary people because of their extreme simplicity and their total deficiency in worldliness.[23]

Schumann's two paired pieces are simpler in form than the pieces before and after. The first half of the work thus couples two pieces with a high degree of intensity and contrast with a less intense pair moving to a humorous conclusion; it ends where it began, in D flat major. In the second half something similar occurs, but with a stronger sense of dynamism and drama in the first piece, and a progression from F minor through its dominant to a concluding F major.

v: 'In der Nacht' ('At Night')

What occurs 'in the night' appears to be an F minor drama in the relationship between a primary voice and its accompaniment. In bars 1–4, a

---

[21] Goethe, *Die Leiden des Jungen Werther*, letter of 12 August 1771, and *Wilhelm Meister*, IV 1 about the disturbed Augustin, V 9 about Wilhelm, VIII 7 about philistines (*Werke*, IV 187, 281 and 514); *Faust* (*Werke*, II 42).

[22] *Jugendbriefe*, 185 (18 July 1832); *Mottosammlung*, III 54 (compare *GSK*, II 278; I 20, 470 ('Unschuld')); *Mottosammlung*, IX 20 (from *Siebenkäs*); *GSK*, II 425, note 379 ('immer so vor sich hinbrütet, und in der Dämmerstunde den Flügel aufmacht'; the final phrase puns in German on 'opens his wings'); *Briefwechsel*, I 52 (29 November 1837) and *Tagebücher*, II 84.

[23] Hoffmann, *Fantasiestücke*, 187–8, 198 ('Traümerisches Hinbrüten'), 181–2 and 230.

Example 5.8: Schumann, *Fantasiestücke*, v, bars 1–8

swirling accompaniment obscures four pairs of *piano* falling steps f^1-e^1 (Example 5.8).

A motif in triplets rises briefly above the accompaniment (apparently reluctant to follow its metre) from f^1 to g^1 and $a\flat^1$, and sinks back, without completing its descent to $\hat{1}$. This forms a motivic germ that shapes the second half of the work, fully resolved only at the very end. From bar 16, the rising triplets of the primary voice lead into a *piano* descent (19–22) that is perhaps imploring; an answer comes from the remote world of V of D major (23–5). In another variant on the theme (from bar 26), in E flat minor, a chord hammers home, *sforzando*, a repeated G♭ octave (29 and 33), perhaps recalling the percussive chords of 'Aufschwung'.

In what follows the drama takes a puzzling turn. The accompaniment clears to the major (bars 65–8), A♭ yielding to A♮, and a lyrical interlude opens in a slower *piano* duple rhythm. Its theme rises up the tonic triad, F–A♮–C, (69–71) and descends stepwise (71–2), perhaps recalling the opening theme of 'Grillen'. Had it been a simple duet, interrupted in bars 87 and 91 by echoes of the opening triplet motif in the bass, the trajectory would be clear. But it tastes wrong. In bars 73–5 and again in 77–84 a lower voice adds a distorted reflection of the melody – off the beat, with some odd intervals and a strange grace note at the end of bar 74, and then fading away after F♯ is 'corrected' by an accented F♮ in 81, with some elongation and compression (Example 5.9).

Chromatic insertions, starting from the tenor line of bar 69, become more insistent in 75 and 79–81. They generate frequent tritones (bars 71, 75–6, 79–80, 82), and other dissonances that are sharp in themselves, and sometimes in relation to the key as well; their register and persistence leave

Example 5.9: Schumann, *Fantasiestücke*, v, bars 77–84

an acid taste in the mouth – perhaps even metallic, given the role of metals as a symbol in Hoffmann's tale and arguably in Schumann's work.[24] In any case, they seem a distorting medium between the lyrical melody and its twisted reflection. Schumann could write a lyrical cantilena without such discords, or a duet of mirroring voices without such distortions – as for instance in the Trio of op. 21.1, which has a similarly shaped theme and accompaniment, or the middle sections of the first and third pieces of op. 16, or opp. 18 and 19, or the duet of 'Reconnaissance'. But here, as in the middle section of 'Romanze' from op. 32, composed in 1839, something is happening of which sense needs to be made.

The next section is equally puzzling: an oddly static intrusion into an otherwise dynamic piece. From bar 109 the tempo speeds back up for a theme that, for all its busy-ness, goes nowhere. The harmony consists of chords of vi of D flat major (♭VI of the F major of the preceding passage) with G♭ as upper neighbour, alternating every four bars with its dominant. The melody is limited. The contrast between the faster pace and the absence of movement suggests a comedy of helpless scurrying; it resembles the busy and directionless staccato parallel thirds, alternating the tonic minor (vi/♭III) with its dominant, in the opening allegro of Mendelssohn's *Midsummer Night's Dream* Overture, representing the fairies in the nocturnal wood.

Returning to F major in bar 115, expectations build from 122 of a return of the turbulent darkness of the F minor opening music, as the bass mutates

---

[24] Daverio, *Nineteenth-Century Music*, 49–50, emphasises the unusual nature of these discords without trying to make sense of them.

Example 5.10a: Beethoven, Piano Sonata, op. 2.1, iv, opening

Example 5.10b: Beethoven, Piano Sonata, op. 2.1, iv, retransition

into a theme a little reminiscent of the scherzando theme from 'Aufschwung'. Imitations, repetitions, rising and accelerating sequences, a greater density of minor and diminished chords, and increasingly frequent percussive discordant downbeats (bars 126, 130, 132, 134) wind up the expectation. When the opening key and music return, the sense of melodrama is confirmed perhaps in the now more feverish pace. The main voice is eventually overwhelmed (bars 219–22) in repeated hammered E–F steps and a plunge into the bass. The piece ends with a discordant appoggiatura and an abrupt *sforzando* F minor chord. These middle and final sections may undercut the darkness and tragedy, especially if the ending is taken at a faster pace than the opening.

This puzzling piece may be illuminated by some comparisons. The F minor Prestissimo of Beethoven's first sonata begins with an insistent rushing accompaniment in the bass under a *piano* F–E–F motif and repeated *forte* octaves (Example 5.10a). An episode in A flat major serves as the start of a 'development', with a return to F minor with some colour of D flat major. If played prestissimo, rather than in more measured style, this leads to a melodramatic retransition before the 'exposition' returns (Example 5.10b). There is then a plunge into the bass at the end (Example 5.10c).

Example 5.10c: Beethoven, Piano Sonata, op. 2.1, iv, end

I have no idea whether Schumann had that movement in mind; but it illustrates the sort of music against which his own piece may emerge as balanced between dark storms and ironic melodrama. For his music exaggerates features that in the Beethoven can be heard as on the verge of comedy (in particular the retransition and the final plunge), and brings out a newly comic possibility in the move to ♭VI that precedes and delays that retransition.

Some months after 'In der Nacht' was written, Schumann told Clara how he had found in the piece when completed the 'lovely old romantic legend' of Leander and Hero. On other occasions he described how in that 'touching fable', Hero's 'old Papa takes violent action ... and locks her up because she loves someone she should not ... See how she sits in a tower in the water and darns stockings ... and so Hero and Leander, who loved each other so much, are drowned'. Now he told Clara:

> If I play 'Nacht' I can't forget the picture – first how he plunges into the sea – she calls – he answers – he makes it through the waves to dry land – then the *cantilena* where they lie in one another's arms – then how he has to set off again, but can't bear to part from her – till night envelops everything in darkness again. Of course I think of Hero just like you, and if you were stuck in a lighthouse, I'd probably learn to swim even at my age. But tell me whether the picture fits the music for you too.

Tadday, following Schumann's hint, has mapped the story onto the music precisely: the swim (bars 1–68), Hero's call (10–12) and Leander's answer (18–22); lovers' union (69–108); he cannot tear himself away (108–43), and in swimming back he is engulfed (143–223).[25]

Schumann might have pinned the fable onto Beethoven's F minor *prestissimo* instead, describing how Leander swims out, with the calls perhaps in the main second group melody; the lovers share a lyrical night of A flat major union; he cannot tear himself away in the retransition; the piece ends with the swim back and the final drowning. We could have either enjoyed the association, or dismissed it as merely another poetic

---

[25] *Briefwechsel*, I 154 (21 April 1838) (compare *Neue Folge*, 120, of 22 April 1838); *GSK*, II 303 of 1834 and 126–7 of 1843, mentioning Musaeus' version; Tadday, *Das schöne Unendliche*, 141–2.

extravaganza of a later musician. But a composer's own words inevitably carry some authority, and if Schumann invites Hero and Leander to squat in his own piece, I at any rate find it hard to evict them: like Schumann, 'I can't forget the picture'. But I do not find the programme helpful. The story, even if fitting here, makes no sense of the rest of the work; even in this piece, to understand who calls and who answers requires a listener to make impossible distinctions between identities in the music; and if the distinctive musical images of the middle sections are interpreted through their story, Hero seems to taste brine on Leander's limbs during their night of love (admittedly as she did in Musaeus), and their souls mirror one another with inexplicable distortions (bars 69–108); and when he 'has to set off again, but can't bear to leave her' (bars 109–21), he scurries around ineffectually as though looking for his swimming trunks. Rather than taking Hero and Leander too seriously, I prefer to speculate that Schumann was aware of his first audience's tendency to miss the humour in his piece, and used the fable as a corrective hint.

Clara's 'old Papa' had taken almost as drastic action as Hero's to obstruct the course of love; and in the autumn of 1837, Schumann suffered from anxiety as to whether he would ever see Clara again: 'What a terrible night last night was. My head burned, my imagination led me from abyss to abyss... I'm ill, really ill.' In April 1838, in the very letter in which he mentioned Hero and Leander, he told Clara how he himself had called for help from dark forces:[26]

Last night ... I woke up and could not get back to sleep – and then I thought myself deeper and deeper into you and your soul and your dream life, and all of a sudden cried out with profound conviction: 'Clara, I'm calling you' – and then I heard right by me 'Robert, I'm here beside you.' But a kind of horror overtook me, at how spirits can traffic with one another over the great expanses of land.

We need not insist, of course, that the music be seen as conveying autobiography. But Schumann could have associated his experience with Leander's, for like Leander he braved forces of darkness to meet his beloved, and was defeated.

So too did Veronika in Hoffmann's 'Der goldne Topf'. Fearing the loss of Anselm, she followed an old hag out 'in der Nacht' as the storm howled, taking a cauldron of metals to forge a metallic mirror in which to conjure the spirit of her lover. Urged on by the hag, she knelt 'frozen in horror', her 'little hands clasped imploringly above her head'. As the metals seethed,

---

[26] *Briefwechsel*, I 32–3 (7 October 1837), 138 (15 April 1838).

Figure 5.1: Goethe, 'Hexenszene', 1776–8

shapes began to emerge, 'and all of a sudden there stepped from the depths of the cauldron the student Anselm'. (Elsewhere in Hoffmann, metallic mirrors are used to similar effect, and there are several scenes of witchcraft in stormy nights;[27] Goethe's sketch of such a scene, with a witch holding a homunculus above a boiling cauldron, is at Figure 5.1). Hoffmann imagines the reader jumping melodramatically out of a passing coach to rescue Veronika, but ironically admits that the reader was not there. A howling storm, imploring figure, distorted image of a lover in the metal mirror, helpless reader, irony and melodrama may all have counterparts in the music.

Understandably, it was not the association to which Schumann drew his fiancée's attention in April 1838. He could not have wanted to stress the triangular pull between love and art in the *Fantasiestücke*, nor to risk Clara imagining herself cast as the bourgeois Veronika. In March Clara had refused to be reassured when she suspected herself miscast as the prosaic

---

[27] Hoffmann, *Fantasiestücke*, 219–23, 248–9; 'Die Geheimnisse' and 'Der Elementargeist' (*Späte Werke*, 191 and 389), and 'Nachrichten von den neuesten Schicksalen des Hundes Berganza' (*Fantasiestücke*, 86–7). Compare also Kleist's *Das Käthchen von Heilbronn* (1810), with its elderflower bush and witchcraft with cauldrons of metal, and its hero torn between two women.

sister Ambrosia in his essay about *Carnaval*.[28] An association with Anselm would not have helped persuade Clara's father of Schumann's suitability as a husband. Let Clara instead see herself as Hero. For us, however, different interpretive contexts – Beethoven, fable, Hoffmann, the composer's own experience – need not be mutually exclusive.

Veronika, her dark ordeal ended not by Hoffmann's reader but by a mysterious intervention, found herself in her bed in daylight, slipping from dreaming to waking and back again, feverishly unsure which was which.[29] In Schumann's music, the bass appoggiatura to the *sforzando* concluding F minor chord of 'In der Nacht' begins F–G–A♭, recalling the opening motif, and that dissonant G prepares for a transition that will lead to confusion between dreaming and waking.

vi: 'FABEL' ('Fable')

In a slow *piano* awakening into C major, the treble of bar 1 takes the G–A♭ (=G♯) just heard and stretches it out over two slow beats before replacing the A♭ with an A♮, and stretching further up the scale to a relaxed cadence (3–4). The f^1–e^1 step, now part of a C major, not F minor, cadence, is at the same time continued down e^2–d^2–c^2: the melody concludes by falling satisfyingly $\hat{3}$–$\hat{2}$–$\hat{1}$, like an answer to the question of 'Warum?'

A 'schnell' *pianissimo* theme, still in C major, (bars 5ff) brings a sense of innocent play with melody, harmony and metre (and with the f^1–e^1 step). The harmonies are mostly in root position, moving along a conventional path, if spiced with dissonance. The downbeats as heard fall on the second and sixth semiquavers of each notated bar, out of sync with the notated bar line: the teasing metrical complexity may barely be registered at first, but bars 7 and 10 accent the seventh semiquavers, crossing both the metre as previously heard and the stresses on the even-numbered semiquavers arising from the melody and the bass in 8 and 12.

In contrast to these light or clinking sonorities, the repeated percussive chords in A minor that open bar 29 (and indeed every bar up to 41) can sound like the ringing of hammered metal (as in the opening motif of 'Aufschwung' and in the repeated chords of 'In der Nacht': bars 29, 33, 174 and 178). They seem derived, as in a development, from the

---

[28] *Briefwechsel*, I 80–1, 103, 107 (21 January, 12 February and 2 March 1838).
[29] Hoffmann, *Fantasiestücke*, 222–4.

Example 5.11: Schumann, *Fantasiestücke*, vi, bars 60–7

accompaniment of bar 28; and the middle section they initiate (bars 29–69) adopts other traits of a development too (thematic derivation, sequences, changes of texture and mode, shifting tonalities). At the same time it uses clusters of ordinary materials to foreshadow a return to darkness or nightmare: a syncopated accented motif harps on repeated accented Es in bars 29–33, and in 56 emphasises the step f^1-e^1, recalling the same step in 'In der Nacht' and 'Aufschwung'. In bars 122–38 of 'In der Nacht', sequences rising in steps had served, along with the acceleration and the harmonic progression, to build tension for the return of the dark main theme; now in 'FABEL', a stepwise rise in the highest note of each bar in the largely G minor 62–8 likewise threatens a return, presumably again to darkness (Example 5.11).[30]

But the threat turns out to be insubstantial, as daylight and innocence return with the conversion of a G minor chord to a G pedal as V of C major in bar 66. In a bar (69) falling outside the four-bar framework, the rapid semiquaver motif of bars 61–8 slows (in an echo of the semitone rise that opened the piece?) to reveal instead the 'schnell' theme (70–7); and the final

---

[30] Compare bars 93ff of 'Aufschwung', whose stepwise upward motion picks up the similar steps in 90–1 and 60–3; in bars 104ff similar upward steps lead back to the main theme of the piece. Similarly, patterns of rapid semiquavers in 'FABEL' (bars 33ff, 41ff, 61ff) resemble those in bars 116–37 of 'In der Nacht' and 61–114 of 'Aufschwung' (there in quavers); from bar 61 the pattern resembles the rising motif of 'In der Nacht' (bars 3 etc. and 86–7) – strikingly so in bar 63, with a similar rise from $\hat{5}$ to $\hat{1}$, $\hat{2}$ and then $\hat{3}$.

word goes to the 'langsam' music from the very beginning. The opening music sounded like an awakening, and the middle section a nightmare; and when the opening music returns at the end, now moving from the dominant G major (bars 78–81) down to the tonic C major (82ff), with an 'ever slower' tempo, and ending with the descent e^1-d^1-c^1, it perhaps betokens a reverse process of falling asleep, and entering a dream, as the title of the next piece, 'Traumes Wirren', suggests.

In that sense, these pieces confuse dreaming and waking; and in Hoffmann's tale, images of dream and waking are frequent and equally ambivalent.[31] Dreaming was widely recognised as an exalted state of insight, illusion, and delusion, and associated with the creation and reception of art. Goethe's Wilhelm Meister claims that the artist 'lives the dream of life awake', whereas others 'even waking pursue dreams'; his Tasso asks himself, 'Have you awoken from a dream? ... Yes, you wake and sleep at once'; his life was said to lose all balance in a way that can 'bring us at the end to dreaming by the light of day'.[32] Schumann's Florestan, after a reverie about Chopin's op. 2, bids his alter ego 'awake to new dreams, and sleep'. For Schumann, sometimes music 'dreams, and we in it', and the listener 'is in a reverie'.[33] Novalis described the unbounded, integrative, primal nature of Romantic art in terms of 'sleep', which 'is nothing more than the flood of that invisible ocean, and waking is the start of the ebb.' Shakespeare had led the way. Prospero's island is full of 'sounds and sweet airs', as Caliban said, 'that if I had then wak'd after long sleep / Will make me sleep again' and show him dreams that 'when I wak'd / I cried to dream again'; similarly in *Twelfth Night*, 'If it be thus to dream, still let me sleep'. It was an image Schumann echoed (once again about Chopin).[34]

The confusion between dreaming and waking is akin to that between fable and the everyday, and so associated with myth, poetry and symbolism.[35] In its title, 'FABEL', Schumann's piece may recall the fable in Novalis' *Heinrich von Ofterdingen*, where a character of invulnerable childlike playful innocence, called 'Fabel', brings about the liberation of the world from

---

[31] Hoffmann, *Fantasiestücke*, 185, 187, 191, 197–200 (*passim*), 203, 204, 205, 214, 224, 231, 233, 234, 235, 237 ('Traumgestalt'), 239, 249, 250, 251, 253.

[32] Hoffmann, *Die Serapions-Brüder*, 263; Goethe, *Wilhelm Meister*, II/2, *Torquato Tasso*, IV/1 and V/1 (*Werke*, IV 73 and II 766 and 785). The young Schumann wrote in 1828 (*Tagebücher*, I 112): 'Physical sleep is the soul's real vigil, as physical waking is the soul's dreaming'.

[33] *GSK*, I 7, 362; compare 117, 123, 180, 191. The idea of music as dream seems to be concentrated in 1835–7.

[34] Novalis, *Die Lehrlinge zu Sais*, in *Schriften*, I 104; Shakespeare, *The Tempest*, III.ii.147–55; *Twelfth Night*, IV.i.67; *GSK*, I 255.

[35] See Williamson, *The Longing for Myth*, chapter 1.

dangerous forces, and its transfiguration through love and poetry. Novalis wrote that 'a fairy tale is in truth like an image from a dream – without coherence – an assembly of wondrous things and situations – for instance a fantasy in music ... a masked ball'.[36] 'Der goldne Topf', too, associates fable with dreaming. In a room filled with teasing, clinking, delicately dancing sounds, Serpentina tells Anselm the fable of the marriage of her parents, a Salamander and a green snake, of her father's fall, and of the need for the three sisters to marry poetical spirits if redemption is to be found. As she ended, Anselm awoke as from a deep dream and found her vanished – but his duty to copy out the fable she had told him had been magically fulfilled. With Veronica the next day, however, he was sure that 'the fantastic saga ... had been written by him himself... He was amazed at his daydreaming ... and laughed over his wild fantasy that he was in love with a little serpent'.[37] Similarly, at the end of the tale, the author has a vision of Anselm in Atlantis that he thought he had dreamed in his garret, but when he wakes he finds it written out apparently by himself, and each of the book's chapters, named 'Vigils', is presumably the output of a similar nocturnal session. In each case it remains moot whether the vision is higher truth or mere fiction.[38] As fable for Novalis 'contains the history of the primeval world' and its triadic pattern of harmony, fall and restoration, so in 'Der goldne Topf', fable reveals that pattern as the mythic kernel of the story.[39]

But here there is irony. When Serpentina's father told the fable of a primal conflict between Phosphorus, the bringer of light, and the dragon, his listeners scoffed at such 'oriental bombast'; and Anselm was warned that he had 'a dangerous tendency to the Poetical, from which one can so easily decline into the Fantastic and the Novelistic'. Now, however, Anselm appears to witness a fairy tale conflict between Serpentina's father and the forces of witchcraft – if he does not dream it; and images of dream and of

---

[36] Novalis, *Schriften*, V 269(fr. 493); compare III 449, unknown to Schumann in 1837: 'everything poetical must be like a fairy tale'.

[37] Hoffmann, *Fantasiestücke*, 224–34. As Anselm was torn between love and art, so, in Schumann's mind, was the artist-hero of Berlioz's *Symphonie Fantastique* – between a feverish unrequited love for 'the chilly British woman', and a vision of pure, heavenly love of art: *GSK*, II 212–4.

[38] Hoffmann, *Fantasiestücke*, 254 and 197. For Schumann, a composer 'dreamed ... and when he awoke, his concerto was written' (*GSK*, I 152; compare 185). The self-reflexiveness is traditional. Wilhelm Meister found in a tower a scroll with the story of his life on it (*Wilhelm Meister*, VII/9 (*Werke*, IV 443–4)). In Novalis' *Heinrich von Ofterdingen*, Heinrich von Ofterdingen opens an ancient book and finds himself and his story in it: *Schriften*, I 264–5.

[39] Novalis, *Schriften*, V 264(fr. 451); fable was also a philosophic-aesthetic category ('language to a raised power, e.g. Fable, is the expression of an integrated thought'): 231(fr. 249).

conflict, presented with similar irony, occur in Schumann's next piece, whose F major has been prepared by the C major end of 'FABEL'.[40]

vii: 'Traumes Wirren' ('Swirling Dreams')

The opening phrase of 'Traumes Wirren' (rising F–G–A in bars 3–4) is regular in melody, harmony and metre; only the perhaps exaggerated brightness of the treble figuration suggests a dream. But thereafter oneiric features throng (Example 5.12).

A peculiar bar (8) interrupts the figuration to end the answering phrase: does it parody the semitone upward steps of bars 66–9 of 'FABEL'? When a sequence (bars 9ff) moves the opening melody up a tone to G minor, regular bass accents shift in bar 13 to the second quaver, and stress an F♮ in the tenor that clashes with a *sforzando* F♯ an octave above, which itself clashes with a C♮ a tritone below. A similar jangling recurs in the next bar (14). In this dream, unnatural brightness suddenly becomes battle. Under the lively treble figuration martial calls sound in the left hand, in a march rhythm (bars 17–24). But it is an unreal, even grotesque battle. A pedal on a low F♮ every other bar turns jarringly (bar 25) into a pedal on a deep F♯, giving rise to four bars of F sharp major harmony: the melodic jangling of bars 13–14 is written into the harmony. When the martial calls return (31–5), they issue in V^7 for the return of the opening music.

In bar 63, after a modified return of the opening, the music is suddenly in D flat major, *pp*. The immobility of its harmony, melody, rhythm and voice-leading contrasts with the 'extremely lively' opening music. Low tonic and subdominant chords alternate (bars 63–6), plagal harmonies matching limited rhythmic movement. Four bars of uniform crotchets rise in cramped steps, and four fall (67–74), their stiffness accentuated by frequent parallel tritones (Example 5.13).

Even this degree of freedom shrinks, the crotchets scarcely budging within a semitone step up in parallel tritones (bar 75). The step is repeated, first at pitch, then a semitone lower, and then a little higher as the harmony retreats to the subdominant G flat major for five bars of plagal harmonies (bars 87–91). Since bars 67–74 have some thematic resemblance to the stepwise rise to the fifth degree and subsequent descent, all in low crotchet chords, that open 'Grillen', it is as though

[40] Hoffmann, *Fantasiestücke*, 193, 188, 236–43.

Example 5.12: Schumann, *Fantasiestücke*, vii, bars 1–31

Example 5.13: Schumann, *Fantasiestücke*, vii, bars 63–94

the blundering persona of 'Grillen' were now imprisoned in the paralysis of nightmare.[41]

When liveliness returns with the opening theme (bar 95), in D flat major until bar 115, the martial calls at first are given normalised harmony and voice-leading; and when further grotesque martial blasts – featuring tritone harmonies (bars 145, 149, 153, 157) – interrupt the concluding flourishes, they are forced gradually into the depths of the bass. Here their D♭ bass octaves under a treble C recall the sonority of 'Aufschwung'. But in a disarmingly mild, somewhat anticlimactic, conclusion (*mezzo forte*, decrescendo and ritardando) any sense of conflict evaporates like a dream. As in 'FABEL', the conflict is only a fairy tale; the threat of nightmare vanishes.

Hoffmann's tale has recurrent images of conflict, but throughout the final fairy-tale battle between the Salamander and the old hag with her dark forces, Anselm is confined in a crystal bottle:

---

[41] Perhaps the G flat major harmony and stiff movements also recall bars 60ff of 'Grillen', and the featureless rhythm, rise and fall, and plagal harmonies may echo the ineffectual movement of bars 108ff of 'In der Nacht', with its emphasis on G♭ and subdominant harmonies.

His limbs drew closer and closer together . . . he could not stir or move . . . He could not budge a limb, but his thoughts beat against the glass, deluding him with dissonant sounds, and . . . he heard only the dull noise of madness.

He was not released until the Salamander finally defeated the forces of witchcraft. The voice of a student suggests to the reader, however, that Anselm hallucinated the bottle while in fact standing on the Elbe bridge: his liberation may then have been a leap to his death in the water.[42]

'Traumes Wirren', despite its relatively static form, to my ear is too insubstantial – too dreamlike – to bring a fully settled closure to the work. In the concluding piece, by contrast, solid signs of closure accompany a static form to reinforce the F major conclusion.

viii: 'Ende vom Lied' ('End of the Song')

Hoffmann signs off his tale with 'Ende des Märchens', and Schumann's title may in some sense parallel that. The opening music can be heard as akin to that of 'Grillen' – in its marking, *Mit gutem Humor*, low register, crotchet movement and thick chords, and even melodic pattern, rising through $\hat{1}$ to $\hat{5}$, followed by a stepwise descent. But awkwardness has been transformed into loose-limbed strength, and D flat major into F major. The theme sprawls up the octaves (bars 1–3, 5–7 etc.) in a confident *forte*, a swinging rhythm, sustained notes and cacophonous harmonies (on the third beats of bars 1 and 5). In contrast with the stiff confinement of bars 67–86 of 'Traumes Wirren' (which also perhaps echoed 'Grillen'), the metre conveys a free movement, the first downbeat obscured by a rest in the bass, and the melody's stresses initially on the second and fourth beats (Example 5.14).

The theme is built around harmonies and pitches of F major and G minor; but its cadences are inconclusive, both emphasising the pitch of a^1: bar 4 on V of ii, and bar 8 on an accented weak beat. The melody of bars 9–12, with chorale-like harmonies, sounds like a peal of bells, perhaps wedding bells; its concluding G pedal (V of V) prepares, with some melodrama, for the return of the opening theme. That theme is now (bars 16ff) clarified: the notes of the melody clearly differentiated from the accompaniment, the chords sharply defined, the harmonies and

---

[42] Hoffmann, *Fantasiestücke*, 193, 230–1, 236–43; on the story's first page (179) the hag's curse had condemned Anselm to 'fall into crystal': 'Ins Kristall bald dein Fall – ins Kristall!'. The 'beautiful soul' in Book VI of Goethe's *Wilhelm Meister* feels trapped in a glass bottle which she need only burst apart in order to be free.

Example 5.14: Schumann, *Fantasiestücke*, viii, bars 1–16

voice-leading more normal and the phrasing unambiguous. The loose-limbed metre, with the bar line still initially displaced by a beat, is the more striking. The thick chords and awkward rhythm are once again reminiscent of 'Grillen'; but the ungainly octave leap of bar 7 of 'Grillen' is turned in bar 17 of this piece into exultant strength.

But so simple a happy ending is apparently not what Schumann intended. Nor is it what Clara heard. She was, she said, reminded of Zumsteeg in places; and Schumann replied:[43]

It is good that Zumsteeg came into your mind – it's true, I thought there, well, everything will after all be resolved in the end in a cheerful wedding – but then at the end the pain about you returned and so it sounds like wedding bells and a death knell mixed together.

They were presumably both thinking of Zumsteeg's setting of Bürger's gothic ballad *Lenore*.[44] In it, a soldier returns to claim his bride at dead of night, and ride away with her. But he is a corpse, and takes her to her death. 'The dead ride rapidly', we are told, and 'the bridges thunder' under their horses'

---

[43] *Briefwechsel*, I 112, 121 (4 and 17 March 1838).   [44] As Heller, 'Fantasiestücke', 70, suggests.

Example 5.15: Zumsteeg, *Lenore*, page 29

hooves, with a variety of galloping and cantering motifs, which close on G minor to give way to a dirge in E flat minor (♭vi). Between its phrases a major phrase intones: 'Hark the tolling bell! Hark the dirge!' (Example 5.15).

Schumann does not copy or allude to Zumsteeg, but Clara's association was natural. For Schumann's B flat major middle section (bars 24–60) opens with a simple melody and tonic harmony over a cantering bass, with percussive repeated chords (now no longer discords). After a passage like a development (bars 33–44), a pedal on C and G (44–8) underlies the dominant preparation for the return, issuing in a rising bass (48–52) and then (52–60) thundering *fortissimo* reaffirmation of the B flat major theme. This might recall or spoof Zumsteeg's galloping horses, thundering bridges and deathly wedding, and that association complicates the impact of the return of the opening section (bars 60–84) with its wedding bells, chorale and emphasis on the pitches F, G and A. Then suddenly (bar 85), as in Zumsteeg, the rhythm is far slower; by 87 the bass A sinks to A♭, and the tonality is ♭VI. Over ten bars, first *p*, then *pp*, and then *ppp*, swaying chords float slowly upwards through a liquefying pedal in various refractions of the submediant D flat major harmony.[45] At bar 95 a bell begins to toll on a low A♮ as the harmony returns to F major. In the depths emerges an outline of the first two bars of the opening theme of the piece (bars 95–100), scarcely perceptible at half speed through the aqueous dimness. A second statement begins (bar 100), more audibly, and comes to a perfect authentic cadence at 105, by which time a third statement is already emerging. The melody and its final cadence emphasise the descent from c^2 to f^1, resolving the a^1 of bars 4 and 8, or the $a\flat^1$ of the opening motif of 'In der Nacht': a fully settled close to the work, with repeated expanded cadential progressions over a tonic pedal and a loosening phrase structure.

---

[45] Compare the sudden *piano*, slower harmonic movement, and low register of the slowly swaying chords in the final couplet of the last song in *Dichterliebe*, op. 48/16 – where we know from the text of the song that we are hearing a coffin sink slowly to rest in deep water.

If Schumann's coda suggests not only resolution but dream and fluidity, those traditional metaphors for art, Hoffmann's ending does likewise. Anselm, in wedded bliss ('Seligkeit'), and now a fully fledged artist, retires with his bride Serpentina to his father-in-law's estates in submarine Atlantis; its sounds, colours, lights and crystal gleams, awoken from sleep, play in childlike 'jubilant upheaval'.[46] Hoffmann's ending has a note of elegy too: Anselm's wedding to Serpentina was also a death to this world, either metaphorically, as the author would have it, or perhaps literally, as the student on the Elbe bridge may have suggested.

The work as a whole

Schumann's title, *Fantasiestücke*, recalls Hoffmann's, and is an apt description for the musical entity I have described, with its vivid dreamlike images; and those images come together in Hoffmann's tale, 'Der goldne Topf'.

If Schumann's thematic families suggest a central persona, and the titles a poetic thread similar to Hoffmann's, the music could moreover be interpreted in the light of the archetypal trajectory of a *Bildungsroman* such as 'Der goldne Topf'.[47] Schumann's work introduces a self mesmerised by crystalline, serpentine beauty, confronted by a magisterial dark presence, brooding like a child, and risibly clumsy; and in the second half that self becomes a victim of dark threatening storms and involved in a distorted love duet; awakens into innocent playfulness, despite the threat of a renewed nightmare; dreams of a fairy-tale conflict, entrapment and liberation; and at the end matures into strength, despite deathly associations and a note of elegy. The trajectory brings a comedy of character that largely depends on taking each passage in relation to the whole rather than as an isolated moment of farce. It may show some overlap too with the novel the young Schumann had in mind (see Chapter 1). In the plot he sketched one could see in embryo ideas that emerge in several pieces (as indicated) of the *Fantasiestücke*:

Florestan is to be that artist, pure, changeable, receptive, inspired, ... driven on by the urge to please his beloved [i]. Krümelchen, the embodiment of the mechanical,

---

[46] *Fantasiestücke*, 250–5. Schumann described his work as 'blissful' ('selig'): *Tagebücher*, II 34.
[47] Hoffmann's *Meister Floh* is another *Bildungsroman*, with many of the same images as 'Der goldne Topf', though not as central to the story: a magical evening scene with silver bells (*Meister Floh*, 678), the magician soaring with his love in his arms (704), the emptiness of the hero's life (687, 739–40), self-absorbed childish daydreaming ('Grillen') (685, 739, 795), a stormy night scene (694–6), 'fabelhafte' (794), 'confused dreams' ('wirren Träumen') (724).

gives him a jolt [ii]. Seraphine, as the image of taste and fashion, almost puts Caecilia in the shade [v]. Raro as an ironic principle, appears last, till in the end Caecilia leads him back to the purity of art [vi].[48]

Moreover, the manuscript title page and the music manuscript itself reveal that the order of the pieces mattered. While Schumann considered several variants of the sequence before he reached the final selection and order, none of the surviving pieces ever moved further than one place from its final position, with the possible exception of 'Warum?', which may have moved two places.[49] The work had, then, some overall trajectory from which Schumann did not consider departing.

But the exact order was not fixed, as it might have been were there a controlling narrative programme. And Schumann's titles do not attribute identities as they do in *Carnaval*; the work invokes no distinct characters or events, and no ambient world. It is tempting to interpret the work's trajectory as primarily musical, but such that its patterns of tonality, theme, form and sonority may bring psychological and imagistic overtones (if the titles are our guide), and resonate with aspects of Schumann's musical and literary culture.

The work need not then be programmatic in the sense of following an external or narrative schema: Schumann neither follows Hoffmann's order, nor builds an expectation as to what scene will be painted next, but follows his own musical processes. How far these processes make sense of each part of the music's sequence is a matter of judgement. The D flat major section of 'Traumes Wirren', for instance, seems to me in place because the piece sets an expectation of discontinuity through its title and its largely paratactic formal construction, and because the expressive opposition between the D flat major and F major sections meets that expectation. Similarly, the expectations generated by the rondo structure of 'Grillen', and the expressive continuity, make sense of its G flat major episode. Such factors do not, in my judgement, help enough with bars 108–15 of 'In der Nacht', which

---

[48] *Mottosammlung*, IX 26. 'Krümelchen' was Hummel (though for Schumann in 1837 Beethoven might be the greater jolt-giver); 'Caecilia' is Zilia, or Clara. Schumann dished up for Clara a yarn that in June 1837 he nearly proposed to her bourgeois 'lookalike' – a Seraphine or Veronika – but she sensibly doubted the tale: *Briefwechsel*, I 68, 82 (3 and 24 January 1838).

[49] The 'Stichvorlage' was sent for printing on 7 August 1837: *Neue Folge*, 421. It is described in Boetticher, *Robert Schumanns Klavierwerke*, II 207–12, and Schumann, *Fantasiestücke*, ed. Herttrich, 42–3. Its owner restricts access to it, but displayed copies of four sheets in an exhibition in Basel in 2010–11: I am grateful to Roger Harmon for his expert description. It is impossible to be sure on the basis of the available evidence which of the markings in the music manuscript were made or guided by Schumann himself. Similarly late changes were made to op. 6 in September 1837: Roesner, 'The Sources for Schumann's *Davidsbündlertänze*', 58–61.

feel oddly intrusive – especially given Schumann's own imputation of a narrative, which suggests that the music is best understood through narrative even if one tries to set aside the particular programme.[50] And if Hero and Leander become a programmatic basis for one piece, then the work as a whole has less coherence than I have found (for instance in the transition to 'FABEL'); or if instead one hears Veronika and Anselm, that brings difficulties in the other pieces about causation and identity – whether a character persists across the work as a whole, and who is the subject of each piece. Such concerns obscure my appreciation of the work's liveliness: better to find imagistic and psychological resonances without importing narratives or characters.

The sparse critical comment and the resort to a programmatic interpretation involving Hero and Leander suggest that several critics find a difficulty in the music; and that may suggest that the work is transitional between the earlier 'literary' works (*Papillons* and *Carnaval*) and the later (*Kreisleriana* and the *Nachtstücke*). These latter works have richer musical patterns, and a subtly different relationship to literature, and resort to programmatic or narrative explanations is less tempting. This development is part of a wider evolution in Schumann's compositional style in 1836–8; and that is the subject of the next chapter.

---

[50] These bars were indeed a late insertion – but one of many: see Chapter 6, note 20. Compare *GSK*, II 221, demanding an account of coherence between passages short on musical relationships.

6 | 'In possession of the secret', 1836–1838
Schumann's stylistic evolution

In February 1838 Schumann told Clara Wieck 'for about the last eighteen months I've felt as if I were in possession of the secret'.[1] *Carnaval* was largely composed before that eighteen-month period, the *Fantasiestücke* during it, and the later two 'literary' works after. It was a period in which there were significant shifts in Schumann's style, and in the way his music related to literature.

Schumann had become aware how distant the demands of great music were from the literary enthusiasms of his youth. In his writing, fragile butterflies had already yielded as images of art and artists to great oaks and commanding eagles; and masks gave way to faces as characterisations of his poetic music. His musical thought had come over the years to centre less on Schubert as master of the dance sequence, and more on his novel sonata forms, and on Beethoven and Bach.[2] Schumann had studied Bach since youth, and periodically renewed his engagement with his music; but in 1837–8 that engagement was particularly intense.[3] Between February and October 1836 he first heard Beethoven's late quartets in A minor (op. 132) and B flat major (op. 130), and by December 1837 the C sharp minor, op. 131 and E flat major, op. 127. In 1832, following study of the 'Hammerklavier' Sonata, op. 106, he had called Beethoven 'not a guide but the destination itself'; now in 1836, his comment on what he might have seen in the quartets, then only just over ten years old, was laconic: 'Endziel', 'final destination'.[4] Schumann called the quartets, opp. 127 and 131, works 'for whose greatness no words can be found, works which alongside some chorales and original pieces by Sebastian Bach seem the outer limits that human art and imagination have reached to date'.

---

[1] See Appendix 3–6.
[2] *GSK*, I 118 and 128 (1835); *Briefwechsel*, I 127 (18 March 1838); *GSK*, I 328ff (1838); *Briefwechsel*, I 169–70 (11 May 1838); Marston, 'Schumann's Heroes', 49; Brown, 'Higher Echoes', 538–43.
[3] Bischoff, 'Das Bach-Bild Robert Schumanns', 446–52.
[4] *Tagebücher*, I 394, 396, 398; II 23, 28 and 45. I assume that at some point he heard the F major Quartet, op. 135, but not necessarily in time for its three mottoes, headed 'Der schwer gefasste Entschluß', to influence 'Sphinxes' in *Carnaval*. Compare Bischoff, *Monument für Beethoven*, 189–93, 306–10 and 415ff.

Schumann said: 'I am satisfied only by the ultimate – Bach almost always, Beethoven above all in his later works.'[5]

Hoffmann did not, of course, know these late works. But Bach's music is central to the first of Hoffmann's *Kreisleriana*; in the fifth, his counterpoint, with its 'wonderful entwinements', epitomises music's mysterious kinship with the nature of the cosmos:

> There are moments – especially after I have immersed myself in the works of the great Sebastian Bach – when the numerical relationships of music, and indeed the mystic laws of counterpoint, awake in me a deep dread. Music! I invoke you with an eerie shudder, even with horror! You! – Nature's primal language [Sanskritta der Natur] expressed in notes![6]

In the second essay, Beethoven figures as a 'mighty spirit' too powerful for vulnerable minds; the fourth describes how he went beyond his predecessors and 'penetrated the innermost being' of instrumental music. In Haydn, 'the expression of a childlike serenity prevails', and 'the majority of people can measure themselves against Haydn, and grasp him'; while Mozart (who figures repeatedly as a model composer in the penultimate essay) 'lays claim to the supernatural that dwells deep inside human nature', and 'leads us into the depths of the world of spirits' where 'fear embraces us', and 'love and melancholy sound in graceful spirit voices'. Beethoven's works, however, 'awake that infinite yearning that is the essence of Romanticism'.[7]

Schumann's interpretation of recent musical history was similar. In 1838, his eye was caught by Zelter's comment, perhaps influenced by Hoffmann, that Bach was 'dreaded but also divine'. Bach was Schumann's 'daily bread', 'one of the greatest creators of all time', 'inexplicable as ever', with a 'boldly labyrinthine style', many of whose fugues 'are character pieces of the highest kind, sometimes truly poetic creations'.[8] While Schumann thought Haydn one of the great composers, not least of string quartets, he shared something of Hoffmann's idea that his music is a little too comfortable: 'he is like a familiar friend of the family, always received with pleasure and respect, but no longer with any profounder interest for today'. His view of Mozart deepened with age, making room perhaps for Hoffmann's insight that in him grace, while ever present, can

---

[5] *GSK*, I 380 (compare 343 of 1838: 'the highest kind of music, as Bach and Beethoven have given us in some compositions'; and II 420 note 365); *Neue Folge*, 157 (to Krüger, 14 June 1839).
[6] Hoffmann, *Kreisleriana*, I/5, 50 (excerpted by Schumann in *Dichtergarten*, 305); compare I/3, 39.
[7] Hoffmann, *Kreisleriana*, I/2, 33–4; I/4, 42–3 (Appendix 3.4(a)); II/6, 313–21 (Mozart as model).
[8] *Mottosammlung*, I 197 (echoed in *GSK*, I 403); *GSK*, I 305 (1837), 376, 357 and 354 (1838); *Briefwechsel*, I 126 (18 March 1838).

sometimes be driven by dread; but in 1839, he wondered what Mozart might have achieved if he had known Bach in his entirety, rather than in part. In 1835 he had said that Haydn and Mozart brought an elastic grace to music, while Beethoven, entering the Viennese ballroom unkempt like Hamlet, found it constricting, and burst out into the dark night.[9]

Haydn, Mozart and middle-period Beethoven had developed a style in which material, treatment, form and expression were so interdependent that to work out form was also to deal with profound human issues; but as Schumann recognised in relation to sonata form, composers have to rethink forms in cross-fertilisation with evolving aesthetic aims.[10] In the late works, Beethoven reinvented his style. Classical patterns of shape and tonality are refashioned, with some unstable openings that are neither introduction nor exposition, a predilection for mediant relations between large key areas, and for moves to the subdominant where a more classical style would prefer dominant keys; there is a shift of weight to final movements.[11] Relationships between melodic elements may seem 'tenuous' or 'paradoxical', in Kerman's words, rather than clear and logical; they thus create what Chua describes as 'indistinct configurations'. Material spreads across works, sometimes apparently as quotation.[12] Passages may invoke the styles or works of his great predecessors (as in Variations XXII–XXXIII of the 'Diabelli' Variations). Metrical conflict and disruption can be marked, with irruptions of music in a new time signature, as in the last twenty-five bars of the second movement of the String Quartet in A minor, op. 132. Local tonality may seem directionless, or accidental; on a larger scale, the *Heiligerdankgesang* (in the same quartet), whose tonal centre is debated, arguably demands to be taken in more than one tonality at once – in C major, F major and a Lydian mode – if its tensions and its resolution are to be felt.[13] One genre or character may coexist or clash with another, for instance the deeply felt with the banal or excessively repetitious, or the wholly modern with a long-neglected historic manner. Stark juxtapositions, as in collage, may suggest what Chua calls 'immiscible fragments'. Such features teem in that A minor quartet, whose first twenty-two bars, for instance, contain four tempo markings, two time signatures, and five abrupt switches of texture, dynamics and character. Forms may be

---

[9] *GSK*, I 333 (1838) and II 54 (1841); I 328 (1838); *Neue Folge*, 177 (31 January 1840), *GSK*, I 390 (1839); 107 (1835).
[10] *GSK*, I 59, 394–5. [11] Marston, 'Schumann's Monument', 247–64.
[12] Kerman, *Beethoven Quartets*, 241, 304–6, 226; Chua, *Galitzin Quartets*, 47, 50, 195–8 (including note 28), 211–12.
[13] Chua, *Galitzin Quartets*, 110–29, 131–51.

radically reconstructed, or obscured through dislocations of formal function. Dissociation, or extreme contrast, threaten rupture; contrasting movements multiply; and continuity sometimes arises not organically but in 'paradoxical' processes and from secondary elements. Sometimes 'digressions assume a life of their own' to become the life of the work. But there remains a sense that each of the works nevertheless is profoundly right, 'a separate paradigm for wholeness', in Kerman's words.[14]

Schumann saw in Beethoven's last works an exemplary case of 'idiosyncratic forms' serving novel conceptions, but gave little more detail.[15] We cannot, therefore, weigh their relative importance in his stylistic development. If what he saw influenced his style, it was probably as much through reinforcing vectors already at work as through pitching him into a wholly new course. Nevertheless, I will suggest that features of Beethoven's late style, in the areas I have sketched, reappear in Schumann.[16] He integrated them with everything else that he was learning, including through the study of Bach; thus they are not aped in a pastiche, but become his own idiom, and serve his own particular purposes. They are at least as likely to have been major influences on his music as formal 'strategies' taken directly from literature.

In 1836 and early 1837, Schumann pondered ideas for composing trios, and worked over the winter on sonatas, mulling over a couple of movements from an F minor sonata, ordering the G minor sonata, and completing the first movement of the C major *Fantasy*: attempts perhaps to digest what he had learned from Beethoven. He often said that he was not composing much, and he certainly worked hard on criticism; but from some time in the early summer of 1837, his composing flourished again, and he 'composed in a state of bliss as never before'.[17] He began the *Fantasiestücke* and *Davidsbündlertänze*, and then in early 1838 the *Novelletten*, *Kinderszenen* and *Kreisleriana*. These are works in which some significant shifts in style appear, and, in the last, 'new worlds', he thought. He said in 1836 and again in 1838 that he felt 'as though we were at the starting-point, as though we could yet strike strings never heard before'.[18]

---

[14] Chua, *Galitzin Quartets*, 54–5, 88–102, 122, 183–8, 190–3, 198–201, etc.; Kerman, *Beethoven Quartets*, 239, 304–7, 319, 320–5; 229.
[15] *GSK*, I 73.
[16] Compare Marston, 'Schumann's Monument', 247–64 and 'Schumann's Heroes', 54.
[17] *Tagebücher*, II 29–34. 1836 yielded over twice as many pages of reviews for *GSK* as 1838.
[18] *Tagebücher*, II 55; *Neue Folge*, 74 (2 July 1836) ('Mir ist's oft, als ständen wir an den Anfängen, als könnten wir noch Saiten anschlagen, von denen man früher noch nicht gehört') and 110 (8 February 1838). Compare Tunbridge, 'Piano Works II', 86.

Most of the works Schumann composed between 1834 and late 1836 (with the exception of *Carnaval*) had presented themselves as falling within traditional forms and genres such as sonatas, studies and variations. By contrast, most of the works of 1837–9 evade or defeat classification in traditional terms; it seems to me a mark of Schumann's originality that for several years following his immersion in late Beethoven, the only sonata movements he wrote were the light final movement of op. 26 and the revised finale to op. 22. The piano works of these years more often present themselves overtly as 'poetic' or 'literary', picking up in that respect where *Papillons* and *Carnaval* had left off.[19]

Many of these works adopt an expansiveness previously confined largely to Schumann's works in the traditional genres of the classical style. In late summer 1837 as he prepared the *Fantasiestücke* for publication, he apparently lengthened and complicated several of its pieces.[20] The earlier version would have been a fast sequence, almost as fleeting and kaleidoscopic as *Carnaval*, each piece conveying more simply the image or idea suggested in each title; in the final version each piece is more expansive (generally three or four times longer than most of *Carnaval*'s pieces), doing more to develop an image or idea in its own way, and with a more complex form. A listener can 'spread out comfortably' in a steadier musical flow.[21] Again, while in the final version most pieces are self-contained, it seems that in earlier versions most of the first six pieces would have flowed into one another in continuing sequence rather than being detachable units, and only the last two pieces had assertive conclusions.[22] The trend towards expansiveness continued in the *Novelletten*, *Kreisleriana* and *Humoreske*. At the same time, the relationship of part to whole altered: including fewer pieces within each work made a simple contribution to this. The *Humoreske* of 1839 maintains an unbroken flow, with flimsier partitions

---

[19] Brendel, 'Robert Schumann' (1845), 89.

[20] The original 'Aufschwung', it appears, was only about 47 bars long; to 'In der Nacht', Schumann added bars 45–67 and 108–21, and perhaps 93–107, 122–37 and 144–60; to 'Traumeswirren' perhaps 135–42; and to 'Ende vom Lied' a new coda at 85–117. Or so Boetticher, *Robert Schumanns Klavierwerke*, 207–11, seems to imply.

[21] *Briefwechsel*, II 367 (26 January 1839): 'kann man sich aber recht behaglich ausbreiten'. Compare Heller, 'Fantasiestücke', 67. To my taste, though the final piece brings a single definitive moment of conclusive resolution on I, with a linear descent to $\hat{1}$, the sectional and repetitive structure of the last two pieces make for too many returns to F and too long a conclusion for the aesthetic implied by the work. Later works, such as the *Davidsbündlertänze* and *Kreisleriana*, escape that problem.

[22] In earlier versions, the endings of 'Aufschwung' and 'In der Nacht' were less abrupt (a descending bass, ritardando and diminuendo, under a sustained chord in the treble in the former; *pianissimo* in the latter): Boetticher, *Robert Schumanns Klavierwerke*, 210–11.

between sections even than those in Beethoven's late quartets; in *Kreisleriana* and the *Nachtstücke* close-knit continuities link separate pieces, as the following chapters will argue.

Schumann's style changed in other and related ways too. His idiosyncrasies had always been striking, as his contemporaries noted. Brendel said that his 'harmonic idiosyncrasy often put people off', and his treatment of dissonance and counterpoint was indeed daring.[23] Equally, Schumann had enjoyed metrical 'dissonances' capable of variation, intensification, a kind of development, and resolution.[24] He had used mutating and ramifying patterns of loose thematic relationships – with motifs often only suggesting affinities, rather than exposing logical developments or blatant similarities – to carry particular qualities or expressive overtones, or to create cross-links across a work.[25] He had developed novel ways to extend and manipulate forms to meet new needs; for some years his style had encompassed formal dislocations and obscurity, along with extreme contrast, abrupt transitions and a concentration on the seemingly digressive. Indeed, *Carnaval* used the idiosyncratic and the centrifugal as paradoxically unifying forces. In the 'literary' works of the later years of the decade, however – perhaps learning from late Beethoven – he developed bolder ways to use these features within large-scale musical processes, sustaining the flow of a piano cycle in tighter constructions subject to a 'poetic idea' or specific expressive purpose. This was not wholly new from 1837, but comparing *Papillons* and even *Carnaval* with *Kreisleriana* reveals a trend that may owe something to Beethoven.

During 1836–9 he took conventional forms that he considered abused by his contemporaries, and explored challenging transformations of them in the service of his own aesthetic aims and particular conceptions. He developed new ways to use tonality and thematic relationships on a larger scale, serving a stronger flow. While the second movement of the *Fantasy*, op. 17, that 'monument for Beethoven' of late 1836, pays homage to the style of a late Beethoven scherzo, and is not without challenging formal complexities, the first goes further, both inviting and defeating reconstruction as a traditional sonata movement. As befits its title, it is more radical in

---

[23] Castelli ('bizarre originality', 1832) in *GSK*, II 454; Koßmaly, 'Schumann's Claviercompositionen', 1844, 17. Liszt, 'Franz Liszt über Robert Schumann' (1840), 67 and 64; Brendel, 'Robert Schumann' (1845), 92. Compare Bischoff, 'Das Bach-Bild Robert Schumanns', 451 (on the influence of Bach on dissonance); Perry, 'Dissonance Treatment', 279–83 and Alphonce, 'Schumann's Reckless Counterpoint', for whom Schumann's techniques look forward to those of later generations (18).

[24] Krebs, *Fantasy Pieces*, passim and 82–114.

[25] Appel, 'Schumanns Humoreske', 69–75 and 271; Rosen, *Romantic Generation*, 235.

that respect than the preceding F sharp minor, G minor and F minor sonatas. Schumann considered 'Ruins' as a title, and in its multiple fractures and displacements it appears the ruin of some lost sonata movement, in which the fragments now visible might have had functions and a sequence making more conventional causal sense, possibly even with a different tonic – perhaps C minor. In what we have, however, glimpses of the final Beethoven theme flit across the music, like the 'Fata Morgana' Schumann also considered as a title, emerging clearly only at the very end; and till then C major is not stabilised. Thus a tonality and motif crucial to the resolution are not established at the start, but loom through the movement like ruins and mirages of a lost state.[26]

The *Fantasiestücke*, of summer 1837, revolve around the relationship, frequent in late Beethoven, between tonic (F minor) and submediant (D flat major), but begin from the latter. Some of the key changes appear dreamlike rather than architectonic. Formal patterns include stark juxtapositions as in late Beethoven.

The *Davidsbündlertänze* of a few months later may present as a dance sequence, but develop a tonal shape whose innovation and subtlety outdo that of *Carnaval*.[27] The way in which tonal shape contributes to an overall conception picks up where the *Fantasy* left off, and points forward to the *Kreisleriana* of 1838. The fits and starts of tonality, metre and melody of piece 'I', and the awkwardness of 'III', both setting off from G major, frame and accentuate the rapt focus and B minor tonality of 'II', which become a pole of attraction. In pieces 'V'–'IX', there is a descent from D through G to C minor and major, as though C major might be an ultimate destination set up by the opening G major as dominant; but in 'XI'–'XVII' B minor moves back to the centre and exerts its influence, preparing for the return of 'II'. (Both groups of pieces use a mediant E flat major for colour, as prepared in 'I' and 'III'.) In 'IX' and 'XVII'–'XVIII' (and arguably 'I'), these alternative tonal universes are connected, as if by a worm-hole, by V^7 of C, which

---

[26] Marston, *Schumann: Fantasie*, 32, 67 and *passim*; Bischoff, *Monument für Beethoven*, 207–15, especially 209–10, 215. Compare Rosen, *Classical Style*, 452–3. I would then treat the title Schumann considered – 'Ruins' – as a metaphor for musical relationships which can be seen not only as formal or analytical but also as expressive; and in that sense as an image at once of Schumann's monument to Beethoven, his view of Beethoven's aesthetic and his hopes of Clara. (Hepokoski sees ruins as an image of the form and content of Beethoven's overture *Die Ruinen von Athen*, op. 113, in Bergé, ed., *Musical Form*, 77–88.)

[27] My interpretation of the *Davidsbündlertänze* is indebted to analyses in Rosen, *Romantic Generation*, 229–36 and Kaminsky, 'Principles of Formal Structure', 217–24. Compare Daverio, *Crossing Paths*, 135–8.

Example 6.1: Schumann, *Davidsbündlertänze*, XVIII, bars 1–10

can also act as the augmented sixth chord of B minor. The coexistence of tonal alternatives, bound up with subtle thematic relationships, is close to the heart of the work: by opening in G major, closing the first half in C major, and establishing B as an alternative pole, Schumann sets up the C major of the final piece (Example 6.1) to appear as either home or a coda set in a Neapolitan relation to the preceding B minor. The alternative tonal readings – supported by texture, dissonance and melodic echoes – are as delicately poised as a meniscus, a balance of belonging, dream and loss.

Several Beethoven codas, including that of the 'Hammerklavier''s Adagio, involve the same Neapolitan relationship as in the *Davidsbündlertänze* (and some give the augmented sixth chord a similar role), with not dissimilar expressive effect – though Beethoven's conclusions, unlike Schumann's, re-establish an original, unequivocal tonic.[28] (The emergence of Schumann's 'XVIII' from the preceding piece is in some respects foreshadowed in the transition to the closing C major minuet of Beethoven's 'Diabelli' Variations; and though I know of no evidence that Schumann knew Beethoven's work, which like his own unites highly individualised character pieces in a continuous flow, rich in comic gestures, common features might reward exploration.) Musical processes in a passage of the B major 'XVII', moreover, bear comparison with one in the A minor slow movement of Beethoven's Sonata, op. 101 (Examples 6.2 and 6.3). Each

---

[28] Hatten, *Interpreting Musical Gestures*, 167–8.

Example 6.2: Schumann, *Davidsbündlertänze*, XVII, bars 30–50

passage starts at a distance from the tonic, with a pedal – on V^7 of V of F major in Schumann, and on V of C major in Beethoven. Under interwoven repetitions of a melodic fragment, each then harps on what will become the fifth degree of the key of a returning memory, creating a sense of tension without action; and with a largely semitone progression moves away from and then recovers that note in a different register; and as a result, a memory can enter naturally but unbidden, or prepared but unexpected.

Kreisleriana, of 1838, as the next chapter illustrates, consolidates these shifts. Its opening piece is in D minor; but through most of the work, B flat

Example 6.3: Beethoven, Piano Sonata in A major, op. 101, iii, bars 9–18

major alternates with G minor, with some local ambiguity between them; and they coexist as possible home keys well into the second half of the work. A 'tonal pairing' has often been imputed to *Kreisleriana* as a whole – sometimes in an attenuated sense that implies only an alternation of keys – and described for later works, and for individual pieces or groups of pieces within works of the 1830s, such as 'Florestan'–'Coquette'–'Réplique'.[29] I would draw out, however, not so much the bald fact of alternation, or even the persisting uncertainty as to the ultimate destination, as its use to support a distinctive tonal and aesthetic trajectory across an entire work. Schumann invests B flat major and G minor with a significance beyond what accrues from a role in an established formal template (as would attach to the tonic, or the secondary

---

[29] Daverio, *Robert Schumann*, 168 and 178; the essays by Smith, Brown and Kopp in *Rethinking Schumann*; Kinderman and Krebs, eds., *Second Practice of Nineteenth-Century Tonality*, 17–44, on Schubert and the Ballade, op. 38, which Chopin shifted away from monotonality (intriguingly, the year after *Kreisleriana* was dedicated to him); Wadsworth, 'Directional Tonality'.

key area in a sonata form, for instance). Something similar occurs elsewhere of course, including in the works of his great predecessors. Consider for instance minor-key sonata movements (such as Beethoven's C minor sonata, op. 111) whose endings dramatise a move to the tonic major. That move affects the aesthetic shape, even though the tonic major might be taken in classical sonata analysis as formally equivalent to the tonic minor (and could be used to recapitulate material that in the exposition was in the relative major). *Kreisleriana* goes further, creating a striking tonal trajectory, ending not in a B flat major by now associated with the most settled resolutions in the work, but with a G minor characterised by turbulence and alienation.[30]

Described in that way, *Kreisleriana* joins Schumann's opp. 6 and 17. Those others are not naturally described through 'tonal pairing', I think; but each of the three works uses tonality in non-classical ways to serve a musical and aesthetic conception that also informs other musical patterns. The *Humoreske*, op. 20, of 1839, does not go quite as far: it opens and closes in B flat major, and to me scarcely suggests the possibility of an ending in G minor; but it arguably (see Chapter 9) deploys other musical means to make that B flat major conclusion less than satisfying, yielding a non-classical shape.

Kreisleriana's patterns are powerful and musically complex, and it contains multiple echoes of late Beethoven piano sonatas. In common with other Schumann compositions of these years, and like a late Beethoven work, it pits mutually alien kinds of genre or style against one another, confounding historical eras, and it may sometimes exploit deliberate banality and excessive repetition. Like other works Schumann wrote at the time, it exploits fewer thematic cells than *Papillons* or *Carnaval*, and harmony, melody and texture are arguably more closely interwoven, more deeply implicated in a work's fundamental structures.[31] Above all, perhaps, his mastery of linear complexity had grown, with greater variety of voice-leading, pacing, expressive character and texture. There is a balance between the dense and the spare, an ability to weave complex patterns without necessarily appearing learned or rebarbative, and sometimes a telling economy that leaves lines suggested or incomplete (for

---

[30] B flat major and G minor are keys which, in the view of Rosen, *Romantic Generation*, 674, Schumann heard as 'almost interchangeable'; but that seems to me to say only that Schumann's practice treated their difference as significant in ways other than those of 'classical' sonata form. Compare also Brown, 'Higher Echoes', 514, Kopp, 'Intermediate States of Key', 310–13 and Bischoff, *Monument für Beethoven*, 297–306.

[31] Kaminsky, *Principles of Formal Structure*, 220 and 224.

instance in the middle section of the first piece in *Kreisleriana*, or the 'Fughette' of the *Four Pieces*, op. 32). Thus greater linear complexity can be incorporated within any kind of music, not just the deliberately experimental or showy, as complex and varied textures can be fused into compellingly expressive surfaces, or integrated in a coherent and sustained conception. This can be seen by contrasting passages such as the first of the *Intermezzi*, op. 4, of 1832, with the fifth piece of *Kreisleriana* of 1838. They share a motif, but the one appears to value the idiosyncratic and the difficult for themselves where the other uses the complexity to serve a conception. We may perhaps credit the influence of Bach and late Beethoven, as well as six years of learning his craft.

The way Schumann associated others' music with his own may also have evolved over the decade. He often adopted, evoked or imitated musical styles or genres, or recalled, associated or interpolated passages – from his predecessors, from his contemporaries or from himself.[32] But vivid, discontinuous imitations and quotations became rarer in his music after about 1836, except for humorous purposes (such as a flash of the Marseillaise in op. 26), with musical associations more fully integrated in the musical flow.[33] Flavours of Bach and Beethoven in *Kreisleriana*, for instance, are better rooted in the work's musical conception than the sudden presence of Chopin and Paganini in *Carnaval*; echoes of Beethoven's *An die ferne Geliebte* in the *Fantasy*, op. 17 and *Nachtstücke* are more integral than nods to Schubert in the second *Intermezzo*, op. 4, or to Schubert or Beethoven in 'Préambule' or 'Marche'.[34] Studies of Schumann's borrowings from Clara Wieck over the 1830s, and of his echoes of his own works, might reveal analogous developments: away from the esoteric and flamboyant, perhaps, and towards fuller integration into a musical and expressive flow.[35]

Finally, Schumann's use of words in his scores became more sparing from about 1837. His critical views on such additions had always been nuanced. He thought words could be of service to a musical work, but that ill-chosen, misleading or inexact headings could straitjacket responses, suggest misplaced shadings, or set the wrong tone (he took to heart such a criticism of his own works). Words cannot redeem bland music, but if

---

[32] This is of course contentious: Newcomb, 'The Hunt for Reminiscences'. See Lippman, 'Theory and Practice', 311–14; Todd, 'On Quotation in Schumann's Music', 80–112; Daverio, *Nineteenth-Century Music*, 59–61; and Chapter 8 below.
[33] Compare Tunbridge, 'Piano Works II', 87.
[34] Compare Hoeckner, *Programming the Absolute*, 95–108.
[35] Compare Daverio, *Crossing Paths*, 130–9.

carefully chosen, subtle, and well-suited to the nature and quality of the music, they can enhance the effect of the music and the listener's pleasure in understanding it.[36] A verbal hint might, Schumann thought, suggest a voice or movement (a call, the majestic gait of a god), an emotion (anger), or an image, scene or landscape, and thereby clarify the content of an image, for instance, or speed recognition of more arcane states of mind.[37] A title ('Witches' Dance' or 'Ave Maria') or other added words might suggest a context within which a work could be understood the more sensitively and fully; or a simple heading may point to a literary work, for instance, so that music imbued with a book's spirit can stimulate the listener's imagination to work in its own way with the characters and images.[38] In 1838, Schumann reviewed Moscheles' *Charakteristische Studien*, op. 95. He cited the preface, in which the composer hoped that the titles and expressive markings delicately suggested feelings which 'hovered before' him, but recognised that using words to explain his deeper feelings more definitely would trespass on the essence of music. Schumann's review sympathised, saying: 'If poets seek to wrap the meaning of the whole poem in a title, why should musicians not do it too?' The inference is that he saw a 'wrapping' as something different from but suggestive of 'the meaning': headings should not seem to contain 'the meaning' of the work.[39] Words carrying the authority of the composer could 'set limits to imaginative appreciation', Schumann thought: he loved 'the *Pastoral* and *Eroica* symphonies less, precisely because it was Beethoven himself who so characterised them'.[40] Similarly, Kahlert in 1835 said that Beethoven set a dangerous precedent in activating a demand for consciousness of content, and using words to point the way to a work's content, which could degenerate into cases where 'the content of the music is predetermined'.[41] Schumann often insisted of his own works that the music came first and the titles later, but sometimes with the gloss that nevertheless an external text, image or association might have lain at the back of his mind as he composed.[42] But his titles 'aroused opposition', a

---

[36] *Neue Folge*, 170 (5 September 1839); *GSK*, I 99–100 ('bezeichnendere'); II 224 (own work), 240; I 360–1, 369 and 406 (Kittl), 390 ('gutgewählte'), 420–1 ('Waldnymphe').

[37] *GSK*, I 41, 422–3; II 24, 221.

[38] *GSK*, I 389 ('objektivere'), 146–7, 344 (Faust), 435 ('Den Grund'), 474 ('l'Adieu').

[39] *GSK*, I 361.

[40] *GSK*, I 65, 83, 191 (a composer's intention should not be too blatant, in the music or otherwise); 28.

[41] Kahlert, 'Recensionen', 109–10 and 107.

[42] *GSK*, II 332; *Neue Folge*, 54 (22 August 1834), 92 (23 August 1837) and 148 (15 March 1839); 170 (5 September 1839); compare 223 (23 November 1842) and *GSK*, II 429, note 400. *GSK*, II

sympathetic contemporary noted in 1845, especially from those who 'took them for the pre-existing schema to which the music adhered', rather than for 'a result of reflection on the music'.[43]

In any case, from 1837, as his music became capable in itself of more powerful expression, his works were progressively more restrained in the use of words. Up to then, his expressive markings had been denser and more poetic than in other composers. Thus the markings in for instance Moscheles' *Charakteristische Studien*, op. 95, of about 1836, employ some poetic metaphor ('sussurando' and 'come un zeffiretto'); and striking markings draw attention to themselves in Chopin's op. 15/3 of 1832–3 ('languido e rubato, religioso'), though these are rare in his *oeuvre*; but Schumann's markings had been more idiosyncratic. Some are not directly playable (for instance, op. 9, 'Thême du XVIIème siècle'), others unusually specific about style or mood (op. 5 'quasi satira', op. 6 'etwas hahnbüchen'); some suggest a speaking or otherwise particular voice ('bassi vivi', 'basso parlando', 'Stimme aus der Ferne'), or point to imitation of a musical instrument. But his markings became less extravagant from about 1837; those in the *Fantasiestücke* are relatively conventional, almost all offering standard instructions as to tempo, dynamics or manner. By 1842 he was venting his impatience at composers' profligacy with expressive markings: 'always a bad sign'.[44]

Up to 1837, moreover, Schumann added inscriptions and mottoes to several works, and in some cycles individual pieces have titles. In *Carnaval* titles identify personae or events, so that an almost narrative thread accompanies the threads of tonality, melody and form. *Fantasiestücke* too has titles to its individual pieces, though they avoid such identification, and the score contains no poetic inscriptions. We can trace minor adjustments Schumann made to its titles to convey exactly what he wanted, as though they were relevant to interpretation.[45] But after 1837, though Schumann added poetic titles to the individual pieces of *Kinderszenen*, he did not do so again for several years; and the 'Davidsbündler', Florestan and Eusebius, disappeared from his works – youthful masks fleeing, perhaps, before the sterner gaze of Beethoven and Bach. The one-word

---

74 guesses that the titles only came after the music was finished, for a composer (Hirschbach) whom he saw at the time as a kindred spirit.

[43] Brendel, 'Robert Schumann', 90–1. See Appendix 3–4(d).   [44] *GSK*, II 249.

[45] According to Boetticher (*Robert Schumanns Klavierwerke*, 214, 207), 'Des Abends' was in one autograph headed 'Einmal des Abends', and Schumann may have considered 'Des Nachts' for 'In der Nacht'. But of those rejected titles, the one is perhaps too narrative in its suggestions, the other not enough. Clearly, however, he sought to avoid suggesting a description of 'Evening' or 'Night'.

titles of *Kreisleriana* and the *Nachtstücke* each suffice to suggest a context for interpretation of the musical flow and symbolism of the entire work. And the revised edition of the *Davidsbündlertänze* in 1850 deletes 'tänze' from the title, adds 'Characterstücke', and removes the signatures to each piece ('F' or 'E') and the poetic inscriptions: if we had never known the earlier version, the revised version would suggest a miscellany of individual genre pieces, and the drama of a single subject evoked by the music would wilt. Schumann's later aesthetic clashed with the earlier.

The upshot of all these changes is an alteration in the way in which the works hang together. Schumann strengthened his control of musical means – including form, harmony, melody, rhythm, texture and linear complexity – and their interaction in a tighter construction. In *Carnaval*, suitably, genre, form, musical treatment and image are centrifugal; tonality, thematic patterns and gestures may root the first piece and the last three in their positions, but some other pieces could probably have changed places. In later works musical means are more closely intertwined; and trajectories and patterns in the sequence of the work are more deeply embedded, limiting the scope to imagine alternative orderings. This in part reflects differences between the particular conceptions of the works, but those differences in turn reflect a shift in more general aesthetic aims marching in step with increasingly powerful musical means.

At the same time, core musical features came to spin more compelling patterns, and expressive qualities to develop more in them, rather than through incidental musical features, verbal additions or literary allusions. A listener can make sense of the music without having to hold external content in mind. It is probably not a coincidence that during these years the emphasis in Schumann's criticism on how music represents external material was being softened, while that on the use of musical means in the service of a unifying conception was strong.

Thus it is hard to explain why dances 6–10 in *Papillons* (of 1832) appear in that sequence except through a narrative which a programme proffered by the composer invites us to trace. A giant boot and an exchange of masks are scarcely intrinsically musical, lack wider expressive resonance, and are connected to each other only through a particular chapter in a particular book, on which their significance and coherence depend. A 'key' seems to be 'missing' (in Rellstab's words); and the 'key', once supplied by the composer, does not quite fit. *Carnaval*, of 1834–7, solves one problem by supplying titles as a key to its own vestigial narrative, with identities and events as well as images; but like *Papillons*, it invites a listener to trace a sequence of images running parallel to musical threads, and only loosely related to them; without its verbal framework, the work would be much the poorer, offering too little foothold or framework for understanding. By 1837, with 'In der Nacht', a puzzling musical sequence is accompanied by apparently specific images (distorted reflections, fruitless scurrying, perhaps); and a particular narrative (whether Veronika's equinoctial sorcery or Leander's visit to Hero) may be needed to make sense of those images, and perhaps even of the balance between darkness and melodramatic irony, or the odd psychological progression. On this account, the literary relationship is not wholly successful here, but less awkward than in *Papillons*.

As we shall see, nothing of the sort seems to occur in *Kreisleriana* (1838), and if there is a hint of it in the *Nachtstücke* (1839), it is only in the second episode of the third piece, and much milder: a listener's engagement with the peculiar psychological progression of the music may be aided by a similar progression in Hoffmann's fiction, but there is no need to underlay a particular narrative to Schumann's piece. In these works an intrinsically musical 'Geist' or conception is strong enough to integrate cultural associations with core musical processes; they have no verbal apparatus beyond their one-word titles, but no sense of a 'missing key'; they can afford to point more clearly to particular books because there is little risk of a distracting programme; and a literary relationship can flow from the work's musical conception.

7 | New worlds, 1838
Kreisleriana, *op. 16*

From an early stage of composition, the music that became Schumann's *Kreisleriana* was connected to Bach and to Hoffmann. The material took shape in Spring 1838. Entries in Schumann's diary note for late March a study of 'Bach's Well-Tempered Clavier and Chorale Book again from start to finish', and for early April 'fugues and canonic spirit in all my improvising' – in tune with his remark, 'whoever has learnt to wallow in Bach will surely take something of that delight over into his own imagination'.[1] A connection to Hoffmann's *Kreisleriana* was in Schumann's mind by 13 April, when he told Clara he had a whole volume of new things ready, which he would call 'Kreisleriana'; his music now seemed to him 'wonderfully entwined despite all its simplicity' ('wunderbar verschlungen') – presumably echoing Hoffmann's description, in *Kreisleriana*, of counterpoint as 'wunderlich verschlungenen'.[2]

Three days later he told a friend that a new work, 'Kreisleriana', had been finished in a few days: 'there is material to ponder' ('da gibts zu denken dabei'). Later in April Schumann referred in his diary to a Presto that became the first piece of the set. On 3 May he said: 'Kreisleriana done in four days', meaning presumably that material generated through the process of improvisation had been rapidly shaped into a number of pieces. An entry shortly after refers to a 'Kreislerstück in G minor in $^6_8$', which sounds like a version of the final piece. The work was largely ready by about July, when he sent it to Clara and to the publisher.[3]

Schumann put the connection with Hoffmann's Kreisler beyond doubt in his letter to his Belgian admirer, Simonin de Sire, of 15 March 1839:

---

[1] *Tagebücher*, II 53; *GSK*, I 283 (1837).
[2] *Briefwechsel*, I 138 (15 April 1838); Hoffmann, *Kreisleriana*, I/3, 39 (compare I Introduction, 26, I/3, 37, I/4, 45 and I/5, 50; other echoes of 'wunderlich verschlungenen' in Schumann include *GSK*, II 81 (1842)). Hoffmann's *Kreisleriana* were collected in two series in his *Fantasiestücke in Callots Manier* (1814–15); throughout this chapter, references to them give series and essay numbers (e.g. '*Kreisleriana* I/3' or '*Kreisleriana* II/7') and the page in *Fantasiestücke*. Key passages are at Appendix 3–7.
[3] *Neue Folge*, 119 to Fischhof (16 April 1838); *Tagebücher*, II 55.

The title can only be understood by Germans. Kreisler is a figure created by E. T. A. Hoffmann, an eccentric, wild, inspired [geistreicher] Kapellmeister.[4]

Hoffmann's *Kreisleriana* essays contain stories, fictional letters, aesthetics and music criticism, and feature the spirits of Bach, Haydn, Mozart and Beethoven; most are by or about the fictional Kapellmeister Johannes Kreisler, of whom they form a portrait.[5]

Kreisler is devoted to great art for its own sake and to the works of his great predecessors in musical history: Bach and Beethoven above all. Unlike them, however, he suffers from an instability that upsets the self-possession needed for artistic creation. He is at odds with a philistine society that treats art as mere amusement. Companionship for him is rare; love is doomed to disappointment; loneliness may be his ultimate destiny. I will explore ways in which these aspects of the portrait of Kreisler resonate with Schumann's culture, his experience and his *Kreisleriana*.

Though Kreisler could sometimes find serenity in a realm of 'intricate contrapuntal twists and imitations', 'his imagination became over-wrought' through music; his improvisations drove him mad, and the notes often leapt 'off the white page like little black many-tailed demons', whirling him along in 'wild manic gyration'. His 'life as an artist kicked so hard against the pricks of all that counts as good sense and taste that there could be little doubt that his mind was deeply unsettled'.[6] Great music sharpened the danger: 'What would have become of me if . . . Beethoven's mighty spirit had . . . seized me as if with arms of red-hot metal?' Kreisler's 'friends maintained that in putting him together Nature had tried out a new recipe, and the attempt had failed'; and he 'was tossed hither and thither by inner imaginings and dreams as if on an ever restless sea'.[7] The idea and the image were traditional,

---

[4] *Neue Folge*, 148 (15 March 1839); compare 464 (to Whistling, 20 November 1849). That letter claimed that the headings of his compositions only came into his head after the composing was finished. The first edition (Leipzig, 1886) has 'my other compositions', the second 'all my compositions', implying that Schumann included *Kreisleriana* within the claim; if so, one would have to take it either as a routine claim, wrongly applied in this case, a year after the event, or as a memory that in early April he had improvised a good deal of music that only by 13 April was to be given the title *Kreisleriana*.

[5] Hoffmann may have built on the *Herzensergießungen eines kunstliebenden Klosterbruders*, a set of essays published by Wackenroder and Tieck in 1796: this popularised a Romantic picture of artists, featured the spirits of Raphael, Leonardo, Dürer and Michelangelo, deployed anecdotes, fictional letters, aesthetics and art-criticism, and ended with a novella about a fictional musician in a philistine society.

[6] Hoffmann, *Kreisleriana*, I Introduction, 26, II/2 291–2, II Introduction, 284.

[7] Hoffmann, *Kreisleriana*, I/2, 33–4; I Introduction, 25. Schumann (perhaps wrongly) thought the picture of Kreisler based on an eccentric pianist called Böhner, whose imagination he compared, 'in its dislocation, darkness and bleakness, confusion of the old and the new, to a storm or shipwreck' (*Jugendbriefe*, 254 (September 1834); *GSK*, I 366 (1838)).

familiar from Wackenroder's Piero di Cosimo and Joseph Berglinger.[8] Jean Paul wrote, as Schumann noted, 'true genius calms itself from within; not the towering wave but the smooth sea mirrors the world', but Kreisler could not achieve self-possession ('Besonnenheit'), nor reach 'the port which might offer him at last that peace and serenity without which an artist can create nothing'.[9] Kreisler's balance suffered too from disappointed love. A woman's voice might promise him healing, but he could be 'driven to the highest pitch of madness through a quite fantastic love for a singer'. For him, when 'the heavenly form that had penetrated my innermost heart ... dissolved into mist', 'every desolate sigh of that yearning ... was turned into the raging pain of wrath'.[10]

The mild 'young poet' Baron Wallborn, had suffered similarly, and became Kreisler's 'friend and companion'.[11] Kreisler's letter to him described a 'feeling of great strangeness yet great familiarity', as a 'young nobleman' approached: an 'odd sequence of chords' began to swell higher and higher'; the sequence 'melted into gentle angel harmonies that spoke magically of the poet's life and nature', and as he recognised Wallborn it became clear to Kreisler 'from what key the whole set forth'.[12] The soothing effect of companionship on Kreisler's troubled mind replaced the pain of separation, as symbolised respectively by thirds and sevenths. He wrote:

You, Sir, to whom I will sing in all those friendly thirds, are none other than that Baron Wallborn whom I have carried in my heart so long that it seems as if all my melodies are shaped like him ... as if I were him himself... So you see, Baron Wallborn, I promise you solemnly that I will be you, and just as full of love, mildness and respect as you ... All the sevenths evaporate into proper thirds.

But it was not to last:

How much I had still to say – unresolved dissonances howled unremittingly at my innermost self, but just as all the snake-fanged sevenths were about to settle into a whole lucid world of friendly thirds – right then you, Sir, were gone – gone – and the snakes' fangs bit and pierced!

---

[8] Piero was taken 'to be a highly confused and almost mad figure', 'ceaselessly plagued, hounded and exhausted by a restless dark imagination' – to the detriment of his creative power, as 'heaven is not reflected in a raging and foaming sea'; Berglinger was 'tossed on the sea of inner doubts, sometimes lifted on the waves high above other men, sometimes plunged into the deepest abyss': Wackenroder, *Herzensergießungen*, 57, 59, 61, 153.
[9] Jean Paul, *Vorschule*, §12, *Mottosammlung*, IX 16; Hoffmann, *Kreisleriana*, I Introduction, 25–6.
[10] Hoffmann, *Kreisleriana*, I/1, 31–2, II Introduction, 284–5, II/2, 291.
[11] Hoffmann, *Kreisleriana*, II Introduction, 284–5, II/1, 287–8.
[12] Hoffmann, *Kreisleriana*, II/2, 290.

Kreisler had once confessed that in his desolation 'he had resolved upon death and would stab himself in the nearby forest with an augmented fifth'. Nevertheless, he signed his letter off with 'Let this be the serene and reassuring final chord in the tonic'.[13] The odd sequence of chords melting into gentle harmonies to speak of the poet, the thirds and sevenths, the stab of desolation of an augmented fifth, and the serene final chord are all expressive musical symbols readily available to a composer contemplating a 'Kreisleriana'.

The letters to each other of Kreisler and Wallborn were never delivered, and they themselves vanished, in the ultimate expression of isolation. Wallborn, who signed his letter to Kreisler as from 'the *lonely* Wallborn', disappeared; as for Kreisler, the essays had opened with the emblematic question: 'Where is he from? Nobody knows'; now the editor noted of Kreisler that 'once, no one knew how or why, he had disappeared'.[14] On one occasion, after a paroxysm of agitated derangement, Kreisler describes himself, again in musical symbols available to a composer, as a 'harmless melody' craving freedom, or as a 'basso ostinato' repeatedly or compulsively circling (in an echo of his name, 'Kreisler', or 'Circler'):

'A dark shadow has passed over my life! Don't you think a poor innocent melody that craves no place on earth might be granted its freedom to waft harmlessly through the great expanses of the heavens? Oh, I'd like to sail away through that window right now.'

'As a harmless melody?' interrupted his true friend, smiling;

'Or as basso ostinato, if you prefer, but I must move on soon one way or another'.

And it soon turned out as he had spoken.[15]

Kreisler, that is, vanished.

For Hoffmann's Kreisler, the great composers and their music loom as emblems of different kinds of music and symbols of different modes of imaginative apprehension, of relating to the world. Between the giants of musical history (Bach, Mozart, Beethoven) and the philistine yawns a gulf. One essay ironically allows a philistine to speak:[16]

Some unfortunate enthusiasts ... call the wholly useless games of counterpoint – that do nothing to cheer the listener up and so completely miss the real purpose of

---

[13] Hoffmann, *Kreisleriana*, II Introduction, 284, II/2, 289–92.

[14] Hoffmann, *Kreisleriana*, II/2, 289; I Introduction, 25–6 (imitating Diderot's *Jacques le fataliste*). Schumann perhaps echoed the idea, talking of his mysterious friend, the old Captain: 'Nobody asked where he came from, or where he went': *GSK*, I 261 (1837).

[15] Hoffmann, *Kreisleriana*, II/3, 296–7.   [16] Hoffmann, *Kreisleriana*, I/3, 36–41.

music – thrilling arcane combinations, and are ready to compare them with wonderfully entwined mosses, herbs and flowers.

By contrast, 'a successful composition ... keeps demurely within bounds and has one pleasant melody after another'. The philistine lauded music produced from simple prefabricated components, a means to rest, recreation, entertainment, or mood-management: 'let me take you into the domestic circle, where Father, tired from the serious business of the day ... cheerfully smokes his pipe to the *Murki* of his son'.[17] Bourgeois society requires that an artist supply such a commodity, and if instead he pours his heart into playing masterpieces, it yawns, or chatters:

Has it never happened to you, that you went off six or seven rooms away from the chattering company to play or to hear some piece of music, only to find the company had come running to hear – and gossiped as loudly as they could?

Such a world, said Wallborn, is 'horribly cramped for people like us'.[18]

But Wallborn speaks up for amateur music-making:

Look, Johannes, you seem to me very harsh in your zeal against all music that is not the work of genius ... Such tootling, whether dance or march, reminds us of the highest that lies within us.

And Kreisler concedes the point:

The music-making of hoi polloi often drives me to furious rage, but ... when I've been properly battered and beaten by some bravura aria or concerto or sonata without redeeming features, then some unpretentious little melody, sung by a mediocre voice or played with uncertain stumbles, but meant well and honestly and genuinely felt, could often comfort and heal me.[19]

These themes in Kreisler's nature were commonplaces of the traditional picture of the artist. The conflict between philistine and artist arises for instance in Moritz's *Die Neue Cecilia*; Goethe's Wilhelm Meister is warned in his 'Lehrbrief' against 'mediocrity', teases a philistine for turning everything into a commodity, and regrets the manifold pressures on artists to embrace 'the mediocre', including society's tendency to 'reduce everything' to its own mental capacity, 'to so-called effect, so that everything becomes relative'; and in Wackenroder's *Herzensergießungen*, the aspiring composer Berglinger sets his emotional reaction to music against the prevailing

---

[17] *Murkis* – derided by eighteenth-century German theorists as banal – have a bass of broken octaves, normally rising by steps; see Halski, 'Murky', 35–7.
[18] Hoffmann, *Kreisleriana*, II/1, 286–7.   [19] Hoffmann, *Kreisleriana*, II/1, 288, II/2, 291.

empty-headed insensitivity.[20] Schumann's criticism frequently opposed the 'philistine' to great art, and was in large part 'a seawall against the mediocre'.[21] As Florestan, Schumann excoriated himself: 'Did you study Marpurg, dissect the *Well-Tempered Clavier*, learn Bach and Beethoven by heart, just to weep at a miserable aria by Donizetti?', and vented his self-disgust by parodying the aria; Schumann the hack reviewer complained, 'if you had any idea with what reluctance I turn to such miserable compositions, you'd feel sorry for me. But after taking them to pieces, I usually reach for my old Bach: he gives me back strength to work and zest for art and life'.[22]

But the everyday may not be dismissed. In 1835–8, Schumann noted indulgent remarks from Goethe ('there are pieces that are empty without being bad') and Thibaut ('even mediocre stuff may retain some respect, as long as it is not degenerate or distorted. A person is not required to read the Psalms or Homer every second of the day'). And Thibaut had refused to 'criticise some currently well-loved songs half as sharply as art-lovers may have': 'a large part of the public has taste and capacity only for the mediocre.' Goethe's *Wilhem Meister* (VI) described an education of taste from mediocre pietistic hymns to masterpieces by Italian Renaissance composers; and Schumann agreed that music 'should exist to suit every stage of development': 'the more widespread the taste for art, the better'. He knew that serious music could use the trivial for its own purposes, admittedly including parody.[23]

Likewise, mental disturbance was a long-standing literary theme, a traditional characteristic of lovers, artists and artists in love, as in Shakespeare and Novalis.[24] It loomed large at the end of the eighteenth

---

[20] Boulby, *Moritz*, 222; Goethe, *Wilhelm Meister*, VII/9, VIII/1 and 7 (*Werke*, IV 444, 448 and 513–14; compare Watkins, *Metaphors of Depth*, 92–3); Wackenroder, *Herzensergießungen*, 101–2 (compare Ziolkowski, *German Romanticism*, 341 and 256). In Novalis' *Heinrich von Ofterdingen*, the merchants are subtly philistine: *Schriften*, I 207–10; this is imitated in Hoffmann's 'Der Artushof': *Die Serapions-Brüder*, 151–2.

[21] For instance *GSK*, I 347 (1838); 384 (1839); see also 85, 219 (1835–6) and 438 (1839). *Neue Folge*, 123 (to Hirschbach, 13 June 1838) calls for a campaign against the philistines. Compare *Mottosammlung*, I 212 (1838).

[22] *GSK*, II 283 (1835); *Neue Folge*, 103 (4 December 1837).

[23] *Mottosammlung*, I 202 (from Zelter's letter to Goethe of 7 June 1828, which itself echoed Goethe); V 255–6 (compare *GSK*, II 137); *GSK*, I 96 and I 79 (1835), 182 and 185 (1836). Several years earlier Schumann had noted Novalis' remark that 'there is room for some fine achievements in the field of bad and mediocre writing. To date there has been little but bad and mediocre writing about it – but a philosophy of the bad, the mediocre and the vulgar would be of the highest importance': *Mottosammlung*, IX 193, from Novalis, *Schriften*, V 234(fr. 269).

[24] Ziolkowski, *German Romanticism*, chapter 4; Blackall, *Novels of the German Romantics*, chapter 9; *A Midsummer Night's Dream* V. i. 7–8; Novalis, *Schriften*, V 269–70(fr. 499: 'madness and enchantment have much in common. A magician is an artist of madness').

century, reacting with new interests in the *Bildungsroman*, in psychology and in the border between physics and the occult. Goethe's *Wilhelm Meister* contains a disquisition on the treatment and types of madness, and several of its characters are on the brink. The *Nachtwachen von Bonaventura* featured a madhouse with several different typologies of madness satirically represented among its inmates, one a poet, another a victim of disappointed love. In Goethe's *Tasso* the poet-hero is driven mad in part, as Schumann noted in 1835, by unrequited love: 'But She, but She! Hence it was that Tasso entered the madhouse.'[25] Schumann confessed to Clara in February 1838 that in 1833 he too had felt in danger of 'losing his reason'. A doctor had given him the conventional advice that he find a good woman. In 1836 an agitated depression recurred ('a deep depression out of which I can't lift myself for work'), perhaps precipitated by the death of his mother and his enforced separation from Clara. He told his sister-in-law Therese, 'I have no womanly presence to guard me'; 'in my deadly agitation [tödtlichen Herzensangst] . . . I have no one but you to take me by the hand and protect me'. He confided in his landlady his 'deadly agitation' (tödtliche Angst) and 'wonderful hours' of what we might call hyperactivity: 'when my mood is elated, it often develops into a sort of over-confidence in which I could take the whole world by storm; and the reaction follows hard on its heels, and then the artificial treatments. The right treatment for such dangerous extremes is, I well know, a loving woman.' Schumann's diary laconically captured a 'change in my nature' from July 1837 on, 'and genuine yearning for a wife'.[26]

Literature was rich too in images of artists estranged from the world, and of men disappearing into isolation or death, like Augustin in Goethe's *Wilhelm Meister*, or the heroes of Hölderlin's *Empedocles* and Tieck's *William Lovell* and 'Der Runenberg'.[27] Such literary images may have struck Schumann because they resonated with his own experience. From his youth, he had known of the artist's need for 'isolation as an active, contemplative, creative peace, the friend of Art'; and he had told his mother once he became

---

[25] Goethe, *Wilhelm Meister*, V/16 (*Werke*, IV 310–13); *Nachtwachen* (2004), IX; *GSK*, II 214. Schumann reread Goethe's *Tasso* shortly after completing his *Kreisleriana: Mottosammlung*, III 5ff. The *Nachtwachen von Bonaventura* was published under that pseudonym in 1804, leading to discussion ever since as to who wrote it.

[26] *Briefwechsel*, I 95 (11 February 1838; compare *Tagebücher*, I 419; in Goethe a good woman is the best cure: *Wilhelm Meister*, VIII/10 (*Werke*, IV, 542)); *Neue Folge*, 74 (2 July 1836) ('tiefen Seelenschmerz'; compare *Briefwechsel*, I 33 (11 October 1837): 'depressive to the point of illness'); *Neue Folge*, 72 (1 April 1836), and 83 (31 December 1836); 73 (1836 undated); compare *Briefwechsel*, I 101 (12 February 1838); *Tagebücher*, II 33.

[27] See Ziolkowski, *German Romanticism*, 163–70.

a published composer, 'From here on ... I stand alone'. He wrote in 1834: 'The artist should communicate with people and the world in a friendly manner, like a Greek god; but if the world dares to interfere, he may have to disappear.'[28] Now, around the time of his work on *Kreisleriana*, he often expressed the artist's need for isolation but also companionship and love. An artist, if he is to create, must have 'the deepest isolation', he wrote in public; but he told Clara, 'I am so isolated and lonely on my path', and he had nobody to talk to about his music; he wrote to a friend of his 'fairly lonely path', on which 'a real companion in art is a rarity', and 'only my great predecessors Bach and Beethoven look on me from afar and offer support'; and he gratefully accepted Henriette Voigt's appreciation of his op. 12, saying, presumably in an allusion to the woman who succoured the wounded and isolated Wilhelm Meister, 'I have need of such Amazons.' [29]

At the end of Hoffmann's essays, their themes are encapsulated in a fable.[30] Kreisler writes a certificate ('Lehrbrief') for his apprentice, Johannes Kreisler, and recounts how the young Chrysostom came and told him a story. A strange musician came to a castle, where the lord's daughter fell in love with him; she was heard singing to his lute under a tree at midnight. One day the pair vanished. The lord galloped into the wood with his horsemen, and under the tree they found a stone, blood welling from it, and below it the stabbed girl's body and the stranger's shattered lute. Since then a nightingale has sung from the tree at midnight, its laments piercing the heart, and from the blood have grown strange mosses and grasses entwined around the stone. For Chrysostom, the mosses united with the songs of the nightingale and the girl to bring him exquisite music which he could not reproduce; but perhaps that inspiration, allied with technical skills in counterpoint, would eventually lead him to artistic fulfilment. Kreisler detects 'the voice of the poet buried within' his apprentice, sends him on his journey to Sais, and bids him farewell 'as if we were in the end but one person'; then he too disappears.[31]

---

[28] *GSK*, II 188 (1827–8); *Jugendbriefe*, 172ff (8 May 1832); *GSK*, I 19 (1834).

[29] *GSK*, I 358 (1838) (isolation: echoing Goethe's idea in *Wilhelm Meister* II/2 (*Werke*, IV 72)); *Briefwechsel*, I 52, 105 (29 November 1837 and 12 February 1838); *Neue Folge*, 109–10, to Simonin de Sire (8 February 1838; compare 'einsam' at 101, 22 September 1837 and in Goethe's comment excerpted in February 1838, *Mottosammlung*, I 153); *Neue Folge*, 121 (11 June 1838).

[30] Hoffmann, *Kreisleriana*, II/7, 321–7.

[31] The temple of Isis at Sais was a familiar symbol of personal and artistic maturity and self-discovery. Goethe's Wilhelm Meister penetrated behind the curtain to find the image of his father and his son and to receive a 'Lehrbrief' (VII/9); Novalis' Hyazinth discovered himself and his beloved Rosenblüthe behind the veil at Sais. These images lived in Schumann's mind too. He looked in the mirror and wrote himself a sort of 'Lehrbrief' in 1830; he used the image of the veil in his criticism; and in February 1838, he said, 'for about the last year and a half I've felt as if the

Kreisler's disappearance, like that of the stranger in the fable, evokes the whole network of disappearances in Hoffmann's *Kreisleriana*. It is an ambivalent image. Perhaps Kreisler abandons his friends and disappears to death, maybe even with violence – as a result of madness following disappointment in love, or the loss of companionship, or alienation from the bourgeois world. Or perhaps Kreisler is now ready to voyage to the world of art – the temple of Isis at Sais – as a mature artist.[32] Or perhaps to commit oneself to art is to disappear in some more mysterious way from the world of ordinary life;[33] for if Kreisler's spirit lives on, in the nightingale, or Chrysostom, or the apprentice Kreisler, it has been metamorphosed; and what remains at the site of his disappearance is something inhuman – a bird, a stone, a moss.[34]

The form of Hoffmann's *Kreisleriana* is an expression of the ambivalence of Kreisler's nature and fate. The essays appear to be assembled at random. As first published, half of the essays appear in the middle of volume I of the *Fantasiestücke*, the other half at the end of volume IV. There may be structural patterns – links from the end of one piece to the opening of the next; patterns of self-parody; an articulation through the presence of letters at the end of the first series, and the beginning, midpoint and end of the second – but any such patterns are veiled.[35] The tone fluctuates abruptly, between the bitter, the polemical, the realistic and the ironic; musical analysis is mixed with fable, letters and satire. The first essay opens in mid-flow ('they are all gone'); the last offers no clear narrative resolution. Causality and temporality are indistinct; identities often confused (between Kreisler and his apprentice, Kreisler and Wallborn, or one beloved and another); intimations of narrative, symbols and images are repeated and jumbled.

Moreover, musical symbols permeating Hoffmann's essays give expression to these same aspects of Kreisler's nature. Contrasts in the essays between consonances and dissonances, thirds and sevenths, a love song

---

secret were in my possession': *Tagebücher*, I 242–3; *GSK*, I 148 (1836); *Briefwechsel*, I 100 (11 February 1838).

[32] As Charlton argues in *Hoffmann's Musical Writings*, 28.

[33] Schumann's review of Berlioz's *Symphonie Fantastique*, with its imagery of violence, disappearance, death and the dissolution of the mind into music, may imply as much: *GSK*, II 213–14. See Maus, 'Intersubjectivity and Analysis', 136.

[34] Sais also appeared earlier in Hoffmann's essays: *Kreisleriana* (II/5, 313) referred to the stone found by the young pupil at Sais as a symbol of the discovery of the secret of art. Kreisler contemplating himself or his apprentice in the mirror may evoke the same cluster of imagery.

[35] See Kolb, 'E. T. A. Hoffmann's *Kreisleriana*', 34–44. Charlton, *Hoffmann's Musical Writings*, 25, is sceptical of claims of overall formal parallels between Hoffmann's essays and the 'Goldbergs'.

and a violent musical paroxysm, learned counterpoint and popular dance music might all be readily understood as expressive symbols of companionship and loneliness, mental turbulence, and conflict with philistinism. For literature to use musical features as symbols of human states was not unusual. Heinse used the persisting Pythagorean image of 'the world [as] all music', embedding dissonance and consonance in the cosmos, and probably influenced the symbol of dissonance and resolution that frames Hölderlin's novel *Hyperion*.[36] A scale and final discord are similarly symbolic in the *Nachtwachen von Bonaventura* (X, 119). Julius Becker's *Der Neuromantiker* (1840) – which has a chapter on Schumann's *Kreisleriana* – used intervals as symbols (the minor seventh for instance as life's discords). Writing to Wallborn, Hoffmann's Kreisler had excused his use of musical symbols, hoping that Wallborn will not 'take it amiss if I express myself in very musical terms' ('sehr musikalisch ausdrücken'): 'everything for me takes the shape of music' ('alles, alles sich mir wie Musik gestalte'). Kreisler signed off that letter, he said, with a 'serene and reassuring final chord in the tonic'. Schumann too had described a letter as beginning with a discord and ending with the tonic chord. He said of Berlioz in 1835 that 'he had to express himself musically' ('musikalisch aussprechen'), even if he were renouncing music, and of himself in 1839 that he could not find rest, and 'must express it through music' ('durch Musik aussprechen').[37]

Above all, a contrast in Hoffmann's essays between Bach's 'Goldberg' Variations and trivial variations on a popular tune encapsulates Kreisler's devotion to great music as against philistinism. The 'Goldbergs' serve as Kreisler's writing-paper: as the essays' fictional 'editor' reports, 'on the plain reverse side of several sheets of music, brief essays had been hastily scribbled'; and Kreisler himself talks of scribbling an essay on the back of his copy of the 'Goldbergs'. And when Kreisler tries to withdraw from a philistine musical tea party, he finds that:

some devil in the guise of a dandy... has nosed out the Bach variations under my hat in the adjoining room; he thinks they are pretty little variations, 'Nel cor mi non piu sento', 'Ah vous dirai-je, maman' and the like, and demands that I rattle through them... Right, I think to myself, you can listen and burst with boredom.

---

[36] Heinse, *Ardinghello*, 256 (compare *Tagebücher*, I 96). Charlton, *Hoffmann's Musical Writings*, 36, notes Hoffmann's use of musical procedures as Romantic metaphors.
[37] Hoffmann, *Kreisleriana*, II/2, 289, 292; *Jugendbriefe*, 15 (17 March 1828); *GSK*, II 213 (1835); *Neue Folge*, 151 (31 March 1839). Schumann asked a colleague to reply to a request 'not in a stern C sharp major but a mild D flat major, for in life too most ... things can be enharmonically switched': *Neue Folge*, 65 (14 September 1835).

Example 7.1: 'Ah vous dirai-je, maman'

Example 7.2: Bach, 'Goldberg' Variations, 'Quodlibet', bars 1–4

Kreisler plays first the complete 'Goldberg' Variations, and then, provoked by 'number 30' (the 'Quodlibet'), 'thousands' of improvised variations – until everyone is gone.[38] The 'Goldbergs' thus function not only as Kreisler's notepaper, but as a symbol of great music contrasted with trivial variations such as those on 'Ah vous dirai-je, maman' (Example 7.1) which the dandy expected from Kreisler and which Hoffmann elsewhere reviewed with disdain.[39]

The contrast between great and trivial is sharpened because Bach's 'Quodlibet' includes, alongside another folk tune and the bass from the 'Aria', the tune of a comic German song sharing the patterns of 'Ah vous dirai-je, maman' (Example 7.2). This ordinary material, audible perhaps in a graver aspect in the 'Aria', sets off profundity, and the two are interlinked, lending the 'Goldbergs' an elusive complexity, depth and connectedness.

---

[38] *Kreisleriana*, I/1, 26–7, 30.
[39] Hoffmann, *Schriften zur Musik*, 256–7 (1814); compare Schumann's contempt for the poverty and ineptitude of most contemporary sets: *GSK*, I 219. 'Nel cor mi non piu sento' drew variation sets from composers including Beethoven.

Several commentators have pointed out that Schumann's *Kreisleriana* savours of Bach.[40] For me, it echoes the 'Goldberg' Variations in particular. Critics often find family resemblances between melodies in *Kreisleriana*, and though each identifies a different pattern, many overlap in $\hat{5}-\hat{6}-\hat{5}$ and $\hat{4}-\hat{3}-\hat{2}-\hat{1}$: and these are core motifs in 'Ah vous dirai-je, maman' and in the 'Quodlibet' from which Kreisler's improvisations started.[41] Differing aspects of those patterns appear throughout the work, as bearers of musical structure, triggers for quasi-improvisation, or embodiments of differing musical styles or characters, each with its own expressive or symbolic force.[42] These patterns are common to much music, and are not the only ones visible in Schumann's *Kreisleriana*; that it is impossible to be sure how far they underlie it is part of their point. The fugitive nature of their appearances, in various loose transformations and obscure guises, adds an echo perhaps of Kreisler's irony; and elusiveness and difficulty were parts of Schumann's aesthetic too. But Schumann's use throughout his work of patterns also featuring in an everyday tune shows how the simple can be a basis for the profound as well as the trivial: a main point in Hoffmann's essays, where Kreisler notes 'the mysterious magic at the master's command – that he can lend to the simplest melody, the most artless structure, this indescribable power of irresistible impact on every receptive spirit'.[43]

Alongside these melodic patterns, many other kinds of musical patterns can be discerned in *Kreisleriana*, not least of tonality. In the first piece, the outer sections are in D minor, which could support any one of several different tonal trajectories for the work as a whole. Three come to seem leading possibilities. The opening tonality could be confirmed by a final key of D; its major form could become the dominant of G minor; or it could turn out to be a mediant of B flat major.

---

[40] See especially Daverio, *Robert Schumann*, 167.
[41] See for instance Hering, 'Das Variative in Schumanns frühem Klavierwerk', 351–2; Meier, *Schumann*, 65; Münch, 'Fantasiestücke in Kreislers Manier'; 262–64; Deahl, 'Principles of Organisation', 57–69; von Adam-Schmidmeier, 'Kreisleriana', 95. Carey, 'An Improbable Intertwining', 23–37, sees the same patterns as I, but in the first two pieces only and without the associations. Schumann might have been thinking of this relationship with the 'Quodlibet' when he suggested that 'the profound power of combination in recent music, the poetic and the humorous, have their origin above all in Bach . . . Bach is incommensurable': *Neue Folge*, 177–8 (to Keferstein, 31 January 1840). (Throughout this chapter, and indeed the book, I have used careted numbers to refer to pitch levels within a particular scale, generally without Schenkerian connotations.)
[42] On improvisation, compare Münch, 'Fantasiestücke in Kreislers Manier'; Gooley, 'Schumann and Agencies of Improvisation', 149–52. Schumann saw dangers in improvisation as a basis for composition: see *GSK*, I 231 (1836) and *Briefwechsel*, I 307 (3 December 1838).
[43] Hoffmann, *Kreisleriana*, I/2, 34.

The coexistence of different tonal possibilities meshes with repeated outcrops of the melodic patterns. $\hat{5}$–$\hat{6}$–$\hat{5}$ often lights up $\hat{6}$ (B♭ in D minor, and G in B flat major); differing treatments of the potentially cadential $\hat{4}$–$\hat{3}$–$\hat{2}$–$\hat{1}$ in B flat major and G minor affect the sense of resolution in each key. In the D minor first piece, which introduces the melodic patterns, $\hat{6}$ is B♭, which becomes the keynote of its middle section and of the second piece, whose $\hat{6}$ in turn provides the keynote of the G minor third piece. The fourth piece evades a decision between those two, reinstating at its end a bare chord of D. The tonal possibilities remain open as at the start, and persist into the work's second half as alternatives for an ultimate tonal destination (D being recalled by crucial cadences in the fourth and fifth pieces, and at bars 119ff of the second piece, 63ff of the fifth, and 72ff of the eighth). Tonal alternatives mesh too with contrasts of character and style: G minor (a key Schumann once characterised as 'dark, wild') becomes associated, by and large, with more agitated tempi, a lower register, louder and more contrasted dynamics, stronger accents and more staccato articulation, harsher metrical and harmonic dissonance and sharper tonal definition, and B flat major with greater mildness in each aspect, and a soft tonal focus; meanwhile the bare chord of D at the end of the fourth piece brings an aura of mystery.[44] The tonal trajectory, as associated with these contrasts of character, resonates with aspects of the essays, and not least with the central ambiguity about Kreisler's fate: whether ultimately violent and disturbed, settled in mildness and maturity, or mysterious.

In the first half, the first three pieces make up an A-B-A form. Thus pieces 'i' and 'iii' open with a turbulence and violence that energise the entire work; each features dissonance and metrical conflict in minor-mode outer sections surrounding a calmer interlude; while the intervening 'ii' contrasts consonance with dissonance in a more complex form. The fourth piece adds a coda moving into a different sphere.

The first piece contrasts turbulence with a clarity that evokes Bach. The regularity of the overall shape, with three eight-bar sections to open, three in an interlude (bars 25–48), and an exact repeat of the opening three to conclude, only sets that turbulence – as extreme as in any previous opening Schumann had published – in sharp relief. The piece seems to begin in the middle of a rushing movement. An opening fragment $\hat{5}$–$\hat{6}$ unleashes an eight-bar surge of energy. The tonality is clouded, the harmonies unresolved, the metre confused and the rhythm disjointed: the bass octaves are

---

[44] *GSK*, II 333. Compare Deahl, 'Principles of Organisation', 21 and 78–86.

Example 7.3: Schumann, *Kreisleriana*, i, bars 1–4, from first edition

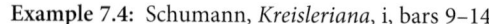

Example 7.4: Schumann, *Kreisleriana*, i, bars 9–14

syncopated against and often dissonant with the main treble accents on the first and third beats (Example 7.3).[45]

It is not until bars 10–12 that a melodic fragment appears: $\hat{5}$–$\hat{6}$–$\hat{5}$–$\hat{4}$–$\hat{3}$–$\hat{2}$–$\hat{1}$ in the minor mode (though arguably this pattern underlies the opening bars too[46]) (Example 7.4). If this were from a conventional set of variations on a major tune like 'Ah vous dirai-je, maman', these bars would be from a minor variation in the middle of the work, as in Mozart (Example 7.5). To think along those lines is to reinforce the sense that this first melodic fragment in the Schumann is not the origin of the work, but

---

[45] See Rosen, *Romantic Generation*, 670–1. I use the first edition here in case any reader likes to see Schumann's notes on 'the white page like little black many-tailed demons' as in Hoffmann, *Kreisleriana*, II/2.

[46] Carey, 'An Improbable Intertwining', 27–30.

Example 7.5: Mozart, Variations, K 265, VIII, bars 9–12

Example 7.6: Schumann, *Kreisleriana*, i, bars 25–6

Example 7.7: Bach, 'Goldberg' Variations, XXIX, bars 17–18

would conventionally come late in a set. Schumann's bars 1–8 would then have occurred in the middle of such a late minor variation. The music began, that is, very much *in medias res*.

The lyrical B flat major interlude that follows has something of Bach about it (Example 7.6). It resembles the 'Gigue' of the B flat major Partita, but still more – in its stepwise melody, rhythm, and triplet figuration divided between voices – 'Goldbergs' XXIX (Example 7.7). Schumann's melody opens with $\hat{6}$–$\hat{5}$, and continues with $\hat{4}$–$\hat{3}$–$\hat{2}$, but then plays with the avoidance of the final $\hat{1}$.

Schumann's second piece, in B flat major, *sehr innig*, creates a conflict between thirds and sevenths that works both as expressive music and as symbolism. In the opening section, middle voices move broadly in parallel and often a third apart. Thirds or sixths figure in three-quarters of the chords in bars 1–8, and dominate 12–16; for seven bars from 29, there is an unbroken run of parallel thirds on every quaver in the inner voices. In bars 1–6, successive waves of swelling melody are grouped in $\frac{3}{4}$ bars, but the

Example 7.8: Schumann, *Kreisleriana*, ii, bars 1–8

treble implies stresses on every fifth quaver, and hence $\frac{2}{4}$, reaching up from $\hat{1}$ to $\hat{6}$ and falling back to $\hat{5}$ on the implied downbeats.[47] In bars 6–8, $\hat{5}$–$\hat{4}$–$\hat{3}$–$\hat{2}$–$\hat{1}$ supervenes, but melodic resolution is undercut by dislocated tonal and metrical developments (Example 7.8).

The waves thereafter are extended, compressed or overlain, with the soprano reaffirming (bars 9–20) the same pattern of $\hat{1}$–$\hat{5}$–$\hat{6}$–$\hat{5}$–$\hat{1}$. The harmonic lucidity is no more unqualified than the metric, as in bars 12–20 an upper voice creates passing dissonances of seconds and sevenths.[48]

The flowing legato waves, reaching up, contrast with the downward push of two *intermezzi*. The first is a brisk $\frac{2}{4}$, staccato and *forte*.[49] In the

---

[47] Schumann plays on traditional associations of this melodic pattern with pastoralism and parallel thirds (for which see Day-O'Connell, 'The Rise of $\hat{6}$', 43–5).

[48] Alphonce, 'Dissonance', 8. Some have heard in the metrical ambiguity, the 'odd commingling of pacification and disturbance', and in the continual undermining of the dominant harmony, an undercurrent of persistent quiet madness: Rodgers, '"This Body that Beats"', 90.

[49] Its initial melody might recall, in its upbeat, and the shape of its opening and closing bars (37–8 and 40–1), the lyrical interlude of the first piece (24–6 and 31–2). But in place of the expansive bars 28–30 of that interlude, with its melodic repetitions and lilting rhythm, here there is a merely functional join (39–40) to the end of the melody, and the regular markings of *forte* or *sforzando* on the last quaver of each of bars 37–46 undercut and so flatten the metre. Compared to the lyrical interlude, or the opening legato waves, it is almost perfunctory.

second, in G minor (bars 91–118), the density of dissonance, metrical and harmonic, and in particular of sevenths, builds up. It opens with a dotted motif (like a minor version of that in 'Goldbergs' XXVI) treated sequentially; the model begins and ends on $\hat{6}$ and the sequence falls through $\hat{5}$, $\hat{4}$, and $\hat{3}$ but then sticks, repeatedly starting from $\hat{2}$. From bar 100, accents stress the second beat of each bar, while the bass (whose off-beat semitone rise recalls that of the opening of the first piece, though here *pp*) obstinately emphasises the third beats as well. Metrical and harmonic conflict gradually intensify, with (bars 100–6) an extraordinarily high density of sevenths among other dissonances. In bars 103–8 the accented second beats are harsh dissonances, metrically exacerbated in two unmarked bars of $\frac{2}{4}$ (107–8).[50] The canon at the seventh in the 'Goldbergs' (XXI) has a similar relative density of dissonance, compared to the thirds and sixths that dominate IX and XVIII.

Other aspects of the piece introduce as expressive music images figuring in Hoffmann's essays. After the second *intermezzo*, though the opening tempo and rhythm return, the opening material remains absent while the music instead descends twice into airless depths (bars 119–26). It works its way out of this depression, briefly tonicising several keys before, in a sudden vision, the opening motif appears, initially in the foreign key of F sharp major, then enharmonically notated in G flat major, and then again in the B flat major of bars 1–2. It is 'an odd sequence of chords', 'melting into gentle angel harmonies', as at Kreisler's meeting with the poet Wallborn. And indeed the music breaks down, and a brief cadenza (bars 140–1) adopts an air of recitative, with a turn and accelerando arpeggios in the bass; then two bars of adagio hint at the motif, and the tentative style, in which the poet steps forward to speak, as at the end of the contemporary *Kinderszenen*.

In bars 24–37 and 78–91 the opening material's waves reach an expressive climax where three voices rise to a high A, then, over a deep bass pedal on I, the treble falls on alternate downbeats to $\hat{6}$, $\hat{5}$ and $\hat{4}$; but instead of reaching $\hat{3}$ and falling to $\hat{1}$, the return home goes awry. As the music slows, the hands converge, as though about to be united on a tonic chord on the third quaver of bars 35 and 89; but they cross and are swept apart (the notation emphasising the symbolism, rather than placing the upper voice in the right hand) (Example 7.9).

In an adagio bar an accented flattened sixth might recall the cadence in 'Goldbergs' XIII (bars 16 and 32); perhaps the gesture is of a stab of desolation

---

[50] Perry, 'Dissonance Treatment', 219–20 and Alphonce, 'Dissonance', 13–14.

Example 7.9: Schumann, *Kreisleriana*, ii, bars 33–7

Example 7.10: Schumann, *Kreisleriana*, ii, bars 158–65

at a promised but unrealised convergence of hands and souls. This sequence recurs at the end of the piece: in a coda tinged with a melancholy that persists even through the serene final tonic chord, the hands again converge and are swept apart. The flattened sixth is converted (bar 161) into an augmented sixth, from which spins out a perfect authentic cadence on the tonic B flat major, with $\hat{3}$–$\hat{2}$–$\hat{1}$ in the treble (Example 7.10).

In any other work a 'serene and reassuring final chord in the tonic', in Kreisler's words to Wallborn, might be ordinary; but in Schumann's first edition it is highlighted because the fourth and fifth pieces have no such cadence, while the first and third have cadences that are abrupt or violent, the sixth, on $\hat{3}$, tinged with ♭II, the seventh a weak cadence in the wrong key and the last ambivalent.

As Schumann's first piece juxtaposes turbulence and clarity, so his third varies that structure and character, thus framing the second. The third opens with a G minor theme: the tenor accents G–A–B♭, and then the bass moves from $\hat{1}$ to $\hat{5}$ and back (bars 1–4), and reaches $\hat{6}$ in an unbalanced answer (5–10). A variant of this dislocated, low, percussive music ends dissonantly with three violently accented off-beat bass octaves (18–21). A B flat major interlude, by contrast, rises in flowing steps first to a *sforzando* $\hat{6}$ (bar 35), and then to a *sforzando* $\hat{5}$ (39), and repeats the $\hat{6}$ and $\hat{5}$ (41 and 43). Voices cross and intertwine; quintuplets, turns and delays add a sense

Example 7.11: Schumann, *Kreisleriana*, iii, bars 61–6

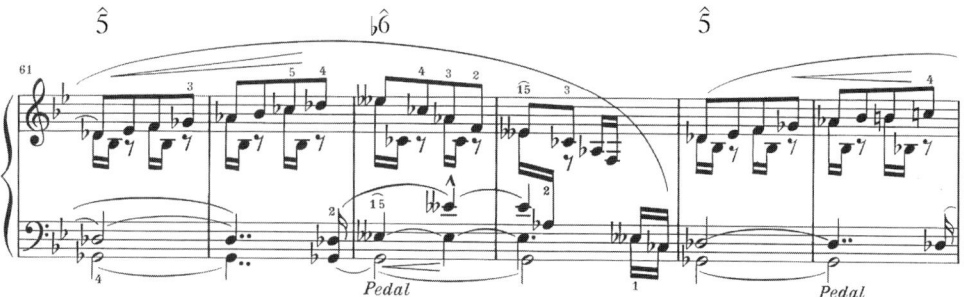

Example 7.12: Schumann, *Kreisleriana*, iii, bars 77–82

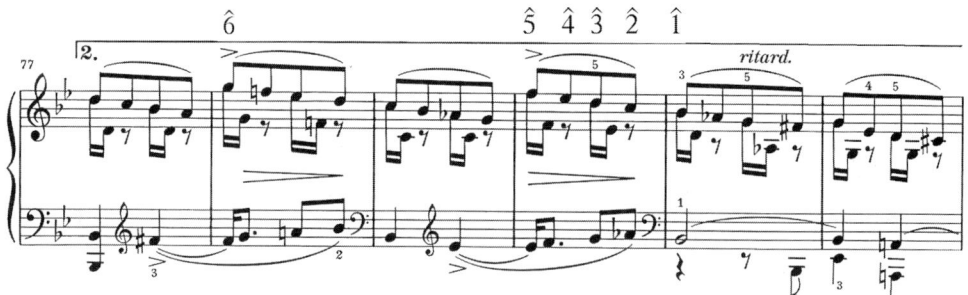

of free improvisation. A middle section of the song flattens $\hat{6}$ (bar 51),[51] and then shifts to G flat major to dramatise $\hat{5}$–$\flat\hat{6}$–$\hat{5}$, doubled in the bass (bars 62–3) (Example 7.11). A stepwise descent (78–81) includes $\hat{4}$–$\hat{3}$–$\hat{2}$–$\hat{1}$ but the harmony sweeps on past to E flat and then G minor (Example 7.12). The texture, movement and quasi-plucked alto line might suggest a love song. Unlike the first piece, this third interrupts the reprise of the opening music with a 'noch schneller' coda, whose final twenty bars pound down and up the registers, accenting beats and off-beats indifferently, and violently affirming G minor in what Kreisler might have called a 'raging pain of wrath'.

From that furore emerges a fourth piece that opens in B flat major, but has no cadence on that key (except in the middle of a middle section not in that key), and no instance of the melodic pattern $\hat{4}$–$\hat{3}$–$\hat{2}$–$\hat{1}$. Instead, F ($\hat{5}$) runs through the fabric of bars 1–2; G ($\hat{6}$) sounds and fades (Example 7.13).

---

[51] One thread in the work as a whole may be the contrast between melodies that reach $\hat{6}$ and those that instead reach $\flat\hat{6}$, major or minor. The $\flat\hat{6}$ in cadences in bars 36, 90 and 160 of 'ii', 38 of 'vi', and 113 and 115 of 'vii' may be related to this pattern.

Example 7.13: Schumann, *Kreisleriana*, iv, bars 1–2

The slow melody leaves bar line and metre unclear; the improvisatory style and melodic shape, including the turn, may again recall *Der Dichter Spricht* from *Kinderszenen*. A subdominant answer suggests an unsettled, sombre dialogue; but by bar 10 it issues in monologue when the upper voice disappears, while the bass traces a G minor answer without accompaniment, coming to a halt on a low unharmonised and tonally mysterious B♭.[52] Nothing is explained. There are long rests. Something has passed out of our world into the depths, and silence supervenes.

Thereafter even crotchets climb up different scales in the soprano and bass. Five times the soprano crotchets start and end on D, creating a sense of linear rather than tonal directedness. The music is suspended between keys, and more B flat major or G minor than D, but there are three cadences on D (in bars 13, 19 and 23), one on B flat major (15), and one on V of G minor (17). A new motif climbs by semitones, with a rest in the figuration like a catch in the throat (third beats of bars 20 and 21) before jumping to a *pianissimo* d^2 (21) over a pedalled chord of V^7 of C, with a C in the bass. As that chord is released (bar 22) into a C minor triad, and the simple soprano melody restarts along with its basso ostinato, there is a sense of untying, of floating up (the more so with the first edition's ritardando at the end of 21)[53] (Example 7.14). This expressive music resonates with the 'innocent melody' and 'basso ostinato' (see page 144 above) of Hoffmann's essays.

When Schumann's opening music returns, there is only the first entry and a subdominant answer descending into the bass. It fades away, slowing to adagio and ends, in the first edition, on a bare chord which, missing the third degree, could be either D major or minor. The cadence is reminiscent,

---

[52] See Rosen, *Romantic Generation*, 674–7; Moraal, 'Life and Afterlife', 180 and Kopp, 'Intermediate States of Key', 315–21.

[53] Compare the 'lift' and 'suspension' Hatten (*Interpreting Musical Gestures*, 203–4) finds in Beethoven's C major Cello Sonata, op. 102, and elsewhere.

Example 7.14: Schumann, *Kreisleriana*, iv, bars 18–23

perhaps (despite differing tonal environments) of the overdue resolutions and bare final chord of D in bars 181–2 of the slow movement of Beethoven's op. 132, with its incorporation of modal music in a diatonic context. Through the cadence, an after-image of the disappearance in bars 8–11 may remain in the mind. Cycling as it does back to the tonality of the first piece, it could have been the end of the work. But Schumann has more to say; and Beethoven's late quartets might well have taught him how to follow such an adagio: with a sardonic scherzo.

The second half of Schumann's work evokes different musical styles and aesthetics, setting echoes of great composers (Bach and Beethoven for instance) against the more trivial, as expressions of differing musical aesthetics. It both confirms and transcends the thematic, tonal and structural patterns of the first. Its first three pieces form an A-B-A shape, as in the first half. The more complex forms are in the outer pieces, 'v' and 'vii'. The fifth piece centres on G minor, but in place of the turbulence associated with that key in the first half is a contrast between uncompromisingly learned styles and a simple dance; and its final cadence in the first edition is on D, which might seem odd did it not pick up the end of the fourth piece. Similarly the sixth piece in B flat major has little contrasting minor, and little harmonic or metrical dissonance; though there is a cadence in bar 5 on D, near its B flat major end it foregrounds (if somewhat undercuts) the potentially cadential pattern $\hat{4}$–$\hat{3}$–$\hat{2}$–$\hat{1}$. The work does not end there, as it might have done. The seventh piece, like the third, reverts to the minor (C minor and G minor), but ends with a very different sort of coda, reiterating

Example 7.15: Schumann, *Kreisleriana*, v, bars 28–36

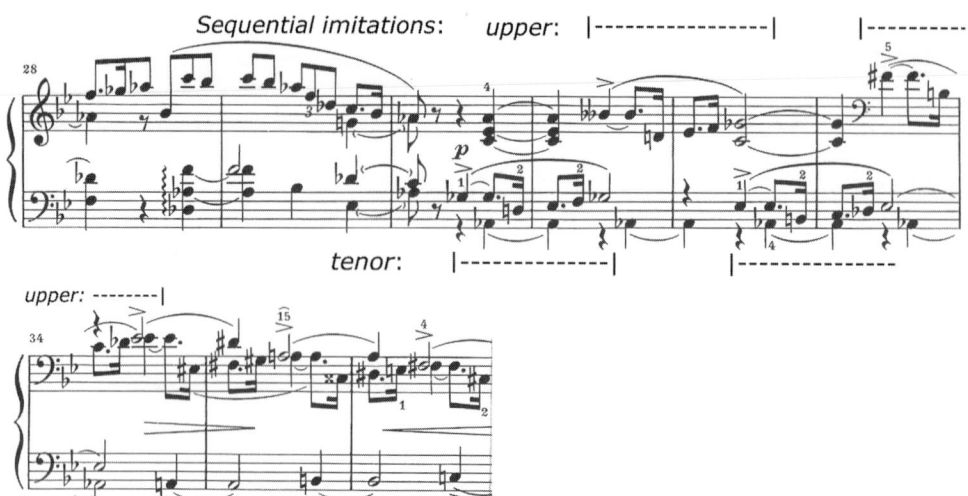

$\hat{4}$–$\hat{3}$–$\hat{2}$–$\hat{1}$, first in B flat major and then in its subdominant. That inconclusive major coda, however, is followed by a final G minor piece, like a coda to the entire work that is both fitting and an alienation. The seventh piece descends from the opening C minor to B flat major in the coda; and the final piece picks up that descent, its first episode emphasising B♭, its second continuing down to A minor, and its ending returning to G minor, as though the minor $\hat{4}$–$\hat{3}$–$\hat{2}$–$\hat{1}$ were written into the harmony.

The fifth piece opens in G minor with a staccato figure whose first three bars feature d¹, a¹ and g¹. Bar 4 offers $\hat{6}$–$\hat{5}$–$\hat{4}$–$\hat{3}$–$\hat{2}$–$\hat{1}$, and the alto voice in bars 12–13 has $\hat{4}$–$\hat{3}$–$\hat{2}$–$\hat{1}$ in a V-i cadence; but neither stops there. Bachian imitations perhaps represent Bach as seen in a late Beethoven scherzo, such as the Vivace alla Marcia from Beethoven's Piano Sonata op. 101; and a second section opening in B flat major (bars 15–37) reinforces that sense of old learning. It has two voices in canonic imitation, a texture opened by rests, insistent dotted rhythms, accented cross-rhythms, and sharp dynamic contrasts. Bars 26ff in particular share the key (D flat major), melodic shape and rhythm of Beethoven's bars 30-3, and bars 30-6 their imitative and sequential treatment and function as retransition (Examples 7.15–16).

As Hoffmann's philistine contrasted such arcane music with 'pleasant melodies', so Schumann's third section (bars 51ff) juxtaposes to these evocations of Bach and Beethoven an undemanding G minor waltz, very

Example 7.16: Beethoven, Piano Sonata in A major, op. 101, Vivace alla Marcia, bars 30–3

different in texture from the sophisticated music that came before. A square two-bar motif occurs thirteen times in thirty bars. Root-position harmonies largely repeat simple harmonic moves, with block chords followed by unison octaves. Is it an ironic parody (similar to those found in the *Humoreske*)?[54] Is the irony the sharper if this melody too emphasises, on every other downbeat, $\hat{1}, \hat{5}, \hat{6}$ and $\hat{5}$ again, as though derived from the same germ as the most profound music in the work? It eventually gives rise to a fourth section: an outburst in E flat major in which the waltz pattern is pounded *fortissimo* (bars 63–8) and then torn apart in accented hemiolas, with a *Murki* in the treble. But if this is an example of those 'amusing *Murkis* and waltzes' of which Kreisler ironically spoke, it is here subjected to scorn: the conventional ascending broken octaves have been given idiosyncratic features, mocked by a bass with two strands of irregular upward movement in semitone steps.[55] The music then retraces its steps from this fourth section through returns of the third, second (bar 105), and finally first sections (128).[56] At the end the descending dotted overlapping sequences halt (bar 140) on a cadence which in the first edition is on D, and as much in that key as in G minor: an inconclusive end that links the piece to its predecessor.

That final D is picked up by the first note of the sixth piece. From it winds a slow movement: in musical and emotional terms, a still centre as

---

[54] Appel, 'Schumanns Humoreske', 289, 293–4.
[55] Hoffmann, *Kreisleriana*, II/2, 290. Schumann shared Kreisler's suspicion of 'amusement', deriving the French word from the Greek for 'without muse': 'in that sense many a concert is indeed an amusement': *Mottosammlung*, IX 227 (source unknown, copied 1834 or before); compare *GSK*, I 500 ('Amüsement') and 437 ('ergötzen', Hoffmann's German word, used with equal ambivalence). Beethoven's Vivace alla Marcia has a *Murki* near its end.
[56] Could Schumann have meant us to imagine the sardonic opening and the learned material continuing all the while in different rooms through which a listener moves, reaching the one in which the *Murki* follows the waltz, and then retracing the path – as partygoers in Hoffmann's *Kreisleriana* (I/1, 30; II/1, 286–7) move from one room to another in search of diverting music?

Example 7.17: Beethoven, Piano Sonata, op. 111, *Arietta*, bars 16–18

[musical notation with markings "dolce" and "sempre legato"]

close to home as the work permits. A *pianissimo* B flat major melody unfolds in a $^{12}_{8}$ marked 'sehr langsam, durchaus leise zu halten'. Bars 1–2 sustain an F, $\hat{5}$, while bars 3–4 emphasise $\hat{6}$ and then fall back $\hat{5}$–$\hat{4}$–$\hat{3}$. Tonic, dominant and subdominant sound in glowing tenths, perhaps related to the thirds in the second piece. As in that piece, and the fourth (bars 1–10), voices move together in metrical consonance. Here a baroque-style improvisation provides contrast, alternating demisemiquaver runs and accented chords (not unlike the seventh or sixteenth variations of the 'Goldbergs'). A sequence of harmonies, described by Deahl as 'kaleidoscopic',[57] eventually melt back into B flat major (bars 8–11). The ♭II harmony, descending octave arpeggios, ritardando and dynamics in bars 8–9 resemble bars 131–4 of 'ii', perhaps with similarly Kreislerian associations. For me it can be heard as recapitulating 'ii', not methodically but allusively; similarly the cadence at bar 5 may echo that at the end of 'iv', thus serving as another allusive recapitulation of the other major piece in the set.

A third statement of the opening music seems to begin at bar 17, but immediately starts to dance in a quicker $^{6}_{8}$ that contrasts with the slower, freer $^{12}_{8}$ rhythms. The pattern of a faster brusque movement (piece 'v') followed by a slow one (piece 'vi') gradually animated into a spiritualised dance occurs in Beethoven's Piano Sonata, op. 111; now from bar 17, Schumann's quicker movement and carolling rhythm, in syncopation against a dominant pedal, are comparable in their effect with bars 16ff of Beethoven's *Arietta*; even the melodic shape of bars 28–9 might resemble Beethoven's (especially in Clara Schumann's edition, in which the final a♭^{1} of bar 28 continues into the first beat of 29, matching the sequence in 30–1 as it appears in all editions) (Examples 7.17–18).[58]

---

[57] Deahl, 'Robert Schumann's *Kreisleriana*', 138.

[58] Schumann presumably knew the sonata by 1838, though his first attested encounter is 1842: Bischoff, *Monument für Beethoven*, 448, using *GSK*, II 81.

Example 7.18: Schumann, *Kreisleriana*, vi, bars 21–30

Each strain of the dance (bars 19–26 and 27–34) ends with an accented statement of $\hat{4}$–$\hat{3}$–$\hat{2}$–$\hat{1}$, which might have presaged a homecoming, if only melody and harmony had been synchronised; and similarly the adagio final cadence (once again shadowed in bar 38 by $\flat\hat{6}$, as at the end of 'Goldbergs' XIII) forms a settled conclusion in B flat major, which one might now take as the home key of the work.

But *Kreisleriana* does not stop there, and will not reach that home again; for Schumann's aesthetic is not Beethoven's. The major *Arietta* of Beethoven's op. 111 follows a C minor opening movement (Example 7.19). But Schumann now moves the other way, from the major key of the sixth piece to a seventh opening in C minor. His opening rhythm, key and melodic shape somewhat resemble bars 19ff of Beethoven's exposition (Example 7.20). More clearly, Schumann's theme recalls *Kreisleriana*'s third piece, in its accented stepwise upward motif in the tenor, rapid treble figuration, discrete chords in the bass, and of course minor mode. For me, any resemblance to Beethoven serves mainly to amplify the idea (already implicit in the reversal of the sonata's sequence) that the later aesthetic has departed from the earlier.

The following G minor passage (bars 9–33) has a similar motif to Mozart's G minor Symphony, K 550, and may share something of its character (perhaps a sort of driven grace, such as Hoffmann seems to have found typical of Mozart) (Examples 7.21a–b).

A new episode (bars 40–68) begins as if a fugato, with a C minor theme whose core varies $\hat{5}$–$\hat{4}$–$\hat{3}$–$\hat{2}$–$\hat{1}$ (Example 7.22). This theme too resembles

Example 7.19: Beethoven, Piano Sonata, op. 111, i, bars 17–26

Example 7.20: Schumann, *Kreisleriana*, vii, bars 1–4

Beethoven's exposition (bars 23ff: Example 7.19). Rising sequences and a circle of fifths in bars 52–61 lead to the home dominant (59–67) and evoke a 'retransition' to a tonic 'recapitulation' of material previously played in G minor; but the accelerated tempo (69–88) creates little sense of a classical resolution. Instead a 'coda' emerges (bar 89) in B flat major. It is based on a melody akin to the opening motif (1–2), but is a different world: a simple tune played in three pairs of regular phrases, and treated to simple textbook harmonisation.[59] Downbeats fall on the familiar pattern (Example 7.23).

---

[59] Rosen describes 'turbulent violence' succeeded by 'a distant chorale': *Romantic Generation*, 678.

Example 7.21a: Schumann, *Kreisleriana*, vii, bars 9–14

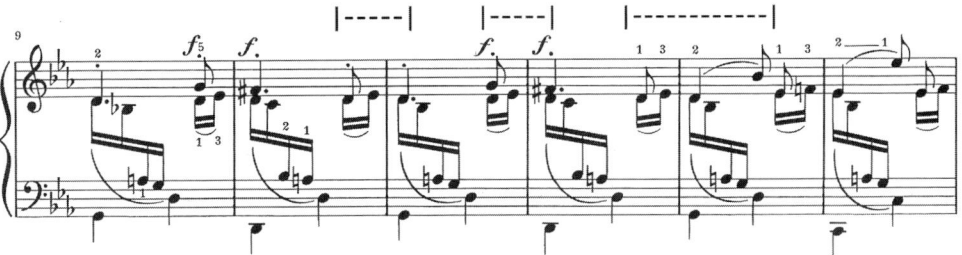

Example 7.21b: Mozart, Symphony, K 550, i, bars 1–3

When the descent reaches $\hat{1}$ there is a perfect authentic cadence in B flat major; but that cannot, and does not, conclude a C minor piece. Beginning again in C minor's relative major, E♭, at bar 100, this 'unpretentious little melody' shows unexpected capacity to 'comfort or heal', in Kreisler's words.[60] The harmony becomes less schoolbook from bar 105; there are markings of ritardando, a chromatic grace note in 109 and a ♭$\hat{6}$ in the final cadence, as in piece 'vi' and 'Goldbergs' XIII. The final $^6_4$ chord is in a key that is home neither for the piece nor the work as a whole; but it links the seventh piece not only to its predecessor, which likewise added ♭$\hat{6}$ to a cadence ending on $\hat{3}$, but also to the fourth and fifth pieces.

One could see the coda as continuing and developing the debate about simple and arcane music that had opened up in Schumann's fourth and fifth pieces: in the fourth an unassuming melody circled and was released; in the fifth a repetitive waltz was juxtaposed with 'convoluted' counterpoint and hammered to destruction, and a *Murki* treated to mockingly idiosyncratic treatment. Now in the seventh, there is an acknowledgment of the power of even the simplest music, or of what both Schumann and Hoffmann saw as the familiar humanity of Haydn, in the face of the driven

---

[60] In Tunbridge's words, by lifting the C minor opening theme to its relative major, the coda serves to confirm its relationship to the theme 'and perhaps grant it redemption': 'Piano Works II', 91.

Example 7.22: Schumann, *Kreisleriana*, vii, bars 40–2

(Mozartean?) energy of the rest of the piece. The time and key signatures, melodic shape and length, repeated rhythmic pattern, simple accompaniment and bass descent through ♭$\hat{6}$ to the cadence, all resemble the opening of Haydn's String Quartet, op. 76/6 (Example 7.24).

Haydn conjoins simplicity and sophistication: he sets a potentially jaunty popular theme to a simple accompaniment, and finally speeds it up for a partly contrapuntal allegro conclusion. Schumann reverses that order; his tiny divergence from Haydn's rhythm makes it less jaunty; and richer harmonies, grace notes, and ritardando markings add poignancy. His echo (if that is what it is) looks on Haydn's easy combination of the popular and the sophisticated perhaps with regret, so embodying his more isolated standing in the world, his view of the recent history of Austro-German music, and an aspect of Kreisler's aesthetics.

That isolation seems confirmed in Schumann's final piece. A staccato theme in G minor hops up the octave and down again; $\hat{5}$–$\hat{6}$–$\hat{5}$ can be heard in bar 2 if the inner voice E♭ is conjoined with soprano Ds; the theme concludes with $\hat{4}$–$\hat{3}$–$\hat{2}$–$\hat{1}$ (c^2 – b♭^{1} – a^1 – g^1) harmonised to yield a perfect authentic cadence (bars 3–4 and 7–8). But in bars 10–12, accents pick out barely coherent hints of another inner voice, which seem a denial of meaning: as Rosen says, they 'come from nowhere and lead to nothing'; they 'hint at forces that will not discover themselves'. The marking of 'schnell und spielend' seems to mean that the music plays with us, not we with it. A bass that Schumann marks as 'light and free' goes its own way, out of sync with the treble and with the metre. It resembles the similar bass voice of previous movements; but here, where there is less regularity, pattern or direction, its contradiction of the treble draws out an opposition (in Rosen's words again) of 'rational and irrational, conscious and unconscious'.[61] As the treble repeats literally through the piece, while the bass shifts unpredictably, both come to

---

[61] Rosen, *Romantic Generation*, 682–3. Compare bass voices in bars 1ff of piece 'i', 48–9, 99ff of 'ii' and 69ff of 'v'.

New worlds, 1838: Kreisleriana, op. 16   169

Example 7.23: Schumann, *Kreisleriana*, vii, bars 89–116

Example 7.24: Haydn, String Quartet, op. 76/6, i, bars 1–8

seem alien; Schumann does not resolve the contradictions as the material recurs, but sharpens them.

From bar 25, while the hopping alto persists in $^6_8$ regardless, Schumann sets below it an ardent $^2_4$ song in B flat major with a strummed accompaniment. Here, unlike in the song in the third piece, there is a note of power or triumph; but after a while the opening music is there again (bar 48), still hopping, as though it had carried on all the while. Once again, from bar 73, it gives way to, or metamorphoses into, a violent canter in D minor and F major, 'mit aller Kraft'. In bars 81–7, the bass hammers $\hat{5}$–$\hat{6}$–$\hat{5}$ while a tenor voice repeats an accented off-beat motif rising by semitones – which may recall rising tenor motifs in the opening bars of the third and seventh pieces. By bar 89, this section, given the repeat, has already lasted for twenty-four bars, as long as the B flat major song; but Schumann extends it for a further twenty-two bars, ten bars of which (100–9) alternate V and i in A minor. There is no preparation until bar 111 for the return of the opening motif or its key. Return it does (bar 112), however, apparently indestructible, initially in C minor, and then again in G minor. Although the theme's cadence ought to complete what began in the G minor fifth piece, repetition has not reinforced but diminished its conclusiveness: by the time it occurs for the last time (bars 139–40), it has already occurred in the same form (barring unaccountable changes in the bass) four times before without bringing a conclusion. Then, as voices disappear one by one, the music passes out of our world, descending into and beyond the bass clef, diminishing to *pianissimo*, and ending not with a cadence but a mere residue of G minor.

It is a far cry from the firm B flat major cadence in the second piece and homecoming in the sixth, and differs too, despite a similar descent, from the passage from dialogue to monologue and then to silence in the fourth piece.[62] What ends the last piece is less personal, a final blank: 'a surprising expression of negation' of the sort that Goethe noted in music by Zelter, or a *danse macabre*, picking up elements of fear that have run through the work.[63] As the music vanishes into nothingness, it conveys perhaps an ultimate isolation characteristic of the Romantic artist's self-perception, in which creativity and adherence to great art demand a kind of withdrawal from the personal; and in this it perhaps resonates with Kreisler's

---

[62] Rosen, *Romantic Generation*, 673–4 and 682; Moraal, 'Life and Afterlife', 183 and Crisp, 'Kreisleriana', 17, both invoke Kreisler's disappearances.

[63] Goethe to Zelter 6 March 1810, a letter Schumann excerpted in 1838 (*Mottosammlung*, I 160). Moraal's word is 'spooky', 'Life and Afterlife', 183. Compare the 1838–9 'Fughette' in op. 32.

disappearances. To Clara Wieck, on 18 September 1838, the eve of Schumann's emigration to Vienna, the pieces seemed sad, as if they might be the very last gift she received from him – a fitting reaction to the suggestion of the disappearance of the artist from the everyday world.[64]

In *Kreisleriana*, the texture of poetic and musical thought is dense. It does not invite a listener to superimpose a literary narrative or programme; rather it creates its own musical patterns, following its own order, embodying as expressive music some of the essays' symbols, and fusing literary, symbolic, expressive and music-historical aspects. These are indeed 'new worlds' in Schumann's development.[65]

* * *

'Stimme aus der Ferne'

Critics often interpret the form of Schumann's work in terms of Hoffmann's novel *Kater Murr*, which also contains, according to its sub-title, *A Fragmentary Biography of the Kapellmeister Johannes Kreisler in Accidental Interleavings*.[66] Some find a formal parallel with Hoffmann's interleaving, either within specific pieces or for the Schumann work as a whole; others go further and compare the music with Hoffmann's 'double-novel structure'.[67] But Schumann was fastidious about titles, and criticised composers who were not: it is perverse to suppose that in this case he carelessly pointed listeners to the essays if he primarily meant the novel – and the less persuasive if there is any reasonable reading of the music in terms of the essays. Of course there are resonances with the novel; but I preferred other descriptions for the forms of 'v' or 'vii' than the particular metaphor of 'interleaving'; and if one sees interleaving in several other Schumann works as well, the term is stretched too thin to carry plausibility and significance. To find a double-novel structure in the work is possible; but if a parallel with *Kater Murr* injects into 'iii', 'v' and 'viii' feline associations – with the complacent Murr in particular – the result,

---

[64] *Briefwechsel*, I 239 (18 September 1838). [65] *Tagebücher*, II 55.
[66] Whoever illustrated the 1838 edition of Schumann's work connected it primarily to Hoffmann's *Kreisleriana*, whereas Konewka, illustrator of the 1863 edition, highlighted the novel; but he was a silhouette-cutter, like Abraham in the novel, which seems to have influenced his choice of subjects.
[67] Daverio (*Nineteenth-Century Music*, 61–2, and *Robert Schumann*, 168) and Tunbridge ('Piano Works II', 90) (interleaving); Deahl ('Robert Schumann's *Kreisleriana*', 131–45) (double novel).

for me at least, is to trivialise 'iii' and 'viii' and to banish a richer symbolism.[68]

I am tempted, however, by an admittedly baseless speculation about a connection between the novel and another Schumann piece. Around the time of writing *Kreisleriana*, Schumann completed eight *Novelletten*, op. 21, and the last may bear comparison with aspects of the novel, including its interleaving of two opposed strands. In the novel, that interleaving is not merely an abstract formal device. Instead, a coherent, complete account of the pompous Murr alternates with disjointed and incomplete fragments about the unsettled but inspired Kreisler. The alternation is such that Murr's interrupted sentences are completed when he resumes after an interleaving, while those beginning and ending the Kreisler passages are not. The interleaving thus expresses something of the character of the protagonists; and it expresses too the tearing grief of the emotional climax of the book. For at that point, Meister Abraham hears the distant voice of Chiara, the 'invisible maiden' whom he had loved, wed and lost. As he laments in his loneliness that he will never hear her sweet voice again, a melodious sound comes to him, reminding him of it, albeit from afar, as 'her words sounded yet softer, yet further'. But 'here the cat tore out another couple of the interleaved sheets', and the continuation is lost. When Abraham later begs the voice to return, it is to no avail; and Murr, who has been seduced by a miaowing 'sweet voice', continues with his own trivial love story, in a painful travesty of Abraham's grief.[69]

The last of the *Novelletten* shows Schumann 'playing with forms'.[70] Resulting from the combination of two previously composed pieces, it is 'a series of interlocking Novelletten within a Novellette'.[71] Its first part contrasts a passionate, aspiring F sharp minor passage, in the spirit of Schumann's Kreisler, with two jolly trios with dotted rhythms and simple harmonic patterns. The transition from the first trio back to the passionate F sharp minor music (bar 94) creates an interleaving effect similar to two joints in *Kater Murr* where interleaving sections (as it were accidentally) complete the sentences they interrupt.[72] The second trio is subjected to an interleaving as well: repeated cadences in its home key of D major are diverted (from 196) into a quite different world: a B minor 'Stimme aus der Ferne' ('Voice from Afar') echoes a melody from Clara's 'Nocturne', apparently with melancholy. Thereafter (255) the interrupted music from

---

[68] Deahl ('Robert Schumann's *Kreisleriana*', 139); Rosen (*Romantic Generation*, 677).
[69] *Kater Murr*, 619–21, 636, 645.
[70] *Briefwechsel*, I 100, of 11 February 1838, the period of composition of the *Novelletten*.
[71] Hoeckner, *Programming the Absolute*, 110.   [72] *Kater Murr*, 448 and 456–7.

the trio resumes its own key, tempo and cadential pattern, this time reaching a conclusion.[73] Schumann then opens a complete new part, in its own time-signature and complex form (A-B-A-C-A-B-A, D-E-Stimme-E-D, A-B-A). The form is further complicated by a progressive acceleration, so that each section on its return seems more frantic. Once again, an echo of Clara's 'Nocturne' (resuming the A major chord it had left off at bar 254) breaks into a section which resumes its tempo, key and melody when the voice disappears, though this time the voice may sound as if it comes from within rather than from outside.[74] Thus in this work, sections that alternate contrasting characters interrupt one another, preventing completion, and later resume, sometimes where they left off: two striking signs of interleaving absent in most cases where interleaving is claimed.

Schumann left no indication of a link between this last *Novellette* and *Kater Murr*, and any idea of an association must remain tentative.[75] But like Abraham, he feared the loss of his own unseen maiden, his Chiara; and he let her voice (her 'Nocturne') sound in this piece, calling to him from afar. Unlike many commentators, I hear the insistently repetitive, frantically cheerful ('munter') music of bars 282ff as redolent not of blissful ('selig') fulfilled love, but of the triviality remaining after such loss: a heartrending form of irony.[76] On that reading, interleaving, in itself and as bringing associations with the form and impact of *Kater Murr*, is a powerful vehicle for the expressive force of the piece.

---

[73] Conceivably, Schumann's marking, 'Continuation', echoes Hoffmann's notation for the resumption of a text after interleaving: 'Murr continues'.

[74] Tunbridge, 'Piano Works II', 89. Hoeckner, *Programming the Absolute*, 112, hears 'extroversion'. The two readings may be interdependent rather than opposed.

[75] He claimed however – albeit perhaps teasingly – that the *Novelletten* contained 'tales of Egmont', that Egmont whose vision of his lost Clara so moved him at this time; and this may be one possible connection (for another, see Brown, 'Higher Echoes', 553): *Briefwechsel*, I 73 (5 January), 90, 97–8 (6 and 11 February 1838). He said (100) that he loved Clara's 'Nocturne' above all her works, apparently hoping it was her lament for the love they lost in 1836.

[76] Kreisler's 'munter' at *Kreisleriana*, II/2 290 may be ironic. Compare Schumann's setting of 'munter' in the last stanza of his song, 'Auf einer Burg', in the 1840 'Eichendorff *Liederkreis*, op. 39/vii; and Appel, 'Schumanns Humoreske', 279–80, 289, 291–4 for examples of the deliberately banal in the *Humoreske*.

8 | Associations and expressiveness in Schumann's 'Hoffmann works'

I have interpreted Schumann's 'Hoffmann works', and not least *Kreisleriana*, as rich in both expressive musical patterns and cultural associations, musical and literary; and this chapter steps back to reflect on those hermeneutic approaches.

Musical and literary associations

Musical resemblances, however striking, may sometimes be just coincidence, or influences without aesthetic significance.[1] Schumann the critic rarely commented on the aesthetic merits of resemblances, but often stressed their dangers, asking of one work that echoed Beethoven, 'Did the composer not notice? If he did, why did he let it stand?' But Schumann the composer must have had answers to the critic's question, for he acknowledged, often in his scores, echoes of Schubert (in op. 4), his own work (in 'Florestan'), Clara Wieck (in opp. 6, 14 and 21), and other composers ('Chopin', 'Paganini', Zumsteeg).[2]

Even where intended, resemblances may enhance instrumental music's aesthetic impact only through determinate means: as quotation or reference; as allusion to texted music that thereby imports the meaning of the text; as the play of concealment, disguise or ciphers for its own sake; or as private communication or even denotation to a select audience (as

---

[1] Given both works' prevalent thirds and alto accompaniment, the rising bass under a repeated soprano note of bars 9–11 of *Kreisleriana* 'ii' strikingly resembles Schubert's *Impromptu* in G flat major, op. 90/3, bars 35–8, in shape, dynamics, subdominant colour and musical function. But Schumann probably did not know the Schubert piece.

[2] *GSK*, II 76. Compare Newcomb, 'The Hunt for Reminiscences'. Schumann's criticism came to stress that if good music resembles other music, it should be in order to achieve a similar effect, evoke a spirit, or associate a feature of what is echoed; resemblances should not be too marked or frequent, or pointlessly slavish: *GSK*, II 86 ('Marlboroughlied'), 126 ('Coriolanus'); I 396 (Weber), 424, 428; compare 240 (Bratchi), 307 (Ries), 320–1 (Marseillaise), 388 ('Bach'), and 453.

a composer in the German tradition may use the notes B–A–C–H to signify the great composer).[3]

But in my understanding, a Schumann work of the 1830s may also use musical features suggestively, to associate an expressiveness developed in the earlier piece, and so to amplify or clarify its own musical qualities for a listener. The qualities may already inhere (at least as perceived within some culture) in musical features embedded in each work. Such features may involve a single aspect taken by itself, such as a melodic pattern; or a passage as a whole; or how a passage's expressiveness is enhanced through musical processes around it; or a work's style, genre, or even reception history.

Thus the motif from *Carnaval* (Example 3.8: bars 5ff) quoted in the third piece of the *Davidsbündlertänze* is to me expressive in itself of a crude self-assertion, and appears as such in both works. Moreover in 'Promenade' it had become (through its opposition to the opening phrase and its development as the music continues, as interpreted in the light of the title) expressive of something like strutting. These associations are carried over into *Davidsbündlertänze*, both through the expressiveness of the motif, and through a resonance with 'Promenade' as a whole. In the later work, Schumann's first edition also clarifies the quality of expression as 'Etwas hahnbüchen', which in my reading characterises both passages in any case. The quotation from *Papillons* in *Carnaval*'s 'Florestan' may work similarly. Echoes of Mendelssohn, Beethoven and Zumsteeg in the *Fantasiestücke* bring out expressive or aesthetic possibilities that complicate and enrich interpretation.

The first movement of the C major *Fantasy*, a 'monument to Beethoven', culminates in an expressive two-bar melodic idea resembling one from Beethoven's *An die ferne Geliebte*. Beethoven set a text that translates:

Take them then, these songs
That I, my love, have sung for you.
Sing them again at evening time
To the lute's sweet sounds . . .

At these songs, all gives way
That sets us far apart;
And a loving heart will win
What's been hallowed in a loving heart.

---

[3] These are the main focus in Reynolds, *Motives for Allusion* (though he allows for musical expressiveness: 7–10).

Example 8.1: Beethoven, *An die ferne Geliebte*, op. 98, bars 266–7

Example 8.2: Schumann, *Fantasy*, op. 17, i, end

He features a poignantly aspiring rise to $\hat{1}$ and a descent, which, though it opens the sixth song, already sounds cadential (Example 8.1).

Schumann enhances the expressiveness through the long-term and immediate preparation for the idea's appearance near the movement's end (including a gradual deceleration to adagio). Small departures from Beethoven's idea have similar effects (including a change of rhythm, a shift of the bar line half a bar earlier to make a repetition of $\hat{1}$ into a downbeat on a harmony of V^{6-7}_{4}); and a continuation in the closing bars converts the end of the idea into a perfect authentic cadence in C major, the first in the work, which is repeated first in the previous note values, and then augmented – with further ritardandos, pauses, ornaments and poignant neighbour notes (Example 8.2).

If Schumann seems to echo Beethoven's 'Nimm sie hin', his work may then be enhanced not just by the words, but also by the music's expressive nature as he has developed it. The musical resonance may be as important as the verbal, and the two are mutually reinforcing: if Beethoven had set the very same words, *per impossibile*, to a rollicking tune, which Schumann had then echoed, both the song cycle and the *Fantasy* would be quite different works. As it is, musical expressiveness and associations contribute to an understanding of both a local musical process and an entire movement.

The repeated chords in Schumann's third last bar – a dominant seventh over a tonic pedal, in a high register, and triplet groupings, losing pace and volume to reach a tonic close – resemble the last eight bars of Beethoven's Sonata in F major, op. 54 (first movement); but here I assume a more distant association, or perhaps only a coincidence. In the case of 'Aufschwung' in the *Fantasiestücke*, the 'retransition' may be heard as suggesting aspects of Beethoven's manner, which I illustrated from one particular sonata without hearing an allusion to that sonata; instead, I interpreted Schumann as introducing associations between his piece and the style of the 'eagle' that Beethoven represented, in order then to express, with mild irony, ways in which his own aesthetic diverged from Beethoven's or in which the achievements of the epigone fall lamely short. Again, the sixth and seventh pieces of *Kreisleriana* seem to me to touch the character of Beethoven's last sonata only tangentially, but perhaps enough to recall the aesthetic expressed in the sonata's sequence, so that Schumann's work can then mark its distance from that sequence and that aesthetic – not as part of an 'anxiety of influence' but as an expression of pain at the fall from classical integration. Something similar may be going on in the coda to the seventh piece in *Kreisleriana*, if it is heard as bringing connotations of the style of Haydn through echoes of one quartet movement in particular. Elsewhere in *Kreisleriana*, suggestions of Bach often seem to invoke a style rather than allude to or quote a particular work, while the use of the folk tune also used in the 'Quodlibet' of the 'Goldbergs' was treated in the previous chapter as a rather complex mix of literary and musical allusions.

Musical threads, interpreted as expressive, can also suggest juxtapositions with ideas and images from books, or from a culture more widely. There is no royal road to making a case that musical or literary associations can enrich understanding, or showing how they might do so, or even that they are present or relevant, or in what sense. Sometimes a general character in the music and the fiction, aided by a title and a remark of the composer, puts an association beyond reasonable doubt, such as between Hoffmann's Kreisler and Schumann's *Kreisleriana*. Or an association may centre on particular musical features, such as the contrast between thirds and sevenths in the second of the *Kreisleriana*, or between relatively specific sonorities, as in *Fantasiestücke*, or particular images or events, as in *Papillons*. Sometimes an association comes to mind the more strongly because of the cumulative effect of other connections between the music and the book: an association between metrical imbalances in *Carnaval* and the literary spirit of carnival would be a stretch were it not for Schumann's titles and the rest of the music.

My choice of literary juxtapositions is sparked by the imagination, guided by Schumann's titles and a sense of the work as a whole, and tested against historical evidence where available. It concentrates on kinds of juxtaposition which Schumann himself emphasised in his criticism and letters; on those authors from the German, English and ancient traditions whose writings demonstrably mattered to him; and on what we know were Schumann's concerns around the time of composition, documented in his letters, diaries, critical writings, and collections of mottoes, or *Mottosammlung*. That does not imply a view that the aesthetic impact of the musical works centrally includes the expression of autobiography. That needs to be insisted upon: the relationship between the music and the biography is tangled and obscure, and it is no part of my purpose to try to disentangle it. But if it could be proved that Schumann never read Hoffmann's *Kreisleriana*, my discussion of it would look misdirected, and quite different questions about Schumann's title and music would loom larger. Similarly, if we knew from his criticism, not that his view of recent musical history was broadly in tune with Hoffmann's (as suggested in Chapter 6), but that he despised Bach and Beethoven, my reading of his *Kreisleriana* would surely be off-beam.

Literary associations may involve not Hoffmann alone but a wider culture as well. Looking at the titles of Schumann's four 'Hoffmann works', only 'Kreisleriana' must point to Hoffmann, the others being more broadly suggestive. Indeed, in all four works, it is only because the music is expressive in ways that are not primarily literary that they are able to make a compelling connection to books as well – because they somehow relate to 'remote interests' touched by the books too. In fact, Hoffmann's books are rich in musical imagery pointing to such interests (as thirds and sevenths point to personal states in *Kreisleriana*); and as a result musical expressiveness and associations are at the core of the literary connection.

The echo chamber of a wider culture can amplify musical features such as motivic patterns in *Kreisleriana*, or the thirds or the sevenths in the second piece – as music and literature ring together. It can elicit, highlight and enrich implicit relationships or 'overtones' between musical features (as between those thirds and sevenths, between contrasting percussive and bell-like sonorities of the *Fantasiestücke*, or between metrical stumbles in 'Grillen' and the 'interrogative' features of 'Warum?'): clarifying, confirming or threading together disparate qualities of expressiveness. And it can enlarge the cultural space in which musical features reverberate. Thus the tonal shape of *Kreisleriana* may also speak of an artist's uncertain destiny, or the image of 'soaring' in the second of the *Fantasiestücke* can also be taken as symbolic, with artistic maturity well within its penumbra of associations (so chiming with overtones of the surrounding pieces). *Carnaval* may resonate with ideas of carnival, and thereby with specific works of the German literary tradition in which those ideas feature. Normally, resonance achieves all these effects simultaneously and more or less indistinguishably. (Where the music can perform the same function for the literature, the process is reciprocal.) Resonant associations, in sum, are both aspects and enhancements of music's expressiveness; and because musical expressiveness is therefore central to my interpretations, it needs more discursive treatment.

Expressiveness

To the extent that expressiveness is a useful hermeneutic tool, it can be imputed to any musical features, however extended or elusive or however far below a surface, and to features described through any analytical tool. The most abstract or abstruse of patterns – puzzling forms in Beethoven's later works, or recondite contrapuntal convolutions in Bach – may in the context of a work be seen as expressive. So expressiveness sometimes seems almost indistinguishable from aesthetic quality; and to appreciate it is not to be distracted from the music but to attend to it all the more closely. Hence my sympathy for calling musical form the seat of musical expression (though to turn the claim into a kind of slogan risks overstating the case). This fits with what Schumann implied in writing of the complementarity of analytic and poetic approaches to music.[4]

And his own works are, in Kaminsky's words, a 'union of structure and symbol'.[5] In Schumann's 'Hoffmann works', expressiveness or evocation may reside in aspects or complexes of harmony, metre, melody, sonority, form, character, style or genre – even visual and tactile aspects, the more

---

[4] *GSK*, I 44, 422–3; II 263.   [5] Kaminsky, *Principles of Formal Structure*, 225.

plausibly in that Schumann's standard mode of musical appreciation was either playing himself or standing by the piano as someone else played, score and hands in sight.[6] Usually a complex is required because a set of pitches, for instance, is not sufficiently expressive in itself; Schumann himself proved that point in *Carnaval* by using two such sets (the Sphinxes) each for multiple different expressive purposes. Schumann the critic sometimes isolates musical features in other composers' works and interprets their expressiveness by describing them metaphorically, for instance as 'breaking off', 'threatening', 'interrogative' or 'pert'.[7] Similarly, I have often used a metaphor both to describe a musical aspect and to intimate how that aspect can evoke for instance a manner (funereal, rustic), a pattern of speech, gesture or movement (even of immobility), a characteristic or state (awkwardness, dream, turbulence) or a process (disappearance). I described the melody in 'Aufschwung' as becoming 'airborne' in bar 4, for instance, and the metaphor may both characterise a musical feature, and make sense of its connections with other complexes (such as in bars 5–8 and 71–4) and with Schumann's title. Such complexes may interact with one another across a work, and their affinity, development, variation or contrast, for instance, may constitute musical patterns or threads.

There are however difficulties in talking about music's expressiveness – in denying it as well as in affirming it. Denial seems counter to widespread (though perhaps not universal) experience of much music, and to an understanding of music active in Schumann's world. Schumann himself often treated the music of his culture as expressive: hence his comment that many of Bach's fugues are 'character pieces of the highest kind ... each requiring its own expression'.[8] He presented many of his own works as expressive; that, I presume, is why he was ready to supply imagistic titles, but to suppress them where he concluded that the music speaks better for itself. On the other hand, affirmation brings hazards. It can claim too much too definitely, and distort musical understanding by distracting from musical processes. There is, it seems, no perfectly satisfactory way to talk about expressiveness; there are only metaphors, each with its own strengths and weaknesses.

One can think of it as like a multipolar gravitational, magnetic or other field – diffused across a work, in some places unobtrusive, elsewhere

---

[6] GSK, I 5–7 (listeners round the piano), 197 and II 212 (visual aspects); compare Kranefeld, *Der nachschaffende Hörer*, 38ff and 57ff; Ferris, 'Public Performance', 354, 372–81.
[7] GSK, I 361–2 and 112–14. On metaphor, compare Watkins, *Metaphors of Depth*, 8–14.
[8] GSK, I 354.

intense, with no definable edges or single centre, its nature in each passage dependent on that passage's location in the work as a whole and on the work's overall aesthetic mass or charge.

Or one could think of expressiveness as pointing to what might be called an enactment or embodiment in music of qualities, or of a state, usually of sensibility (what Schumann often called 'Seelenzustände'). This metaphor too has both value and limitations. 'Enactment' or 'embodiment' might be used literally of a face, gesture or voice, implying an actual personality; in music, however, personality, or persona, is present if at all only in a transferred sense. To say that a piece of music lightly dances may be a good way to describe its expressive nature, but to envisage a particular dancer embodied in it, with feet, legs and face, would often import jarring qualities. The movements of instrumental music affect us because they are free of the associations of an actual embodiment in a particular body, perceived or imagined.

Or music's expressiveness can be treated as akin to linguistic meaning. Analogies between music and language have been tempting and habitual for centuries; they bring familiar problems.[9] For where linguistic meaning, taken in a narrow sense, is built from linear sequences of discrete, arbitrary signifiers, ordered by rules like those of syntax and semantics, music is different. It comprises fluidly interacting features working in many dimensions simultaneously, and not yielding anything like meaning in the narrow sense; as Schumann pointed out, music does not normally signify or 'translate' content that can be articulated verbally; and there is no sense in which we can dispense with the signifier once we grasp what is signified. Musical expressiveness can be appreciated despite a difficulty in isolating configurations that contribute to it, or defining how they do so.

Schumann's world had wrestled with the idea that music is expressive or evocative without taking language's path through semantics and reference.[10] In 1842, Schumann published in the *Neue Zeitschrift* articles on Hegel's philosophy of music – by Eduard Krüger, whom he called the journal's 'most respected contributor' – arguing that music could contain thought not limited to what can be expressed in words. Music's 'content' is some higher and more elusive element: 'what is outside the scope of words

---

[9] See for instance Bonds, *Wordless Rhetoric*, 53–131; Kramer, *Musical Meaning*, 11–20; Abbate, 'Music – Drastic or Gnostic?', 514–23; Agawu, *Music as Discourse*, 3–5, 15–17; Tudor, *Sound and Sense*, chapters 7–8; Hyer, 'Second Immediacies in the *Eroica*', 84–7.

[10] Compare sources cited in Charlton, *Hoffmann's Musical Writings*, 12–14 and Tudor, *Sound and Sense*, 327–30 (Rousseau, Hiller, Herder and Schiller).

is not the meanest part of the mind'.[11] In the 1780s, Karl Philipp Moritz had agonised about thought without words; in the 1790s, Wackenroder, for whom music's communication, its 'unnameable import', is not reducible to the 'alien medium' of verbal formulations, had asked whether 'sceptical rationalists', who wanted music explained in words, had 'never felt without words'.[12] Tieck pursued the same tack. 'Our inner spirit', he wrote, 'hearkens to' music, and 'seeks to grasp and hold fast to its subtler and purer thoughts through thoughts and words, those coarser instruments – and cannot of course succeed that way.' Elusive, purer 'thoughts', conveyed by music are not a translation of or translatable into 'coarser' verbal thoughts; the latter are, he implies, only intimations, or a necessarily inadequate hermeneutic tool to approach the former. He encapsulated the same idea, with the same double sense of 'thought', in a poem that appears twice among Schumann's excerpts, first from about 1836–8, and then again from about 1850: 'Love thinks in sweet music – as thought is too remote – and only in music will she gladly beautify whatever she will.'[13] It is not clear whether 'thought without words' is helpful philosophically; but the insistence that what music does cannot be translated into words does appear valid.

Of course, Schiller had dwelt on how words too can achieve an indefinite, expressive, symbolic meaning not confined to rule-bound, arbitrary, one-dimensional signification; Wackenroder, Hoffmann and Schumann sometimes forgot that, tending to view verbal meaning as more exclusively fixed and definite than it is. There is a narrower sense in which one asks the meaning of a foreign, new, complex or ambiguous word or sentence or passage, or discusses that of empirical statements ('It is snowing in Newark'), of logical deductions, and of the words and statements in this paragraph; but there is also a broader sense in which one might talk of a poem's 'meaning', or expressive drift, as distinct from the meaning of its constituent sentences. That expressive drift depends in part on multidimensional patterns of metre, rhythm, sentence rhythm, alliteration, assonance, rhyme, phrase groupings and stanza. And in those respects,

---

[11] See Pederson, 'Romantic Music under siege in 1848', in Bent, ed., *Music Theory*, 61–3. Compare Tadday, *Das schöne Unendliche*, 123–7.

[12] Moritz, *Anton Reiser* (*Werke*, vol. I), 216; Wackenroder, 'Wesen der Tonkunst', in *Herzensergießungen*, 148.

[13] Tieck, 'Die Töne', 269 and 273 ('Liebe denkt in süßen Tönen / Denn Gedanken stehn zu fern. / Nur in Tönen mag sie gern / Alles, was sie will, verschönen'; *Mottosammlung*, I 109 and XI 39). His *Die verkehrte Welt* (1798) (in *Die Märchen aus dem Phantasus*) opens with a 'Symphonie' suggesting that if thinking in music, and making music in words, were impossible, both music and language would be impoverished. Compare Rosen, *Romantic Generation*, 72–5.

poetry may, as Schumann and his contemporaries might have said, be analogous to music; but it is at the point in which linguistic meaning, in a narrow sense, is isolated as part of the poetic mix that the analogy with music breaks down. It is probably better to say that music generally is meaningful than the contrary; but to say that a particular piece has 'a meaning' risks entangling a narrower sense of 'meaning' with a broader, and imputing to music the property of pointing to something more or less separable from it, and adequately specifiable in words. These are imputations that must be at least partially withdrawn again if the nature of music is not to be falsified.[14]

Again, Schumann and his contemporaries sometimes imputed not just images to music, but scenarios or narratives as well, as one way of expressing the trajectory or drama of a work. Today too, music's expressive import is sometimes conjecturally recovered through imputed narratives or scenarios; but definite figures and coherent narrative connections, once introduced, must, like meanings, be withdrawn again if they are not to straitjacket and falsify the music.[15] They rarely work for any but the person who invents them. Instrumental music by itself could of course conceivably contain vestigial narratives; but the more developed the narrative the worse the music is likely to be. 'Narrative' and 'narrativity' in some broader sense are however sometimes applied to instrumental music.[16] This seems unimpeachable if used casually, but if turned into systematic theory it risks confusion with the narrower (literal) senses of the terms; and for my purposes, where interpretations that relate somehow to actual narratives are at issue, it is better not to invite that confusion.

I prefer likewise not to theorise music as metaphor to explain its expressiveness. Metaphor is (centrally) a figure of speech in which a term (or sign) with a literal sense in one context is transferred to another context in which that literal sense does not apply; but in music there are no terms with literal or transferred senses. What is said about music, however, is often metaphorical. A composer may suggest (for instance through a title such as 'Ruins', 'Ave Maria', 'Aufschwung' or 'Warum?'), or a critic adopt, a context that provisionally fixes a domain within which to analyse or

---

[14] Thus Fisk describes how 'musical experience ... thrives on loss of meaning ... that is, on forgetting what might have been meant while at the same time drawing energy from, or even, in a sublimated way, resolving conflicts within, that lost or forgotten meaning': 'Schubert's Last Sonata', 194–5.
[15] *GSK*, I 85, 121–2, 202–3, 462; II 263; compare Maus, 'Music as Drama'.
[16] See Newcomb, 'Schumann and Late Eighteenth-Century Narrative Strategies', 164–74. Compare Cook, 'Uncanny Moments', 111–13; Nattiez, 'Can One Speak of Narrativity in Music?' and Lester, 'Schumann and Sonata Forms', note 10.

interpret the music; and some of what is said about the music within some such domains is arguably metaphorical.[17] A sub-group of such metaphors may be 'poetic' in the sense that they generate an indeterminate range of connotations or implications, so resembling Goethe's less purely linguistic concept of symbolism described below.

What linguistic terms like 'meaning', 'metaphor' and 'narrative' offer musical hermeneutics is perhaps not so much coherent theory as suggestive paradox: meaningfulness without meanings, metaphor without terms or literal senses, dramatic shape or trajectory without story. Much as they seem familiar enough to enter any field without their credentials being checked – as they routinely do in modern work – meaning and metaphor are radically contentious in the philosophy of language; and pending some unlikely triumph of clarification, their application to music will remain doubly obscure.

Schumann successfully used titles to guide appreciation of his music's expressiveness into one field or another, when without the title listeners might differ as to that large context for interpretation. Given that prompt, a complex expressiveness can emerge in Schumann's instrumental music; but even so, it rarely expresses some complex verbal entity; using words to try to pin down what is expressed will necessarily be more or less off-target, and can only be suggestive. I would not want to assert either that expressiveness in the music of Schumann's 'Hoffmann works' expresses something separately specifiable, or that it is expressive but not of any object. It can clearly be expressive of a character, style, state of mind, gesture, voice, sound or process: it is odd to deny funereal associations in a funeral march, or that the piece called 'Aufschwung' evokes Aufschwung; but every attempt to say what the music expresses is more or less off-target, either for everyone or for many people. Insofar as poetic music transubstantiates external content into itself, it is expressive of something precisely because it is first expressive of itself.

Indeed, 'expressiveness', whatever it drives at in this context, is best taken as no more than a provisional manner of speaking about musical qualities – rarely simple, never definitive, not exactly literal, and not implying entities that are expressed.[18] One could go further and argue that as music is in essence not verbal, and its essence cannot be captured in

---

[17] Schroeder, 'Music and Metaphor'; Davies, *Musical Meaning*, 148–9; Kramer, *Classical Music and Postmodern Knowledge*, 69–70. Music and metaphor may sometimes seem, like the oracles described by Heraclitus, neither to declare nor to conceal but to intimate: Diels, *Die Fragmente der Vorsokratiker*, DK22B93.

[18] Compare Rosen, *Classical Style*, 21.

words, it is better to renounce words and simply perform or appreciate it, resorting to a wordless 'drastic' alternative, or a 'body that beats'.[19] Nobody writing a book about musical works can go that far – least of all a book about connections between music and literature. But in using words I acknowledge their limitations. 'Expressiveness', useful in practice, is untidy in theory. It may be a way of getting at aspects of some works of music, but it is only one way; what makes works matter – or become meaningful, communicative or compelling, or whatever words one chooses – could be put in other ways too, none finally more satisfying.

Schumann's predecessors used various images to talk about music's expressiveness. One was sympathetic vibration, a phenomenon related to resonance. The physics of the acoustic phenomenon may have become clearer since the Romantic age, but the psychological mystery as to how music affects the human heart, which it tried to address, has if anything become more elusive. The loss in part reflects the evaporation since the eighteenth century of a version of 'solidist' physiology. That version, dovetailing with advances in mechanics, suggested a fundamental analogy between human and other nature: fundamental fibres of the body, including therefore of the sentiments, respond to sensory stimulation (touch, light, colour, sound) through induced or sympathetic vibration; that vibration can elicit other associated vibrations through memory; and music may have a particularly powerful effect because of a 'consonance' between musical vibrations and those of the body's fibres.[20]

'Solidist' physiology evaporated as knowledge, but remained a metaphor. Wackenroder saw an 'inexplicable sympathy between mathematical relations of music' and 'the fibres of the human heart' (were those fibres already only an image, or still taken as science?). For him as for Tieck, music, while nothing but a web of numerical relationships represented on wood, gut strings and wire, can seem the speech of angels.[21] Novalis described nature as an Aeolian or wind harp, whose notes are also the hammers that strike strings in our own higher natures.[22] In 1795 Coleridge used the Aeolian harp as the title of a poem about music's intimate relation

---

[19] Abbate, 'Music – Drastic or Gnostic?'; Barthes, *Responsibility of Forms*.
[20] See for instance Fantini, 'Forms of Thought Between Music and Science', especially 258–61.
[21] Wackenroder, 'Wesen der Tonkunst' and 'Die Wunder der Tonkunst' in *Herzensergießungen*, 144, 147–8, 132–4; Tieck, 'Die Töne', 269 and 273. Shakespeare of course had written: 'Is it not strange that sheep's guts should hale souls out of men's bodies?': *Much Ado About Nothing*, II.iii.61–3. Compare the views of Herder and others in Watkins, *Metaphors of Depth*, 31–2.
[22] Novalis, *Schriften*, V 230(fr. 239). See the *New Grove* entry on the Aeolian harp.

with nature and humanity – and incorporated a synaesthesia that Hoffmann might have approved:

O! The one life within us and abroad,
Which meets all motion and becomes its soul,
A light in sound, a sound-like power in light,
Rhythm in all thought, and joyance everywhere –
. . .
Where the breeze warbles, and the mute still air
Is music slumbering on her instrument.

He reused the image, in a gloomier mood, in his *Dejection: An Ode*, of 1802, where 'the dull sobbing draft' 'moans and rakes / Upon the strings of this Aeolian lute, / Which better far were mute.' Shelley's *Ode to the West Wind* of 1819 prays, 'Make me thy lyre, even as the forest is.'[23] Similarly, Hoffmann in 'Die Automate' pictured the apparently random play of the then mysterious Aeolian harp as revealing 'profound acoustic secrets hidden everywhere in nature'; and 'the music dwelling within us, which rings out through the effect of musical instruments as if in the force-field of a powerful magic, is none other than that hidden like a profound . . . secret in nature'. Music can 'touch all the strings hidden in the human heart and make them sound'.[24] The mystery of such music that seems to address each individual personally is not unlike the effect of nature on the wind harp, or indeed that of the automaton in the story, who seems to speak a personal truth to each individual: in each case a source of energy mysteriously elicits sympathetic vibrations. Elsewhere, Hoffmann pictures a butterfly trapped in the strings of a clavichord, its wing-beats eliciting just audible tones and chords, and eventually wounded to death by stronger vibrations: it is an emblem of humanity in Nature's gigantic clavichord, and of music's ability to play on our psychic strings, universally, uncontrollably and inexplicably.[25] In another story, the sound of a name awakens sympathetic vibrations in musical instruments left in a theatre.[26] Likewise, in Schumann's *Carnaval* the magician 'Paganini' elicits an unstruck chord in undamped strings through sympathetic vibration with overtones of the notes last sounded.[27]

Romantics often presented the sympathy between humans, nature and music as a residue of a primal state. In that state, all human

---

[23] Coleridge, *Poetical Works*, 100 and 363; *Shelley's Poetry*, 223.
[24] Hoffmann, 'Die Automate', *Die Serapions-Brüder*, 347–50.   [25] See Appendix 3–8.
[26] Hoffmann, *Fantasiestücke*, 74 ('Don Juan').
[27] See Chapter 3. Schumann compared Chopin's music to an Aeolian harp: *GSK*, I 254–5 (1837).

capacities – including speech, scientific thought and music, and the senses now only reunited in synaesthesia – were undifferentiated, and attuned to Mother Nature; sign and object were one, and communication was absolute.[28] For Tieck, music speaks 'the ancient language that our minds once understood', its 'thoughts' inaccessible to coarse post-lapsarian language. Novalis exploited the same image of the primal, non-verbal language:

The language of music is universal. It arouses the mind in free and uncircumscribed [unbestimmt] ways, but feels to it so right, so familiar, so ancestral [vaterländisch] that for brief moments the mind is in its Indian home.

'Indian' plays on the recent discovery of an Indo-European family of languages, with ancient Sanskrit near its origin, and for Novalis Sanskrit evokes not only an ancestral language but also a primal form of direct, universal communication prior to all languages. Though Tieck's edition omitted 'Indian' before 'home', obscuring the allusion, Hoffmann both echoed the words and adopted the underlying thought. 'In each language', he wrote, 'there is so intrinsic a link between sound and word that no thought is produced in us unaccompanied by its signifying script', but 'music remains a universal language of Nature'. For him, Bach's music with its 'numerical relationships' and mysterious patterns is quintessentially primal communication, 'Nature's Sanskrit'.[29] Schumann too noted Novalis' words, and imitated them closely: 'Music speaks the most universal language, and through it the soul is stimulated in a free and uncircumscribed way; but it feels itself at home.'[30]

In Novalis' *Die Lehrlinge zu Sais*, several voices explore from different angles the idea that the primal state, though now vanished, can still be glimpsed. The play of mathematical, poetic, musical or natural signs, if enjoyed for its own sake ('the true Sanskrit would speak for the joy of speaking'), can give intimations of Nature's truth as it was once visible. Other voices are sceptical, and modern critics, accustomed to a postmodern semiotics, detect ambivalence.[31] But in Tieck's versions of Novalis, something like Platonism seems reinforced in the prose fragments he placed in the same slim volume (as tabulated in Appendix 1). These

---

[28] Compare Scott Burnham, 'How Music Matters', 193–5; Watkins, *Metaphors of Depth*, 96–8.
[29] Tieck, 'Die Töne', 269; Novalis, *Schriften*, III 283–4; *Schriften*, V 230(fr. 242); Hoffmann, *Kreisleriana*, II/7, 326, I/5, 50, I/3, 39. See also Charlton, *Hoffmann's Musical Writings*, 35; Rosen, *Romantic Generation*, 59–68.
[30] *Mottosammlung*, IX 190 (1832–4); *GSK*, I 19 (1832).
[31] Novalis, *Die Lehrlinge zu Sais* (*Schriften*, I), *passim* and 79; O'Brien, *Novalis*, 206–9, detects irony.

describe how poetry, fable and true philosophy, on which 'all sciences' converge, give 'intimations' and 'dreams of that world, lying everywhere and nowhere, where we would be at home'. It would be a 'regeneration of Paradise', a 'marriage of nature and mind', in which 'magic words' provided 'real definitions', not mere ciphers only arbitrarily linked to things, and the analytical and synthetic sides of our being, reasoning and instinct, were reunited. But it is a 'Protean' ideal that always eludes our grasp. In its absence, we can only 'divine' 'analogies', 'affinities', 'kinships' and symbolic relationships between different areas of thought, whether philosophy, natural and human sciences, politics, ethics and religion, or art, music and poetry. In a comment which Schumann excerpted, Novalis unites music, mathematics, creativity and philosophy as vehicles of truth: 'In music, mathematics appears really as revelation, as creative Idealism, and is accredited as heaven's ambassador to humanity.'[32]

Jean Paul reflects similar presumptions in a passage which Schumann will have read. In this imperfect world, he says, sign and signified, thing and meaning, nature and mind, are sundered, and we reach out intuitively in search of their reintegration:

Sowie es kein absolutes Zeichen gibt – denn jedes ist auch eine Sache – so gibt es im Endlichen keine absolute Sache, sondern jede bedeutet und bezeichnet, wie im Menschen das göttliche Ebenbild, so in der Natur das menschliche. Der Mensch wohnt hier auf einer Geisterinsel, nichts ist leblos und unbedeutend, Stimmen ohne Gestalten, Gestalten, welche schweigen, gehören vielleicht zusammen, und wir sollen ahnen; denn alles zeigt über die Geisterinsel hinüber, in ein fremdes Meer hinaus. Diesem Gürtel der Venus und diesem Arme der Liebe, welcher Geist an Natur wie ein ungebornes Kind an die Mutter heftet, verdanken wir nicht allein Gott, sondern auch die kleine poetische Blume, die Metapher... Wie schön, daß man nun Metaphern, diese Brotverwandlungen des Geistes, eben den Blumen gleich findet, welche so lieblich den Körper malen und so lieblich den Geist, gleichsam geistige Farben, blühende Geister!

Just as there is no absolute sign – for every sign is also a thing – so in the finite world there is no absolute thing; rather each thing signifies and has meaning, man's image in nature as God's in man. Man dwells here on an isle of spirits; nothing is lifeless or without meaning; voices without form and forms that are silent may

---

[32] Novalis, *Schriften*, V 269(fr. 494, 496: fable and dream of a primal home; compare 207(fr. 28)); 209–10(fr. 47: paradise); 210(fr. 52) and 222(fr. 152) (marriage of mind and nature); 211(fr. 61), 217(fr. 95) (magic and signs); 209(fr. 43: converging sciences; compare 249(fr. 335), I 84 and IV 252); 217(fr. 92) (instinct); 206(fr. 18: Proteus); 207(fr. 23–6), 212(fr. 69), 236(fr. 281), 258 (fr. 405) and 275(fr. 531) (divination and analogy); 248–9(fr. 330: ambassador; *Mottosammlung*, IX 183). Compare *Notes for a Romantic Encyclopedia*, xxiii–xxix; O'Brien, *Novalis*, chapter 4 *passim* and 314–16; Hoffmann, *Kreisleriana*, II/7, 326.

belong together, and we can only accept intimations; for everything points out across the spirit isle, out into an unknown sea.[33]

Such intimations are a divine 'arm of love which joins spirit to nature like an unborn child to his mother', and to it we are indebted for 'that little poetic flower', the metaphor, which he saw as a primal speech form.[34] Jean Paul's own floral metaphor then blossoms in both a restatement and an exemplification of his point: 'how lovely that metaphors ... are thought to resemble flowers, that so sweetly depict body, so sweetly spirit, both pigments for the mind and minds that bloom'. Mixing his metaphors, and echoing his claim that art 'transubstantiates' extraneous material into the poetic (see Chapter 4 above), he also calls metaphor 'the mind's transubstantiations' ('Brotverwandlungen'): it does not so much use a sign to signify something else, but by transmutation creates something new, at once sign and thing.

Jean Paul may have been using 'metaphor' in a broad sense – coloured by the related concept of symbolism, which his contemporaries used to describe how art can communicate. Thus for Goethe, an object is transmuted in alchemical ways into a new symbolic entity that eludes determinate formulation:

Symbolism transforms the perceptible into an idea, and the idea into an image, in such a way that the idea within the image always remains infinitely [unendlich] active and unattainable, and, even expressed in all languages, it would still remain inexpressible.

A symbol is not merely a disposable sign for the denotation of something perceptible; what is symbolised remains limitlessly active in the symbol, beyond grasping through verbal formulations. Goethe elsewhere calls such symbolism 'the nature of poetry'.[35] In contrast,

Allegory transforms the perceptible into a concept, and the concept into an image, but in such a way that the concept always remains confined within the image, completely attainable and contained, and expressible through that image.[36]

---

[33] Jean Paul, *Vorschule*, §49 (compare Watkins, *Metaphors of Depth*, 99–103). His phraseology reflects Augustine, *On Christian Teaching* (1999), I 4 ('every sign is also a thing', but 'it is not true that every thing is also a sign'); his ideas and images reflect ibid., II–III, and *Confessions*, XIII 18–24, interpreting Genesis I 14. Unless Jean Paul's usage differs from standard German, translations of the sentence 'Diesem Gürtel ... verdanken wir ... Gott' often miss the intriguingly radical theology.

[34] Watkins, *Metaphors of Depth*, 100–3, adduces similar floral images from Herder, Hegel, Hoffmann and Heine.

[35] Goethe, *Werke*, III 579(fr. 1113), 487(fr. 279). See Dickson, 'E. T. A. Hoffmann', 251–4. Compare Langer, *Feeling and Form*, 24–31.

[36] Goethe, *Werke*, III 579(fr. 1112).

Jean Paul too contrasted his view of 'metaphor' with allegory, a 'degenerate' and 'arbitrary' form.[37] While programmatic understanding, like allegory, specifies a reference, symbolism is potent in its impact, but resistant to definition and analysis.[38]

Music was often credited with such a symbolic capacity. For Schiller, landscape art and instrumental music express ideas not by arbitrary association but through 'the laws of the symbolising power of imagination' ('Gesetzen der symbolisierenden Einbildungskraft'). According to Michaelis in 1805–6, instrumental music can create ideas in a listener's imagination through 'symbols and intimations of possible objects, and in particular states of mind'. For Hoffmann just as in an old-fashioned aria 'the words are a symbolic indication of inner feeling, so now [in a Lied] the music is the symbol of all the varied emotional implications that the poet's Lied contains'.[39] Goethe too remarked in a letter to Zelter of 6 March 1810, which Schumann excerpted in 1838, on a symbolic relation between a piece of music and the text that it sets:

It is a kind of aural symbolism [eine Art Symbolik fürs Ohr] in which the object . . . is neither imitated nor portrayed, but is conjured up for the imagination in a quite peculiar and incomprehensible way, in that the signified seems to bear almost no relationship to the signifier.[40]

There are (more or less) codifiable procedures for verbal translation, and translation is reversible. But music does not present objects through systems of signs; no *codifiable* procedure could recover this 'object' from that music, or vice versa – though their relationship is not as 'incomprehensible' as Goethe says: much that is comprehensible can be said about it.

I have suggested that music can speak to listeners through an ultimately undifferentiated wash of the formal, the expressive, the associative and the resonant. The early Romantics reflected something similar in an image they often used: fluidity. Novalis' *Die Lehrlinge zu Sais* hymns the

---

[37] Jean Paul, *Vorschule*, §51. See also Watkins, 'Floral Poetics', 36–7.
[38] This resonant symbolic capacity was often described in terms of 'Potenzierung': a large (even exponential) amplification of significance through associations. Compare instances from Novalis and Schumann in Appendix 2 below.
[39] Schiller, *Sämtliche Werke*, V 698 ('Über Mathissons Gedichte'); Michaelis, 'Vermischte Bemerkungen' (1805), 14, 21; Hoffmann, *Schriften zur Musik*, 238 (1814). A symbolic relationship is often imputed to Schumann's songs: for instance, by Youens, 'The Cry of the Schuhu', 40ff. On Schumann's music in general, compare Lippman, 'Theory and Practice', 311 and 340 and Watkins, *Metaphors of Depth*, 104–7. Compare also Reynolds, *Motives for Allusion*, 7–10.
[40] *Mottosammlung*, I 160.

pre-lapsarian state as 'that unseen universal ocean', or primal fluidity ('Urflüssige'):

Selbst der Schlaf ist nichts als die Flut jenes unsichtbaren Weltmeers, und das Erwachen das Eintreten der Ebbe. Wie viele Menschen stehn an den berauschenden Flüssen und hören nicht das Wiegenlied dieser mütterlichen Gewasser, und geniessen nicht das entzückende Spiel ihrer unendlichen Wellen! Wie diese Wellen, lebten wir in der goldnen Zeit ... liebten und erzeugten sich die Geschlechter der Menschen in ewigen Spielen.

How many stand by those entrancing waters [berauschenden Flüssen] and do not hear the lullaby of that maternal liquid, nor enjoy the delightful play of its unending [unendlichen] waves! Like those waves, we lived in the golden age ... and generations of men loved and procreated in eternal play.[41]

The terms 'das Flüssige' and 'das Unendliche' naturally convey the fluid, indeterminate, elusive, infinite and ineffable; Novalis here added connotations of the synaesthesic, cosmic and primal, and even maternal or placental. Moreover, he associated fluidity with the poetic. He thought 'only poets should deal with the fluid', as 'a true poet is all-knowing', 'poetry is by nature fluid', and 'Unendlichkeit' is inherent in poetry.[42]

Such indefinite fluidity was widely seen as quintessential to 'the Romantic', which is, Jean Paul said, and Schumann noted, 'the beautiful without limits, or the beautiful "Unendliche"'. Moonlight, in which the objective world loses its definition, is for Jean Paul 'both image and example of the Romantic'; so is the resonance of a bell that lives in the memory after its sound dies away.[43] Novalis brought out two implications of this 'Unendlichkeit'.[44] The veil of Isis that hovers around an artwork will 'dissolve at the slightest touch, leaving a magical fragrance': a warning for books like this one. But an artwork 'brought to perfection expresses not only itself but an entire associated world': the more a composer creates music that works as music, rather than as a means to convey something, the more expressive or evocative it can be. If this is paradoxical, it is a familiar paradox. For Novalis, 'the true Sanskrit' speaks for the sake of speaking; and he put the point even more clearly in his 'Monolog' (not published until 1846): 'if someone speaks simply for the sake of the speaking, he expresses the most splendid and original truths; if he tries to express

---

[41] Novalis, *Die Lehrlinge zu Sais* (*Schriften*, I 104–5).
[42] Novalis, *Schriften*, I 105; V 265(fr. 463) and 264(fr. 456); IV 246.
[43] Jean Paul, *Vorschule*, §22 (*Mottosammlung*, IX 29), 25, 31 ('Wir haben der romantischen Poesie im Gegensatz der plastischen die Unendlichkeit des Subjekts zum Spielraum gegeben, worin die Objektenwelt wie in einem Mondlicht ihre Grenzen verliert'); *Nachschule*, 7.
[44] Novalis, *Schriften*, V 264(fr. 455).

something definite, capricious language has him utter ridiculous and distorted stuff. As Scott Burnham has written in our own times, 'we need to understand music as music ... if we want to grant it the power of speaking of other things'.[45]

Schiller had pointed out that poetry and painting have an indefinable ('unendlich') 'possible content' alongside their more specific ('endlich') 'express meaning'; but music in particular was seen as embodying 'das Flüssige' and 'das Unendliche'. Schumann copied out Novalis' aphorism that 'music [is] the fluid given shape', and 'Pater' Kircher's description of music as 'an inexhaustible ocean'. He probably knew Tieck's comparison of music to 'a fine, fluid element', and himself contrasted it as a 'fluid, indefinable element' ('flüssigen, unendlichen Element') with the fixity of words; in music 'otherwise solid objects appear strange'.[46] He noted Rochlitz's aphorisms about 'music extending the delimited to the undelimited', and 'spiritualising the material', in contrast to the plastic arts.[47]

Obscurity, exaggeration and mythology may linger in this cluster of notions; but music can indeed be seen as fluid in a rich variety of senses. It is, of course, essentially transient, and sometimes music sucks from that aspect of its fluidity a poignancy unparalleled perhaps in any other art form. Language may in some kinds of use consist of discrete, rule-bound and arbitrary signifiers; music by contrast involves features that are not finally separable one from another, but interact elusively in a multidimensional flow. Its potential expressiveness is inherent but allergic to definitive specifications of either 'sign' or 'signified': for 'form' and 'content', expressiveness and resonance flow one into another. Some uses of language, especially in some kinds of poetry, also have some of these characteristics; but some music has them to a greater degree and more nearly as an essential characteristic. Schumann's 'Hoffmann works' exploit music's fluidity in several senses; at their most successful, as in *Kreisleriana*, it seems to me, form and content flow into one another virtually inseparably, and so too do the contributions of parallels of form and content to their literary connection and its aesthetic impact.

---

[45] Novalis, *Schriften*, II 672. Scott Burnham, 'How Music Matters', 215.

[46] Schiller, *Über Matthissons Gedichte*, 1794 (*Sämtliche Werke*, V 698); 'Die Sculptur ist das gebildete Starre, die Musik das gebildete Flüssige', Novalis, *Schriften*, V 229(fr. 232) (*Mottosammlung*, IX 188); 'oceanus inexhaustus': *Mottosammlung*, IX 258 (from Müller, *Wissenschaft der Tonkunst*, Leipzig, 1830); Tieck, 'Die Töne', 272; *GSK*, I 110, 250.

[47] *Mottosammlung*, IX 285; Franz Brendel used similar concepts as the basis for his contrast between the 'objective' Mendelssohn and the 'subjective' Schumann: 'Robert Schumann' (1845), 64 (Appendix 3–4(d)).

The first three pieces in Schumann's 1839 *Nachtstücke*, to which the next chapter turns, are the opposite of fluid: they take on the characteristically antinomian challenge of making music seem bald and hard edged. This work is the antimatter of his aesthetics in more ways than one. Its conception is no less strong than that of *Kreisleriana*, but it may be less appealing.

9 | Antimatter, 1839–1840
Nachtstücke, *op. 23*

One tendency in Schumann's output of 1839 was to music simpler in structure than before, and less demanding in conception, if imaginative and sometimes elaborate in detail: local colour replacing poetic threads. Looking back in 1839 he saw progressive 'softening and lightening'.[1] On 4 April, Clara Wieck, pushing him in directions in which he was already going, begged him to write something that 'is easily understandable, and has no titles, but is a complete and coherent piece'.[2] Admittedly, the *Four Pieces*, op. 32, and *Drei Romanzen*, op. 28, contain experimental elements; but the *Arabesque* and *Blumenstück*, opp. 18 and 19, are relatively straightforward; and the *Fachingsschwank aus Wien*, op. 26, unlike its near namesake, *Carnaval*, has no esoteric titles, no fleeting short pieces, and little that challenges the listener to search for threads, musical or poetic.

The *Humoreske*, op. 20, composed in early 1839, is plain in some ways, and relatively expansive, but subtle, and full of 'import', Schumann said.[3] Schumann inscribed in his *Brautbuch* a version of the B flat major opening: an exquisite, balanced duet, integrated with a passage (bars 28–36) in the rhythms of a speaking voice. The upbeat to the theme is F♯, and bars 8ff shift to G flat major, while the final cadence figures a G♭. The tonality of B flat major thus inflected with ♭VI remains associated with the memory of the duet throughout the work: it recurs in colours of ♭VI, and in G flat major music, inserted into B flat major passages or cadences. Despite these tonal reminiscences, and despite a dense network of motivic affinities throughout the work, that exquisite texture of duet integrated with prose rhythms is not recovered after its return to complete the first section in bars 239–50 (though there are approaches towards it, for instance in bars 667–74 and 683–92). The B flat major 'In Conclusion' (bars 861–end) has the familiar Schumannesque rhythms of poetic monologue, but little texture of duet; and its ♭III colour is no more than a residue of the ♭VI of

---

[1] *Neue Folge*, 150 (15 March 1839: 'immer leichter und weicher') and 197 (28 September 1840, seeing the change as evident in op. 15, though he saw that as 'mere Bagatelles': 'heiterer, weicher, melodischer'), and *Briefwechsel*, I 100 (11 February 1838). Compare Koßmaly, 'Schumann's Claviercompositionen', (1844), 20 and Newcomb, 'Schumann and the Marketplace', 266–8.
[2] *Briefwechsel*, II 469 (4 April 1839).   [3] *Neue Folge*, 167 and 169 (11 and 15 August 1839).

the opening. The work, that is, sets up a yearning for the tonality and fulfilment of the opening duet, which remains a presence precisely through its absence.

Meanwhile, the G minor themes of the second and third sections (bars 251–513 and 514–642), their tonality foreshadowed by the F# of the duet's upbeat, are expressive of something like emptiness – as symbolised by the missing 'inner voice' in the second section. And several B flat major passages have an air of parody, or of the trivial or futile;[4] while a regularity that sometimes seems mechanical is contrasted with irregular phrase lengths of declamation, oratorical or hesitant. Thus the B flat major in which the first and last main sections (bars 1–250, and 643–964) open and close, and to which the work often reverts, progressively acquires an association of the ordinary; it is not dramatised as a potentially satisfying end-point.

Is that a context in which to read what seems to me the puzzle of the final section? Its formal structure and trajectory are unclear;[5] it opens and closes in B flat major, but seems unable to reach a satisfactory cadence in that key, despite a V pedal in bars 797–805, repeated attempts after bar 861, and an emphasis on the subdominant – until the last twelve bars impose a final and perhaps peremptory flourish. If Schumann uses a range of musical means to undermine the ability of his tonic key to generate a satisfactory conclusion, as part of a pattern in which fulfilment is suggested at the opening, but then withdrawn and never recovered, the work may join other Schumann masterpieces of the late 1830s, opp. 17, 6 and 16, in their substitution of their own tonal and aesthetic conception for patterns characteristic of a classical style.

Though the *Nachtstücke*, op. 23, composed in the months after the *Humoreske*, exploits the mechanical and the empty even more starkly, it is not radical in the same way. What makes it an outlier in Schumann's oeuvre is partly that simplification and lightening are pushed to the point of a plainness that baffles.

Schumann's diary for early April 1839 records that he was 'writing a Corpse Fantasy [*Leichenfantasie*] – how remarkable my premonitions were'.[6] His brother Eduard was about to die, as Schumann explained to Clara Wieck on 7 April:

---

[4] Such words are used in Appel, 'Schumanns Humoreske' (281–2, 289, 291–4, 325–6, on bars 89ff, 322–33, and especially 550–614), and Schumann, *Humoreske*, ed. Köhler (45, on bars 104ff, 191ff, 358ff, 693ff and 833ff).
[5] See the summary of previous interpretations in Appel, 'Schumanns Humoreske', 298ff.
[6] *Tagebücher*, II 89.

I don't have much [hope], and yet I can't believe that Eduard could be dead. I'd written to you about a premonition; I had it between 24 and 27 March as I was working on my new composition; there's a passage there that I kept coming back to – where it is as though someone were weighed down with sorrow and groaning 'Oh God' – as I composed I kept on seeing funeral processions, coffins, lost despairing people, and when I had finished and was long searching for a title, I always lit upon: *Corpse Fantasy*. Isn't that odd? As I was composing I was often so shaken that the tears poured out and I didn't know why and had no reason for it – and then came Therese's letter and it all became clear to me.[7]

Meanwhile the work's name had changed to *Nachtstücke*. Much of the composition probably took place well after Schumann hit on the new title, though we do not know how much. In November he was 'putting the set in order', which must have involved selecting, ordering and altering the pieces, and probably new composition – in December he apparently envisaged three pieces, in January four. At some stage, one piece was removed and later used in the *Faschingsschwank*.[8] Then on 7 January 1840 he consulted Clara about giving the individual pieces their own titles:

1. Trauerzug [Funeral procession]
2. Curiose Gesellschaft [Weird company]
3. Nächtliches Gelage [Nocturnal revels]
4. Rundgesang mit Solostimmen [Roundelay with solo voices].[9]

Clara, however, advised against, and Schumann dropped the idea.

The connection between the music and the rejected titles of the second and third pieces needs clarification; and 'Corpse Fantasy' fits the first piece, but not the third or fourth, nor in any obvious sense the second. Moreover, the work seems to repel appreciation and interpretation: Clara predicted, 'the public won't know what you mean by it, and will stumble over it'.[10] Schumann may have intended it so. He praised Chopin's Preludes in 1838 as containing 'the diseased, feverish and repellent' ('Abstoβendes'), for the repellent in life may be attractive in art, he said; and in 1841 he saw something 'repellent' in the funeral march in Chopin's Sonata op. 35.[11] Schumann's composition is bare of the charm, extravagance and sense of imaginative freedom typical of his oeuvre: all four pieces are rondos, and

---

[7] *Briefwechsel*, II 473–4 (7 April 1839).
[8] *Briefwechsel*, II 801 (24 November); *Neue Folge*, 175 (11 December 1840); *GSK*, II 471 note 577; *Tagebücher*, II 494, note 332. *Briefwechsel*, III 845–81 (3–20 January 1840) reveals other aspects of the revision process.
[9] *Briefwechsel*, III 877 (17 January 1840).   [10] *Briefedition*, I/6 540 (19 January 1840).
[11] *GSK*, I 418; II 12, 14.

the first three are rondos of a particular plainness.[12] They share a markedly bald style compared with the variety of forms and linear complexity deployed with such mastery in Kreisleriana. Their major-key refrains are dominated by thematically austere and rhythmically hard-edged phrases, with block chords in largely parallel movement, and little of Schumann's characteristic suppleness and fluidity. The expressive contrast with the episodes is striking; and while the refrains normally reach firm conclusions, creating self-contained units, episodes end in drift, without a cadence in their starting key, and are cut off by the returning refrain. And the repetitions of the refrain are rigidly unvarying, with little development, and virtually no responsiveness between episodes and refrain. Together these factors contribute to a character quite different from that of other rondos.

Thus the work turns to his own purposes a formal property that Schumann's criticism scorned. He lambasted the rondos of his day, issued in industrial quantities: 'boxed between two planks, one stands at the end of the world, and can move neither forward nor backward'; 'moving in a small circle of thoughts'.[13] These stark criticisms of others' works, paradoxically, are a clue to the conception of his own. Intriguingly, they echo passages from Karl Philipp Moritz's *Anton Reiser. Ein Psychologischer Roman* (1785–90). This novel describes a 'labyrinth' out of which the protagonist 'finds no way', a 'plank wall' 'that cut off any further view', his thoughts 'turning in a circle', 'fixated and confined within himself'. In a scene ironically described as 'ein schönes Nachtstück', Reiser tramps obsessively across the fields in the gloom and stops in a churchyard: 'the end of all things seemed to him to lead to just such a point – the stiflingly narrow coffin was the last thing – behind this was nothing further – here was the nailed-up plank wall'.[14] In Moritz, parataxis, tautology and repetition of symbols (circles, labyrinths, walls) express obsession and claustrophobia; his book is shaped by relentless cycles of self-destructive abnegation. The

---

[12] The piece displaced to the *Faschingsschwank* is not a rondo, and was perhaps too impassioned to remain here.

[13] *GSK*, I 291–4 (1837) ('zwischen zwei Brettern eingeklemmt steht man am Ende der Welt und kann weder vor noch zurück'; 'bewegt es sich in einem kleinen Zirkel von Gedanken').

[14] Moritz, *Werke*, I 341, 216 ('wie eine bretterne Wand ... seine weitere Aussicht schloß'), 231 ('und sich alles so im Zirkel drehte'), 224 ('in sich eingeengt und eingebannt'), 306, 303 ('das Ende aller Dinge schien ihm in solch eine Spitze hinauszulaufen – der enge dumpfe Sarg war das letzte – hierhinter war nun nichts weiter – hier war die zugenagelte Bretterwand – die jedem Sterblichen den ferneren Blick versagt'). Schumann knew some of Moritz's work: *Tagebücher*, I 415 (1832).

Example 9.1a: Schumann, *Nachtstücke*, i, bars 1–4

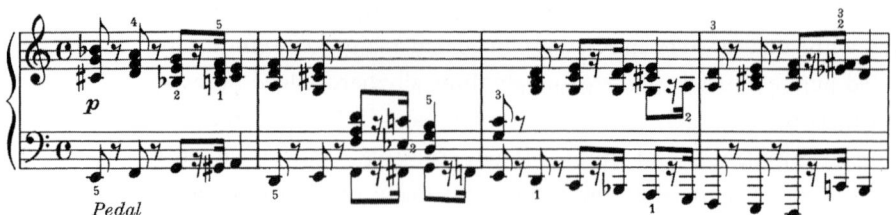

Example 9.1b: Schumann, *Nachtstücke*, ii, bars 1–4

Example 9.1c: Schumann, *Nachtstücke*, iii, bars 1–8

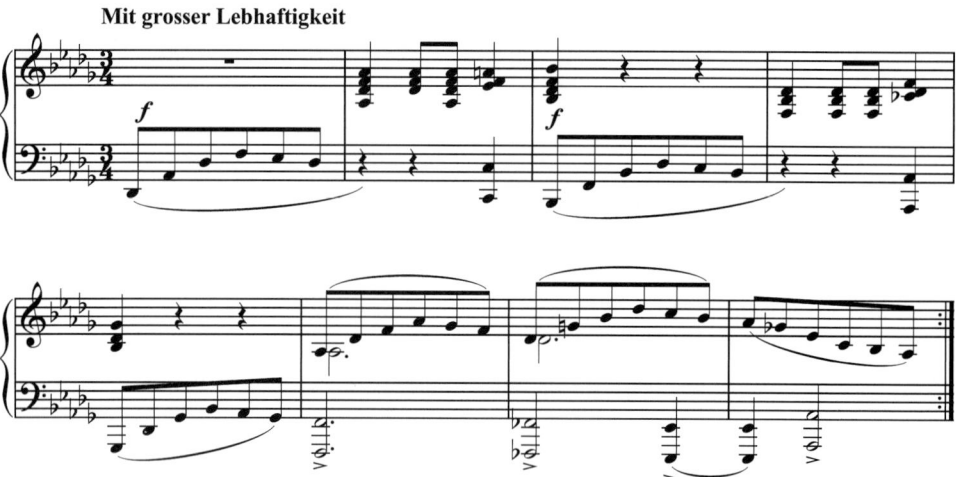

first three rondos of Schumann's *Nachtstücke* are similarly obsessive, or claustrophobic, and their refrains return as relentlessly: the limitations his criticism scorned become a source of the work's unity, individuality and shape.

The work is constructed from minimal musical material: above all, perhaps, scalar descents and semitone slides. The first two pieces open with phrases built on descending scales, both sliding at the bottom by a semitone, and both reascending to $\hat{5}$, with contrary movement in the bass (Examples 9.1a–b); in the third piece, the descending scale, with a semitone slide at the bottom, forms the bass of the opening bars (Example 9.1c), and climbs back up at 26–8.[15] Though the melodic material of the last piece is different, it too has distant echoes of descending scales and semitone slides, and its dotted rhythm is a transformation of the dotted march of the opening piece.[16]

In the first three pieces, transitions between refrain and episode sometimes exploit semitones for the work's most dramatic tonal shifts: from C to D♭ for the shift from C major to G flat major in bars 48–50 of the first piece, and again, with an octave displacement, for that from F major to A flat major in bars 22–3 of the second (Example 9.7); and from E♮ and A♮ to E♭ and A♭ for the switch from A major to D flat major in bars 211–13 of the third. Only as the last piece opens (bars 1–2) are these flatward lurches reversed, as a *forte* bass D♭ at the end of the third blossoms into a *piano* bass C. Tonally the last three pieces are united by a pattern of contrasts between F major and D flat major, leaving the C major of the opening piece appearing as the dominant of F major; and the close link between these tonal developments and the limited thematic material contributes to the work's tight musical form and overall shape. The first three pieces set up an interplay between A♮ and A♭ (and especially a♮^{1} and a♭^{1}) only resolved when the last piece brings a satisfyingly concluding F major cadence, albeit with a coda shadowed by D flat harmonies.

Relationships in the first three pieces between the hard-edged melodies and rhythms of the repeated refrains and the more pliable legato episodes can be understood through ideas from a wider culture. Where the second piece, for instance, deploys musical features that are markedly mechanical, literature, including Hoffmann, can help by showing how ideas like those of the mechanical automaton and the robotic puppet, opposed to living humanity, acted as symbols in musical criticism and psychological fictions; and such lines of thought help to make sense of connections between musical features across the four pieces.[17]

---

[15] Similar material infects bars 9ff, 48ff and (in truncated form) 89ff in the first piece, and the first and second episodes in the second (where there are semitone slides in bars 30, 35, 46–7, 74, etc.). In the third piece, the second episode has variants of the descending and ascending scales.

[16] The accompaniments to the first and second episodes sink down scales (bars 10–12, 22–3, etc.), and there are semitone slides in bars 2–4, etc. The rhythmic relationship is explored in Watkins, *Metaphors of Depth*, 108–13.

[17] In summer 1840 Schumann's acquaintance, Franz Brendel, was awarded a degree for a psychiatric dissertation on somnambulism, and Schumann in recognition took the opportunity to send him a copy of his *Nachtstücke* (*Briefedition*, II/5 213): perhaps Schumann could see his work in the light of a nexus of notions surrounding the psychology of automatism.

The work's title, *Nachtstücke*, helps guide a listener towards such interpretive contexts. For although in music the word could simply be a variant of 'Notturno', its connotations were not confined to gentle romance. Schumann wrote approvingly in 1838 that in Kahlert's set one could 'find more distinctive states of mind than in run-of-the-mill notturnos'.[18] In the visual arts the term characterised for instance Salvator Rosa's gothic images. In literature, Jean Paul applied it to menacing scenes as to idyllic. He put the 'Nachtstück' near the heart of the aesthetic of the time, speculating that Christian Europe opened an imaginative gulf between concrete objectivity and illimitable perspectives where endless possibilities of terror lurked.[19] Hoffmann used the title *Nachtstücke* for a collection of stories published in 1816–17 in which the perils of the mind loom large. Much of German literature had already explored self-destructive psychoses. In 1782–3 Karl Philipp Moritz had compiled case histories of psychological aberrations; his *Anton Reiser* is in part the autobiography of someone blighted by self-contempt. Achim von Arnim's *Hollinsliebeleben* (1802) and Jean Paul's *Titan* (1800–3) feature similarly self-destructive characters. In Tieck's 'Liebeszauber' (1811) dark forces combine with psychosis to destroy the hero, and in 'Der Runenberg' (1802) and 'Der Pokal' (1811), imaginative suggestibility becomes enthralment to a fantasy that takes over, shapes and perhaps destroys life. Similar themes emerge, with a distinctive twist, in stories written by Heinrich von Kleist around 1810, which influenced Hoffmann's *Nachtstücke*.[20] Even Goethe's *Wilhelm Meister*, emblem of the genre of the *Bildungsroman* in which a hero grows to fruitful maturity, deals in part in such self-destructive syndromes. The *Nachtwachen von Bonaventura* (1804), with its bitterly satirical portrayal of descent into madness and devilry, inverts the normal trajectory and wholesome conventions of the *Bildungsroman*; its exposure of the terrifying loneliness of the subjective self parodies the dominant Idealism of Fichte and Schelling.[21] There is no evidence that the book was to Schumann's taste, but its images of chillingly robotic or deathly figures, and of young women condemned to death or madness (*Nachtwachen* V, III, X and XIV), may haunt Hoffmann's *Nachtstücke*, and may be relevant to Schumann's too.

[18] *GSK*, I 188 and 366.
[19] Jean Paul, *Vorschule*, §§5 and 22 (about Ossian); *Titan* (1st, 122nd & 139th Cycles); *Die unsichtbare Loge* (49th Sektor); *Vorschule*, §24 (terror).
[20] *Die Serapions-Brüder*, 1049. Schumann's interest in Kleist is not evidenced until 1839 (*Briefwechsel*, II 360, 19 January) and later (*Tagebücher*, II 431, 436).
[21] 'Das ist ja schrecklich einsam hier im Ich': *Nachtwachen*, X (120). Compare Goethe's 'hohles, leeres Ich': 'Ich sehe nichts vor mir, nichts hinter mir ... als eine unendliche Nacht, in der ich mich in der schrecklichsten Einsamkeit befinde': *Wilhelm Meister*, VII/4 (*Werke*, IV 390).

Thus the title of Hoffmann's book, borrowed by Schumann, brings apt connotations. It would be possible, moreover, to trace quasi-formal parallels. Each of the two halves of Hoffmann's book contains four stories, the first three describing repetitions that seem compulsive, nightmarish, relentless or accursed; only in the last story in each half does repetition bring release. Likewise, Schumann's first three rondos are plain, ironic, mechanical and relentless; only the last piece brings repetition imbued with human warmth. There may be moments or even sequences of scene-painting as well; but the work's musical conception is strong enough not to need the support of a programmatic schema. Both programmatic and formal connections appear to me more powerful when seen as fused, and as consequences of resonances between Schumann's musical conception and ideas from his world.

The evidence that the composition of what became Schumann's op. 23 was influenced at an early stage by premonitions of his brother's impending death cannot be dismissed. But nor can the music in its final form be taken simply as a response: its irony remains uncomfortably dissonant. Whatever the role of Eduard's death in the compositional process, I would not take the final work as presenting autobiography. Nevertheless, Schumann himself said that what 'goes on in the world' finds 'outlets' in his music;[22] and awareness of what was on his mind may give some reassurance that psychological progressions that can be found in the music are ones with which he might plausibly have been concerned then. In summer 1839 Schumann felt 'cut off from every poetic dimension' – so different from his confidence in early March – and these concentrated, stark *Nachtstücke* are the antimatter of the 'Romantic' or 'poetic'.[23]

i: 'Trauerzug' ['Funeral Procession']

If Schumann's first piece is a funeral procession, something is awry. A funeral march, like the slow movements of Beethoven's Sonata, op. 26 or Chopin's Sonata, op. 35, characteristically opens in slow common time with a regular metre, a dotted rhythm, a low register, an unambiguous minor mode, and a melody in a narrow range. A consistently restrained and sombre tone may be confirmed by repetition, and perhaps by a brief

---

[22] *Briefwechsel*, I 146 (16 April 1838).
[23] *Briefwechsel*, II 659 (23 July); contrast *Neue Folge*, 150 of 15 March: 'sogar manchmal ist es mir, als könnte ich immerfort spielen und nie zu Ende kommen'.

Example 9.2: Chopin, C minor Prelude, op. 28, bars 1–4

Example 9.3: Schumann, *Nachtstücke*, i, bars 1–9

breakthrough into a higher register or a major key. Other pieces, though not quite funeral marches, such as Chopin's C minor Prelude, op. 28, may adopt these features even if only to subject them to an unusual twist (Example 9.2).

Schumann's piece likewise has a slow march time, low register and regular four-bar phrases; its rhythm and melody resemble Chopin's (Example 9.3). But anomalous features disturb the funereal tone:[24] a lightness or hollowness to the texture; jarring tritones in the first, third and fourth chords of the first bar; an unsettled tonality (alternate bars highlight A so as to suggest D minor, with a weak C major cadence only in bar 8); and a perhaps obsessive repetition in six of seven consecutive bars of the same rhythm, stepwise pattern in the soprano and contrary motion in the bass. The marking 'oft zurückhaltend', 'often holding back', suggests not the respectful evenness of pace of a funeral cortège but something more complex. The *piano* descent of

---

[24] Contrast the more evenly dark treatment of a similar musical idea – albeit in triple time – in the 1835 'Leides Ahnung'; or the second piece of *Albumblätter*, op 124; or the accompaniment to the thirteenth song of op. 48.

Example 9.4: Schumann, *Nachtstücke*, i, bars 49–60

the bass in bars 3–4 opens a registral space into which the octave doubling in the bass of bars 5–7 lurches, *mezzo forte*, like an invading nightmare. These features connive to leave hints of the sinister, ironic, trite, grotesque and leering: if it is close to the heart of the classical rondo that tonic reappearances of the refrain ground or relax the form, Schumann has in a characteristic antinomy presented a march whose reappearances are more likely a source of dread and confusion.

Bars 9–16 could be taken as either the middle section of a ternary rondo theme, or as a first episode. They treat the same basic material – dotted rhythm, stepwise descent, contrary motion in the bass – as in the march, but with an unambiguous G major, and a lilting legato movement.[25] Any reassurance dissolves, however, when from bars 12–13 the music is repeated in A minor, and drifts further in 16 to a chord of E minor. An episode in bars 25–40 begins in A minor, sounding more like a real funeral march, as though to ground the uncertainty of the opening.[26] But the impetus gets lost in repetitiveness, harmonic drift and metrical displacement and confusion (bars 33–4, and 35–6 and 39–40). The next episode is very different. A held bass octave on C (bar 48) brings, as if from far away (*piano*, and in a remote key that turns out to be G flat major), a simple, barely harmonised descent (Example 9.4).

---

[25] Compare Watkins, *Metaphors of Depth*, 109–11.
[26] Here if anywhere one might hear the 'Choral von Posaunen' which Schumann said he had heard at the moment of his brother's death: *Briefwechsel*, II 478 (10 April 1839).

Its largely even crotchets, ending with a rising fourth and falling fifth, its imitation in the bass and its sixfold repetition of the same motif in different keys, all suggest peals of bells. The peal repeats in C flat major, and in D, followed by G and C, and recedes to *pianissimo*. Those dynamics and shifting tonalities might suggest increasing remoteness, perhaps even something alien; but the descent by fifths to C suggests a return 'home', and the descending scale is related to that of the march – to which it indeed returns.

What returns in this rondo is normally only the eight-bar march-refrain, which thus appears six times – an unusual frequency for a rondo of this length. And the march is almost unaltered on the first four reappearances, making no concession to the intervening music. But each moment of return seems different, partly because of the different tonalities on which it intrudes: menacing at bar 17 (as the exposed bass E on the downbeat draws attention to the bass line and the possibility of E minor prepared by the previous bar), relentless at bar 41 (with D minor prepared by its dominant), and a willed or compulsive repetition at bar 72 (as the march enters early, and pauses as though to be invited back).

Bars 81–8 develop the material of bars 9–10, with the same lilting *legato* and the same relative harmonic normality, as though at last a recapitulation of the middle section of the rondo theme, now in the tonic C major. That sets up an expectation – by now perhaps dread – that the march must again follow it; but the *forte* dynamic, home key, and emphatic and repeated descent to $\hat{1}$ (bars 82 and 84) suggest that the piece might yet resolve reassuringly. When the march nonetheless returns at bar 89, with an accented organ point on G, its grip is unchallenged, and for the first time its final cadence (bar 96) does not seem weak. Suddenly it expands, both in time and in apparent space. The second half of the march had jumped up in the last chords of bars 93 and 94, which in retrospect foreshadowed an unexpected leap in the upper part of 96–7 to beyond the range the march has reached before; the harmony slides to the classically unrelated key of B flat major for two bars (97–8): over a sustained bass octave a mutation of the main theme swings in phrases suddenly twice the expected length, with a high fanfare stretching the registral space (Example 9.5).

The march has swollen to nightmare proportions. But the mood immediately changes again. Though bars 104–5 start with the low E and diminished chord associated with each return of the march, as though to begin all over again, bars 105–6 instead invert the gestures of bars 9–10 and 81ff to

Example 9.5: Schumann, *Nachtstücke*, i, bars 93–100

become a neat cadence on I: it sounds glib after what has gone before.[27] The music ends in deflation. The march, one of its notes missing in each bar, disappears into the distance: in the last four bars, the holes in the upper part leave the semitone slides in the bass more exposed, and the pause before the final *pianissimo* chord is long. The tone remains unreadable. The coda beginning at bar 96 does not bracket off, frame or confirm something already concluded by then; instead it extends fear and ambivalence into the frame.

The spectre of death tainted 1839 for Schumann. His letters to Clara are full of fears that she or he might die of an illness or accident before they overcame her father's attempts to block their marriage; Clara reflected similar fears back to him. She dreamed she died, and from her bier heard bells 'sounding of heaven and horror' ('himmlisch' and 'schauerlich'). In April he wrote to her of Agnes Carus, whom he had loved: 'Now she's dead. One after another they go. What about us in ten years' time?' He awoke on

---

[27] The phrase repeats from bar 107, launched this time from a German augmented sixth. In his own copy of the first edition, Schumann annotated bar 105 with the same chord: Schumann, *Nachtstücke*, 21. This highlights questions about Schumann's compositional practice. It has often been said – rightly in my view – that Schumann characteristically experimented with different versions of a work up to and after 'final' versions were sent to a printer or published: see for instance Roesner, 'The Sources for Schumann's *Davidsbündlertänze*', 62. A possibility is that one purpose was to try out expressive variants. Thus the augmented sixth chord may bring out something like glibness; but does it do so more, or arguably less, if it appears in bar 105 as well? Or should we hear it as injecting common-sense deflation, or leering mockery, or ironic trivialisation?

his birthday in June to the sense of 'peals of inner bells'. But in the same letter he wrote about a pianist's fiancée who drowned herself in a river, and he fretted about a similar rupture of his own engagement. Later he transcribed Henriette Voigt's last diaries, describing them as 'heavy with premonition'.[28] She died that October. In July he gave Clara a description of 'an extraordinary day':

Ich kann kaum mehr beten, so bin ich vom Schmerz niedergebeugt und verstokt. Ich habe doch eine große Schuld auf mir, daß ich Dich von Deinem V. getrennt habe – und dies foltert mich oft ... Da war ein sonderbarer Tag der vorgestrige, einer wo alle Lebenslinien [sich] wie in einem Knäuel zusammen zu laufen schienen. Der Tag war so gespenstisch still, der Himmel ganz weiß umflort; ich sah oft Särge tragen, kam *zufällig* an der Thomaskirche vorbei, hörte Orgel darin, ging herein, da war eben ein Paar getraut worden. Der Altar war mit Blumen überschüttet. Ich stürzte fort. Früh, nachdem ich das Schreiben an das Gericht eingereicht habe, begegne ich *zufällig* Voigt; er bittet mich, seine Frau zu besuchen, die morgen in ein Bad abreiste. Abends geh' ich *zufällig* an Voigts Haus vorbei, denke an die Frau, geh hinauf; sie wird wohl nicht wieder zurückkommen; sie gibt mir noch einen [ein]gedrückten Brief, darin steht die Todesanzeige von Ernestinens Mann, der im 25sten Jahr gestorben – denke Dir das Unglück für Ernestine – mir schwindelte – ich nahm von der Voigt Abschied wie man von einer Sterbenden nimmt – als ich Abends zu Hause ging, rasselt auf einmal der Leichenwagen im Flug an mir vorbei. Welcher Tag – aber die Nacht schlief ich ruhig. Daß ich es gegen Dich aussprechen kann, erleichtert mich auch, denn sonst bin ich jetzt so scheu, so schrecksam, daß ich allen Freunden ausweiche. Auch besuchen mich wenige; sie wißen vielleicht wie mir zu Muthe ist.

I can scarcely pray any more, I'm so oppressed ... by anguish. I'm burdened with the huge guilt that I've separated you from your father – and that often tortures me ... It was a day of such ghostly quiet ... I kept seeing coffins being carried, walked *by chance* past the Thomaskirche, heard an organ, went in, and there a couple had just been married. The altar was covered with flowers. I hurried out ... [Later] I meet Voigt *by chance*; he asks me to visit his wife who is going away to a spa tomorrow. In the evening I walk *by chance* past Voigt's house, remember his wife, go up; she doesn't look as if she'll be coming back; she gives me a ... letter, and in it is the announcement of Ernestine's husband's death, aged 25 – think of the blow to Ernestine – made me feel faint – I parted from Voigt's wife as from one on her deathbed – as I was going home that evening, suddenly the hearse flies rattling past me.

---

[28] *Briefwechsel*, II 368–9 (26 January), 438 (11 March), 474 (7 April), 479 (10 April), 488 (17 April, Agnes Carus), 492, 496 (21–2 April), 558 and 563 (9 June), 657 (23 July); Clara's dream and fears: II 387 (14 February), 420 (28 February), 483 (13 April), 592 (24 June); *GSK*, I 451.

It was a day 'where all the threads of life seemed to run together as if into one ball', by which I suppose Schumann meant something like the wasting of couples' love through death. It is understandable that his state of mind was 'fearful' and 'uncanny' ('unheimlich').[29]

Indeed, Schumann's state anticipates Freud's 1919 characterisation of the uncanny. In wandering around a strange town in Italy Freud became disoriented and found himself in a sinister quarter; trying to leave it, he repeatedly found himself arriving back there, rather as Schumann found himself once more confronting the coffins. As Schumann emphasised 'by chance', as though some part of him doubted it, so Freud interpreted his experience as 'uncanny' – an experience where 'the familiar is made strange'. In experiencing the uncanny, 'the distinction between imagination and reality is effaced', 'something actually happens in our lives which seems to confirm the old discarded beliefs' of superstitious fear, and 'the compulsion to repeat ... lend[s] to certain aspects of the mind their demonic character'. Similarly, Freud once claimed to begin 'to notice that everything with a number — addresses, hotel rooms, compartments in railway trains — invariably has the same one,' '62'. Feeling this to be 'uncanny', he was tempted to see in this 'obstinate recurrence' an omen of death at that age – the age at which he was writing.[30]

Schumann's piece, with its 'obstinate recurrences' and effacement of 'the distinction between imagination and reality', seems similarly to explore the 'compulsion to repeat' and the uncanny. Freud's essay makes no reference to Schumann. But mention of Freud here is neither a mere anachronism, nor is it to claim Schumann's work as a startling – or uncanny – pre-echo of Freud's description. Instead the ways in which Schumann foreshadows Freud reflect both the capacity of each for diagnosing common fears, and the role played in the cultural hinterland of each by 'Der Sandmann', the opening tale of Hoffmann's *Nachtstücke*.

For Freud, 'the uncanny in literature is a much more fertile province than the uncanny in real life', especially where the author 'promises to give us the sober truth, and starts from common reality, and then oversteps it', or 'keeps us in the dark about the presuppositions on which the world he writes about is based'. The work he cites as an archetype of the uncanny is 'Der Sandmann'.[31] That story tells of Nathanael's nightmare sense of being

---

[29] *Briefwechsel*, II 649, 651 (18 July 1839): 'Denn in meinem Kopf sieht es unheimlich aus und ich fürchte mich bei hellem lichten Tag, daß mich alles erschrickt.'
[30] Freud, 'Das Unheimliche', 259–61, 267.
[31] Ibid., 271–3, 251. Prawer, 'Hoffmann's Uncanny Guest', 302, prefers a more Jungian interpretation.

stalked by Coppelius, whom he identifies with the sandman of fable. It describes his shifting, bewildered reaction, and his doomed attempts to escape. The young student Nathanael recalls his childhood terrors:

> 'The sandman is coming'; and I really heard then a heavy slow step clump up the stairs ... Through the hall it went with a slow heavy thudding tread towards the stairs ... Closer, ever closer thudded the steps ... my heart shook with fear.

Nathanael's mother had offered him a reassuring version of the fairy tale of the sandman, while his nurse had scared him with the macabre version in which the sandman plucks out children's eyes. But Coppelius had indeed been a harbinger of death – literally for Nathanael's father, and almost for the child Nathanael too. Now the student Nathanael again heard Coppelius, or someone like him, clump up the stairs, bringing, as Nathanael described it to his fiancée Clara, 'dark premonitions of a terrible fate'. The sensible Clara responded:

> To my mind all the horror and terror you speak of only occurs inside you, and the real outside world probably plays no part in it ... If there's a dark power ... it is the phantom of our own self ... Your Father probably brought death on himself ... and Coppelius is not responsible. If every line of your letter didn't declare the depths of your mental unrest, I'd honestly have to laugh at the story of the sandman ... and Coppelius.[32]

Coppelius however stalked Nathanael again. On the last occasion, he grew suddenly to 'giant stature';[33] and under his nightmare spell, Nathanael leapt over a parapet:

> As he lay on the pavement, his skull shattered, Coppelius melted away in the throng ...
>
> Several years later there was a report that Clara had been seen in a distant place, sitting hand in hand with a benign husband before the door of a nice country house, watching two happy boys at play. It would be reasonable to conclude that Clara found that restful domestic bliss, suited to her untroubled fun-loving nature, which could never have been secured for her by Nathanael's fractured self.

Nathanael's story can be seen as a series of compulsive re-enactments of the childhood nightmare in his father's study when the sandman tore him apart – re-enactments such as Freud sees as a substitute for addressing the trauma. Through this compulsion, Nathanael destroyed both his prospect of marriage to Clara and his own self.

---

[32] Hoffmann, *Nachtstücke*, 331–4, 339–41.   [33] Ibid., 361–3.

The tale withholds any hierarchy or reconciliation between different perspectives, so that the reader remains uncertain whether to see the approach of Coppelius through Nathanael's terror, his mother's reassurances, the old crone's spooky version, or Clara's sensible mockery. And the end derails what should have been Nathanael's happy reunion with Clara not only through his renewed madness and then death, but also – in the final paragraph about Clara's ultimate domestic bliss – through an ironic belittling of all that has gone before. A reader may even toy with the suspicion that a manipulative narrator, seemingly in love with Clara, may also have been an actor in his history, exploiting Nathanael's destruction in order to win her. If so, the uncanny, far from being just part of the story we have read, invades the level of narration, as Freud noted, and thus the level at which we read – it infects our world. If a part of the ordinary world has been infiltrated, becoming alien and inscrutable, perhaps the entire fabric of familiar security is in fact radically alien and hostile.[34] The tale's ambivalence is insidious.

Schumann's music is equally ambivalent. The refrain may suggest the tramp of death, the irony of a satirist, or the leer of a nightmare, and the episodes can be seen as labile reactions to this ambivalence. Other musical features too can be diagnosed in terms of syndromes – including multiple perspectives, compulsion, alienation, hollowness and a breached frame – which the early Romantics elaborated and the twentieth century made its own. Such syndromes are exemplified in 'Der Sandmann'. Just as no single interpretive voice settles whether Nathanael is trapped by his own compulsions or by uncanny forces, so Schumann's excessive repetition of a death-tramp may suggest contrary interpretations: one voice in one's head finds a rondo with six appearances of the march-refrain (in the same key and until bar 101 the same register) compulsive, and sees the piece in terms of death and nightmare; a counter-voice (the voice of the episodes, perhaps) insists that this is an over-interpretation, as repetition does not make a march obsessive; and yet a third voice responds that exactly that oscillation between irrationality and common sense, or imagination and dullness, or emotional engagement and alienation, is what Schumann manipulates in order to convey the sense of neurosis and of the uncanny. At the point in bars 97–100 where the main march is fleetingly swollen to giant stature, the listener is tempted half to share its nightmare exultation, as Nathanael fell once again under the spell of the

---

[34] Hoffmann might have noted such a self-reflexive magnification of the power of the uncanny in Tieck's 'Der Blonde Eckbert' of 1796–7; it has since become archetypal: for instance Susan Hill, *The Woman in Black*.

approaching Coppelius, now grown to giant proportions; and when the threatening tread melts into the distance (bars 109–12), as Coppelius melted away in the crowd, the contrary perspectives are unresolved, and we remain uncertain as to the object of the irony of bars 105–8. And again: the march acquires a certain hollowness as the ambivalent tone separates the musical signs of a funeral march from its mournful effects. Or finally, the frame that limits the imagination to its sphere is breached, as the march interrupts (at bar 89) what might have been a reassuring conclusion, and infiltrates the coda (bars 96ff), as though escaping from one level of narration to invade another.

Whether or not one finds scene-painting in the music, or narrative connections to Hoffmann, it is not difficult to imagine that Schumann in 1839 found Hoffmann's story disturbing.[35] The music presents neither Nathanael nor the sandman, and its rejected title was 'Trauerzug', not 'Sandmann'; but the presentiments of death that Schumann felt over several months in 1839, the confusion of his reaction, and experiences like his 'chance' encounters with coffins and weddings on that 'ghostly' day, could have meshed with Hoffmann's story and the wider culture, and found an outlet in this music.[36]

ii: 'Kuriose Gesellschaft' ('Weird Company')

The second piece juxtaposes apparently opposed natures. It opens with faceless regularity. The volume and texture are unvarying. Block chords moving in parallel reduce linear complexity to a minimum. The harmony changes on every quaver. Accents fall relentlessly on every beat. In a monotonous succession of short two-bar phrases, the melody descends and rises again, with regular cadences (Example 9.6).[37]

It is subjected to mechanistic development; it is repeated (bars 5–18). There is no give, but instead the charm of a jackhammer: a mechanical mimicry of life rather than life itself. Perhaps it parodies piano studies contrasted by Schumann in reviews of 1836–9 with living music: 'all that is mechanically lifeless' ('alles mechanisch Toten'), or 'simulacra of life' ('Scheinleben') as against 'pure poetic creation'.[38]

---

[35] Steinberg, 'Schumann's Homelessness', 68–9, notes parallels between Schumann's own situation and that of Nathanael and *his* Clara (without mentioning the *Nachtstücke*).

[36] *Anton Reiser* too features 'continual recurrences', confining emptiness and repeated affliction by trivial accidents: Moritz, *Werke*, 200–1, 301, 363, 385–6.

[37] With the same descending line, chordal texture and opening diminished 7th chord as the opening of the first piece: Moraal, 'Schumanns Nachtstücke', 78–9.

[38] *GSK*, I 289, 392, 215; compare 304, 389, 437–8 and II 135, 67; and Appel, 'Schumanns Humoreske', 293–4, on 'Automatismus' in the *Humoreske*.

Example 9.6: Schumann, *Nachtstücke*, ii, bars 1–4

Example 9.7: Schumann, *Nachtstücke*, ii, bars 20–8

A D♭ in the bass in bar 23 unseats the harmony, and the regular metre of the first 22 bars becomes a metrical swamp, out of which emerges in A flat major the theme of an episode (bars 25–65) (Example 9.7).

This *piano* music could not be more different from the loud opening. It is in the style of those pieces in which for Schumann 'the poet speaks': its halting, evolutionary style accentuates by contrast the robotic regularity of the opening material. It flows in unaccented legato quavers, a lilting dotted rhythm, and many layers.[39] It unfolds organically, as the upper motif evolves almost unnoticed, one strand growing from what came before (transforming bars 28–32, for instance, into 51–5). Phrase lengths are flexible and ambiguous, and the tone quixotic, with a sort of melancholy in its opening, and glimpses of humour in bars 37–8 and recitative in 45–7. The music is hesitant, with for instance ten markings of ritardando in forty bars; and its main, alto melody, unlike the opening theme, is unable to close, despite repeated attempts at

---

[39] In bars 25–8, for instance, the three main voices are subtly metrically apart, with a middle voice descending in quavers, an upper melody, such as it is, perhaps a crotchet ahead, and a lower voice perhaps five quavers behind.

Example 9.8: Schumann, *Nachtstücke*, ii, bars 71–7

cadences. And it is suggestible. Its material (bars 25ff), if opposed in character to that of the refrain, grows out of bars 20–1 and depends on 1ff, which the bass reproduces in bars 43–5; and cadences in bars 33–4 are seemingly influenced by 8–9 (or even by bar 8 of the first piece), and those in bars 57–9 by 18–21.

The piece is indeed a *Kuriose Gesellschaft* – an ill-matched coupling of the mechanical with a hesitant, human voice. The human voice turns out the weaker. Bars 62–3 replace $a\flat^1$ with $a\natural^1$; and a concise reprise of the refrain, starker for the omission of bars 5–18, sweeps the episode aside. A second episode in D flat major (bars 74–93) is like a robotic dance. It opens in a featureless rhythm with an unusual density of repeated notes in the inner parts, rather mechanical contrary motion between soprano and bass, and for melody little more than ascending and descending scales (Example 9.8).

In bars 80–1 a brief hesitation, with a cadential turn and *ritard.* (the sole expressive marking in this passage), both borrowed from 39–40, leads to a moment of metrical confusion (82–4) – but hesitation is swept aside by the unbending rhythmic regularity of a repeat of 74–81. And the mechanical turns out to have the last word too. An identical repetition of the first episode, differing only in showing fewer *ritardandos*, seems to suggest that the human voice has begun to be taken over by the machine – or perhaps was always an uncanny mechanical imitation or even extension of humanity. Then $a\natural^1$ again replaces $a\flat^1$ and the refrain returns, repeating bars 65–73 exactly, and closing with the same brisk flourish, only now presto.

It is tempting to allow the 'weird coupling' of the rejected title to resonate with the literary tradition. In Hoffmann's story, 'Die Automate', Ludwig comments on odd couplings between people and 'lifeless figures that mimic the human in their form and movement', and on 'something oppressive, uncanny, or horrible' about them:

> It must be possible to give a mannequin a hidden inner mechanism so that it can dance with nimbleness and grace; it could perform a dance with a human ... such that the living dancer grasped his lifeless wooden partner and swayed with her – and would you be able to bear the sight of it for even a minute without a deep shudder?[40]

Ludwig admits that his sensitivity to automata arises in part from his horror of 'all that mechanized music' prevalent in society: a distaste shared by Schumann, for whom in 1839 one singer was 'an automaton'.[41] So Hoffmann's automata may be images of the mechanical in art too, as opposed to the living human voice. For Hoffmann, true melody is ideally 'song, streaming free and unforced straight from the human breast, which is itself the instrument that resonates with Nature's most wonderful and secret lutes.' Ludwig goes on:

> The greatest reproach one can level at a musician is that he plays without expression, and so ... destroys the *music* in music – and yet the most soulless and insensitive performer achieves more than the most perfect machine ... The efforts of technicians to imitate human organs in their production of musical tones, or to replace them through mechanical means, are for me a war waged on the human spirit.[42]

Automata – bodies alienated from souls – arouse the fear of the living dead that haunts a culture of dualism of body and mind; but human and robotic, live and mechanical, are mutually dependent in music and elsewhere, and continuous as well as opposed; the banality of their traffic can make suspected exchanges between them the more uncanny.

In the middle of 'Der Sandmann' Nathanael became infatuated with Olimpia's 'beautifully sculpted features'. Though seeming human, she was

---

[40] Hoffmann, 'Die Automate', *Die Serapions-Brüder*, 346. O'Brien, 'E. T. A. Hoffmann's Critique of Idealism', 375–8 and 398.
[41] *Briefwechsel*, II 473 (7 April 1839). See also *GSK*, I 437–8, 451 (1839).
[42] Hoffmann, *Kreisleriana*, II/6, 318 (which Schumann copied in the 1850s into his *Dichtergarten*); 'Die Automate', *Die Serapions-Brüder*, 347. Kleist ('Ueber das Marionettentheater', *Berliner Abendblätter*, 12 December 1810) characteristically put a perverse twist on similar ideas. He noted the graceful dance of mechanical puppets, so hard to replicate in self-conscious humans, and speculated that tasting of the Tree of Knowledge resulted in a Fall from an unselfconscious state, but innocence and grace might be restored through an infinite extension of 'Knowledge' as in self-reflecting mirrors.

in truth a robotic mannequin, made by Coppelius, and at first her eyes seemed to Nathanael 'oddly fixed and lifeless'. However, when she 'played the piano with great dexterity and sang a bravura aria in a bright, almost diamantine glass harmonica voice', Nathanael 'was bewitched', seeing in her eyes a 'yearning' for him never conveyed by the 'cold' Clara, whom he accused of being a lifeless automaton. But when he grasped Olimpia's hand, 'it was icy; he felt the shudder of a terrible frost of death'. With her as partner, Nathanael, who 'thought he danced rhythmically', quickly 'saw his deficiencies'. His friend later tried gently to bring him to his senses: 'her playing and singing have the unpleasantly rigid, mindless rhythm of a machine, and her dancing too'.[43]

Olimpia's 'diamantine' singing, mechanically dexterous playing and rigid dancing encapsulate the simultaneous allure and horror of the automaton – enacting Ludwig's fear of uncanny partnerships between human and machine in life and art. She symbolises the mechanical as against true art, prose as against poetry, or chilly perfection against life. Hoffmann satirically has the 'Professor of the Poetic and its Discourses' declare of Olimpia that she 'inscribes a project of allegory – of metaphor embodied'; in effect, he interprets her as standing for the created artwork as against its living model. She is also a parody of the classical requirement for an extreme of flawlessness and purity in female beauty, and Hoffmann satirises the anxieties and perversions of relationships to which this gives rise.

The automaton brings associations of the deathly as well as the mechanical. Nathanael fleetingly feels Olimpia's chill as that of the lifeless bride who was the subject of Goethe's 1797 poem, *The Bride of Corinth*. There, a young man travels to meet the bride his parents had long ago chosen for him; he finds himself, in the midst of warm-blooded enjoyment of his youth, making love to a dead woman whose chilly embrace condemns him to death too; for unless she is laid to rest, she will draw one young man after another to perdition. Moritz's Anton Reiser recalls how the disturbed Werther in Goethe's novel saw the world as a play of marionettes: grasping someone's 'wooden hand', he recoils with a shudder.[44]

---

[43] Hoffmann, *Nachtstücke*, 345, 348, 351–6.

[44] Hoffmann, *Nachtstücke*, 355; Moritz, *Werke*, 245–6; Goethe, *Die Leiden des Jungen Werther*, letter of 20 January 1772, *Werke*, III 59. Goethe's poem was known to Schumann: *GSK*, I 269. In that summer of 1839, Clara felt that the misery would leave her a 'Todtenbraut': *Briefwechsel*, II 519 (13 May 1839). In Goethe's *Wilhelm Meister*, Mignon sometimes seemed a marionette, an alternative to adult love for Philine, a projection of Wilhelm's regressive enthralment by childhood puppet shows, of his absorption in an inner world, or narcissism; she herself was unwilling to grow up, and longed for angelic purity and death instead.

Schumann's piece can be interpreted in the light of similar associations and complexes of mental states. His refrain embodies a robotic mechanical dexterity;[45] his first episode is unable to assert a living sense of self, colludes with its lifeless partner in a weird coupling, and by the end of the piece is overwhelmed. In his second episode, a cadence brings only a brief *ritardando* before being rushed back into strict tempo, like a human dancer with a robotic partner. That the refrain and episode are both fashioned from similar thematic material, heard as derived from the death march, brings out an uncanny mutual dependence of human and mechanical, living and dead.

iii: 'Nächtliches Gelage' ('Nocturnal Revels')

In Schumann's third piece the encounter is perhaps between a vulnerable sensibility and a coarseness that comes to seem brutal. A *forte* waltz in D flat major opening on $a\flat^1$ and $a\natural^1$ is marked by tonal simplicity, bluff rhythms and plain fanfares. The bass is assertive in bars 6–8, hits a discordant $F\flat$ in 7, and hurries its next two notes (Example 9.9). There are sharp discords in bars 14–15, and a glaring *sforzando* $C\flat$ in 21. If these are the nocturnal revels of Schumann's suppressed title, there is something coarse or even overbearing about them.[46]

The first episode is very different, opening *piano* in B flat minor. Long accented melodic notes die away before being as it were impulsively renewed, over a rolling accompaniment in the same low register, the bass adding a metrical tension by coming in on the third beat of every other bar. The passion brews as the melody slowly builds, remaining within the bounds of just three adjacent notes for thirty bars (33–64). From bar 81 the piano evokes a soprano voice entering, perhaps tentatively, into a duet. Chromatic arpeggios and a circle of fifths (bars 97–109) suggest the intoxication of the moment and a promise of fulfilment. But the harmony overshoots B flat minor to D flat major, and the melody is displaced to the second beat (109ff), as though rattled by a threatened return to the opening tonality; and the advance of the bass by a beat (bar 117) may seem to hasten the return of the refrain. At bar 121, the refrain brusquely dismisses an

---

[45] Unsurprisingly, perhaps, Offenbach's setting of Olimpia's song 'Les oiseaux dans la charmille' from *Les Contes d'Hoffmann* likewise begins on the tonic, and ascends and descends the scale by steps, in even quavers and a mechanical staccato matching Schumann's regular accents. Presumably both composers expressed the idea of an automaton's music in similar ways.

[46] Appel, 'Nachtstücke', 130, sees the theme as a suggestive of parody.

Example 9.9: Schumann, *Nachtstücke*, iii, bars 1–20

episode which has come to seem not only its victim but also its creature, borrowing its theme, albeit in minor mode.

After an exact repeat of the waltz – ending this time however with a coda whose repeated bass figure (bars 160–4) sounds like ironic vamping – comes a second episode. A staccato phrase in F sharp minor quivers (bars 165–6) and seems to buck as it doubles the pace of its harmonic and metrical movement and jerks up in 167–8 to an echo of bars 14–15 (Example 9.10). Interrupted by hectic passages (bars 173–80 and 189–96) in $\frac{3}{2}$, the staccato phrase sounds on its return all the more convulsive.

But the episode is engulfed when the refrain suddenly starts up again, in an over-bright A major, before being wrenched back, at the dark climax of the piece, to its home key of D flat major, $a\flat^1$ replacing $a\natural^1$ (bars 211–13). Music that originally seemed merely coarse might now appear brutal. In the first two pieces, overbearing refrains interrupt and overwhelm more pliant and dependent episodes; in this third, therefore, a listener may, similarly, hear the first episode as a victim of the refrain, and the convulsive second as a symptom of the tension between that refrain and the sensibility of the first episode. The refrain, of course, has the last word, and this time the vamp that had ended its coda in bars 160–4 crescendos to a bathetic

Example 9.10: Schumann, *Nachtstücke*, iii, bars 165–72

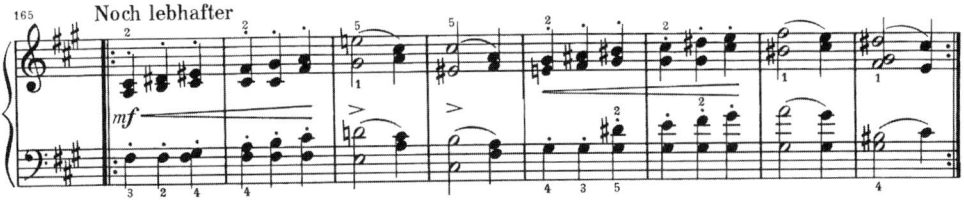

forte low D♭, two beats of silence, and a peremptory $^6_4$ tonic chord. The abruptness may seem ironic, or even cynical.

It is a peculiar psychological sequence, and seems to me one of those instances which for Schumann demanded some account of an underlying coherence.[47] Literary resonances may help. Moritz's *Anton Reiser* sees individuals as repeatedly 'crushed by social constraints'.[48] That sense of oppression had become characteristic of mid-eighteenth-century *Sturm und Drang*, as in Rousseau's protest for 'unhappy peoples groaning under an iron yoke, mankind crushed by a handful of oppressors'.[49] Figures in literature were often described as oppressed by forces such as disease, society or male power. Gretchen in Goethe's *Faust* is a prime example. Heinse's 1785 *Ardinghello* has a woman wasted by frustrated love, and confined, as Hamlet would have confined Ophelia, to a nunnery, where she eats nothing, wrings her hands, sighs and stares. In the *Nachtwachen von Bonaventura*, brutal forces crush pairs of lovers: 'Nachtwache X' evokes Ophelia, her songs turning into the dissonance of lonely death, while 'XIV' juxtaposes dance music with a nun interred alive as punishment for giving birth.

Any of these images might have resonated in Schumann's mind in summer 1839. He felt himself oppressed and made ill by 'an evil spirit which frightened me lest it would not let me go': 'what crushed me was this relentless coarseness', the 'naked bourgeois vulgarity' of Friedrich Wieck's campaign against him. In April, Eduard's death had appeared to him a 'Fieberphantasie'; Wieck's attacks had then made him 'ill', 'devastating his sense and balance', so that he 'lost his creative imagination'; in December an 'evil foe had him in thrall'. That Wieck – an 'evil demon' out of Hoffmann, according to a contemporary reviewer – bedevilled Clara too amplified the distress.[50]

---

[47] *GSK*, II 221. [48] Moritz, *Werke*, 300. [49] Rousseau, *Oeuvres*, III 609–10.
[50] *Briefwechsel*, II 624, 626–7 ('Rohheit'), 639 (7, 10 and 12 July); II 481 (13 April); 770–1 (30 October); 808 (1 December); *Neue Folge*, 165 ('Dein kranker Robert Schumann', 4 August, 'Rohheit', 7 August); Ferris, 'Public Performance', 365–72.

In 'Das Majorat' from Hoffmann's *Nachtstücke*, the Baron, inheritor of a family curse, has arranged for 'a proper ball' in his haunted Baltic castle – like the 'nocturnal revels', perhaps, of Schumann's suppressed title. 'The musicians had arrived with their hoarse fiddles, mistuned basses and bleating hautboys'; meanwhile in a chamber the visiting young musician Theodor sings with the Baroness:

> She had sat down close beside me at the piano . . . and a white ribbon that had freed itself from her delicate ball gown fell on to my shoulder and fluttered, wafted back and forth by my singing and her gentle sighs . . . It was charming to see how she struggled with her shyness . . . but she began to sing with a delicate, pure voice . . . I accompanied the second verse with chords in arpeggios.

Coarse and boisterous music ('a badly tuned shriek of trumpets and horns') announces the ball and cuts the singing short: '"Alas, I must go now", said the Baroness.' For her, the heart's yearning is thus brushed aside. The Baron rebukes Theodor for inflaming the fevered mind of the lonely and delicate young Baroness. And in the darker second half of the tale it emerges that Theodor was meddling in a family blighted by an institution of primogeniture designed to consolidate wealth and by a curse working itself out repeatedly across the generations, killing off every heir and his brothers. When the curse unfolded for the last time, the Baroness died, a 'victim of evil and uncanny forces'; but by then Theodor had left, and when he eventually returned to the now ruined castle, it was all a long time ago and he had made his career elsewhere.[51] My description of the music and the tale could suggest a particular narrative programme; for me, though, a psychological trajectory that can be heard in Schumann's piece – coarse forces brushing aside yearning, engulfing a feverish episode and issuing in an ironic end – is not tied to any particular narrative but may be clarified and amplified by multiple literary resonances.

iv: 'Rundgesang mit Solostimmen' ('Roundelay with Solo Voices')

From the closing D flat of the previous piece, there emerges, by way of the opening diminished seventh chord, a dominant seventh of F. A simple theme (marked 'einfach'), harps on a^1; with its metrical and harmonic consonance, and a softening pedal, it suggests a slow dance (Example 9.11).

---

[51] Hoffmann, *Nachtstücke*, 507, 508–9, 522–3, 558–9.

Example 9.11: Schumann, *Nachtstücke*, iv, bars 1–10

The texture, with broken chords often moving in parallel tenths over bass octaves, evokes a strummed instrument.[52] Semiquavers in the accompaniment in bars 2 and 3 suggest a slight shuffle. The theme's rhythm, with its quavers, rests and trochees, is a memory of the rhythm of the march that opened the first piece; and the cadence at bars 8–9 recalls those of 34 and 40 of the second (in turn developed from bar 8 of the first). But the descending scales and discordant notes are absent; and the intervention of the third piece makes the memories seem remote from the emotions that originally surrounded them. The contrasts of material, style and texture of the first three pieces are softened, as are the tonal wrenches and disorientations.

This last piece too is a rondo – the more obviously so, perhaps, after changes discussed by Clara in January 1840.[53] But there is a mutuality

---

[52] Appel, 'Nachtstücke', 131 calls it a 'guitar'; Moraal prefers a 'harp or guitar': 'Life and Afterlife', 192. One might, though, with Hoffmann in mind (see below), hear it as a theorbo.

[53] *Briefwechsel*, III 845, *Briefedition*, I/6 487–8 (3 January 1840): Clara questions the removal of a repetition, and recommends joining a bar like the current 13, which she describes as the twelfth of the repetition, directly onto a bar like the current bar 37. This leaves it unclear what was the structure of the piece Schumann had sent her in December 1839, but implies that its structure was quite different from what we now have: was it a rondo? This is further evidence of the

previously missing, alongside an interaction of the collective and the individual (Schumann's rejected title, 'Rundgesang mit Solostimmen', suggests both a rondo and a choral refrain alternating with solo verses). Before, the returning refrains had abruptly dismissed the episodes; here there is more overt continuity, and less striking contrast.

The episode in bars 9–13 retains the refrain's strumming accompaniment and the opening dotted leap of a sixth, but the dance of bars 2–9 gives way to intertwining 'solo' voices ('Solostimmen'). The rhythm, with a rest in each voice after its leap in bars 10–11, suggests an expressive catch in the voice; and there is, especially in bar 12, a flow previously absent. Then in bars 13–21, the refrain is varied to accommodate that more flowing polyphony.[54] Bar 22 moves from C to A flat major for the second episode (following the pattern of bars 22–3 of the second piece, but here without the abruptness). Replacing the shuffles and rests of the opening with expressive ornaments and a more flowing quaver movement, this is not so much an elderly dance as a youthful song, or 'Solostimmen' again. A tenor and a soprano respond to and brush against one another (at the third beats of bars 23 and 24). The less regular phrase structure (2+1+2) represents the first time in the work in which the mechanical regularity of the four-bar phrase loosens – excepting only the hesitant and inconclusive first episode of the second piece. In bars 25–6 the harmony briefly moves further to suggest the darker key of D♭. An expressive ritardando and an echo of Beethoven's 'Nimm sie hin, denn, diese Lieder' from *An die ferne Geliebte* (Example 8.1) give the music pause (Example 9.12).[55]

A repeat of the opening chords (bars 31–2) reverses the tonal move, bringing back the refrain; but once again its second half (36–40) has a newly flowing movement like that of bars 21–31 (in place of the original quavers and rests); a linear complexity again suggests 'Solostimmen', in contrast with the unvaried block chords of the returns in the first three rondos; and there are poignant decorations and dissonances.

Unlike previous pieces, this one concludes with a perfect authentic cadence that is neither brisk nor abrupt, a^1 resolved to f^1. In a brief coda, however, shadows fall. The tonic chord on the third beat of bars 40 and 41 is reinterpreted as the dominant of B flat minor, which had figured as the

---

significance of late changes to Schumann's works – not just minor expressive details, but crucial aspects of structure, shape and aesthetic impact.

[54] With more voices and smoother motion in bars 17–21, a ritardando in 20, and the minor harmony of the third beat of bar 2 replaced by a poignant V of ii chord (14 and 18), giving more forward motion to the theme.

[55] Moraal, 'Life and Afterlife', 192, and 'Schumanns Nachtstücke', 82.

Example 9.12: Schumann, *Nachtstücke*, iv, bars 21–8

key of the first episode of the third piece, and the relative minor of the D flat major of the second and third pieces. The bass shudders onto D♭ and G♭ and back to C and F for a return of the cadence of bar 40, now adagio, rhythmically augmented and no longer perfect (41–4): a close not of fulfilment or even regret, but of something more like waste.

Hoffmann's 'Das Steinerne Herz' is likewise a release from the chill of previous stories and an elegy of waste. The 'astonishingly convoluted arabesques' of Max's house 'express the bitterest irony of earthly existence', and his garden is characterised as 'old-world French', its 'serious solemnity' contrasted with the 'empty-headed triviality' of English gardens. In that garden Max had constructed a shrine for a stone icon of his heart, and now holds a party, choreographed like a *Gesamtkunstwerk* accompanied by music.[56] Max's old flame Julie rebukes his attachment to rare visions that made their love impossible; Max claims that he had to 'live alone … as anything that love, that friendship can do falls uselessly away from this stone heart'. 'The sun sank below the horizon', and Julie

> began a great Italian scene by Anfossi, singing with unusual expressiveness. Her voice was old, shaky and uneven … In Max's transfigured look shone the enchantment of youth long passed …

---

[56] Hoffmann, *Nachtstücke*, 587–8. The shrine, music and garden are all images of Hoffmann's exuberant arabesque with its darkly lyrical story. Hoffmann touches on contemporary debates between English and French garden styles, with their musical, cultural and political implications: Richards, *Free Fantasia*, 186–90. In Goethe's *Wilhelm Meister* (VI and VIII/5, *Werke*, IV 360–8 and 484–7), a party unfolds like a *Gesamtkunstwerk* in what becomes a garden of remembrance and shrine for its creator.

The solo voices gave way to a collective dance:

> Max encouraged the company to dance. Four theorbos ... played a sarabande full of pathos. The old danced; the young looked on.

Max had long ago become estranged from his nephew, the young Max, who falls in love with Julie's daughter, also called Julie: the older generation witness in the younger generation the love they never achieved. The old Max encounters his double, young Max, in the garden:

> I heard a softly lamenting voice ... I went closer, and saw – myself! – myself! but as I was thirty years ago, clothed as I was that fateful day when in despair I wanted to end my miserable life, when Julie appeared before me like an angel of light in her bridal dress.

The young Julie's love reconciles him, and he approves the marriage of the two young people, as though it were the marriage he himself had never had. After his death, the young couple weep at the stone below which lies his heart; and 'with his own hand' the young Max 'engraved in the stone' – in which 'he found the whole story of the life-path and pain of his uncle' – the words 'Rest and peace'.[57] The tale is full of the artistry of quotation from previous works; those concluding words allude to the garden, tomb and dark shadows that mark the end of Jean Paul's *Hesperus*.

Schumann too echoes a great predecessor, and in the context of his piece, Beethoven's melody might suggest a young man casting forward to a time when he will look back at the wasted love of youth, as the old Max does in Hoffmann's tale while Julie sings and a theorbo sounds. The words Beethoven set express something consonant with this:

Take them then, these songs
That I, my love, have sung for you.
Sing them again at evening time
To the lute's sweet sounds ...

If Schumann's music, with its strummed instrument and lengthening shadows, creates an emotional world similar to that of Hoffmann's tale, it is not I think to allude to it, re-create its narrative, or muse on it. Instead it is to open cultural and psychological spaces in which the music reverberates, as this final piece at last brings regret for the waste of life and love implied by the previous three rondos' overbearing deadness.

---

[57] Hoffmann, *Nachtstücke*, 589, 597, 602, 604, 609. Compare Tieck's 'Der Pokal' (in *Die Märchen aus dem Phantasus*) of a few years earlier, for a similar recreation of lost love.

10 'The closed book'
Interpreting aesthetic entities

Each of Schumann's four 'Hoffmann works' seems to respond to interpretation as an aesthetic entity shaped and energised by distinctive musical processes; and each forms a whole in a different way. *Carnaval* appears an exhilarating comedy, a carnivalesque centrifuge of structural signals; and *Fantasiestücke* evokes a dreamlike juxtaposition of images of vivid inconsequence, shot through with elusive patterns of tonality, motifs, and sonorities; associations between those images and patterns and Hoffmann's work may bring out hints of a psychological trajectory spanning the work. *Kreisleriana*'s more integrated tonal and thematic shape, resonating with themes from Hoffmann's essays, keeps open as ultimate tonal destinations three expressively contrasted keys. *Nachtstücke* draws disturbance out of three oppressively plain rondos before warmth enters with the last, and its musical patterns evoke psychological complexes resonating with those described in Hoffmann's *Nachtstücke*.

Focusing on these four 'Hoffmann works' (which, with *Papillons*, represent the Schumann works of the 1830s most clearly related to particular books) brings out the interdependence of hermeneutics and history. In a timeless hermeneutic model, resonances with Hoffmann's fictions or a wider culture arise not only in added words, or incidental musical features, but in those giving distinctive shape, flow and energy to a work. These form fluid patterns open to interpretation as indefinitely expressive and resonant, and subsume programmatic elements and formal parallels, so that separate schemata are not necessary to make sense of the work. Musical analysis and cultural interpretation are thus fused together. But this formulation may itself be too timeless, too absolute and too definite.

Seen over time, the varying nature of the whole as between the four works, and perhaps covarying relationship to cultural and literary associations, reflect both divergent aims and stylistic evolutions. Thus there are stories to tell that have not had much attention in Schumann studies to date, and some of them can be traced in this book. *Papillons* does not quite work, despite its charm, and despite Schumann's pointers to Jean Paul's novel. *Carnaval* is a triumph, but could not do without the titles to its individual pieces, which colour its particular aesthetic shape, and set up a strand of understanding running partly in parallel to musical patterns. In *Fantasiestücke* suggestive titles to individual pieces do not specify characters, events or (except for 'Aufschwung') even determinate visual images; but without these titles its expressive musical features and patterns might not show strong enough 'coupling' with Schumann's literary culture to generate resonances. The later two works, by contrast, need no verbal clues beyond an overall title. This implies stories about Schumann's willingness to add words to his scores, and about his capacity to shape musical patterns – including patterns of form, tonality, melody, pitch level, rhythm and metre, sonority, character and style – and to mesh them together in the service of an overall aesthetic conception. *Carnaval* revels in the absence of such integration, but *Kreisleriana*'s various musical patterns are fused with each other and with expressive, resonant cultural overtones. (A sub-plot here is about Schumann's development of radical approaches to tonal patterns in his opp. 17, 6, 16 and 20 in the service of a post-classical aesthetic.) Running alongside these stories is yet another, about the evolution over the 1830s in his criticism, from emphasis on music's ability to 'translate' definite things, to notions of its 'transmutation' of unspecifiable experience into a fusion of form and content.

Treating the works as aesthetic entities brings consequences: interpretation is necessarily plural and relative; analysis must depend on imagination as well as on rigorous derivation from a given set of explicit theoretical models; and the analytic and the interpretive are not ultimately separable. This raises issues that are the subject of this conclusion, and brings hazards which can probably not be wholly avoided, even by a critic or analyst of greater stature than mine. The chapter follows paths well-trodden in current musicology, not hoping to push the theoretical arguments forward, let alone resolve them, but only to clarify where my approach sits along ranges of possibilities, and why. It closes the book rather than opening it because it was not a starting-point, driven by its own theoretical motivations; and coming at the start it would inevitably have distorted the book's focus, towards philosophical aesthetics and away from the four works. But though it closes the book, it cannot close the issues: challenging topics rarely settle, these works resist resolution, and in any case treating them as aesthetic entities precludes the possibility of finality.

In recent decades, Schumann studies have tended to treat literary connections as trivial, or as primarily about programmes or generic parallels of form or style. My approach represents a departure. Different approaches, I would argue, amount to different answers to a question about how best to interpret the works as aesthetic entities; and though there can be comparison, dialogue and even rivalry between approaches, there need be no ultimate confrontation unless one school claims a monopoly.

Or should a composer's own views be seen as settling the question authoritatively? Schumann's frequent and generally consistent discussions of how musical works (his own and others') relate to literature often emphasise links of 'Geist', character, scene and psychological sequence; meanwhile they generally dismiss programmatic links, and give almost no hint that he thought about formal parallels. But none of this settles the issue. A composer's silences may have many different kinds of motivations and causes. And despite his reservations about programmes, his letter to Clara imputes the story of Hero and Leander to 'In der Nacht' (though if that letter had not survived, I do not suppose anyone would have thought of hearing that story there, so it is scarcely a useable model for interpreting his other works). The proof of this pudding lies in the eating, not in recipes derived from Schumann's comments.[1]

Matters of personal taste make some difference here. Schumann appears to have enjoyed his own visual and even narrative imputations, if not others'. I prefer to allow aspects of Hoffmann's fictions to contribute to a richer understanding of musical features and patterns, and then often to recede, without obtruding visual and narrative associations, leaving behind resonant musical patterns. Acculturation matters too. Works of art, as inherently cultural and historical constructs, cannot be interpreted or even analysed as aesthetic objects from an inaccessible position outside all cultural assumptions; differences in the ways in which music is heard depend on the cultural landscape in which a listener – consciously or subconsciously – locates it. The temptation to take one's own landscape as universal should perhaps be recognised. This applies to analyses of musical patterns as well as understanding of expressiveness and interpretation of literary connections. A rich work offers analysts myriad patterns, threads and qualities; and there are infinite different individual standpoints from which to interpret it, each depending in part on individual musical and other acculturation, taste, psychic chemistry and history. Interpretations are incorrigibly plural, and stubbornly relative.

This does not mean that interpretations must be purely subjective, nor just about one individual imagination as fed by the music, with nothing to say to anyone else (though some may be); relativity need not mean that

---

[1] On a strong argument from critical comment to compositional intention, Schumann the critic of mechanical rondos could be read as ruling out the composer's relentless sequence of plain rondos in the *Nachtstücke*.

each individual is mutely isolated in his own solipsistic world of private taste. Instead a work's patterns and expressiveness can be seen as not just in a listener's mind, but as potentially inhering in the work as understood through ideas from a culture.[2] Where habits of appreciation are not shared, interpretations seem lifeless at best, absurd at worst; but many such habits can indeed be adumbrated, discussed, tried out, adopted, internalised and developed.[3] Interpretation is communicable in large part, though fully adequate verbal formulation may be less an attainable destination than a limit of possibility, or ever-receding horizon. It can be put to objective tests, and modified or rejected; and it will flourish or die according to intersubjective consensus, at least within a common culture. These tests may include those of comprehensibility or acceptability to people familiar with the culture, and of plausibility in the light of for instance musicological and historical evidence. One might deploy a 'principle of charity' – a presumption that unless tests suggest serious doubt, an interpretation of a musical work is at least *prima facie* worth attention if it helps to explain to others the richness of the work's aesthetic qualities.

Similar forms of interpretive pluralism and relativity were accepted by some in Schumann's world. C. F. Michaelis said in 1805–6 that each musical work requires the listener to re-create it as a complete whole; its effect depends on the diverse capacities of different individuals' imaginations; 'the music is just the composer's means to set the imagination in motion ... The imagination works further on what he only intimated to me, or sketched'.[4] Schumann adopted a similar view. He insisted that music can be appreciated on paper, as it sounds, and as listeners later re-create ('nachschaffen') a work reflectively in their own individual creative imaginations.[5] Schumann said of his criticism that 'it seemed not inappropriate to invent contrasting figures to give voice to diverse approaches to views of art', in the shape of 'Eusebius', 'Florestan' and 'Raro', who

---

[2] To split hairs, interpretation is not simply a product of 'poetic reflection stimulated by the musical form', in Tadday's words: *Das schöne Unendliche*, 143. Compare Hatten, *Interpreting Musical Gestures*, 4–8.

[3] Is that not a common experience with Schenkerian approaches? Proust famously dismissed the idea of 'aesthetic merits as material objects which an unclouded vision could not fail to discern, without one's needing to nurture equivalents of them and let them slowly ripen in one's own heart': *Swann's Way*, 175. In a different context, Augustine of Hippo said 'believe so that you may understand', and 'it is impossible to love what is entirely unknown ... but when what is known, if even so little, is also loved, this very capacity for love makes it better and more fully known': Augustine, *Tractatus in Ioannis Evangelium*, 29/6 and 96/4.

[4] Michaelis, 'Vermischte Bemerkungen' (1805), 14, 21 and 'Nachtrag', 138.

[5] *GSK*, I 186; compare 146 ('das ihrige'). See also Tadday, *Das schöne Unendliche*, 142–3, Kranefeld, *Der nachschaffende Hörer* and Newcomb, 'Schumann and the Marketplace', 278.

debate between themselves. Koßmaly, in his 1844 review of Schumann's piano compositions, thought 'several different interpretations of one and the same work' imaginable, and cited Novalis' claim that a work is the better 'the more ways it has of being understood'.[6] Schumann often said that a broad culture is essential to musical understanding; the implication is that associations will depend on the cultural riches available to the listener, and interpretation of purely musical features will alter with musical tastes over the centuries. (His colleague, Keferstein, expressed a similar view about the nature of comedy in music.)[7] But imaginative interpretation need not exclude reasoned debate and evidence, at least within some broadly shared assumptions.[8]

Thus my interpretations would seem to me more successful if they stimulated dialogue, alternatives and challenge on musicological, literary and historical grounds. One could question whether for instance the motivic patterns I stress in *Kreisleriana* occur significantly enough to justify my emphasis on them; or whether musical features as I describe them meet the conditions I suggest for 'resonance', match well with literary features and can be seen as emblems of wider significance. And it would be fascinating to see alternative interpretations. Perhaps the musical style and trajectory of *Carnaval* could be interpreted as if it were an 'opera without text' (in Schumann's phrase of July 1832),[9] setting aspects of its style, that is, in the light of developments in operatic and theatrical fashion in the five or six decades before its composition – including those on which *Brambilla* plays, and including of course the contribution of Mozart to comic opera. In the *Nachtstücke*, Holly Watkins draws out contrasts between the first piece and the fourth, describing them in terms of the separation of spirit and body and their reunification.[10] She relates that to an aspect of the aesthetics of Jean Paul in which metaphor is seen as a marriage of spirit and body. This is a rather different context to that which I have drawn on; but I see no reason to have to choose between these contexts. Taking a quite

---

[6] *GSK*, I 2; Koßmaly, 'Schumann's Claviercompositionen', 35; Novalis, *Schriften*, V 236(fr. 281).

[7] *GSK*, I 143, 422; II 115 (broad culture), 221 (insufficient understanding); I 22, 371 (changing musical tastes); 'K. Stein', 'Versuch über das Komische' (1833), 240–1.

[8] Such a hermeneutic approach was exemplified in the dialogue form of art-criticism developed around 1800. August Wilhelm Schlegel's 'Die Gemälde. Gespräch' concerns the reciprocal relationship between visual art and words, the dependence of the individual work on the historical and cultural tradition, the hermeneutics of analysis and interpretation and above all the possibility of reasoned debate: *Athenaeum*, II.1, 1799. Compare colloquies in Novalis' *Die Lehrlinge zu Sais*, Tieck's *Der Phantasus* and Hoffmann's *Die Serapions-Brüder*. See also Ziolkowski, *German Romanticism*, 355–72.

[9] *Tagebücher*, I 411. [10] Watkins, *Metaphors of Depth*, 108–13.

different tack on that same work, one could follow Schumann's hints and enquire whether either the formalities of the concert hall or comforts of home make a suitable ambience for its performance: what kind of surroundings might work better?[11]

Various hermeneutic approaches can coexist. It might sometimes be valuable to try describing a work of art using the most sparing possible framework of assumed cultural contexts, aiming for maximum objectivity (but meaner assumptions may give a meaner description). Others may prefer to weave aspects of Schumann into a re-creation of more modern ideas, or to depend on arbitrary association of ideas. This book has taken the works as expressive, not regardless of culture, but for cultural worlds within the range of Schumann's. It assumes that the worlds in which Schumann's work is rooted are still partially accessible, and fruitful for its understanding: postmodernism, in upholding diverse rights, risks exaggerating how far awareness of past cultures is unnecessary or impossible.[12]

But Schumann's cultural worlds need not monopolise our thinking to the exclusion of cultures that can find connections with them. Affinities and differences between modern ideas and nineteenth-century conceptions cast a revealing raking light on Schumann's music. One can see something of the postmodernist revolt against modernism, for instance, in the Romantic rebellion against Enlightenment claims to universal, rational, systematic objectivity, championing the partial, instinctive, non-axiomatic and subjective.[13] Modern semiotic theories of the arbitrariness of signs may seem prefigured in Novalis' *Monolog*, where the play of mathematical and verbal signs is for its own sake. The Romantics' fascination with the psychology of outsiders and their plight in the face of bourgeois social interests resonates with concerns of the Frankfurt school. Highly self-conscious in their hermeneutics, the early Romantics including Friedrich Schlegel explored non-classical aesthetic ideas such as fragmentation, self-reflexiveness, alienation and defamiliarisation; and so did early

---

[11] *GSK*, II 350 ('räumlichen und anderen Nebenumstände').

[12] Extreme versions of 'aesthetic autonomy' or 'decontextualisation' are not necessary here. Hoeckner (*Programming the Absolute*, 63–71) reads Schumann's remark that Schubert's 'Great' C major Symphony leads us into a region where we have not previously been (see Appendix 3–4(c)) as an assertion of the aesthetic autonomy of music in general, as a decontextualised world, thus downplaying cultural and historical understanding in Schumann's hermeneutics. But for me, Schumann's remark expresses his admiration of that symphony's uniqueness.

[13] Compare, for instance, the summary of postmodernism in Kramer, *Classical Music and Postmodern Knowledge*, chapter 1.

twentieth-century thinkers in Russia and Germany.[14] It is not surprising then that there have been interpretations of Schumann's aesthetics through Kristeva, or Benjamin, or the Russian Formalists, or current ideas akin to those of Schlegel; and to explore the works in that light, though it exceeds historical evidence, need not conflict with it, if handled with sensitivity to Schumann's views and cultural inheritance.[15]

Following this line, ideas from Freud such as compulsion, trauma, oscillation, alienation and hollowness might enrich interpretation not just of the first rondo of the *Nachtstücke*, but the other three as well. So might the 'Ostranenie' or defamiliarisation described by Russian Formalists, Brecht's 'Verfremdung', and similar concepts in Barthes. Adorno's description of the Brecht / Weill 'Moritat', highlighting 'unrelated juxtaposition[s]', banal sonorities, 'wrong notes' and 'glibness' in the rhythm, resonates with Schumann's work.[16] The rondos could be seen also through ideas in Deleuze about refrains and machines, through Calasso's postmodern Marxist interpretations of fetishism and of sacrificial repetition in myth, or through the instinct of Kleist, Tolstoy and Thomas Mann that music can induce a loss of identity bordering on automatism.[17] Automatism might be seen not only in the second piece, but in the death march of the first too, complicating the relationship between the march refrain and the other material of the piece, and perhaps seeing the last return of the march less as a disappearance than as a winding-down of the machine.[18] Modern perspectives might be illuminating for the other works too. For instance, Žižek's interpretation of *Carnaval* links Deleuze and Lacan to Schelling's Idealism and Hoffmann's puppets;[19] and it would be interesting to explore how far images of carnival from Schumann's culture

---

[14] For defamiliarisation, see for instance Novalis, *Schriften*, V 267(fr. 482), and Hoffmann, *Fantasiestücke*, 12 ('etwas fremdartig Bekanntes' of Callot's representations).

[15] For instance, Reiman, *Schumann's Piano Cycles*, chapter 3 (Russian Formalists); Daverio, *Crossing Paths*, chapter 5 (the Frankfurt school); Bekker-Adden, *Nahtstellen* (Kristeva and Lévi-Strauss); Daverio, *Nineteenth-Century Music*, chapter 3 (F. Schlegel), on which compare Muxfeldt, 'Review', 149–60. Schumann appears not to have read Schlegel's philosophy or aesthetics, and probably adopted Jean Paul's disdain for the latter; Russian Formalists' attempts to reduce art to the mechanical would presumably have been unsympathetic to him; and the Novalis he read in Tieck's coherent and Idealist version diverges from the disjointed fragments and almost postmodern semiotics that sometimes appears from modern versions.

[16] Cited in Kramer, *Musical Meaning*, 217; compare 216–20, and the musical analysis of Weill's 'Moritat' at 220–7.

[17] Deleuze and Guattari, *A Thousand Plateaus*, 330–86; Calasso, *The Ruin of Kasch*, 186–205 and *passim*; Kramer, *Classical Music and Postmodern Knowledge*, 56.

[18] I have here elaborated a comment made to me by Nicholas Marston.

[19] Žižek, 'Robert Schumann: The Romantic Anti-Humanist' in *The Plague of Fantasies*, 84, 265–9.

can be related to Lacan's specularity, modern equivalents of magic lanterns, or to Kramer's interpretation of the work in terms of a late nineteenth-century view of mirrors, Bakhtin's understanding of Rabelais and Terry Castle's of English masquerade.[20] *Kreisleriana* could be seen in terms of Kristeva's concept of the 'abject', relating it to Romantic notions including the isolation of the artist.[21] Or the *Fantasiestücke* could be viewed in terms of modern ideas of dreaming, or of the yearning for a primal undifferentiated state, such as Kristeva's (or Plato's) 'chora', and how these might relate to ancient mythological images of serpent and water, or to the Romantics' concept of 'das Flüssige'.

If I have here preferred a more historical approach, that has not stretched to trying to analyse the four 'Hoffmann works' only in ways rooted in the techniques or concepts of Schumann's day, or to treating historically documented interpretive approaches as a final court of appeal. The attempt would be in vain. No one can wholly inhabit a past culture, or wholly escape the presumptions of their own time; theory rarely marches closely enough in step with practice to justify such a restriction; and composers cannot be relied on to articulate as theory enough of their compositional approach. I will argue against restricting myself to what can be derived from stated theoretical models; still less should I restrict myself to the stated theories of two centuries ago.

An interpretation wholly derived from articulated theory might lay claim to a reassuring degree of objectivity, transparency, rigour and authority; and particular aspects of music, such as classical tonality, encourage a hope that they might be reducible to a combination of hard empirical fact and deductive argument within articulated theoretical systems – some of them fascinating and compelling.

But it should not be taken for granted that more easily systematised features, such as relationships of pitch level and tonality, are prime drivers of the shape or energy of Schumann's piano works, or as important as in, say, Beethoven. What matters is what is dramatised in a work. In some (for instance Schumann's opp. 6 and 17), energy appears to arise less from a particular 'Ursatz' or tonal opposition than from the attraction of a pole that may be expressive as much as tonal (and may be initially unestablished, or apparently secondary). And relationships of pitch level and tonality may be less important in works consisting of many short pieces,

---

[20] Kramer, *Classical Music and Postmodern Knowledge*, 67–8 and 264, note 45, 'Carnaval, Cross-Dressing', 305–25, and 'Rethinking Schumann's *Carnaval*', 100–32.

[21] Compare Bekker-Adden, *Nahtstellen*, 192ff, 263ff; Kramer, *Classical Music and Postmodern Knowledge*, chapter 2.

and in general less again in the 'Hoffmann' works (*Kreisleriana* perhaps excepted), where tonal patterns seem to reinforce a shape rather than drive it. Other musical dimensions may play important parts as sources of a work's aesthetic drive or shape – including rhythm, sonority and texture (as in the *Fantasiestücke*), and expressive quality, gesture and associations.[22]

More generally, it is not obvious that any single theory or specified set of theories will sustain a rich account of the shape and energy, or 'conception' of such complex and expressive aesthetic entities as these works. Have theories yet been adequately articulated in all the requisite dimensions – to cover and then unite register, dynamics, texture, attack and release, and dissonance in the construction of sonority, for instance; or to unite tonality, form, formal function, melodic shape, rhythm and thematic development? It may not be possible to achieve any wide consensus on the adequacy of any one theory, let alone on a complete set and its internal relationships.[23] Arguably any such theoretical framework will be less than absolute, complete or adequate; to be useful as a model, it must deliberately exclude some aesthetic factors from consideration.[24] Dependence on a system can appear to subordinate or misrepresent individual works as mere instantiations of theory, and to confine understanding to what can be inferred from the theory, dismiss higher-level qualities emerging from a synthetic view of a work, or downplay expressiveness, associations, culture and the imagination – even though the analytic and the hermeneutic or interpretive are often ultimately inseparable.[25]

---

[22] Compare Cohn, 'Autonomy of Motives', 167–70, Lester, 'Schumann and Sonata Forms', 208–10, and Rosen's view (*Romantic Generation*, 40) on timbre, register, spacing and sonority in Schumann; in a passage in Schumann's op. 1 and in 'Eusebius' from *Carnaval*, 'sonority plays a structural role as important as pitch and rhythm' (12). In quasi-Schenkerian terms, my treatments have focused on the foreground and deeper middleground; it might be interesting to try drawing out more explicit relationships to other middleground layers – conceivably while still taking some account of sonority and expressiveness. Trying such Schenkerian analyses would also yield insights into how the works divide up: while *Carnaval* could presumably be analysed as one, and perhaps the *Nachtstücke* too (probably with some softening of Schenker's principles), the other two works might be better divided, for instance into two halves each.

[23] See Caplin, in Bergé, ed., *Musical Form*, 145: 'I doubt whether such a utopian agreement [consensus on fundamental theoretical perspectives] could ever (or even should) be achieved.'

[24] For both points, see for instance, Bergé, ed., *Musical Form*, 165–7.

[25] Treitler, *Music and the Historical Imagination*, 32–3 and Cook, *Music, Imagination and Culture*, 240–3, argue such cases. Hepokoski in Bergé, ed., *Musical Form*, 146–51, acknowledges that analysis needs on occasion to 'leave the domain of empirically safe, evidentiary fact' for an 'analytically responsible' hermeneutic interpretation.

And the impression of rigour results in part from obscuring some of the choices being made. For every theoretical system remains relative to musicological perspective and acculturation; and 'scientific' or 'hard-edged' analyses are scarcely independent of implicit aesthetic judgements. Any interesting analysis selects features from myriad possibilities in a work, including some less amenable to traditional analytical theories; and it shows how features, under convincing descriptions and in well-judged groupings, contribute to significant aesthetic patterns or effects. One cannot deduce from theory which patterns and features to select as significant, nor in which groupings, nor how to describe them and their relations; theory can only set limits to the sorts of features that might count towards a given pattern. The selections are acts of imaginative interpretation, implicating an indefinite range of conscious and unconscious assumptions, including those about the nature of, for instance, harmony, metre, melody and sonority in the work and its culture. Only within those selections, and given those ranges of assumptions, can analytical observations constitute objective facts or falsehoods; the selections and assumptions themselves are matters of judgement. In an evolving iterative process, they rest on intuitions and inferences about how a work can be synthesised as an individual whole, and in turn modify those inferences.[26]

Much as a work of music can be analysed into elements treated as extensional, or as more fundamental than the work, no single analysis can exhaust the valid possibilities, as the history of analysis proves time and again. An aesthetic entity, essentially involving an indefinite range of connotations, is nearer the intensional than the extensional: it is ultimately irreducible to any given set of such analyses.[27] There can be no definitive articulation in words of its aesthetic impact, or 'Geist', to borrow Schumann's term. Such impact is not inaccessible, as there is plenty that can be said about it, discussed, tested and refuted or widely rejected or accepted; but interpretations are from particular standpoints rather than absolute. That state of affairs is not so well conveyed by notions borrowed from harder sciences, which tend to suggest a reassuring transparency and

---

[26] Hatten, *Interpreting Musical Gestures*, 2–8, Treitler, *Music and the Historical Imagination*, 69 and Cook, *Music, Imagination and Culture*, 154–60.

[27] Compare the argument in Cook, *Musical Analysis*, chapter 6. On intensionality in this context, see Dodd, *Works of Music*, 40–1. Such a non-reductive approach may owe something to Aristotle (see for instance Barnes, *Aristotle*, 100–1, 134–5, 183; and compare 70–1, 111–12, 174–5). A glance at this book's index will suggest how many aspects of its stances can be traced back to positions developed or sketched – at least arguably – by that great, if sometimes obscure, thinker. Of course, I am skating lightly over the many aspects of his thought that remain contentious.

rigour, laying implicit claim to the extensional, definite and absolute. A work seen as an aesthetic entity is not ultimately an engineering structure. If it fails, it fails only contestably, not as incontrovertibly as a bridge collapses; and it fails because it is *arguably* aesthetically inadequate, rather than because it is built with scientifically *demonstrable* deficiencies. Nor is it ultimately just a sample of a common kind, essentially explicable through study of common practice of the day: it stands or falls on its own aesthetic merits, which may be more or less idiosyncratic. I stress 'ultimately', in order not to seem to reject studies of musical engineering or common practice, both of which are potentially valuable. But to some extent both depend on first adopting, even if only implicitly, some view of aesthetic impact.

If aesthetic entities *essentially* have aesthetic qualities (even if no particular set is essential to a given entity), and may stand or fall by them, some attempt to come to grips with aesthetic qualities has to be made by some people some of the time.[28] Perhaps such an attempt should be made only outside the scholarly community, as scholarly disciplines have nothing to say about the subject, risk corruption from it, and should focus only on what derives definitive results from stated premises; but I would regret such segregation. Both camps would be impoverished.

Analyses like mine, neither abstruse nor derived from theory in a sophisticated way, may be charged with obviousness.[29] That the third scale-degree figures in a certain passage of a movement is banal, if true; that it forms part of a significant pattern in which there is a linear descent to the tonic over the rest of the movement may be obvious when pointed out, or may be disputed, as such analyses are matters of judgement, not fact. But even if obvious, it may still focus a listener's attention on a satisfying pattern. That the middle section of 'Grillen' ends with a tonic cadence in that section's home key is banal; and it plays no role in my interpretation such that it could be anything other than banal. The mere (quasi-extensional) fact that the same is not true of many episodes in the *Nachtstücke* is equally banal; but an (intensional) interpretation of that fact need not be: the fact contributes to aesthetic patterns important in my interpretation of the work as a whole which so far as I know have not been brought out before. Those patterns are arguably part of the conception of the work (its 'Geist'), and help to bring resonant associations. Ideally, such

---

[28] See the previous note for this quasi-Aristotelian position.
[29] Even analyses based in sophisticated models risk being dismissed as obvious – see for instance the exchange between Hepokoski and Webster in Bergé, ed., *Musical Form*, 146 and 156–7.

an interpretation, once stated and internalised, will seem both obvious and illuminating.

For all these reasons, I have not tried to limit myself to any one or more articulated systems of theory, nor claimed to derive my analyses, or indeed my methodological choices, from such models, preferring an eclectic approach that exploits whatever analytical tools come to hand. Those tools derive, of course, from theoretical models of music developed and restated over centuries: I mean to question a tyranny of musicological theory, not its contribution. Suspicion of the monopoly of theory – as in Novalis' 'infinite automaton' – was a commonplace of Schumann's culture.[30] Schumann himself built no theoretical systems, and in the controversy of the early 1830s over comedy in music, he simply offered insights into instances of comic music in Beethoven, where others started from abstract theoretical definitions in order to generate inevitably inadequate specifications as to how comedy arises in music in general.[31] In 1831 Schumann noted the remark from Wolfgang Menzel's *Aesthetics* that between aesthetic theory and practice, or rule and instance, there persists an irreducible ('unendlicher') gap that is 'perhaps worth more than the whole' (presumably 'the whole theory').[32]

Schumann's works, as I have described them, often seem to exploit precisely that gap, embodying an antinomian or paradoxical conception, or upending assumptions about a genre. Their features may resist definitive determination in analytic terms – as evidenced for large-scale form by

---

[30] Novalis' 'crude discursive thinker' (*Schriften*, V 205(fr. 15)) builds an artificial nature from atomic propositions, in quest of a mechanically deductive model of the universe ('unendliches Automat': a Turing machine); but such a deductive system cannot explain nature, and negates its life; it is better to hover between analysis and an intuitive grasp of the whole. *Die Lehrlinge zu Sais* (*Schriften*, I 84) has a character contrast natural scientists 'seeking to examine the internal structure through precise incisions' with poets 'pursuing the fluid and the fleeting with agile minds'. Wackenroder contrasted 'dry' or 'everyday' verbal systems with the fineness and fluidity of music, a 'sounding sea' or 'streaming river': 'Die Wunder der Tonkunst' in *Herzensergießungen*, 41–2 and 131, and 'Wesen der Tonkunst', 148; and Tieck made similar points: 'Die Töne', 273. Compare 'the technological swerve' described by Abbate, 'Music – Drastic or Gnostic?', 527–9.

[31] *GSK*, I 112–14, as expounded by Appel, 'Schumanns Humoreske', 179–91. Compare ibid., 35–6, and *GSK*, II 387, note 178, on Schumann's aversion to theory and the influence of F. H. Jacobi. Schumann rebuked critics for always wanting to pin down what cannot be said, and denounced slavish adherence to theoretical systems. As he said, 'beauty mocks all aesthetic theory'; give yourself a box, and you may have to live in it: *GSK*, I 422; 499, 22.

[32] *Mottosammlung*, IX 152 – a remark Schumann used in the *Neue Zeitschrift* in 1835, and recopied in 1850 (VI 20). He may not have known Friedrich Schlegel's fragment, 'Intellectually, it is equally lethal to have a system and to have none'; but in December 1838 he copied out C. F. D. Schubart's similar sayings: *Mottosammlung*, III 61–2 and 73 (compare IV 10, 13 and 18).

debates over opp. 17 and 20. Likewise, for large-scale tonal movement, the aesthetic impact of the final keys of the *Fantasy*'s first movement, *Davidsbündlertänze* and *Kreisleriana* may be inseparable from persisting ambiguity as to each work's tonic. More locally, states of key may be clouded, 'intermediate' or 'directional' as has recently been argued.[33] Thematic relationships too may be elusive. The time signature of 'Des Abends' does not reveal a 'true' metre so much as ensure the constant self-assertion of duple time against an otherwise dominant triple time; in 'Warum?', alternative phrase structures are equally valid. There is a doctrine that ambiguities in musical features are always decidable within a theoretical framework; but any such decision may represent the music as an aesthetic entity less adequately than 'pre-theoretical' indecision.[34]

This may be related to Brendel's 1845 claim that some passages of Schumann's piano music 'lose themselves in fluidly dissolving outlines'.[35] His works embody a particular aspiration to 'fluidity', to a liminal world of suggestiveness, sometimes shading into half-lights and dream, or fading into the recession of distance, memory or the play of ideas; they are best understood by divining analogies between different areas of thought; and their musical features, expressiveness and resonances sometimes depend on elusive affinities rather than logical and structural developments. In all of this Schumann's works resemble Novalis' ideas quoted on page 188. A listener is invited to re-create threads from which they seem to hang, or access a flow by which to be carried. As Schumann's friend Keferstein wrote, in some works 'one feels caught in acute tension, even though one has fully grasped their musical structure. One dwells on them again and again until eventually one succeeds in finding the right poetic key to their thought.'[36] Schumann's own criticism praised music whose threads, musical and poetic, are not 'coarse' or 'blatant', but 'fine', 'light', 'hidden' or 'arcane'.[37] He admired works in which obscurity of form, melody, harmony or rhythm serves to draw attention to some 'deeper'

---

[33] Compare Appel, 'Schumanns Humoreske', 69–75 and 271 (thematic); Rosen, *Romantic Generation*, 227 (phrase structure), 275–6 (metre), 229–36 (tonality); Kopp, 'Intermediate States of Key', and Wadsworth, 'Directional Tonality'.

[34] Agawu, 'Ambiguity in Tonal Music', 107; Cook, 'Uncanny Moments', 107–10; compare Hepokoski in Bergé, ed., *Musical Form*, 110.

[35] Brendel, 'Robert Schumann' (1845), 89–90, adding that Schumann's use of the pedal in his own playing 'often prevented the harmonies from standing out distinctly'. See Appendix 3–4(d).

[36] 'K. Stein', 'Bemerkungen eines irrenden Theoretikers' (1837), 29–30.

[37] *GSK*, I 155, 233, 143, 251, 72 ('Spuren'), 400; II 221. Goethe (*Wilhelm Meister*, V/4, in *Werke*, IV 265) described *Hamlet* as held together by threads that 'are tenuous and loose, but run through the whole'. Compare Hoffmann, *Die Serapions-Brüder*, 842.

psychological progression, or 'more poetic' or 'dramatic' development; a superficial absence, peculiarity or grotesqueness of form, as in Beethoven or Berlioz, may point to an underlying conceptual coherence, or to unusual connections of thought.[38]

Even the status of a Schumann work as an entity is often unfixed, with questions as to how far it is fruitful to take a synoptic view of musical or aesthetic patterns, and how far they give each work shape, energy and individuality. A recent scholarly trend has stressed fragmentation in Schumann's works of the 1830s.[39] For the 'Hoffmann works', I have explored the possibility that fragmentation may have served aesthetic purposes within a whole that each nevertheless forms, however qualified; but I have fought shy of any general theory of unity, which would have to tackle various sets of questions.[40] One set concerns how far a piece of music is self-contained, rather than joined to, part of or dependent on other music; this book has explored the notion that each of the four works is a whole in that the individual pieces within each are less self-contained than the whole. To that end I addressed another set of concerns, tracing how far each work is internally unified or coherent, and by what sorts of connections between what sorts of elements, and how clear, definite or explicit those connections might be. And here I touch on a third set of questions, about the sorts of concepts or metaphors through which the music and its connections can be described.[41] Evocations in some of Schumann's works of the 1830s of suspension of causality and the irruption of the unbidden or subliminal may suggest dreams as soon as planned or teleological constructions; their shape might be captured in images such as waves, torrents or subterranean streams, as well as in more conventional musicological metaphors from architecture or engineering such as structure, shape and line.

Elusive fluidity is found not only in Schumann's music, of course; but in his 'poetic' and 'Hoffmann works' he may have sought to heighten those characteristics. His generation had inherited an already outmoded classical ideal of drama, irony or tension held within the symmetry, clarity and

---

[38] *GSK*, I 73 (metre, and Beethoven's 'idiosyncratic' forms); 77–8 (Berlioz's thematic development); 251 (harmony); 73–4 ('geistigen Zusammenhang'), 347 ('contrapuntal refinement').

[39] Well captured in Muxfeldt, 'Review', 153–7.

[40] See for instance Schmalfeldt, *In the Process of Becoming*, 6–8; Morgan, 'The Concept of Unity', 7–50; Korsyn, 'The Death of Musical Analysis?', 337–51.

[41] I have largely left aside further sets of questions, around how far a piece is or presents itself as finished, crafted or repeatable rather than a sketch or improvisation, what conceivable variations on it would leave it the same work, rather than creating a new work, and how far a work should be seen as an evolving cultural construction.

resolution of a whole. Under that classical ideal, individual works negotiated a stylistic force-field: the tendency was towards a clear starting point that also implied a destination, at which, despite prolongations, interruptions, delays and digressions there would eventually be a single point of definitive arrival; towards seeing anything occurring before or after this journey as a preparation for it or confirmation of its end; and towards a convergence of different kinds of musical means in support of the trajectory. In hindsight, this force-field ossified into magisterial, deadening rules; and Schumann – an original genius, of his time, and a devotee of late Beethoven – found innovative and sometimes radical ways to reshape it to new purposes. He softened, stretched or upended each of its tendencies; and he learnt to deploy the idiosyncratic, fragmentary or antinomian, the elusive and the allusive, as constituents of striking musical patterns, and in the service of individual musical conceptions.

Music is a medium of its own, and so in a sense forever inaccessible to verbal description: in that sense it is stubbornly transcendent. This need not imply mystical visions, taking music as from another world, or beyond the bounds of experience, history or culture. Music is not so ineffable that nothing can be said about it: much may be said about its qualities. But trying to get at its aesthetic impact through using words tempts – or perhaps requires – a critic to try to capture and convey an interpretation of that impact. A critic may be fatally tempted into purple prose, or may substitute his own vision for that of the composer. I have shaded my musical interpretations with characterisations and metaphors designed to bring out expressive associations with Schumann's culture, as stimulated by his titles; but from a narrowly musicological viewpoint, and especially one that abstracts from the literary cultures of his day, these shadings may seem extravagant or banal.

Even short of those dangers, verbal interpretation can be damaging, if it seems to give words primacy over music, set barriers of thought between music and listener, or neglect or negate music's elusive 'fluidity', 'indefinable yearning' (in Hoffmann's phrase), 'charme' or 'infinite plenitude of meaning' (Jankélévitch's term) – its subtle and varied aesthetic and expressive beauty.[42] Analysis demands that aspects be identified; words offer nouns for those aspects, which therefore crystallise as separable, reified

---

[42] Jankélévitch, *Music and the Ineffable*, 52–3, 72, 93–102 and *passim* (in protest perhaps against a Germanic notion of 'frozen architecture', he exaggerates fluidity at the expense of shape). Compare Rosen, *Classical Style*, 176 and 324; Wackenroder's letter to Tieck of 12 May 1792 (*Herzensergießungen*, xxi–xxii); Kramer, *Classical Music and Postmodern Knowledge*, 63–5; Abbate, 'Music – Drastic or Gnostic?', 510–11.

entities imputed to music (form, tonality, theme, line, programme, meaning or conception); the fluid is solidified, the indefinable defined ('unendlich' becoming 'endlich'); symbol becomes allegory; and the life drains away. Thus music might be reduced through analytical techniques deduced from a theoretical model to Novalis' 'infinite automaton'. Alternatively, it might be seen as a blank screen onto which the interpreter projects his own arbitrary imaginings, treating artworks as Hoffmann's Nathanael treated the puppet Olimpia, who rewarded him, whatever he said, with her indifferent, soulful 'Ach!'. Either way, music's inherent expressiveness gets short shrift. Or separate schemata of meaning might dominate interpretation, isolating the spirit as external to the music, and leaving the music (in Rellstab's picture) as dead as 'a corpse on a bier'. These three death's-heads cannot be finally shut out: they can only be acknowledged – regarded in the mirror, with a degree of irony, as one's own image, sobering if no longer spooking us.

A more encouraging image is that of Proteus, a primal divinity of the sea, embodying the fluid and indefinite. He was capable of endless elusive self-metamorphosis; but he might, if wrestled into a transient stasis, adopt a definite shape and speak to his captor in ways that seemed oracular.[43] He became an image for many people of the sea, of art and of the unconscious, for Novalis of elusive truth – and for a correspondent of Schumann's *Neue Zeitschrift*, of Beethoven's musical humour.[44] Like Proteus, and like truth, an artwork both invites and eludes understanding; wrestled into stasis, it seems to speak oracles; but each interpretation is only one possible shape, and only temporarily fixed, always leaving more to find. The interpretive process, while tied to palpable features, is complex, intuitive and unfinished, iterating between and meshing different dimensions – analysis, imagination and interpretation – any one of which alone will drain the life out of it. It takes on aspects of 'the fluid' and 'the indeterminate', aiming to use the demonstrable in order, in Jean Paul's words, to point beyond it, 'out into an unknown sea'.

Several of Schumann's works of the 1830s, much as they speak directly, remain in some senses a 'closed book'.[45] In his songs of 1840, even if musical patterns are as radically elusive, the singer provides threads of line, voice, subject and poetry, helping to open the book. But if the piano works connect with 'remote interests' through expressive features, elusive

---

[43] Virgil, *Georgics*, IV 387–414 (after Homer, *Odyssey*, IV 382ff).
[44] Griepenkerl, 'Musikalisches Leben in Braunschweig' (1837), 70.
[45] In Schubring's words: 'Schumanniana No. 4' (1861), 213.

symbols and suggestive resonances, rather than through definite meanings or programmes, that may erect barriers. The literature, images and ideas on which they trade were never widely familiar, and have now receded even further from the common stock, internalised by very few, so that living resonance is likely to be taken as dead reference. In any case, today's culture may find the hermeneutics of reference more congenial than resonance: and a tendency to see 'absolute' and 'programme music' as polar opposites may still hamper understanding. It is one thing to anatomise 'the poetic' in music in general, but quite another (particularly within an academic tradition) to attempt an aesthetic interpretation of a 'poetic' work, and especially works of such an antinomian, idiosyncratic and elusive nature. Even where interpretations aspire to a protean fluidity, they all too easily ossify into one of those lifeless automata, puppets and corpses, as mine too, for all their disclaimers, may seem to do. If more prudent critics give these dangers a wider berth than I have, that may be a reason why a closed book remains closed.

Appendices

Appendix 1: Concordance of citations from Novalis

Chapter and note number		Citation opening	Schriften, V, 1988 (=Tieck 1802)	Schriften, I, II or III, 1960, or IV, 1975	Schriften, Reimer, 1837 (Tieck)	Gesammelte Werke, 1967
1	9	[Wilhelm Meister]	233(fr. 263–4)	III 638–9 (505), 646–7 (536)	II 181–3	412–3
	16	Wenn der Mensch erst ein wahrhaftes innerliches Du hat	216(fr. 88)	III 577 (172)	II 139	391
3	51	Musik und Poesie mögen wohl ziemlich eins sein	–	I 211	I 34	189
	54, 66	Ein Alkahest	–	I 79	II 54	145
	63	Jeder feste Punkt	–	I 101	II 92	165
	64	Am Quell der Freiheit	–	I 89	II 72	154
	64	Der denkende Mensch	–	I 101	II 92	165
	64	Das Theater ist die tätige Reflexion	266(fr. 476)	III 681 (642)	II 224	443
	64	Fast jeder Mensch ist ... Künstler	229(fr. 228)	II 574 (226)	II 171	403
	64	Jeder Mensch sollte Künstler seyn	249(fr. 336)	II 497 (39)	II 232	370
	64	[Poesie] ist die eigentümliche Handlungsweise des menschlichen Geistes	–	I 287	I 161	256
	66	See under chapter 8 below				
	68	10/12/98 letter	–	IV 269	–	–
4	21	Nirgend aber ist es auffallender	228–9(fr. 228)	II 573–4 (226)	II 170–1	402
	51	Der wahre Leser muß der erweiterte Autor	232–3(fr. 260)	II 470 (125)	II 180	357
	55	Jedes Kunstwerk hat ein Ideal	229(fr. 230)	II 648 (476)	II 172	405
	55	Überhaupt können die Dichter	–	I 286	I 159–60	255
	67	Die Poesie ganz auf Erfahrung beruht	–	I 285–6	I 159–60	–
5	18	Wie ein Kind mit dem Zauberstabe	–	I 100	II 90	164
	34	Selbst der Schlaf	–	I 104	II 97	167–8
	36	Alles poetische muß märchenhaft	–	III 449 (940)	–	452
	36	Ein Märchen ist wie ein Traumbild	269 (493)	III 454 (986)	II 230	446–7
	38	[Heinrich finds book]	–	I 264–5	I 121–3	236–7
	39	Die Fabellehre	264 (451)	II 456 (100)	II 218	351
	39	Sprache in der zweiten Potenz	231 (249)	II 588 (264)	II 177	407
7	20	[Philistine merchants]	–	I 207–10	I 29–32	184ff
	23	An schlechten und mittelmäßigen	234 (269)	II 598–9 (340)	II 185	415

(cont.)

Chapter and note number		Citation opening	Schriften, V, 1988 (=Tieck 1802)	Schriften, I, II or III, 1960, or IV, 1975	Schriften, Reimer, 1837 (Tieck)	Gesammelte Werke, 1967
8	24	Wahnsinn und Bezauberung	269–70 (499)	III 639 (508)	II 268	448
	22	Die Natur ist eine Äolsharfe	230 (239)	III 452 (966)	II 174	406
	29	Die Musik redet eine allgemeine Sprache	230 (242)	III 283–4 (245)	II 175	407
	31	Die echte Sanskrit	-	I 79	II 55	145
	32	In einem echten Märchen tritt … die Zeit vor der Welt ein	269 (494)	III 280 (234)	II 230	447
	32	Alle Märchen sind nur Träume von jener heimatlichen Welt	269 (496)	II 564 (196)	II 231	447
	32	Die Philosophie ist … Heimweh	207 (28)	III 434 (857)	II 116	381
	32	Das Paradies war das Ideal	209–10 (47)	III 446–7 (929)	II 122	384
	32	Die höhere Philosophie behandelt die Ehe von Natur und Geist	210 (52)	III 247 (50)	II 124	385
	32	Wir selbst sind ein … Keim der Liebe zwischen Natur und Geist oder Kunst	222 (152)	III 253 (79)	II 155	396
	32	Die reale Definition ist ein Zauberwort	211 (61)	II 592 (297–8)	II 126	385
	32	Die Zeit ist nicht mehr … Die Bedeutung der Hieroglyphe fehlt.	217 (95)	II 545 (104)	II 141	392
	32	Philosophie … ist eine unbestimmte Wissenschaft der Wissenschaften	209 (43)	III 666	II 120	382–3
	32	Ist nicht alles voll von Bedeutung	249 (335)	III 665 (603)	II 148	423–4
	32	Die Wissenschaften	-	IV 252	-	-
	32	Naturforscher und Dichter	-	I 84	II 63	149
	32	Mit Instinct hat der Mensch angefangen	217 (92)	III 301 (340)	II 140	392
	32	Sie wagen es nie, diesen Proteus	206 (18)	III 338 (468)	II 114	379–80
	32	Die Analysis ist die Divinations-Kunst auf Regeln gebracht	207 (23)	III 434 (858)	II 115	380
	32	Alle Ideen sind verwandt	207 (24)	II 540 (72)	II 115	380
	32	Die Philosophie ist die Wissenschaft des allgemeinen Divinations-Sinn	207 (25)	III 464–5 (1061)	II 115–16	380

	32	Synthetische Gedanken ... Affinitäten und Sippschaften	207 (26)	III 558 (20)	II 116	-
	32	Meine Erkenntniß des Ganzen würde ... den Charakter der Analogie haben ... Analogie ist symbolisch	212 (69)	II 551 (118)	II 129	386
	32	Der Mensch ist eine Analogie-Quell für das Weltall	236 (281)	II 610 (401)	II 190	417
	32	Der echte Divinationssinn	258 (405)	III 250 (61)	II 252	-
	32	An die Geschichte ... lernt den Zauberstab der Analogie	275 (531)	III 518	II 281	-
	32	In der Musik erscheint sie	248–9 (330)	III 593 (241)	II 147	423
	41	Wie viele Menschen	-	I 104	II 97	167–8
	42	Nur Dichter sollten mit dem Flüßigen	-	I 105	II 98	168
	42	Der echte Dichter ist allwissend	265 (463)	II 592 (296)	II 221	441
	42	Poesie ... ist von Natur flüßig	-	IV 246	-	-
	42	Der Sinn für Poesie	264 (456)	III 685–6 (671)	II 219–20	440
	44	Alles Vollendete spricht sich	264 (455)	III 410–11 (737)	II 218	440
	45	Wenn einer bloß spricht (*Monolog*)		II 672–3	III 120–22 (1846)	
	46	Die Sculptur und die Musik	229 (232)	III 259 (102)	II 172	405
10	6	Eine Idee ist desto gediegener	236 (281)	II 610 (401)	II 190	417
	14	Die Kunst, auf eine angenehme	267 (482)	III 685 (668)	II 225	444
	30	Wenn diese mehr das Flüßige	-	I 84	II 63	150
	30	Der rohe diskursive Denker	205 (15)	II 524–5 (13)	II 109–12	377

Appendix 2: Novalis and the Schumann of 1828

Schumann	Novalis
Philosophie ist Musik des Geistes, Musik Philosophie des Gemüthes.[1]	Die Poesie ist der Held der Philosophie.[7] Poesie ist Darstellung des Gemüths.[8]
Musik ist die höhere Potenz der Poesie.[2]	Sprache in der zweiten Potenz, z.B. Fabel, ist Ausdruck eines ganzen Gedankens.[9]
Ton ist überhaupt componirtes Wort.[3] Die Tanzmusik ist verkörperte, bewegliche Musick; jede Bewegung muß Harmonie seyn.[4] Tanz ist gefrorne Musik.[5]	Der Ton scheint nichts als eine gebrochene Bewegung zu seyn, in dem Sinn, wie die Farbe gebrochenes Licht ist.[10] Die Sculptur ist das gebildete Starre. Die Musik das gebildete Flüßige.[11]
Ein zufälliger, unberechneter Strich führt den Maler oft auf ein schönes Gesicht, so auch beim Musiker ein falscher Griff u. beym Dichter ein zufälliger Reim auf einen hohen Gedanken.[6]	Die Hand wird beim Maler Sitz eines Instinkts, so auch beim Musiker, der Fuß beim Tänzer, das Gesicht beim Schauspieler.[12]

Appendix 3: Extracts from selected German original texts

Chapter 2

3–2 (a)   Schumann's review of Berlioz's *Symphonie Fantastique*

Der vielfache Stoff, den diese Sinfonie zum Nachdenken bietet, könnte sich in der Folge leicht zu sehr verwickeln, daher ich es vorziehe, sie in einzelnen Teilen, so oft auch einer von dem andern zur Erklärung borgen muß, durchzugehen, nämlich nach den vier Gesichtspunkten, unter denen man ein Musikwerk betrachten kann, d.i. je nach der Form (des Ganzen, der einzelnen Teile, der Periode, der Phrase), je nach der musikalischen Komposition (Harmonie, Melodie, Satz, Arbeit, Stil), nach

---

[1] *Tagebücher*, I 96.
[2] Ibid.; Schumann began writing 'Philosophy', which is even nearer Novalis, but wisely changed his mind.
[3] Ibid.   [4] Ibid.   [5] Ibid., 105.   [6] Ibid., 97.
[7] Novalis, *Schriften*, V 266(fr. 466); II 590; Reimer (1837), II 222; *Werke* (1967), 442.
[8] Novalis, *Schriften*, V 265(fr. 459); III 650(fr. 553); Reimer (1837), II 220; *Werke* (1967), 441.
[9] Novalis, *Schriften*, V 231(fr. 249); II 588(fr. 264); Reimer (1837), II 177; *Werke* (1967), 407.
[10] Novalis, *Schriften*, V 231(fr. 250); III 561(fr. 43); Reimer (1837), II 177; *Werke* (1967), 408; *Mottosammlung*, IX 192.
[11] Novalis, *Schriften*, V 229(fr. 232); III 259(fr. 102); Reimer (1837), II 172; *Werke* (1967), 405; *Mottosammlung*, IX 188.
[12] Novalis, *Schriften*, V 228(fr. 227); III 276(fr. 204); Reimer (1837), II 170; *Mottosammlung*, IX 184.

der besonderen Idee, die der Künstler darstellen wollte, und nach dem Geiste, der über Form, Stoff und Idee waltet.

Die Form ist das Gefäß des Geistes. Größere Räume fordern, sie zu füllen, größern Geist.

...

Wir schließen mit einigen Worten über Idee und Geist.

Berlioz selbst hat in einem Programme niedergeschrieben, was er wünscht, daß man sich bei seiner Sinfonie denken soll. Wir teilen es in Kürze mit.

Der Komponist wollte einige Momente aus dem Leben eines Künstlers durch Musik schildern. Es scheint nötig, daß der Plan zu einem Instrumentaldrama vorher durch Worte erläutert werde. Man sehe das folgende Programm wie den die Musiksätze einleitenden Text in der Oper an. Erste Abteilung...

...

Soweit das Programm. Ganz Deutschland schenkt es ihm: solche Wegweiser haben immer etwas Unwürdiges und Charlatanmäßiges. Jedenfalls hätten die fünf Hauptüberschriften genügt; die genaueren Umstände, die allerdings der Person des Komponisten halber, der die Sinfonie selbst durchlebt, interessieren müssen, würden sich schon durch mündliche Tradition fortgepflanzt haben. Mit einem Worte, der zärtsinnige, aller Persönlichkeit abholde Deutsche will in seinen Gedanken nicht so grob geleitet sein; schon bei der Pastoralsinfonie beleidigte es ihn, daß ihm Beethoven nicht zutraute, ihren Charackter ohne sein Zutun zu erraten...

Ob diese [die Musik] nun in einem, der die Absicht des Komponisten nicht kennt, ähnliche Bilder erwecken wird, als er zeichnen wollte, mag ich, der ich das Programm vor dem Hören gelesen, nicht entscheiden. Ist einmal das Auge auf einen Punkt geleitet, so urteilt das Ohr nicht mehr selbständig. Fragt man aber, ob die Musik das, was Berlioz in seiner Sinfonie von ihr fordert, wirklich leisten könne, so versuche man ihr andere oder entgegengesetzte Bilder unterzulegen. Am Anfange verleidete auch mir das Programm allen Genuß, alle freie Aussicht. Als diese aber immer mehr in den Hintergrund trat und die eigene Phantasie zu schaffen anfing, fand ich nicht nur alles, sondern viel mehr und fast überall lebendigen, warmen Ton. Was überhaupt die schwierige Frage, wieweit die Instrumentalmusik in Darstellung von Gedanken und Begebenheiten gehen dürfe, anlangt, so sehen hier viele zu ängstlich. Man irrt sich gewiß, wenn man glaubt, die Komponisten legten sich Feder und Papier in der elenden Absicht zurecht, dies oder jenes auszudrücken, zu schildern, zu malen. Doch schlage man zufällige Einflüsse und Eindrücke von außen nicht zu gering an. Unbewußt neben der musikalischen Phantasie wirkt oft eine Idee fort, neben dem Ohre das Auge, und dieses, das immer tätige Organ, hält dann mitten unter den Klängen und Tönen gewisse Umrisse fest, die sich mit dem vorrückenden Musik zu deutlichen Gestalten verdichten und ausbilden können. Je mehr nun der Musik verwandte Elemente die mit den Tönen erzeugten Gedanken oder Gebilde in sich tragen, von je poetischerem oder plastischerem Ausdrucke wird die Komposition sein, – und je phantastischer oder schärfer der Musiker überhaupt auffaßt, um so mehr wird sein Werk erheben oder ergreifen. Warum könnte nicht einen Beethoven inmitten seiner Phantasien der Gedanke an Unsterblichkeit überfallen? Warum nicht das Andenken einer großen gefallenen Helden ihn zu einem Werke begeistern? Warum nicht einen anderen die Erinnerung an eine selig verlebte Zeit? Oder wollen wir undankbar sein gegen Shakespeare, daß er aus der Brust eines jungen Tondichters ein seiner würdiges Werk hervorrief, – undankbar gegen die Natur und leugnen, daß wir von ihrer Schönheit und Erhabenheit zu unseren Werken borgten? Italien, die Alpen, das Bild des Meeres, eine Frühlingsdämmerung – hätte uns die Musik noch nichts von allem diesem erzählt? Ja selbst kleinere, speziellere Bilder können der Musik eine so reizend festen Charakter verleihen, daß man überrascht wird, wie sie solche Züge auszudrücken vermag ...

Ob nun in dem Programme zur Berliozschen Sinfonie viele poetische Momente liegen, lassen wir dahingestellt. Die Hauptsache bleibt, ob die Musik ohne Text und Erläuterung an sich etwas ist, und vorzüglich, ob ihr Geist inwohnt.[13]

3–2 (b) Schumann on programmes

Wir gestehen, ein Vorurteil gegen diese Art des Schaffens zu haben, und teilen dies vielleicht mit hundert gelehrten Köpfen, die freilich oft sonderbare Vorstellungen vom Komponieren haben, und sich immer auf Mozart berufen, der sich nichts bei seiner Musik gedacht haben soll. Wie gesagt indes, das Vorurteil haben wohl manche, auch nicht-Gelehrte, und hält uns daher ein Komponist *vor* seiner Musik ein Programm entgegen, so sag' ich: Vor allem laß mich hören, daß du schöne Musik gemacht, hinterher soll mir auch dein Programm angenehm sein. Es ist eben ein Unterschied, ob ein Goethe nach aufgegebenen Endreimen einmal dichtet oder ein anderer ... Über all dieses ist schon bei der Weihe der Töne hin und her geredet worden, und der Kampf fängt schon wieder an aufzulodern über das Etwas-sich-nicht-denken-sollen beim Komponieren und das Gegenteil. Die Philosophen denken sich die Sache auch schlimmer, als sie ist, gewiß, sie irren, wenn sie glauben, ein Komponist, der nach einer Idee arbeitet, setzte sich hin wie ein Prediger am Sonnabendnachmittag und schematisiere sein Thema nach den gewöhnlichen drei Teilen und arbeite es überhaupt gehörig aus; gewiß, sie irren. Das Schaffen des Musikers ist ein ganz anderes, und schwebt ihm ein Bild, eine Idee vor, so wird er sich doch nur erst dann glücklich in seiner Arbeit fühlen, wenn sie ihm in schönen Melodien entgegenkommt, von denselben unsichtbaren Händen getragen, wie die ‚goldenen Eimer' von denen Goethe irgendwo spricht.[14]

---

[13] *GSK*, I 69–84.   [14] *GSK*, II 129–30.

Chapter 3

3-3 Goethe on the Roman Carnival

Das Römische Karneval ist ein Fest, das dem Volke eigentlich nicht gegeben ist, sondern das sich das Volk selbst gibt ... Hier wird ... nur ein Zeichen gegeben, daß jeder so töricht und toll sein dürfe, als er wolle, und daß außer Schlägen und Messerstichen fast alles erlaubt sei. Der Unterschied zwischen Hohen und Niedern scheint einen Augenblick aufgehoben: alles nähert sich einander, jeder nimmt was ihm begegnet leicht auf, und die wechselseitige Frechheit und Freiheit wird durch eine allgemeine gute Laune im Gleichgewicht erhalten.

Dieser Abendspazierfahrt ... lockt viele Füßgänger in den Corso; jedermann kommt, um zu sehen oder gesehen zu werden. Das Karneval ist ... eigentlich nur eine Fortsetzung oder vielmehr der Gipfel jener gewöhnlichen sonn- und festtägigen Freuden; es ist nichts Neues, nichts Fremdes, nichts Einziges, sondern es schließt sich nur an die Römische Lebensweise ganz natürlich an.

... Alle Kinder sind auf der Straße, die nun aufhört eine Straße zu sein; sie gleicht vielmehr einem großen Festsaal, einer ungeheuren ausgeschmückten Galerie ...

Nun fangen die Masken an sich zu vermehren. Junge Männer, geputzt in Festtageskleidern der Weiber aus der untersten Klasse, mit entblößtem Busen und frecher Selbstgenügsamkeit, lassen sich meist zuerst sehen. Sie liebkosen die ihnen begegnenden Männer, tun gemein, und vertraut mit den Weibern als mit ihresgleichen, treiben sonst, was ihnen Laune, Witz oder Unart eingeben.

Da die Frauen ebensoviel Lust haben, sich in Mannskleidern zu zeigen, ..., so haben die beliebte Tracht des Pulcinells sich anzupassen nicht verfehlt, und man muß bekennen, daß es ihnen gelingt, in dieser Zwittergestalt oft höchst reizend zu sein ...

Manchmal wird eine Maske vom Theater nachgeahmt ...

Ein Zauberer mischt sich unter die Menge, läßt das Volk ein Buch mit Zahlen sehn und erinnert uns an seine Leidenschaft zum Lottospiel ...

Weil die Fremden Maler ... in Rom überall öffentlich sitzen und zeichnen, so werden sie auch unter der Karnevalsmenge emsig vorgestellt ...

Unweit der französischen Akademie tritt in spanischer Tracht, mit Federhut, Degen und großen Handschuhen, unversehens mitten aus den von einem Gerüste zuschauenden Masken der sogenannte Capitano des italienischen Theaters auf und fängt an, seine großen Taten zu Land und Wasser in emphatischen Ton zu erzählen. Es währt nicht lange, so erhebt sich gegen ihm über ein Pulcinell, bringt Zweifel und Einwendungen vor, und indem er ihm alles zuzugeben scheint, macht er die Großsprecherei jenes Helden durch Wortspiele und eingeschobene Plattheiten lächerlich.

Das entsetzliche Gedränge ... zwingt ... eine Menge Masken aus dem Corso hinaus in die benachbarten Straßen. Da gehen verliebte Paare ruhiger und vertrauter zusammen, da finden lustige Gesellen Platz, allerlei tolle Schauspiele vorzustellen . . .

Auf einmal entzweien sich die Männer, es entsteht ein lebhafter Wortwechsel, die Frauen mischen sich hinein, der Handel wird immer ärger, endlich ziehen die Streitenden große Messer von versilberten Pappe und fallen einander an . . .

Die Nacht ist eingetreten . . . und ein großer Teil des Publikums eilt nach dem Theater . . . Die Theater Alberti und Argentina geben ernsthafte Opern . . . Valle und Capranica Komödien und Tragödien mit komischen subordinierte Schauspiele . . .

Die Leidenschaft der Römer für das Theater ist groß und war ehemals in der Karnevalszeit noch heftiger, weil sie in dieser einzigen Epoche befriedigt werden konnte . . .

Die Tänze bei diesen Festen werden gewöhnlich in langen Reihen, nach Art der englischen, getanzt; nur unterscheiden sie sich dadurch, daß sie in ihren wenigen Touren meistenteils etwas Charakteristisches pantomimisch ausdrücken; zum Beispiel, es entzweien und versöhnen sich zwei Liebende, sie scheiden und finden sich wieder . . .

Besonders wird der Menuett ganz eigentlich als ein Kunstwerk betrachtet, und nur von wenigen Paaren gleichsam aufgeführt. Ein solches Paar wird dann von der übrigen Gesellschaft in einen Kreis geschlossen, bewundert und am Ende applaudiert . . .

Aschermittwoch: So ist denn ein ausschweifendes Fest wie ein Traum, wie ein Märchen vorüber.[15]

Chapter 4

3–4 (a)   Hoffmann on Bach, Haydn, Mozart and Beethoven

Es gibt Augenblicke – vorzüglich wenn ich viel in des großen Sebastian Bachs Werken gelesen – in denen mir die musikalischen Zahlenverhältnisse, ja die mystischen Regeln des Kontrapunkts ein inneres Grauen erwecken. – Musik! – mit geheimnisvollen Schauer, ja mit Grausen nenne ich dich! – Dich! – in Tönen ausgesprochene Sanskritta der Natur![16]

Sollte, wenn von der Musik als einer selbstständigen Kunst die Rede ist, nicht immer nur die Instrumental-Musik gemeint sein, welche jede Hülfe, jede Einmischung einer anderen Kunst (der Poesie) verschmähend, das eigentümliche, nur in ihr zu erkennende Wesen dieser Kunst rein ausspricht? Sie ist die romantischste aller Künste, beinahe möchte man sagen, allein echt romantisch, denn nur das Unendliche ist ihr Vorwurf. – Orpheus' Lyra öffnete die Tore

---

[15] Goethe, *Das Römische Karneval* (*Werke*, VI 495–523).
[16] Hoffmann, *Kreisleriana*, I/5, 50, excerpted by Schumann in *Dichtergarten*, 305.

des Orkus. Die Musik schließt dem Menschen ein unbekanntes Reich auf, eine Welt, die nichts gemein mit dem äußern Sinnenwelt, die ihn umgibt, und in der er aller *bestimmten* Gefühle zurückläßt, um sich einer unaussprechlichen Sehnsucht hinzugeben.

Habt ihr dies eigentümliche Wesen nur geahnt, ihr armen Instrumentalkomponisten, die ihr euch mühsam abquältet, bestimmten Empfindungen, ja sogar Begebenheiten darzustellen? Wie konnte es auch denn nur einfallen, die der Plastik geradezu entgegengesetzte Kunst plastisch zu behandeln? Eure Sonnenaufgänge, eure Gewitter, eure Bataille des trois Empereurs u.s.w. waren wohl gewiß gar lächerliche Verirrungen und sind wohlverdienterweise mit gänzlichem Vergessen bestraft.

In dem Gesange, wo die Poesie bestimmte Affekt durch Worte andeutet, wirkt die magische Kraft der Musik, wie das wunderbare Elixier der Weisen, von dem etliche Tropfen jeden Trank köstlicher und herrlicher machen. Jede Leidenschaft – Liebe – Haß – Zorn – Verzweiflung und so weiter, wie die Oper sie uns gibt, kleidert die Musik in den Purpurschimmer der Romantik, und selbst das im Leben Empfundene führt uns hinaus aus dem Leben in das Reich des Unendlichen. So stark ist der Zauber der Musik, und, immer mächtiger wirkend, müßte er jede Fessel einer andern Kunst zerreißen . . .

Mozart und Haydn, die Schöpfer der jetzigen Instrumental-Musik, zeigten uns zuerst die Kunst in ihrer vollen Glorie; wer sie da mit voller Liebe anschaute und eindrang in ihr innigstes Wesen ist – Beethoven! – Die Instrumentalkompositionen aller drei Meister atmen einen gleichen romantischen Geist . . .

So öffnet uns auch Beethovens Instrumental-Musik das Reich des Ungeheuern und Unermeßlichen. Glühende Strahlen schießen durch dieses Reiches tiefe Nacht, und wir werden Riesenschatten gewahr, die auf- und abwogen, enger und enger uns einschließen und *uns* vernichten, aber nicht den Schmerz der unendlichen Sehnsucht, in welcher jede Lust, die schnell in jauchzenden Tönen emporgestiegen, hinsinkt und untergeht, und nur in diesem Schmerz, der Liebe, Hoffnung, Freude, in sich verzehrend, aber nicht zerstörend, unsere Brust mit einem vollstimmigen Zusammenklange aller Leidenschaften zersprengen will, leben wir fort und sind entzückte Geisterseher!

Haydn faßt das Menschliche im menschlichen Leben romantisch auf; er ist kommensurabler, faßlicher für die Mehrzahl. Mozart nimmt mehr das Übermenschliche, das Wunderbare, welches im innern Geiste wohnt, in Anspruch.

Beethovens Musik bewegt die Hebel der Furcht, des Schauders, des Entsetzens, des Schmerzes, und erweckt eben jene unendliche Sehnsucht, welche das Wesen der Romantik ist. Er ist daher ein rein romantischer (und deshalb ein wahrhaft musikalischer) Komponist, und daher mag es kommen, daß ihm Vokalmusik, die unbestimmtes Sehnen nicht zuläßt, sondern nur durch Worte bestimmte Affekte als in dem Reiche des Unendlichen empfunden darstellt, weniger gelingt?[17]

---

[17] Hoffmann, *Kreisleriana*, I/4, 41–3.

3-4 (b) C. F. Michaelis on music

Die Musik wirkt, weil sie nicht bestimmte Gegenstände der äußern oder innern Anschauung unmittelbar darstellt, sondern in den Tönen und Melodien nur Zeichen, nur Andeutungen von möglichen Gegenständen (besonders von inneren Empfindungen, Affekten, Leidenschaften und überhaupt Gemüthsstimmungen) giebt, ganz vorzüglich auf die Reproduktionsfähigkeit und auf das Dichtungsvermögen der Seele, welche das Angedeutete aus eigener Kraft ausführt und vollendet. Ihr Effekt ist daher so zauberreich groß, größer als gewöhnlich in den bildenden Künsten, in wiefern diese mehr die Objekte für die Sinne selbst, als die bloßen Zeichen für die Einbildungskraft darstellen, und selten ihre Darstellungsmittel symbolisch gebrauchen . . .

Die Tonkunst . . . giebt den aus der Natur abstrahirten Lauten und Tönen in der musikalischen Composition eine gewiße Selbständigkeit, schafft und bildet aus den Tönen eine unsichtbare geistige Welt.[18]

3-4 (c) Schumann on Schubert's C major Symphony

Aber daß die Außenwelt, wie sie heute strahlt, morgen dunkelt, oft hineingreift in das Innere des Dichters und Musikers, das wolle man nur auch glauben, und daß in dieser Sinfonie mehr als bloßer schöner Gesang, mehr als bloßer Leid und Freud, wie es die Musik schon hundertfällig ausgesprochen, verborgen liegt, ja daß sie uns in einer Region führt, wo wir vorher gewesen zu sein uns nirgends erinnern können, dies zugegeben, höre man solche Sinfonie. Hier ist außer meisterlicher musikalischer Technik der Komposition, noch Leben in aller Fasern, Kolorit bis in die feinste Abstufung, Bedeutung überall.[19]

3-4 (d) Brendel on Schumann

Die Ungenbundenheit des Subjects, das schranken- und fessellose Ergehen desselben, das freie Waltenlassen des Genius ist das Characteristische der modernen Zeit, und dafür ist vorzugsweise die Instrumentalmusik geeignet. In dem Gesangswerke ist durch den Text ein bestimmter Inhalt gegeben; bestimmte Formen sind vorgezeichnet, und der Componist ist an einen bestimmten Fortgang, an eine bestimmte Entwicklung gebunden. In der Instrumentalmusik dagegen ist Alles der Eingebung des Componisten überlassen. So weit nur die künstlerischen Ausdrucksmittel ausreichen, kann er sein Inneres entfalten, und zuletzt in der freien Phantasie ganz den Launen und Eingebungen des Augenblicks huldigen. Wenn alle Kunst die Aufgabe hat, das Endliche in das Unendliche emporzuheben, wenn aber andere Künste an einer bestimmten Endlichkeit

---

[18] C. F. Michaelis, 'Vermischte Bemerkungen' (1805), 21–2.   [19] *GSK*, I 462.

anknüpfen, und diese ins Unendliche auflösen, einen bestimmten Lebensinhalt zur Darstellung bringen, welcher von dem Unendlichen durchdrungen wird und in diesem aufgeht, so zeigt die Instrumentalmusik das Emporstreben des Subjects zum Unendlichen überhaupt, weniger eine bestimmte Endlichkeit, sondern die endliche, von einen höheren erfüllte Natur im Allgemeinen ...

In Beethoven herrscht der Inhalt die Form ...

Ich bin hiermit unmittelbar bei den künstlerischen Anfängen Schumann's angelangt; – die frühesten Compositionen desselben sind ... Erzählungen, oder ein Cyklus von unter sich zusammenhängenden lyrischen Gedichten. Der poetische Gedanke wird der herrschende, und die Theile sind nicht mehr technisch, sondern durch einen poetischen Faden verbunden ... Hin und wieder zwar werden auch Aueßerlichkeiten gezeichnet, aber es verschwimmt im Ganzen Subjectives und Objectives phantastisch zusammen.

[In den Phantasiestücken] ... ['In der Nacht'] bringt uns ... beängstetes Traumwachen ... [und] der vorigen Nummer [referring to 'Des Abends'] entgengesetzte Seelenzustände. Sch.'s Compositionen sind häufig landschaftlichen Gemälden, in welchen der Vordergrund in scharfbegrenzten, klaren Umrissen hervortritt, der Hintergrund dagegen verschwimmt, und in eine unbegrenzte Perspective sich verliert, sind einer von Nebeln verschleierten Landschaft zu vergleichen, aus der nur hier und da ein Gegenstand sonnenbeleuchtet hervortritt ... Dieser inneren Eigenthümlichkeit entspricht die äußere, daß Sch., sehr mit aufgehobenen Pedal zu spielen liebt, um die Harmonien öfter nicht ganz deutlich hervortreten zu lassen ...

Hier bei Sch. ... dienen sie [Benennungen der Tonstücke] oftmals, wie z. B. in den Kinderscenen, dazu, um die letzte Bestimmtheit hinzufügen. Diese Benennungen haben zum Theil heftigen Widerspruch erfahren; man sah nicht ein, daß sie nur Resultat der Reflexion über das schon vorhandene Kunstwerk waren, und hielt sie für das vorher vorhandene Schema, nach welchem der Componist arbeitete ...

Ich glaube durch das Bisherige den Punct, welcher bei der Kunstentwicklung der Gegenwart hauptsächlich in Frage kommt, zur Sprache gebracht, eine erste Ausführung des Programms in Nr. 1 u. 2 dies. Bl. gegeben zu haben.[20]

Chapter 6

3–6 Schumann's style

Der Brief von Simonin de S. hat mich sehr gefreut – überhaupt sehe ich mit Freude, wie sich meine Compositionen hier und da Bahn brechen – ich schreibe jetzt bei weitem leichter, klarer und, glaube ich, anmuthiger; sonst löthete ich Alles

---

[20] Brendel, 'Robert Schumann' (1845), 64; 67; 82–3; 89–91; 149.

lothweise an einander und da ist viel Wunderliche und wenig Schönes herausgekommen; indeß auch die Irrthümer des Künstlers gehören der Welt, wenn es gerade keine Häßlichkeiten sind. Seit 4 Wochen habe ich fast nichts als componirt, wie ich Dir schon schrieb; es strömte mir zu, ich sang dabei immer mit – und da ist's meistens gelungen. Mit den Formen spiel' ich. Überhaupt ist es mir seit etwa anderthalb Jahren, als wär ich im Besitz des Geheimnißes; das klingt sonderbar. Vieles liegt noch in mir. Bleibst Du mir treu, so kömmt alles an den Tag; wo nicht, bleibts begraben. Das Nächste, ich mache 3 Violinquartetten.[21]

Chapter 7

3-7 Hoffmann's Kreisler

Wo ist er her? – Niemand weiß es! Wer waren seine Eltern? – Es ist unbekannt! ...

Die Freunde behaupteten: die Natur habe bei seiner Organisation ein neues Rezept versucht und der Versuch sei mißlungen, indem seinem überreizbaren Gemüte, seiner bis zur zerstörenden Flamme aufglühenden Fantasie zu wenig Phlegma beigemischt und so das Gleichgewicht zerstört worden, das dem Künstler durchaus nötig sei, um mit der Welt zu leben und ihr Werke dichten, wie sie dieselben, selbst in höhern Sinn, eigentlich brauche. Dem sei wie ihm wollen – genug, Johannes wurde von seinen innern Erscheinungen und Träume, wie auf einem ewig wogenden Meer dahin-dorthin getrieben, und er schien vergebens den Port zu suchen, der ihm endlich *die* Ruhe und Heiterkeit geben sollte, ohne welche der Künstler nichts zu schaffen vermag ...

Auf einmal war er, man wußte nicht wie und warum, verschwunden. Viele behaupteten, Spuren des Wahnsinns an ihm bemerkt zu haben ...[22]

Sie sind alle fortgegangen. – ...

Hab ich doch während des Spielens meinen Bleistift hervorgezogen, und Seite 63 unter dem letzten System ein paar gute Ausweichungen in Ziffern notiert mit der rechten Hand, während die Linke in Strome der Töne fortarbeitete! Hinten auf der leeren Seite fahr ich schreibend fort. Ich verlasse Ziffern und Töne, und mit wahrer Lust, wie der genesene Kranke, der nun nicht aufhören kann zu erzählen, was er gelitten, notiere ich hier umständlich die höllischen Qualen des heutigen Tees. Aber nicht für mich allein, sondern für alle, die sich hier zuweilen an meinem Exemplar der Johann Sebastian Bachschen Variationen für das Klavier, erschienen bei Nägeli in Zürch, ergötzen und erbauen, bei dem Schluß der 30sten Variation meine Ziffer finden, und, geleitet von dem großen lateinischen Verte (ich schreib es gleich hin, wenn meine Klageschrift zu Ende ist), das Blatt umwenden und lesen ...

---

[21] *Briefwechsel*, I 100 (11 February 1838). [22] Hoffmann, *Kreisleriana*, I Introduction, 25–6.

Da tritt der Baron ... auf mich und sagt: „O bester Herr Kapellmeister, Sie sollen ganz himmlisch fantasieren; o fantasieren Sie uns doch eins! Nur ein wenig! Ich bitte!" Ich versetzte ganz trocken, die Fantasie sei mir heute rein ausgegangen; und indem wir so darüber sprechen, hat ein Teufel in der Gestalt eines Elegants mit zwei Westen im Nebenzimmer unter meinem Hut die Bachschen Variationen ausgewittert; der denkt, es sind so Variatiönchen: nel cor mi non più sento – 'Ah vous dirai-je, maman' etc. und will haben, ich soll darauf losspielen. Ich weigere mich: da fallen sie alle über mich her. Nun so hört und berstet vor Langeweile, denk ich, und arbeite drauf los.[23]

Der Zweck der Kunst überhaupt ist doch kein anderer, als dem Menschen eine angenehme Unterhaltung zu verschaffen, und ihn von den ernsten, oder vielmehr den einzigen ihm anständigen Geschäften, nämlich solchen, die ihm Brot und Ehre im Staat erwerben, auf eine angenehme Art zu zerstreuen, so daß er nachher mit gedoppelter Aufmerksamkeit und Anstrengung zu dem eigentlichen Zweck seines Daseins zurückkehren ... kann.

Was nun aber die Musik betrifft, so können nur jene heillosen Verächter dieser edeln Kunst leugnen, daß eine gelungene Komposition, d.h. eine solche, die sich gehörig in Schranken hält, und eine angenehme Melodie nach der andern folgen läßt, ohne zu toben, oder sich in allerlei kontrapunktischen Gängen und Auflösungen närrisch zu gebärden, einen wunderbaren Reiz verursacht ...

Euch, ihr heillosen Verächter der edlen Kunst, führe ich nun in den häuslichen Zirkel, wo der Vater, müde von den ernsten Geschäften des Tages, im Schlafrock und in Pantoffeln, fröhlich und guten Muts zum *Murki* seines ältesten Sohnes seine Pfeife raucht ...[24]

Schon lange galt der arme Johannes allgemein für wahnsinnig, und in der Tat stach auch sein ganzes Tun und Treiben, vorzüglich seine Leben in der Kunst, so grell gegen alles ab, was vernünftig und schicklich heißt, daß an den innern Zerrüttung seines Geistes kaum zu zweifeln war. Immer exzentrischer, immer verwirrter wurde sein Ideengang; so z. B., sprach er, kurz vor seiner Flucht aus dem Orte, viel von der unglücklichen Liebe einer Nachtigall zu einer Purpurnelke, das Ganze sei aber (meinte er) nichts als ein Adagio, und dies nun wieder eigentlich ein einziger lang ausgehaltener Ton Juliens, auf dem Romeo in den höchsten Himmel voll Liebe und Seligkeit hinaufschwebe. Endlich gestand er mir, wie er seinen Tod beschlossen und sich im nächsten Walde mit einer übermäßigen Quinte erdolchen werde ...

So wie übrigens Wallborn in verfehlter Liebe den Wahnsinn fand, so scheint auch Kreisler durch eine ganz fantastische Liebe zu einer Sängerin auf die höchste Spitze des Wahnsinns getrieben worden zu sein.[25]

Ach, es geschah Euch vielleicht noch nie, daß Ihr irgend ein Lied singen wolltet vor Augen, die Euch aus dem Himmel herab anzublicken schienen, die Euer

---

[23] Hoffmann, *Kreisleriana*, I/1, 27–30.   [24] Hoffmann, *Kreisleriana*, I/3, 36–7.
[25] Hoffmann, *Kreisleriana*, II Introduction, 284–5.

ganzes, besseres Sein verschönt auf Euch herniederstrahlten, und daß Ihr auch wirklich anfingt, und glaubtet, o Johannes, nun habe Euer Laut die geliebte Seele durchdrungen, und nun, eben nun werde des Klanges höchster Schwung Tauperlen um jene zwei Sterne ziehen, mildernd und schmückend den seligen Glanz – und die Sterne wandten sich geruhig nach irgend einer Läpperei hin, etwa nach einer gefallenen Masche, und die Engelslippen verkniffen, unhold lächelnd, ein übermächtiges Gähnen – und, Herr, es war weiter nichts, als Ihr hattet die gnädige Frau ennuiert ... Und im Vertrauen, Herr, hier liegt der Grund, warum ich das geworden bin, was die Leute toll nennen. Aber ich bin selten wild dabei. Meist weine ich ganz still. ...

Sieh, Johannes, Du kommst mir mit dem, was Du gegen alle ungeniale Musik eiferst, bisweilen sehr hart vor ... Ich kann dir mit voller Wahrheit sagen, daß auch der schlechteste Klang einer verstimmten Geige mir lieber ist, als gar keine Musik ... Eine solche Dudelei, heiße sie nun Tanz oder Marsch, erinnert an das Höchste, was in uns liegt.[26]

Nehmen Ew. Hoch- und Wohlgeboren es aber doch ja nicht übel, wenn ich mich sehr musikalisch ausdrücken sollte, denn Sie wissen es ja wohl schon, daß die Leute behaupten, die Musik, die sonst in meinen Innern verschlossen, sei zu mächtig und stark herausgegangen, und habe mich so umsponnen und eingepuppt, daß ich nicht mehr heraus könne, und alles, alles sich mir wie Musik gestalte ... Doch ... ich muß an Ew. Hoch- und Wohlgeboren schreiben, denn wie soll ich anders die Last, die sich schwer und drückend auf meine Brust gelegt, in dem Augenblick als die Gardine fiel, und Ew. Hoch- und Wohlgeboren auf unbegreifliche Weise verschwunden waren, los werden.

Wie viel hatte ich noch zu sagen, unaufgelöste Dissonanzen schrieen recht widrig in mein Inneres hinein, aber eben als all die schlangenzüngigen Septimen herabschweben wollten in eine ganze lichte Welt freundlicher Terzen, da waren Ew. Hoch- und Wohlgeboren fort – fort – und die Schlangenzungen stachen und stachelten mich sehr! Ew. Hoch- und Wohlgeboren, den ich jetzt mit all jenen freundlichen Terzen ansingen will, sind doch kein anderer, als der Baron Wallborn, den ich längst in meinem Innern getragen, daß er mir, wenn alle meine Melodien sich wie *er* gestalten und nun keck und gewaltig hervorströmten, oft schien: ich sei ja eben er selbst. – Als heute im Theater eine kräftige jugendliche Gestalt in Uniform, das klirrende Schwert an der Seite, recht mannlich und ritterhaft auf mich zutrat, da ging es so fremd und doch so bekannt durch mein Inneres, und ich wußte selbst nicht, welcher sonderbare Akkordwechsel sich zu regen und immer höher und höher anzuschwellen anfing. Doch der junge Ritter gesellte sich immer mehr und mehr zu mir, und in seinem Auge ging mir eine herrliche Welt, ein ganzes Eldorado süßer wonnevoller Träume auf – der wilde Akkordwechsel zerfloß in zarte Engelsharmonien, die gar wunderbarlich von dem Sein und Leben des Dichters sprachen, und nun wurde mir, da

---

[26] Hoffmann, *Kreisleriana*, II/1, 287–8.

ich, wie Ew. Hoch- und Wohlgeboren versichert sein können, ein tüchtiger Praktikus in der Musik bin, die Tonart, aus der das Ganze ging, gleich klar. Ich meine nämlich, daß ich in dem jungen Ritter gleich Ew. Hoch- und Wohlgeboren den Baron Wallborn erkannte. Als ich einige Ausweichungen versuchte, und als meine innere Musik lustig und sich recht kindisch und kindlich freuend in allerlei munteren Melodien, ergötzlichen *Murkis* und Walzern hervorströmte, da fielen Ew. Hoch- und Wohlgeboren überall in Takt und Tonart so richtig ein, daß ich gar keinen Zweifel hege, wie Sie mich auch als den Kapellmeister Johannes Kreisler erkannt und sich nicht an den Spuk gekehrt haben werden, den heute Abend der Geist Droll nebst einigen seiner Konsorten mit mir trieb. – In solch einer Lage, wenn ich nämlich in den Kreis irgend eines Spuks geraten, pflege ich, wie ich wohl weiß, einige besondere Gesichter zu schneiden ...

Ach, Baron Wallborn, auch Ihnen bin ich wohl, vom Heiligsten sprechend, was in mir glüht, zu hart, zu zornig erschienen! ... – Ach, Baron Wallborn, ... auch mir zerrann in Nebel die himmlische Gestalt, die in mein tiefstes Innerstes gedrungen, die geheimsten Herzensfasern des Lebens erfassend. Namenloser Schmerz zerriß meine Brust, und jeder wehmutsvolle Seufzer der ewig dürstenden Sehnsucht wurde zum tobenden Schmerz des Zorns, den die entsetzliche Qual entflammt hatte ...

Du weißt, Baron Wallborn, daß ich mehrenteils über das Musiktreiben des Pöbels zornig und toll wurde, aber ich kann es dir sagen, daß wenn ich oft von heillosen Bravour-Arien, Konzerten und Sonaten ordentlich zerschlagen und zerwalkt worden, oft eine kleine unbedeutende Melodie, von mittelmäßiger Stimme gesungen, oder unsicher und stümperhaft gespielt, aber treulich und gut gemeint und recht aus dem Innern heraus empfunden, mich tröstete und heilte ...

Denn sieh, Baron Wallborn! ich verspreche es Dir hiemit heilig, daß *ich* dann *Du* sein will, und ebenso voll Liebe, Milde und Frömmigkeit, wie Du. Ach, ich bin es ja wohl ohnedem! – Manches liegt bloß an dem Spuk, den oft meine eigene Noten treiben; die werde oft lebendig, und springen wie kleine schwarze vielgeschwänzte Teufelchen empor aus den weißen Blättern – sie reißen mich fort im wilden unsinnigen Dreher, und ich mache ganz ungemeine Bocksprünge und schneide umziemliche Gesichter, aber ein einziger Ton, aus heiliger Glut seinen Strahl schießend, löst diesen Wirrwarr, und ich bin fromm und gut und geduldig. – Du siehst, Baron Wallborn, daß das alles wahrhafte Terzen sind, in die alle Septime verschweben; und damit du diese Terzen recht deutlich vernehmen möchtest, deshalb schrieb ich Dir! ...

Gott segne Dich und erleuchte die Menschen, daß sie Dich genügsam erkennen mögen in Deinem herrlichen Tun und Treiben. Dies sei der heitre beruhigende Schluß-Akkord in der Tonika.[27]

‚Ach Freund!' erwiderte Kreisler, ‚ein düstrer Wolkenschatten geht über mein Leben hin! – Glaubst Du nicht, daß es einer armen unschuldigen Melodie, welche

---

[27] Hoffmann, *Kreisleriana*, II/2, 289–92.

keinen – keinen Platz auf der Erde begehrt, vergönnt sein dürfte, frei und harmlos durch den weiten Himmelsraum zu ziehen? – Ei, ich möchte nur gleich auf meinem chinesischen Schlafrock wie auf einem Mephistophelesmantel hinausfahren durch jenes Fenster dort!' – ‚Als harmlose Melodie?' fiel der treue Freund lächelnd ein. ‚Oder als basso ostinato, wenn du lieber willst', erwiderte Kreisler, ‚aber fort muß ich bald auf irgend eine Weise'. Es geschah auch bald, wie er gesprochen.[28]

Chapter 8

3–8 Hoffmann's butterfly

Ich sah einmal einen kleinen buntgefärbten Schmetterling, der sich zwischen den Saiten Eures Doppelklavichords eingefangen hatte. Das kleine Ding flatterte lustig auf und nieder und mit den glänzenden Flügelein um sich schlagend berührte es bald die obern bald die untern Saiten, die dann leise nur dem schärfsten geübtesten Ohr vernehmbare Töne und Akkorde hauchten, so daß zuletzt das Tierchen nur in den Schwingungen wie in sanftwogenden Wellen zu schwimmen oder vielmehr von ihnen getragen zu werden schien. Aber oft kam es, daß ein stärker berührte Saite, wie erzürnt in die Flügel des fröhlichen Schwimmers schlug, so daß sie wund geworden den Schmuck des bunten Blütenstaubs von sich streuten, doch dessen nicht achtend kreiste der Schmetterling fort und fort im fröhlichen Klingen und Singen bis schärfer und schärfer die Saiten ihn verwundeten, und er lautlos hinabsank in die Öffnung des Resonanzboden … Von einer besonderen Anwendung ist hier nicht die Rede … Ich wollte … nur im allgemeinen eine Idee andeuten … Ihr könnt das Ganze aber auch für eine Allegorie ansehen, und es in das Stammbuch irgend einer reisenden Virtuosin hineinzeichnen.[29]

[28] Hoffmann, *Kreisleriana*, II/3, 296–7. [29] Hoffmann, *Fantasiestücke*, 441–2.

Bibliography

I: Primary sources

A: Schumann compositions and writings

Compositions

Piano Music of Robert Schumann, ed. Clara Schumann, 3 vols. (Dover, New York, 1972 and 1980) (reproduced from the Breitkopf & Härtel edition of 1879–87).

Carnaval
Schumann, Robert, *Carnaval Opus 9*, ed. Ernst Herttrich (G. Henle, Munich, 2004).

Fantasiestücke
Fantasiestücke Opus 12, ed. Ernst Herttrich (G. Henle, Munich, 2004).

Humoreske
Humoreske Opus 20, ed. Hans Joachim Köhler (C. F. Peters, Leipzig, 1981).

Kreisleriana
Kreisleriana Opus 16, ed. Ernst Herttrich (G. Henle, Munich, 2004).

Nachtstücke
Nachtstücke Opus 23, ed. Ernst Herttrich (G. Henle, Munich, 2008).

Writings

Briefedition
Schumann Briefedition, multiple vols. (Robert-Schumann-Haus Zwickau, Dohr, Cologne), of which:

I/2 *Briefwechsel Robert und Clara Schumanns mit der Familie Wieck*, ed. Eberhard Möller (2011).

I/4–6 *Briefwechsel von Clara und Robert Schumann*, ed. Anja Mühlenweg and Thomas Synofzik (2012–14).

II/5 *Briefwechsel Robert und Clara Schumanns mit Franz Brendel, Hermann Levi, Franz Liszt, Richard Pohl und Richard Wagner*, ed. Thomas Synofzik, Axel Schröter and Klaus Döge (2014).

III/8 *Verlage im Ausland 1832–53*, ed. Michael Heinemann and Thomas Synofzik (2010).

Briefwechsel
Schumann, Clara and Robert, *Briefwechsel: Kritische Gesamtausgabe*, ed. Eva Weissweiler, 3 vols. (Stroemfeld/Roter Stern, Basel and Frankfurt, 1984–2001).

Dichtergarten
Schumann, Robert, *Dichtergarten für Musik. Eine Anthologie für Freunde der Literatur und Musik*, ed. Gerd Nauhaus and Ingrid Bodsch (Stadtmuseum Bonn and Stroemfeld, Frankfurt and Basel, 2007).

Erler
Erler, Hermann, *Robert Schumann's Leben aus seinem Briefen geschildert*, 2 vols. in 1 (Ries and Erler, Berlin, 1887).

GSK
Schumann, Robert, *Gesammelte Schriften über Musik und Musiker von Robert Schumann*, 5th edn, 2 vols., ed. Martin Kreisig (Breitkopf & Härtel, Leipzig, 1914).

Jugendbriefe
Jugendbriefe, ed. Clara Schumann, 2nd edn (Breitkopf & Härtel, Leipzig, 1886).

Mottosammlung
Hotaki, Leander, *Robert Schumanns Mottosammlung. Übertragung, Kommentar, Einführung* (Rombach, Freiburg im Breisgau, 1998).

Neue Folge
Schumann, Robert, *Briefe, Neue Folge*, ed. Gustav Jansen, 2nd edn (Breitkopf & Härtel, Leipzig, 1904).

Tagebücher
Tagebücher, ed. Georg Eisman and Gerd Nauhaus, 3 vols. (Stroemfeld/Roter Stern, Basel and Frankfurt, 1971–87).

Unpublished
Schumann, Robert, Letter to Emilie Schumann, Leipzig, 15 July 1835, Robert-Schumann-Haus Zwickau, 280 A-2.

B: E. T. A. Hoffmann

Hoffmann, E. T. A., *Nachtstücke*, ed. Gerhard R. Kaiser (Reclam, Stuttgart, 1990).

Sämtliche Werke, ed. W. Müller-Seidel and W. Segebrecht (Winkler, Munich, 1960–5), of which:

Brambilla, Meister Floh
Späte Werke (1965).

Kater Murr
Elixiere des Teufels / Kater Murr (1961).

Kreisleriana, Fantasiestücke, Nachtstücke
Fantasie- und Nachtstücke (1960).

Schriften zur Musik
Schriften zur Musik. Nachlese (1963).

Die Serapions-Brüder
Die Serapions-Brüder (1963).

C: Other

Aristotle, *The 'Poetics' of Aristotle*, ed. S. H. Butcher (Macmillan, London, 1929).
Augustine, (Saint), *Confessions*, trans. R. S. Pine-Coffin (Penguin Books, Harmondsworth, 1961).
  On Christian Teaching, trans. R. P. H. Green (Oxford University Press, 1999).
  Tractatus in Ioannis Evangelium CXXIV, ed. Radbodus Willens (Brepols, Turnhout, 1954).
Becker, Julius, *Der Neuromantiker. Musikalischer Roman* (J. J. Weber, Leipzig, 1840).
Bonaventura: see under *Nachtwachen von Bonaventura* below.
Brendel, Franz, 'Die Neuromantiker. Musikalischer Roman von Julius Becker', *Neue Zeitschrift für Musik*, 11 (1839), 190–2.
  'Robert Schumann mit Rücksicht auf Mendelssohn-Bartholdy und die Entwicklung der modernen Tonkunst überhaupt', *Neue Zeitschrift für Musik*, 22 (1845), 63–7; 81–3; 89–92; 113–16; 121–3; 145–7 and 149–50.
Coleridge, Samuel Taylor, *Poetical Works*, ed. Ernest Hartley Coleridge (Oxford University Press, London, New York and Toronto, 1967).
Freud, Sigmund, 'Beyond the Pleasure Principle', in Adam Phillips (ed.), *The Penguin Freud Reader* (Penguin, Harmondsworth, 2006), 132–95.
  'Das Unheimliche', in Alexander Mitscherlich (ed.), *Sigmund Freud: Studienausgabe*, IV (Frankfurt, 1970), 241–74.
Goethe, Johann Wolfgang, *Werke* (Winkler, Munich), 6 vols., of which:
  I *Gedichte, West-östlicher Divan, Epen*, ed. Victor Lange and Eva-Maria Lenz (1972).
  II *Dramen*, 4th edn, ed. Victor Lange and Ilse-Marie Barth (1981).

III *Dichterische Prosa, Maximen und Reflexionen*, ed. Victor Lange and Annalisa Viviani (1972).

IV *Wilhelm Meister, Lehrjahre, Wanderjahre*, ed. Victor Lange and Annalisa Viviani (1973).

VI *Reisen*, ed. Victor Lange, Eva-Maria Lenz and Annalisa Viviani (1973).

Gozzi, Carlo, *Five Tales for the Theatre*, ed. and trans. Albert Bremel and Ted Emery (University of Chicago Press, 1989).

Griepenkerl, Friedrich, 'Musikalisches Leben in Braunschweig', *Neue Zeitschrift für Musik*, 6 (1837), 17, 70.

Heine, Heinrich, 'Die romantische Schule', in Manfred Windfuhr (ed.), *Historisch-kritische Gesamtausgabe der Werke*, vol. VIII/1 (Hoffmann and Campe, Hamburg, 1979).

Heinse, Wilhelm, *Ardinghello und die Glückseligen Inseln* (Insel Verlag, Leipzig, 1962).

Hölderlin, Friedrich, *Hyperion* (Bibliothek der Erstausgaben, dtv, Munich, 2005).

'Urteil und Sein', in Friedrich Beißner (ed.), *Sämtliche Werke. Stuttgarter Hölderlin-Ausgabe*, vol. IV (Stuttgart, 1961).

Homer, *Iliad*, ed. Walter Leaf and M.A. Bayfield (Macmillan, London, 1965), vol. I. *Odyssey*, ed. A.T. Murray (Heinemann, London, 1919).

Jean Paul, *Flegeljahre, eine Biographie*, ed. Thomas Koebner (Reclam, Stuttgart, 1994).

Kleine Nachschule zur Ästhetischen Vorschule, in *Vorschule der Ästhetik* (see below).

Die unsichtbare Loge, ed. Norbert Miller (Piper, Munich and Zürich, 1986).

Vorschule der Ästhetik; Kleine Nachschule zur Ästhetischen Vorschule, ed. Norbert Miller (Hanser, Munich, 1963) [contains *Vorschule der Ästhetik, Nebst einigen Vorlesungen in Leipzig über die Parteien der Zeit* (2nd edn of 1813) and *Kleine Nachschule* of 1825].

Kahlert, August, 'Die Genrebilder in der Modernen Musik', *Neue Zeitschrift für Musik*, 2 (1835), 189 ff.

'Recensionen', *Cäcilia*, 66 (1835), 106–15.

Kapp, Julius, ed., *Gesammelte Schriften von Franz Liszt* (Breitkopf & Härtel, Leipzig, 1910).

Koßmaly, Carl, 'Ueber Robert Schumann's Claviercompositionen', *Allgemeine musikalische Zeitung* (Leipzig), 1–3 (1844), 1–5, 17–21, 33–7.

Liszt, Franz, 'Compositions pour piano de M. Robert Schumann', *Revue et Gazette Musicale de Paris* (1837), 488–90.

'Franz Liszt über Robert Schumann', *Literatur und Kunstblatt zur Zeitschrift, "Der Eisenbahn"*, 16–17 (1840), 63–4, 67–8.

'Robert Schumann' (1855), in Julius Kapp (ed.), *Gesammelte Schriften von Franz Liszt* (Breitkopf & Härtel, Leipzig, 1910), vol. IV, 166–243.

Marx, A. B., *Musical Form in the Age of Beethoven: Selected Writings on Theory and Method*, ed. Scott Burnham (Cambridge University Press, 1997).

Michaelis, Christian Friedrich, 'Einige Bemerkungen über das Erhabene der Musik', in *Berlinische musikalische Zeitung, herausgegeben von Johann Friedrich Reichardt, Zwei Jahrgänge in einem Band* (Georg Olms, Hildesheim, 1969).

'Nachtrag zu den vermischten Bemerkungen über Musik', in *Berlinische musikalische Zeitung, herausgegeben von Johann Friedrich Reichardt, Zwei Jahrgänge in einem Band* (Georg Olms, Hildesheim, 1969).

'Vermischte Bemerkungen über Musik', in *Berlinische musikalische Zeitung, herausgegeben von Johann Friedrich Reichardt, Zwei Jahrgänge in einem Band* (Georg Olms, Hildesheim, 1969).

Moritz, Karl Philipp, *Werke*, ed. Horst Günther (Insel Verlag, Frankfurt-am-Main, 1981), vol. I.

Moscheles, Ignaz, *Charakteristische Studien für das Pianoforte, Opus 95* (Kistner, Leipzig, c. 1836).

'Pianoforte Sonate, Clara zugeeignet von Florestan und Eusebius, Op. XI', *Neue Zeitschrift für Musik*, 5 (1836), 136.

Nachtwachen von Bonaventura, ed. Peter Küpper (Wissenschaftliche Buchgesellschaft, Darmstadt, 2004).

Novalis, *Gesammelte Werke*, ed. H. and W. Kohlschmidt (Sigbert Mohn Verlag, Gütersloh, 1967).

Notes for a Romantic Encyclopedia, 'Das Allgemeine Brouillon', ed. David W. Wood (State University of New York Press, Albany, 2007).

Schriften, ed. Ludwig Tieck and Friedrich Schlegel, 2 vols. (G. Reimer, Berlin, 1837).

Schriften, ed. Ludwig Tieck and Eduard von Bülow, vol. III (G. Reimer, Berlin, 1846).

Schriften, I, Das Dichterische Werk, ed. Paul Kluckhohn and Richard Samuel (Kohlhammer, Stuttgart, 1960).

Schriften, II-III, Das Philosophische Werk, ed. Paul Kluckhohn and Richard Samuel (Kohlhammer, Stuttgart, 1960).

Schriften, IV, Tagebücher, Briefwechsel, Zeitgenössische Zeugnisse, ed. Richard Samuel (Kohlhammer, Stuttgart, 1975).

Schriften, V, Materialien und Register, ed. Hans-Joachim Mähl and Richard Samuel (Kohlhammer, Stuttgart, 1988).

Ovid, *Metamorphoses, Books I–VIII*, ed. Frank Miller (Harvard University Press, Cambridge, Mass. and London, 1977).

Proust, Marcel, *In Search of Lost Time. I: Swann's Way*, trans. C. K. Scott Moncrieff and Terence Kilmartin, rev. D. J. Enright (Chatto and Windus, London, 1992).

Rellstab, Ludwig, review in *Iris*, 21 (25 May 1832), in Schumann, *Tagebücher*, I 425.

Rousseau, Jean-Jacques, *Oeuvres complètes,* vol. III, *Du contrat social; Écrits politiques,* ed. Bernard Gagnebin and Marcel Raymond (Gallimard, Paris, 1964).
Schiller, Friedrich, *Sämtliche Werke,* ed. Benno von Wiese and Helmut Koopmann, vol. V, *Philosophische Schriften, Vermischte Schriften* (Winkler, Munich, 1968).
Schlegel, August Wilhelm, 'Die Gemälde. Gespräch', *Athenaeum* (Berlin), 2.1 (1799).
Schubring, Adolf, 'Schumanniana No. 4', *Neue Zeitschrift für Musik,* 54 (1861), 213.
Schütze, Stephan, 'Über das Verhältnis der Komik zur Musik', *Cäcilia,* 63 (1834), 197–205.
von Seyfried, Ignaz, 'Schumann, Robert, Kreisleriana, Phantasie für Pianoforte, 16. Werk', *Allgemeine musikalischer Anzeiger,* 29 (1840), 113–14.
Shakespeare, William, *Complete Works,* ed. W. J. Craig (Oxford University Press, London, New York and Toronto, 1966).
  Shakespeare's dramatische Werke, trans. A. W. Schlegel and J. J. Eschenburg, 20 vols. (Vienna, 1811–12).
Shelley, Percy Bysshe, *Shelley's Poetry and Prose, Authoritative Texts and Criticism,* ed. Donald H. Reiman and Sharon B. Powers (W. W. Norton, New York, London, 1977).
'Stein, K.' (pseud. of Gustav Adolph Keferstein), 'Bemerkungen eines irrenden Theoretikers: sollen Musikstücken wirkliche Gedanken zum Grunde liegen?', *Cäcilia,* 73 (1837), 14–44.
  'Versuch über das Komische in der Musik', *Cäcilia,* 60 (1833), 221–66.
Tieck, Ludwig, *Die Märchen aus dem Phantasus. Dramen,* ed. Marianne Thalmann (Winkler, Munich, 1964).
  'Die Töne', from 'Phantasien über die Kunst für Freunde der Kunst', in Eduard Berend (ed.), *Tiecks Werke* (Deutsches Verlagshaus Bong, Berlin, 1908), vol. I.
Virgil, *Bucolica et Georgica,* ed. T. E. Page (Macmillan, London, 1968).
Wackenroder, Wilhelm Heinrich, and Tieck, Ludwig, *Herzensergießungen eines Kunstliebenden Klosterbruders,* together with Wackenroder's contributions to the *Phantasien über die Kunst für Freunde der Kunst,* ed. A. Gillies (Blackwell, Oxford, 1948), including:
  'Die Wunder der Tonkunst', 130–5;
  'Das eigentümliche innere Wesen der Tonkunst und die Seelenlehre der heutigen Instrumentalmusik', 143–52;
  'Ein Brief Joseph Berglingers', 152–6.
Zumsteeg, Johann Rudolf, *Lenore von G. A. Bürger* (Breitkopf & Härtel, Leipzig, 1809).

II: Secondary sources

Abbate, Carolyn, 'Music – Drastic or Gnostic?', *Critical Inquiry,* 30.3 (2004), 505–36.

Unsung Voices: Opera and Musical Narrative in the Nineteenth Century (Princeton University Press, 1991).
von Adam-Schmidmeier, Eva-Maria, 'Kreisleriana, Op. 16', in Helmut Loos (ed.), *Robert Schumann. Interpretationen seiner Werke*, 2 vols. (Laaber, 2005), vol. I, 92–8.
Agawu, V. Kofi, 'Ambiguity in Tonal Music: A Preliminary Study', in Anthony Pople (ed.), *Theory, Analysis, and Meaning in Music* (Cambridge University Press, 1994), 86–107.
  Music as Discourse: Semiotic Adventures in Romantic Music (Oxford University Press, 2008).
  Playing with Signs: a Semiotic Interpretation of Classical Music (Princeton University Press, 1991).
Almén, Byron and Pearsall, Edward, eds., *Approaches to Musical Meaning* (Indiana University Press, Bloomington and Indianapolis, 2006).
Alphonce, Bo, 'Dissonance and Schumann's Reckless Counterpoint', *Music Theory Online*, 7 (March 1994), 1–19.
Altenburg, Detlef, 'Robert Schumann und Franz Liszt. Die Idee der poetischen Musik im Spannungsfeld von deutscher und französischer Musikanschauung', in Ute Bär (ed.), *Robert Schumann und die französische Romantik. Bericht über das 5. Internationale Schumann-Symposium der Robert-Schumann-Gesellschaft am 9. und 10. Juli 1994 in Düsseldorf*, Schumann Forschungen VI (Schott, Mainz, London, Madrid, 1997).
Appel, Bernhard, 'Carnaval, Op. 9', in Helmut Loos (ed.), *Robert Schumann. Interpretationen seiner Werke* (Laaber, 2005), vol. I, 49–55.
  'Nachtstücke, op. 23', in Helmut Loos (ed.), *Robert Schumann. Interpretationen seiner Werke* (Laaber, 2005), vol. I, 129–31.
  'R. Schumanns Humoreske für Klavier, Op. 20. Zum musikalischen Humor in der ersten Hälfte des 19. Jahrhunderts unter besonderer Berücksichtigung des Formproblems', unpublished PhD thesis, Universität Saarbrücken (1980–1).
  ed., *Robert Schumann und die Dichter. Ein Musiker als Leser: Katalog zur Ausstellung des Heinrich-Heine-Instituts in Verbindung mit dem Robert-Schumann-Haus in Zwickau und der Robert-Schumann-Forschungsstelle in Düsseldorf* (Droste, Düsseldorf, 1991).
  'Schumanns Davidsbund. Geistes- und sozialgeschichtliche Voraussetzungen einer romantischen Idee', *Archiv für Musikwissenschaft*, 38.1 (1981), 1–23.
Arnsdorf, Mary Hunter, 'Schumann's Kreisleriana, Op. 16, Analysis and Performance', unpublished dissertation, Columbia University (1976).
Bär, Ute, ed., *Robert Schumann und die französische Romantik. Bericht über das 5. Internationale Schumann-Symposium der Robert-Schumann-Gesellschaft am 9. und 10. Juli 1994 in Düsseldorf*, Schumann Forschungen VI (Schott, Mainz, London, Madrid, 1997).
Barnes, Jonathan, ed., *The Cambridge Companion to Aristotle* (Cambridge University Press, 1995).

Barthes, Roland, *The Responsibility of Forms: Critical Essays on Music, Art and Representation*, trans. Richard Howard (Hill and Wang, New York, 1985).
Beaufils, M, *La musique de piano de Schumann* (Larousse, Paris, 1951).
Bekker-Adden, Meike, *Nahtstellen: Strukturelle Analogien der Kreisleriana von E. T. A. Hoffmann und Robert Schumann* (Bielefeld, 2006).
Bent, Ian, ed., *Music Analysis in the Nineteenth Century*, 2 vols. (Cambridge University Press, 1994).
  ed., *Music Theory in the Age of Romanticism* (Cambridge University Press, 1996).
Bergé, Pierre, ed., William E. Caplin, James Hepokoski, James Webster (contributors), *Musical Form, Forms and Formenlehre: Three Methodological Reflections* (Leuven University Press, 2009).
Berger, Karol and Newcomb, Anthony, eds., *Music and the Aesthetics of Modernity*, Isham Library Paper 6 (Harvard University Press, Cambridge, Mass. and London, 2005).
Bischoff, Bodo, 'Das Bach-Bild Robert Schumanns', in Michael Heinemann and Hans-Joachim Hinrichsen (eds.), *Bach und die Nachwelt* (Laaber, 1997), vol. I, 421–99.
  Monument für Beethoven. Die Entwicklung der Beethoven-Rezeption Robert Schumanns (Dohr, Cologne, 1994).
Blackall, Eric A., *The Novels of the German Romantics* (Cornell University Press, Ithaca, NY, 1983).
Boetticher, Wolfgang, *Robert Schumanns Klavierwerke, Teil II, Opus 7–13, Neue biographische und textkritische Untersuchungen* (Heinrichshofen's Verlag, Wilhelmshaven, 1984).
  'Weitere Forschungen an Dokumenten zum Leben und Schaffen Robert Schumanns', in *Robert Schumann: ein romantisches Erbe in neuer Forschung: Acht Studien* (Robert-Schumann-Gesellschaft, Düsseldorf, Mainz, London, 1984).
Bonds, Mark Evan, 'Idealism and the Aesthetics of Instrumental Music at the Turn of the Nineteenth Century', *Journal of the American Musicological Society*, 50 (1997), 387–420.
  Music as Thought: Listening to the Symphony in the Age of Beethoven (Princeton University Press, 2015).
  Wordless Rhetoric: Musical Form and the Metaphor of the Oration (Harvard University Press, Cambridge, Mass., 1991).
Botstein, Leo, 'History, Rhetoric and the Self: Robert Schumann and Music Making in German-Speaking Europe, 1800–60', in R. Larry Todd (ed.), *Schumann and His World* (Princeton University Press, 1994), 3–46.
Boulby, Mark, *Karl Philipp Moritz: At the Fringe of Genius* (University of Toronto Press, 1979).
Bowie, Andrew, *Music, Philosophy, and Modernity* (Cambridge University Press, 2007).

Brion, Marcel, *Schumann et l'âme romantique* (Albin Michel, Paris, 1954).

Brown, Hilda Meldrum, *E. T. A. Hoffmann and the Serapiontic Principle: Critique and Creativity* (Camden House, Rochester, NY, 2006).

Brown, Julie Hedges, 'Higher Echoes of the Past in the Finale of Schumann's 1842 Piano Quartet', *Journal of the American Musicological Society*, 57.3 (2004), 511–64.

'Schumann and the Style Hongrois', in Roe-Min Kok and Laura Tunbridge (eds.), *Rethinking Schumann* (Oxford University Press, 2011), 265–99.

Burkholder, J. Peter, 'A Simple Model for Associative Musical Meaning', in Byron Almén and Edward Pearsall (eds.), *Approaches to Musical Meaning* (Indiana University Press, Bloomington and Indianapolis, 2006), 76–106.

Burnham, Scott, *Beethoven Hero* (Princeton University Press, 1995).

'Criticism, Faith and the "Idee": A. B. Marx's Early Reception of Beethoven', *19th-Century Music*, 13 (1990), 183–92.

'"E. T. A. Hoffmann's Musical Writings: Kreisleriana, The Poet and the Composer, Musical Criticism", by David Charlton, Martyn Clarke: Review', *19th-Century Music*, 14 (1991), 286–96.

'How Music Matters: Poetic Content Revisited', in Nicholas Cook and Mark Everist (eds.), *Rethinking Music* (Oxford University Press, 1999), 193–216.

Calasso, Roberto, *The Ruin of Kasch*, trans. William Weaver and Stephen Sartarelli (Vintage, London, 1995).

Carey, Norman, 'An Improbable Intertwining: An Analysis of Schumann's *Kreisleriana* I and II', *Theory and Practice*, 32 (2007), 19–50.

Célis, Raphaël, 'L'art et l'aspiration à l'unité « magique » de la vie dans le romantisme allemand. Méditations sur les affinités destinales des *Kreisleriana* d'E. T. A. Hoffmann et de R. Schumann', in Raphaël Célis (ed.), *Littérature et musique* (Facultés universitaire Saint-Louis, Brussels, 1982).

Chailley, Jacques, *Carnaval de Schumann* (Alphonse Leduc, Paris, 1971).

'Zum Symbolismus bei Robert Schumann mit besonderer Berücksichtigung der *Papillons*, Op. 2', in *Robert Schumann: ein romantisches Erbe in neuer Forschung: Acht Studien* (Robert-Schumann-Gesellschaft, Düsseldorf, Mainz, London, 1984), 57–66.

Charlton, David, ed., *E. T. A. Hoffmann's Musical Writings* (Cambridge University Press, 1989).

Chernaik, Judith, 'Schumann's "Papillons", Op. 2: A Case Study', *The Musical Times*, 153 no. 1920 (2012), 67–86.

Chua, Daniel K. L., *The Galitzin Quartets of Beethoven, Opp. 127, 132, 130* (Princeton University Press, 1995).

Cochrane, Tom, Fantini, Bernardino and Scherer, Klaus R., eds., *The Emotional Power of Music: Multidisciplinary Perspectives on Musical Arousal, Expression and Social Control* (Oxford University Press, 2013).

Cohn, Richard, 'The Autonomy of Motives in Schenkerian Accounts of Tonal Music', *Music Theory Spectrum*, 14 (1992), 150–70.

Columbus, Claudette Kemper, '"Die Flegeljahre", "Papillons", "Carnaval" as Masques', *Mosaic, a Journal for the Interdisciplinary Study of Literature*, 10.1 (1976), 69–91.

Cook, Nicholas, *A Guide to Musical Analysis* (J. M. Dent, London, 1987).

Music, Imagination and Culture (Oxford University Press, 1992).

'Uncanny Moments: Juxtaposition and the Collage Principle in Music', in Byron Almén and Edward Pearsall (eds.), *Approaches to Musical Meaning* (Indiana University Press, Bloomington and Indianapolis, 2006), 107–34.

Cook, Nicholas and Everist, Mark, eds., *Rethinking Music* (Oxford University Press, 1999).

Cramer, Alfred W., 'Of Serpentina and Stenography: Shapes of Handwriting in Romantic Melody', *19th-Century Music*, 30 (2006), 133–65.

Crisp, Deborah, 'The *Kreisleriana* of Robert Schumann and E. T. A. Hoffmann: Some Musical and Literary Parallels', *Musicology Australia*, 16 (1993), 3–18.

Dahlhaus, Carl, *Klassische und romantische Musikästhetik* (Laaber, 1988).

Daverio, John, *Crossing Paths* (Oxford University Press, 2002).

Nineteenth-Century Music and the German Romantic Ideology (Schirmer Books, New York, 1993).

'Piano Works I: a World of Images', in Beate Perrey (ed.), *The Cambridge Companion to Schumann* (Cambridge University Press, 2007), 65–85.

Robert Schumann, Herald of a 'New Poetic Age' (Oxford University Press, 1997).

Davies, Stephen, *Musical Meaning and Expression* (Cornell University Press, Ithaca, NY and London, 1994).

Day-O'Connell, Jeremy, 'The Rise of 6̂ in the Nineteenth Century', *Music Theory Spectrum* 24 (2002), 35–67.

Deahl, Lora Gay, 'Principles of Organization in Robert Schumann's Davidsbündlertänze, Opus 6, and Kreisleriana, Opus 16', unpublished dissertation, University of Texas at Austin (1988).

'Robert Schumann's *Kreisleriana* and Double Novel Structure', *International Journal of Musicology*, 5 (1996), 131–45.

Deleuze, Gilles and Guattari, Félix, *A Thousand Plateaus*, trans. Brian Massumi (Continuum, London and New York, 2004).

Dickson, Sheila, 'E. T. A. Hoffmann: Mind, Mythology and Meaning', *Forum for Modern Language Studies*, 32 (1996), 251–63.

Diels, Hermann and Kranz, Walther, *Die Fragmente der Vorsokratiker* (Weidmann, Zurich, 1985).

Dill, Heinz J., 'Romantic Irony in the Works of Robert Schumann', *Musical Quarterly*, 63 (1989), 172–95.

Dodd, Julian, *Works of Music: An Essay in Ontology* (Oxford University Press, 2007).

Draheim, Joachim, 'Schumann und Shakespeare', *Neue Zeitschrift für Musik*, 3 (1981), 237–44.

Erhardt, Damien, 'Die französische und die deutsche Erstdruck von *Carnaval*', in Ute Bär (ed.), *Robert Schumann und die französische Romantik* (Schott Music, London, 1997).

Fabre, Florence, '"L'Enfant Étranger" d'Hoffmann, les "Scènes d'Enfants" de Schumann: Une "Transformation Topologique"?', *Revue International d'Études Musicales*, 22 (2004), 219–33.

Fantini, Bernardino, 'Forms of Thought Between Music and Science', in Tom Cochrane, Bernardino Fantini and Klaus R. Scherer (eds.), *The Emotional Power of Music* (Oxford University Press, 2013), 257–69.

Ferris, David, 'Public Performance and Private Understanding: Clara Wieck's Concerts in Berlin', *Journal of the American Musicological Society*, 56.2 (2003), 351–408.

Finson, Jon W., 'Schumann and Shakespeare', in Jon W. Finson and R. Larry Todd (eds.), *Mendelssohn and Schumann: Essays on Their Music and Its Context* (Duke University Press, Durham, NC, 1984), 125–36.

Finson, Jon W. and Todd, R. Larry, eds., *Mendelssohn and Schumann: Essays on Their Music and Its Context* (Duke University Press, Durham, NC, 1984).

Fisk, Charles, 'What Schubert's Last Sonata Might Hold', in Jenefer Robinson (ed.), *Music and Meaning* (Cornell University Press, Ithaca, NY and London, 1997), 179–200.

Floros, Constantin, 'Schumanns musikalische Poetik', in Heinz K. Metzger and Rainer Riehn (eds.), *Musik-Konzepte Sonderband Robert Schumann* (edition text + kritik, Munich, 1981–2), vol. I, 90–104.

Giani, Maurizio, 'L'Italia di Robert Schumann. Riflessioni sui Tagebücher', in *Schumann, Brahms e l'Italia. Atti dei convegni lincei 165, Convegno internazionale, Rom, 4–5 November 1999* (Accademia Nazionale dei Lincei, Rome, 2001).

Gooley, Dana, '*La Commedia del Violino*: Paganini's Comic Strains', *Musical Quarterly*, 88.3 (2005), 370–427.

 'Schumann and Agencies of Improvisation', in Roe-Min Kok and Laura Tunbridge (eds.), *Rethinking Schumann* (Oxford University Press, 2011), 129–56.

Grey, Thomas, '"Wie ein rother Faden": On the Origins of the "Leitmotif" as Critical Construct and Musical Practice', in Ian Bent (ed.), *Music Theory in the Age of Romanticism* (Cambridge University Press, 1996), 187–210.

Gutman, Robert W., *Mozart: A Cultural Biography* (Harcourt, San Diego, New York, London, 1999).

Halski, Czeslaw Raymond, 'Murky: A Polish Musical Freak', *Music and Letters*, 39 (1958), 35–7.

Hatten, Robert, *Interpreting Musical Gestures, Topics and Tropes* (Indiana University Press, Bloomington, 2004).

Heller, Karl, '*Fantasiestücke*, Op. 12', in Helmut Loos (ed.), *Robert Schumann. Interpretationen seiner Werke* (Laaber, 2005), vol. I, 65–71.

Hering, Hans, 'Das Variative in Schumanns frühem Klavierwerk', *Melos / NZ für Musik*, 1 (1975), 347–54.

Hoeckner, Berthold, *Programming the Absolute: Nineteenth Century German Music and the Hermeneutics of the Moment* (Princeton University Press, 2002).

 'Schumann and Romantic Distance', *Journal of the American Musicological Society*, 50.1 (1997), 55–132.

Hyer, Bryan, 'Second Immediacies in the Eroica', in Ian Bent (ed.), *Music Theory in the Age of Romanticism* (Cambridge University Press, 1996), 84–7.

Jankélévitch, Vladimir, *Music and the Ineffable*, trans. Carolyn Abbate (Princeton University Press, 2003).

Jensen, Eric Frederick, 'Explicating Jean Paul: Robert Schumann's Program for Papillons, Op. 2', *19th-Century Music*, 22 (1998), 127–43.

 Schumann (Oxford University Press, 2001).

Kaminsky, Peter, 'Principles of Formal Structure in Schumann's Early Piano Cycles', *Music Theory Spectrum*, 11.2 (Autumn 1989), 207–25.

Kapp, Reinhard, 'Schumann in His Time and Since', in Beate Perrey (ed.), *The Cambridge Companion to Schumann* (Cambridge University Press, 2007), 223–51.

Kerman, Joseph, *The Beethoven Quartets* (Norton, New York and London, 1979).

Kinderman, William and Krebs, Harald, eds., *The Second Practice of Nineteenth-Century Tonality* (University of Nebraska Press, Lincoln and London, 1996).

Kinsky, G., 'Ein unbekanntes Fantasiestück aus Schumanns Jugendzeit', *Schweizerische Musikzeitung*, 75.24 (1935), 769–75.

Knapp, Raymond, 'Brahms and the Anxiety of Allusion', *Journal of Musicological Research*, 18 (1998), 1–30.

 Brahms and the Challenge of the Symphony (Pendragon Press, Stuyvesant, NY, 1997).

Kok, Roe-Min and Tunbridge, Laura, eds., *Rethinking Schumann* (Oxford University Press, 2011).

Kolb, Jocelyne, 'E. T. A. Hoffmann's Kreisleriana: à la Recherche d'une Forme Perdue', *Monatshefte*, 69.1 (Spring 1977), 34–44.

Kopp, David, 'Intermediate States of Key in Schumann', in Roe-Min Kok and Laura Tunbridge (eds.), *Rethinking Schumann* (Oxford University Press, 2011) 300–25.

Korsyn, Kevin, 'The Death of Musical Analysis? The Concept of Unity Revisited', *Music Analysis*, 23.2–3 (2004), 337–51.

Krahe, K., 'Robert Schumanns Schulaufsatz: Warum erbittert uns Tadel in Sachen des Geschmakes mehr, als in anderen Dingen?', in Bernhard Appel (ed.), *Robert Schumann und die Dichter* (Droste, Düsseldorf, 1991), 33–40.

Kramer, Lawrence, '*Carnaval*, Cross-Dressing, and the Woman in the Mirror' in Ruth A. Solie (ed.), *Musicology and Difference* (University of California Press, Berkeley, 1993), 305–26.

Classical Music and Postmodern Knowledge (University of California Press, Berkeley, 1995).

Interpreting Music (University of California Press, Berkeley, 2011).

Music and Poetry: The Nineteenth Century and After (University of California Press, Berkeley, 1984).

Musical Meaning: Toward a Critical History (University of California Press, Berkeley, 2002).

'Rethinking Schumann's *Carnaval*: Identity, Meaning and the Social Order', in Lawrence Kramer *Musical Meaning: Toward a Critical History* (University of California Press, Berkeley, 2002), 100–32.

Kranefeld, Ulrike, *Der nachschaffende Hörer. Rezeptionsästhetische Studien zur Musik Robert Schumann* (J. B. Metzler, Stuttgart, Weimar, 2000).

Krebs, Harald, *Fantasy Pieces: Metrical Dissonance in the Music of Robert Schumann* (Oxford University Press, 1999).

Kruse, Joseph A., 'Robert Schumanns Lektüre', in Bernhard Appel (ed.), *Robert Schumann und die Dichter* (Droste, Düsseldorf, 1991), 123–34.

Langer, Susanne K., *Feeling and Form: A Theory of Art* (Routledge and Kegan Paul, London, 1953).

Leopoldseder, Hannes, *Groteske Welt. Ein Beitrag zur Entwicklungsgeschichte des Nachtstücks in der Romantik* (Bouvier, Bonn, 1973).

Lester, Joel, 'Robert Schumann and Sonata Forms', *19th-Century Music*, 18 (1995), 189–210.

Levy, Morten, 'Music and Pattern', *Musik and Forskning* (1977–1), 96–112.

Lippman, Edward A., 'Theory and Practice in Schumann's Aesthetics', *Journal of the American Musicological Society* (October 1964), 310–45.

Loos, Helmut, ed., *Robert Schumann. Interpretationen seiner Werke*, vol. I (Laaber, 2005).

Marston, Nicholas, 'An die ferne Geliebte', in Scott Burnham and M. Steinberg (eds.), *Beethoven and His World* (Princeton University Press, 2000).

Schumann: Fantasie, Op. 17 (Cambridge University Press, 1992).

'Schumann's Heroes: Schubert, Beethoven, Bach', in Beate Perrey (ed.), *The Cambridge Companion to Schumann* (Cambridge University Press, 2007), 48–61.

'Schumann's Monument to Beethoven', *19th-Century Music*, 14 (1991), 247–64.

Maus, Fred Everett, 'Intersubjectivity and Analysis', in Ian Bent (ed.), *Music Theory in the Age of Romanticism* (Cambridge University Press, 1996), 125–37.

'Music as Drama', in Jenefer Robinson (ed.), *Music and Meaning* (Cornell University Press, Ithaca, NY and London, 1997), 105–30.

Mayeda, Akio, '*Papillons*, Op. 2', in Helmut Loos (ed.), *Robert Schumann. Interpretationen seiner Werke* (Laaber, 2005), vol. I, 9–16.

McCorkle, Margit L., *Robert Schumann. Thematisch-bibliographische Werkverzeichnis* (Robert-Schumann-Gesellschaft, Düsseldorf; G. Henle Verlag, Munich, 2003).

McCreless, Patrick, 'Song Order and the Song Cycle: Schumann's "Liederkreis", Op. 39', *Music Analysis*, 5.1 (March 1986), 5–28.

Meier, Barbara, *Robert Schumann* (Rowohlt Taschenbuch, Reinbek bei Hamburg, 1995).

Messing, Scott, *Schubert in the European Imagination*, 2 vols. (University of Rochester Press, Rochester, NY, 2006), vol. I.

Metzger, Heinz K. and Riehn, Rainer, eds., *Musik-Konzepte Sonderband Robert Schumann*, 2 vols. (edition text + kritik, Munich, 1981–2).

Moraal, Christine, 'The Life and Afterlife of Johannes Kreisler: Affinities Between E. T. A. Hoffmann and Carl Maria von Weber, Hector Berlioz and Robert Schumann', unpublished dissertation, University of Michigan (1994).

  'Romantische Ironie in Robert Schumanns "Nachtstücke", Op. 23', *Archiv für Musikwissenschaft*, 54 (1997), 68–83.

Morgan, Robert P., 'The Concept of Unity and Musical Analysis', *Music Analysis*, 22.1–2 (2003), 7–50.

Müller-Sievers, Helmut, 'Verstimmung: E. T. A. Hoffmann und die Trivialisierung der Musik', *Deutsche Vierteljahrschrift für Literaturwissenschaft und Geistesgeschichte*, 63 (1989), 98–119.

Münch, Stephan, 'Fantasiestücke in Kreislers Manier: Robert Schumanns Kreisleriana Op. 16 und die Musikanschauung E. T. A. Hoffmanns', *Die Musikforschung*, 45 (1992), 255–75.

Musgrave, Michael, *The Life of Schumann* (Cambridge University Press, 2011).

Muxfeldt, Kristina, Review of 'Nineteenth-Century Music and the German Romantic Ideology' by John Daverio, *Journal of Music Theory*, 40.1 (Spring 1996), 149–60.

Nattiez, Jean-Jacques, 'Can One Speak of Narrativity in Music?', trans. Katherine Ellis, *Journal of the Royal Musical Association*, 115.2 (1990), 240–57.

Nauhaus, Gerd, 'Schumanns Lektürebüchlein', in Bernhard Appel (ed.), *Robert Schumann und die Dichter* (Droste, Düsseldorf, 1991), 50–87.

Neergaard, Balder, 'In the Footsteps of Jean Paul: Sonority and Pedalling in Robert Schumann's "Papillons", Op. 2', in Andrew Woolley and John Kitchen (eds.), *Interpreting Historical Keyboard Music: Sources, Contexts and Performance* (Ashgate, Farnham and Burlington, 2013), 243–57.

The New Grove Dictionary of Music and Musicians, ed. Stanley Sadie (executive editor: John Tyrrell), 2nd edn, 29 vols. (Macmillan, London, 2001).

Newcomb, Anthony, 'The Hunt for Reminiscences in Nineteenth-Century Germany', in Karol Berger and Anthony Newcomb (eds.), *Music and the Aesthetics of Modernity*, Isham Library Paper 6 (Harvard University Press, Cambridge, Mass. and London, 2005), 111–35.

  'Once More "Between Absolute and Program Music": Schumann's Second Symphony', *19th-Century Music*, 7 (1984), 233–50.

  'Schumann and Late Eighteenth-Century Narrative Strategies', *19th-Century Music*, 11 (1987), 164–74.

'Schumann and the Marketplace: From Butterflies to Hausmusik', in R. Larry Todd (ed.), *Nineteenth-Century Piano Music* (Routledge, New York and London, 2004), 258–315.

'"Those Images that Yet Fresh Images Begat"', *Journal of Musicology*, 2.3 (1983), 227–45.

Niecks, Frederick, *Programme Music in the Last Four Centuries* (Novello, London, 1907).

O'Brien, William Arctander, 'E. T. A. Hoffmann's Critique of Idealism: Psychology, Allegory and Philosophy in "Die Automate"', *Euphorion*, 83.4 (1989), 369–406.

Novalis: Signs of Revolution (Duke University Press, Durham, NC, 1995).

Otto, Frauke, *Robert Schumann als Jean Paul Leser* (Haag and Herchen, 1984).

Paulin, Roger, *Ludwig Tieck* (Oxford University Press, 1985).

Pederson, Sanna, 'Defining the Term "Absolute Music" Historically', *Music and Letters*, 15.2 (2009), 240–63.

Perrey, Beate Julia, *Schumann's 'Dichterliebe' and Early Romantic Poetics: Fragmentation of Desire* (Cambridge University Press, 2002).

ed., *The Cambridge Companion to Schumann* (Cambridge University Press, 2007).

Perry, Mary, 'Dissonance Treatment in Robert Schumann's Piano Music', unpublished dissertation, New York University (1991).

Pfau, Thomas, 'From Autonomous Subjects to Self-Regulating Structures: Rationality and Development in German Idealism', in Michael Ferber (ed.), *A Companion to European Romanticism* (Blackwell, Oxford, 2005), 101–22.

Place, Jean-Michel, *Robert Schumann. Ostinato Rigore 22* (Jean-Michel Place, Paris, 2004).

Plantinga, Leon B., *Schumann as Critic* (Yale University Press, New Haven, Conn., 1967).

Prawer, S. S., 'Hoffmann's Uncanny Guest: A Reading of "Der Sandmann"', *German Life and Letters*, 18 (1964–5), 297–308.

Rastelli, Anna, '"Carnaval" e "La principessa Brambilla": Ragione e intuizione nel pensiero di Schumann e Hoffmann', *Cristallo* (Bolzano), 29.1 (1987), 61–6.

Reiman, Erika, *Schumann's Piano Cycles and the Novels of Jean Paul* (University of Rochester Press, Rochester, NY, and Woodbridge, 2004).

Reynolds, Christopher Alan, *Motives for Allusion* (Harvard University Press, Cambridge, Mass., 2003).

Richards, Annette, *The Free Fantasia and the Musical Picturesque* (Cambridge University Press, 2001).

Robinson, Jenefer, ed., *Music and Meaning* (Cornell University Press, Ithaca, NY and London, 1997).

Rodgers, Stephen, '"This Body that Beats": Roland Barthes and Robert Schumann's *Kreisleriana*', *Indiana Theory Review*, 18.2 (1997), 75–91.

Roesner, Linda Correll, 'Schumann's "Parallel" Forms', *19th-Century Music*, 14 (1991), 265–78.
  'The Sources for Schumann's *Davidsbündlertänze*, Op. 6: Composition, Textual Problems, and the Role of Composer as Editor', in Jon W. Finson and R. Larry Todd (eds.), *Mendelssohn and Schumann: Essays on Their Music and Its Context* (Duke University Press, Durham, NC, 1984), 53–70.
Rosen, Charles, *The Classical Style: Haydn, Mozart, Beethoven* (Faber, London, 1972).
  The Romantic Generation (Harper Collins, London, 1996).
Rumph, Stephen, 'A Kingdom Not of This World: The Political Context of E. T. A. Hoffmann's Beethoven Criticism', *19th-Century Music*, 19.1 (1995), 50–67.
Ruprecht, Lucia, *Dances of the Self in Heinrich von Kleist, E. T. A. Hoffmann and Heinrich Heine* (Ashgate, Aldershot, 2006).
Schmalfeldt, Janet, *In the Process of Becoming: Analytic and Philosophical Perspectives on Form in Early Nineteenth-Century Music* (Oxford University Press, 2011).
Schoenberg, A., 'Brahms the Progressive', in Leonard Stein (ed.), Leo Black (trans.), *Style and Idea: Selected Writings of Arnold Schoenberg* (Faber, London, 1975).
Schroeder, Severin, 'Music and Metaphor', *British Journal of Aesthetics*, 53.1 (2013), 1–19.
Scruton, Roger, *The Aesthetics of Music* (Oxford University Press, 1999).
Severtson, David M., 'Robert Schumann's *Kreisleriana*: Using Hoffmann's Kreisler as a Model for the Unification of Contrasts', *Music Research Forum, University of Cincinnati*, 17 (2002), 33–47.
Shilo, Nilly Epstein, 'Rendition, Form and Temporal Modification in Robert Schumann's Kreisleriana, Opus 16', unpublished dissertation, Boston University (1993).
Simonett, Hans Peter, 'Taktgruppengliederung und Form in Schumanns "Carnaval"', unpublished dissertation, Freie Universität Berlin (1978).
Smith, P., 'Associative Harmony, Tonal Pairing, and Middleground Structure in Schumann's Sonata Expositions: The Role of the Mediant in the First Movements of the Piano Quintet, Piano Quartet, and "Rhenish" Symphony', in Roe-Min Kok and Laura Tunbridge (eds.), *Rethinking Schumann* (Oxford University Press, 2011), 235–64.
Solomon, Maynard, *Late Beethoven: Music, Thought and Imagination* (University of California Press, Berkeley, Los Angeles and London, 2003).
Steinberg, Michael P., 'Schumann's Homelessness', in R. Larry Todd (ed.), *Schumann and His World* (Princeton University Press, 1994), 47–79.
Struck, Michael, 'Litterarischer Eindruck, poetischer Ausdruck und Struktur in Robert Schumanns Instrumentalmusik', in Bernhard Appel (ed.), *Robert Schumann und die Dichter* (Droste, Düsseldorf, 1991), 111–22.
Summer, Averill Vanderipe, 'A Discussion and Analysis of Selected Unifying Elements in Robert Schumann's "Carnaval", Opus 9', unpublished dissertation, Indiana University (1979).

Swales, Martin, *The German Bildungsroman from Wieland to Hesse* (Princeton University Press, 1978).

Synofzik, Thomas, '" ... den ich nicht hätte herausgeben sollen ... " Robert Schumanns kompositorische Anfänge', in Gerd Nauhaus and Ingrid Bodsch (eds.), *Zwischen Poesie und Musik. Robert Schumann – früh und spät* (Stroemfeld, Frankfurt, 2006).

Tadday, Ulrich, 'Life and Literature, Poetry and Philosophy: Robert Schumann's Aesthetics of Music', in Beate Perrey (ed.), *The Cambridge Companion to Schumann* (Cambridge University Press, 2007), 38–47.

  Das schöne Unendliche: Ästhetik, Kritik, Geschichte der romantischen Musikanschauung (J. B. Metzler, Stuttgart, Weimar, 1999).

  ed., *Schumann Handbuch* (J. B. Metzler, Stuttgart, Weimar, 2006).

Taylor, Ronald, 'Formal Parallels in Literature and Music', *German Life and Letters*, 19 (1965–6), 10–18.

Thym, Jurgen, 'Schumann in Brendel's *Neue Zeitschrift für Musik* from 1845 to 1856', in Jon W. Finson and R. Larry Todd (eds.), *Mendelssohn and Schumann: Essays on Their Music and Its Context* (Duke University Press, Durham, NC, 1984), 21–36.

Todd, R. Larry, ed., *Mendelssohn and His World* (Princeton University Press, 1991).

  'On Quotation in Schumann's Music', in R. Larry Todd (ed.), *Schumann and His World* (Princeton University Press, 1994), 80–112.

  ed., *Schumann and His World* (Princeton University Press, 1994).

Treitler, Leo, *Music and the Historical Imagination* (Harvard University Press, Cambridge, Mass. and London, 1989).

Tudor, J. M., *Sound and Sense: Music and Musical Metaphor in the Thought and Writing of Goethe and His Age* (Peter Lang, Oxford, Bern and Berlin, 2011).

Tunbridge, Laura, 'Piano Works II: Afterimages', in Beate Perrey (ed.), *The Cambridge Companion to Schumann* (Cambridge University Press, 2007), 86–101.

Wadsworth, Benjamin K., 'Directional Tonality in Schumann's Early Works', *Journal of Music Theory Online*, 18.4 (2012).

Warner, Marina, *Phantasmagoria: Spirit Visions, Metaphor and Media* (Oxford University Press, 2006).

Watkins, Holly, 'The Floral Poetics of Schumann's Blumenstück, Op. 19', *19th-Century Music*, 36.1 (2012), 24–45.

  Metaphors of Depth in German Musical Thought: From E. T. A. Hoffmann to Arnold Schoenberg (Cambridge University Press, 2011).

Wendt, Matthias, ed., *Schumann und seine Dichter* (Schott Music, London, 1993).

Williamson, George S., *The Longing for Myth in Germany* (University of Chicago Press, 2004).

Wörner, Karl Heinrich, 'Schumanns *Kreisleriana*', in *Sammelbände der Robert Schumann Gesellschaft*, vol. II (VEB Deutscher Verlag für Musik, Leipzig, 1966), 58–65.

Worthen, John, *Robert Schumann: Life and Death of a Musician* (Yale University Press, New Haven, Conn., 2007).

Youens, Susan, 'The Cry of the *Schuhu*: Dissonant History in a Late Schumann Song', in Roe-Min Kok and Laura Tunbridge (eds.), *Rethinking Schumann* (Oxford University Press, 2011), 30–50.

Ziolkowski, Theodore, *German Romanticism and its Institutions* (Princeton University Press, 1990).

Žižek, Slavoj, *The Plague of Fantasies* (Verso, London, 2008).

Index

Abbate, C., 181, 185, 234, 237, 262, 268
Abrantes, 39
absolute music, 90, 239
Adam-Schmidmeier, E. von, 3, 152, 263
Aeolian harp, 185, 186
Agawu, K., 181, 235, 263
'Ah vous dirai-je, maman', 150, 151, 152, 154, 253
allegory, 186, 189
Allgemeine musikalische Zeitung, 2, 16
allusion, quotation in Schumann's music, 174–7
Alphonce, B., 130, 156, 157, 263
Altenburg, D., 90, 263
Anfossi, Pasquale, 221
Appel, B., 3, 4, 9, 10, 20, 22, 38, 65, 130, 163, 173, 195, 210, 215, 219, 234, 235, 263, 269, 272
Aristotle, 71, 84, 232
  and art as imitation, 84
  and form and matter, 71, 72
  and recognition, 59
  and substance, 85
Arnim, Achim von, 200
Arnsdorf, M. H., 4, 263
associations in music, 7, 19, 26, 27–8, 33, 73, 77, 80, 89, 152, 156, 174–9, 181, 184, 190, 223, 225, 227, 231, 233, 237
  in Schumann's works, 6, 7, 8, 27, 136, 140
    in *Carnaval*, 3, 38, 47, 69
    in *Fantasiestücke*, 92, 93, 95, 96, 121, 122
    in *Kreisleriana*, 164, 171
    in *Nachtstücke*, 5, 215, 223
    in *Novelletten*, 72, 173
Athenaeum, 227, 262
Augustine of Hippo (Saint), 189, 226
autobiography in music, 6, 47, 78, 110, 178, 200, 201
automatism, 186, 199, 200, 210–15, 229, 234, 238, 239, *see also* mechanical

Bach, C. P. E., 20, 74
Bach, J. S., 5, 138, 148, 152, 179, 248, *see also* Hoffmann on Bach
  'Goldberg' Variations, 6, 150–2, 155, 252
  in *Kreisleriana*, 136, 141, 152, 153, 155, 161, 162, 177, 178
  as studied by Schumann, 7, 25, 125–30, 136, 141, 146, 180
  Well-Tempered Clavier, 141, 146
Barnes, J., 71, 232, 263
Barthes, R., 185, 229, 264, 271
Becker, Julius, 89, 150
Beethoven, L. van, 20, 60, 74, 82, 89, 151, 174–8, 251, *see also* Hoffmann on Beethoven
  humour, 64, 234, 238
  influence on Schumann, 20, 21, 112, 123, 125–39
  late works, 7, 127–8, 179
  as seen in Schumann's writings, 29, 74, 98, 146, 148, 245, 246
  style, 20, 22, 74, 100, 103, 161, 162, 177, 230, 236, 237
  works
    An die ferne Geliebte, op. 98, 131, 136, 175, 176, 177, 220
    Cello Sonata, op. 102, 160
    Coriolanus Overture, op. 62, 76
    'Diabelli' Variations, op. 120, 127, 132
    Die Ruinen von Athen, op. 113, 131
    Egmont, op. 84, 76
    Piano Sonata no. 1, op. 2.1, 100, 108, 109
    Piano Sonata no. 12, op. 26, 201
    Piano Sonata no. 21, op. 53 ('Waldstein'), 97
    Piano Sonata no. 22, op. 54, 177
    Piano Sonata no. 28, op. 101, 132, 162, 163
    Piano Sonata no. 29, op. 106 ('Hammerklavier'), 125, 132
    Piano Sonata no. 32, op. 111, 135, 164, 165, 166
    String Quartet no. 12, op. 127, 125
    String Quartet no. 13, op. 130, 125

Beethoven, L. van (cont.)
  String Quartet no. 14, op. 131, 125
  String Quartet no. 15, op. 132, 125, 127, 161
  String Quartet no. 16, op. 135, 125
  Symphony no. 3, op. 55 ('Eroica'), 31
  Symphony no. 5, op. 67, 76, 86
  Symphony no. 6, op. 68 ('Pastoral'), 87
Bekker-Adden, M., 229, 230, 264
Benjamin, W., 229
Bent, I., 28, 29, 83, 149, 181, 182, 264, 267
Bergé, P., 100, 131, 231, 233, 235, 264
Berlinische musikalische Zeitung, 86
Berlioz, H., 17, 22, 77, 115, 149, 150, 236
  Symphonie Fantastique, 28, 30, 31, 33, 70, 71, 79, 80, 83, 244
  Waverley Overture, 77, 80
Bildungsroman, 15, 93, 122, 147, 200
Bischoff, B., 16, 125, 130, 131, 135, 164, 264
Blackall, E., 13, 14, 58, 146, 264
Boetticher, W., 100, 123, 129, 138, 264
Böhner, L., 142
Bonds, M. E., 70, 71, 72, 87, 181, 264
Botstein, L., 2, 264
Brahms, J., 90
Brecht, B., 229
Brendel, F., 2, 17, 19, 64, 78, 82, 89, 90, 91, 129, 130, 138, 192, 199, 235, 250, 251, 258
Brion, M., 34, 52, 59, 265
Brown, H. M., 86, 265
Brown, J. H., 20, 21, 125, 134, 135, 173, 265
Burkholder, J. P., 28, 265
Burnham, Scott, 16, 82, 187, 192, 261, 265, 269
Byrd, William, 32

Calasso, R., 229, 265
Callot, Jacques, 50, 66, 67, 68
Caplin, W. E., 231, 264
capriccio, 37, 38, 65
Carey, N., 3, 152, 154, 265
carnival, 1, 6, 34–69, 178, 179, 223, 229, 247
Carus, Agnes, 205, 206
Castle, Terry, 230
Cervantes, M., 20
Chailley, J., 3, 18, 34, 52, 67, 265
charlatan, 36, 47, 57
Charlton, D., 16, 149, 150, 181, 187, 265
Chernaik, J., 19, 45, 265
childlikeness as quality of artist, 104–5, 114
Chopin, F., 9, 14, 17, 34, 40, 44, 48, 54, 55, 60, 76, 114, 134, 136, 174, 186
  and Clara Wieck, 54
  Nocturne, op. 15.3, 138
  Piano Sonata, op. 35, 196, 201
  Preludes, op. 28, 76, 196, 202
Chua, D., 127, 128, 265
Claude Lorraine, 75
Cohn, R., 231, 265
Coleridge, Samuel Taylor, 185, 186
commedia dell'arte, 1, 22, 34, 35, 37, 40, 47, 49, 52, 68
compulsive behaviour, 14, 201, 204, 207, 208, 209, 229
conception (musical) or 'Geist', 80–3, 231, 233, 238
  in Liszt's words, 90
  in Schumann's music, 6, 72, 131, 135, 136, 140, 194, 195, 224, 234
    in *Carnaval*, 39
    in *Kreisleriana*, 136
    in *Nachtstücke*, 193, 197, 201
    in *Novelletten*, 72
  in Schumann's writings, 70–1, 139
  in von Seyfried, 89
content in music, 2, 4, 6, 7, 13, 70, 71, 73, 74–90, 131, 137, 139, 181, 184, 192, 224
Cook N., 183, 231, 232, 235, 265, 266
Cosimo, Piero di, 143
counterpoint, 21, 22, 24, 25, 130, 150, 167, *see also* Hoffmann on counterpoint
coupling as aspect of resonance, 27, 28, 224
Cramer, A., 95, 266
Crisp, D., 4, 170, 266
crystal as metaphor, 93, 94, 95, 96, 100, 118, 119, 122
culture as background to music, 5, 8, 10, 28, 175, 177, 226, 228–30, 231, 232, 237
  in Schumann's music, 6, 17, 27, 93, 123, 142, 178, 199, 210, 223, 224
  in Schumann's writings, 17, 77, 88, 227

Dahlhaus, C., 64, 86, 266
Daverio, J., 2, 3, 4, 9, 19, 22, 47, 65, 73, 103, 107, 131, 134, 136, 152, 171, 229, 266, 270
Davies, S., 184, 266
Day-O'Connell, J., 156, 266
Deahl, L. G., 4, 152, 153, 164, 171, 172, 266
defamiliarisation as artistic strategy, 13, 37, 73, 228, 229
Deleuze and Guattari, 229, 266
Dickson, S., 59, 189, 266
Diderot, D., 66, 144
digression as artistic strategy, 13, 20, 73, 128, 130
dissonance, 130, 132, 150, 231
  in *Carnaval*, 43, 45, 56, 61, 63

in *Fantasiestücke*, 94, 112
in *Kreisleriana*, 153, 157, 161
Dodd, J., 232, 266
Donizetti, G., 146
Draheim, J., 10, 266
drama in music, 74, 76, 77, 105, 106, 183, 184, 236
dreaming in Schumann's culture and music, 59, 93, 95, 104–5, 112, 122, 131, 230, 235, 236
in *Fantasiestücke*, 6, 91, 93, 114–19, 122, 223
Dürer, A., 142

'ear' as mental function, 29–31, 32, 75, 94
emotion in music, 75–6, 85–8
Empiricism, 11, 230, 231
Erler, H., 17, 80, 258
Ernestine von Fricken *see* Fricken, Ernestine von
Eschenburg, J., 10
expressive markings in Schumann, 138
expressiveness in music, 5–8, 26, 130, 136, 139, 174–92, 223, 225, 226, 228, 230, 231, 238
and form and content, 71–4, 90, 127
in Goethe's words, 170
in Hoffmann's words, 76, 213, 221
in Schumann's words, 27–33, 137
in Schumann's works
in *Fantasiestücke*, 224
in *Kreisleriana*, 144, 150, 152, 157, 161, 171, 223
in *Novelletten*, 173
extension in aesthetics, 30, 232, 233
'eye' as mental function, 29–31, 74, 75, 87, 88, 94

Fantini, B., 185, 265, 267
Ferris, D., 2, 180, 217, 267
Fichte, J. G., 11, 58, 59, 82, 200
Finson, J. W., 10, 267, 272, 273
Fischhof, J., 78, 79, 141
Fisk, C., 183, 267
Floros, C., 1, 90, 267
fluidity (das Flüssige), 30, 57, 122, 190–3, 197, 234, 235, 236–9
foreground analysis, 8, 231
Forkel, J. N., 71
form and structure, 2, 6–8, 20, 25, 30, 70–4, 80, 82–90, 138, 139, 190, 224, 231, 234, 235, 238, 244, 250
in Beethoven and Schumann, 127–31, 134, 179, 251

in *Carnaval*, 38, 41–2, 43, 48, 54, 64, 67, 139
in *Davidsbündlertänze*, 131
in *Fantasiestücke*, 92, 100, 105, 119, 123, 129
in *Fantasy*, op. 17, 130
in *Humoreske*, 195
in *Kreisleriana*, 153, 161, 171
in *Nachtstücke*, 197, 199
in *Novelletten*, 172–3
formal and stylistic parallels, 1, 3, 4, 7, 20, 21, 67, 70, 71–4, 149, 171, 192, 201, 210, 223, 224, 225
Freud, Sigmund, 207, 208, 229
Fricken, Ernestine von, 34, 47, 55, 206

'Geist' *see* conception (musical)
genre (musical), 8, 127, 135, 175, 179, 234
in *Carnaval*, 38, 65, 139
gesture (musical), 8, 30, 56, 60, 157, 160, 180, 181, 184, 231
in *Carnaval*, 38, 43, 60, 63, 66
Giani, M., 34, 46, 50, 65, 267
Goethe, J. W. von, 5, 10, 16, 17, 40, 59, 77, 81, 82, 103, 114, 146, 148, 170, 189, 200, 246
on carnival, 34, 35, 36, 37, 40, 50, 63, 66, 67, 247, 248
'Hexenszene', 111
impact on Schumann, 10
on symbolism, 184, 189–90
works
Die Leiden des jungen Werther, 104, 214
Egmont, 77, 173
Faust, 32, 104, 217
Hermann und Dorothea, 10, 56
Italienische Reise, 36, 40, 50, 64, 66, 248
'The Bride of Corinth', 214
Torquato Tasso, 15, 58, 96, 104, 147
Wilhelm Meisters Lehrjahre, 10, 15, 16, 40, 54, 83, 114, 119, 145, 146, 147, 200, 214, 221, 235
Gooley, D., 60, 152, 267
Gozzi, Carlo, 20, 34, 36, 37, 40, 50, 66, 67
Grey, T., 83, 267
Griepenkerl, F., 238
Gutman, R. W., 40, 267

Halski, C. R., 145, 267
Hanslick, E., 2, 90
Harmon, R., 123
Hatten, R., 56, 60, 132, 160, 226, 232, 267
Haydn, J., 20, 103, 126, 127, 177, 249, *see also* Hoffmann on Haydn
The Creation, 74
The Seasons, 74

Haydn, J. (cont.)
  String Quartet, op. 76.6, 167–9
Hegel, G. W. F., 11, 181, 189
Heine, H., 14, 37, 189
Heinse, W., 16, 81, 150, 217
Heller, K., 4, 120, 129, 267
Hepokoski, J., 100, 131, 231, 233, 235, 264
Heraclitus, 184
Herder, J. G., 30, 59, 181, 185, 189
Hering, H., 152, 268
Hero and Leander, 4, 79, 109–12, 124, 140, 225
Herttrich, E., 5, 123, 257
Hill, Susan, 209
Hiller, F., 181
Hirschbach, H., 138, 146
Hoeckner, B., 5, 136, 172, 173, 228, 268
Hoffmann, E. T. A., 10, 11, 12, 13
  on Bach, 126, 142, 144, 150–2, 187
  on Beethoven, 11, 76–7, 86–7, 100, 126, 142, 144, 248–9
  compositions, 14
  on counterpoint, 126, 141, 144, 148
  fictions, 13–15
  on 'Gemütlichkeit', 64–6
  on Haydn, 74, 126, 142, 249
  on 'Humor', 64–6
  on identity, 13, 52, 149
  impact on Schumann, 14–16
  on 'infinite yearning', 85–7
  on Mozart, 86, 126, 142, 144, 165, 249
  on music and drama, 76
  on music and emotion, 76
  music criticism, 16
  on Novalis, 12
  on pictorial music, 74
  on the 'Serapiontic Principle', 85–6
  works
    Aurora, 14
    'Das Fremde Kind', 93
    'Das Majorat', 218
    'Das steinerne Herz', 221
    'Datura Fastuosa', 14
    'Der Artushof', 146
    'Der Elementargeist', 111
    'Der goldne Topf', 15, 16, 93–124
    'Der Magnetiseur', 93
    'Der Sandmann', 15, 207–15
    'Die Automate', 93, 186, 213–14
    'Die Bergwerke zu Falun', 93
    'Die Geheimnisse', 111
    Die Serapions-Brüder, 14, 227, 235
    Fantasiestücke, 1, 4, 6, 91–124, 149
    Kater Murr, 4, 15, 171–3
    Kreisleriana, 1, 3, 6, 15, 141–72
    Meister Floh, 96, 122
    'Nachrichten von den neuesten Schicksalen des Hundes Berganza', 111
    Nachtstücke, 1, 4, 15, 199–222, 223
    Prinzessin Brambilla, 1, 3, 15, 16, 34–69
Hölderlin, F., 11, 16
  Empedocles, 147
  Hyperion, 150
Homer, 146, 238
Hotaki, L., 258, *see also* Schumann, Robert: Mottosammlung
humour in music, 4, 20, 26, 38, 60, 63–9, 92, 96, 110, 211, 238, *see also* Hoffmann on 'Humor', Jean Paul on 'Humor'
Hyer, B., 181, 268

'Idea' in aesthetics, 29, 30, 31, 33, 70, 71, 77, 80, 88, 89, 90, 130, 189
Idealist philosophy, 11, 12, 13, 14, 37, 54, 59, 60, 64, 70–1, 82, 87, 188, 200, 213, 229
  and recognition, 56–9
identity, plural or split, 10, 13, 36, 37, 38, 40, 48, 52, 57, 148, 149
infinite, indefinite *see* Unendlich
intension in aesthetics, 30, 232, 233
interleaving, 72, 171–3
irony in literature, 12, 13, 14, 15, 37, 73, 93, 111, 115, 149, 152, 187, 209, 221
irony in music, 20, 173, 177, 205, 210, 236
  in *Carnaval*, 55, 64, 69
  in *Fantasiestücke*, 109, 116, 140
  in *Kreisleriana*, 163
  in *Nachtstücke*, 201, 203, 209, 216, 217, 218
  in *Novelletten*, 173
Isis *see* Sais

Jacobi, F. H., 234
Jankélévitch, V., 237, 268
Jean Paul, 3, 5, 10, 13–17, 29, 36, 58, 70, 73, 75, 76, 95, 105, 191, 200, 222, 223, 229
  on allegory, 190
  on Besonnenheit, 64, 104, 143
  on form, content and transubstantiation, 83–5
  on genius, 81, 85, 143
  on 'Humor', 65–6
  on metaphor, 188–90, 227
  on Novalis, 84
  polymeters, 17–25
  works
    Die unsichtbare Loge, 13, 53
    Flegeljahre, 3, 13

Nachschule, 13
Titan, 13
Vorschule der Ästhetik, 13, 47, 70, 71, 78, 80–9, 95, 189, 191, 238
Jensen, E. F., 4, 18, 268
Jung, Carl, 207

Kahlert, August, 88, 89, 137, 200
Kaminsky, P., 3, 19, 38, 42, 49, 51, 131, 135, 179, 268
Kant, Immanuel, 12
Kapp, R., 2, 260, 268
Keferstein, G.A. ('K. Stein'), 73, 88, 152, 227, 235
Kerman, J., 127, 128, 268
key relationships and characters, 30, 127, 135, 235, *see also* tonality
  in *Carnaval*, 35, 56, 60
  in *Davidsbündlertänze*, 132
  in *Fantasiestücke*, 131
  in *Fantasy*, op. 17, 131
  in *Humoreske*, 195
  in *Kreisleriana*, 134, 152, 153, 160, 223
  in *Nachtstücke*, 197, 202, 203, 204, 209, 216, 220, 221
  in *Novelletten*, 173
Kinderman, W., 134, 268
Kircher, 'Pater', 192
Kleist, Heinrich von, 200, 213, 229
  Das Käthchen von Heilbronn, 111
Knapp, R., 27, 268
Knorr, Julius, 19
Köhler, H.-J., 195
Kolb, J., 149, 268
Konewka, Paul, 171
Kopp, D., 134, 135, 160, 235, 268
Korsyn, K., 236, 268
Koßmaly, Carl, 2, 4, 130, 194, 227, 260
Krahe, K., 12, 268
Kramer, L., 3, 28, 48, 56, 60, 64, 181, 184, 228, 229, 230, 237, 268, 269
Kranefeld, U., 83, 180, 226, 269
Krebs, H., 45, 103, 130, 134, 268, 269
Kristeva, J., 229, 230
Krüger, Eduard, 126, 181
Krümelchen *see* Schumann: plans for a novel: Hummel
Kruse, J. A., 9, 13, 17, 269
Kunstblatt, 80

Lacan, J., 229
Langer, S., 72, 189, 269
language and music, 181–5

Leipziger Tageblatt, 39
Leonardo da Vinci, 142
Lester, J., 16, 183, 231, 269
linear complexity in Schumann, 135, 136, 139, 197, 210, 220
Lipinski, Karol, 61
Lippman, E. A., 1, 19, 32, 136, 190, 269
Liszt, Franz, 3, 4, 54, 78, 89, 90, 130
Luther, Martin, 57

madness in literature, 10, 15, 119, 142, 143, 146, 147, 149, 156, 200, 209
Mann, Thomas, 229
Marpurg, F. W., 17, 146
Marschner, Heinrich, 76
Marston, N., 3, 125, 127, 128, 131, 229, 269
Marx, A. B., 58, 72, 80, 82, 83, 88, 261, 265
'material' in aesthetics, 31, 70, 71, 80, 82, 83–9, 139, 189, 192
Maus, F. E., 28, 149, 183, 269
Mayeda, A., 19, 269
meaning in music, 2, 137, 181–4, 188, 192, 237
mechanical, 16, 49, 50, 85, 122, 195, 199, 201, 210–15, 220, 225, 229
mediocrity in art, 10, 17, 144–6
Meier, B., 4, 152, 270
Mendelssohn, Felix, 175, 192
  Melusine Overture, 77, 80
  Midsummer Night's Dream Overture, 107
Menzel, Wolfgang, 234
Messing, S., 60, 270
metals in German culture, 93, 96, 100, 107, 110, 111, 112
metaphor *see also* symbolism
  in art, 188–9
  in musicology, 236, 237
metre and rhythm in the 'Hoffmann works', 8, 25, 130, 131, 179, 194, 224, 232, 235, 236
  in *Carnaval*, 38, 42, 44, 45, 46, 49, 50, 51, 53, 54, 55, 56, 60, 61, 63, 69, 178
  in *Fantasiestücke*, 92, 101, 102, 103, 106, 112, 116, 119, 120, 179
  in *Kreisleriana*, 153, 156, 157, 160, 161, 168
  in *Nachtstücke*, 201, 203, 211, 212, 215, 218
Michaelis, C. F., 73, 86, 190, 226, 250
Michelangelo, 142
middleground analysis, 231
Moraal, C. C., 4, 73, 160, 170, 210, 219, 220, 270
Morgan, R. P., 236, 270
Moritz, Karl Philipp, 146, 182, 197, 200, 210
  Anton Reiser, 182, 197, 200, 214, 217
  Die neue Cecilia, 145
Moscheles, Ignaz, 77, 80, 137, 138

Mozart, W. A., 17, 31, 36, 40, 42, 105, 127, 227, 246, *see also* Hoffmann on Mozart
  Don Giovanni, 30
  String Quartet in D minor, K421, 25
  Symphony no. 40 in G minor, 165
  Variations, K. 265, 154
Münch, S., 3, 152, 270
Murki, 145, 163, 253
Musaeus, 109, *see also* Hero and Leander
Musgrave, M., 9, 270
music as metaphor, 183
music as translation of content, 31, 74, 88, 181, 182, 224
music as transmutation of content, 31, 74, 75, 77, 83–90, 189, 224
musical symbols in literature, 149–51
Muxfeldt, K., 229, 236, 270

Nachtwachen von Bonaventura, 59, 147, 150, 200, 217
Napoleon Bonaparte, 14, 66
narrative in music, 78, 138, 183, 184, 225
  in Schumann's music, 4, 89, 124
    in *Carnaval*, 66, 67, 68, 138, 139
    in *Fantasiestücke*, 123, 124, 140
    in *Kreisleriana*, 171
    in *Nachtstücke*, 140, 210, 218, 222
    in *Papillons*, 17–20, 139
  in Schumann's writings, 77, 80
Nattiez, J-J., 3, 183, 270
Nauhaus, G., 9, 10, 258, 270, 273
Neergaard, B., 19, 270
'Nel cor mi non piu sento', 150, 151
Neue Zeitschrift für Musik, 9, 16, 64, 90
Newcomb, A., 2, 28, 72, 90, 136, 174, 183, 194, 226, 264, 270
Niecks, F., 79, 271
Nissen, G. N. von, 17
Novalis, 5, 10–13, 16, 22, 54, 58, 59, 70, 81, 82, 115, 146, 148, 185–8, 190, 227, 229, 235, 238, 240
  on analysis, 234, 238
  on dreaming, 114
  on fable, 115
  on fluidity, 191, 192
  impact on Schumann, 11, 12, 244
  on mediocrity, 146
  on music, 75, 187
  on philistines, 146
  on primal state, 58, 114, 188
  on recognition, 57
  works
    Die Lehrlinge zu Sais, 57, 104, 114, 187, 190
    Heinrich von Ofterdingen, 12, 13, 15, 93, 95, 114
    'Monolog', 12, 191, 228, 243
    Tieck's edition, 11, 12, 14, 187, 242

O'Brien, W. A., 59, 187, 188, 213, 271
Offenbach, J., 215
Oken, Lorenz, 53
organicism in music, 82, 83, 128
orphan status of music, 88
Otto, F., 13, 22, 65, 271
overtones, 6, 27, 28, 40, 60, 123, 130, 179, 186, 224
Ovid, 20, 74

Paganini, Niccolo, 14, 15, 34, 39, 40, 60, 61, 68, 136, 174, 186
parody in music, 22, 63, 64, 116, 146, 163, 195, 215
Paul (Saint), 57
Paulin, R., 15, 104, 271
Pederson, S., 90, 182, 271
Perrey, B. J., 29, 266, 268, 269, 271, 273
Perry, M., 17, 130, 157, 271
Pfau, T., 53, 271
philistinism, 6, 10, 17, 40, 59, 63, 64, 105, 142, 144–6, 150, 162
phrase structure in Schumann's works, 22, 100, 121, 220, 235
pictorial music, 5, 67, 68, 74–8, 123, 137, 201, 210, 225, 251
Pindar, 97
pitch level, 224, 230
Plantinga, L. B., 28, 271
plastic music, 29–31, 74, 246
Plato, 187, 230
Plotinus, 59
plurality of interpretation, 224–7
'poetic music', 6, 17, 20, 28, 83, 122, 239
  in Bach, 152
  and content, 78, 89, 184
  and 'Geist', 81, 82
  for Schumann's contemporaries, 85, 89–90, 251
  in Schumann's music, 17, 129, 130, 171, 194, 201, 236, 239
  in Schumann's writings, 6, 29, 30, 31, 33, 64, 70, 87, 125, 126, 179, 210, 235, 236
  on Chopin, 76
pot-pourri as musical form, 38, 41

Prawer S. S., 207, 271
primal humanity, 22, 58, 59, 95, 115, 126, 186, 187, 188, 189, 191, 230, 238
programmes in music, 6, 190, 238, 239, 246
    for Schumann's contemporaries, 90
    in Schumann's music, 1, 4, 7, 20, 67, 70, 90, 124, 140, 223, 224
        in *Carnaval*, 3
        in *Fantasiestücke*, 4, 110, 123, 124
        in *Kreisleriana*, 171
        in *Nachtstücke*, 201, 218
        in *Papillons*, 19, 139
    in Schumann's writings, 30, 78–90, 225
Proteus, 188, 238, 242
Proust, Marcel, 226

Rabelais, 66, 230
Raphael, 142
Rastelli, A., 34, 271
recognition, 10, 36, 37, 38, 55–9, 66, 82
Recognition of Sakuntala, by Kalidasa, 59
Reiman, E., 3, 13, 38, 60, 64, 67, 73, 229, 262, 271
relativity of interpretation, 225, 226
Rellstab, Ludwig, 18, 19, 20, 25, 79, 80, 139, 238
resonance between music and culture, 6, 27–8, 30, 90, 175, 177–9, 185, 190–2, 213, 223, 224, 225, 227, 233, 239
    in *Carnaval*, 66, 179
    in *Fantasiestücke*, 93, 94, 123
    in *Fantasy*, op. 17, 177
    in *Kreisleriana*, 6, 142, 153, 160, 170, 171
    in *Nachtstücke*, 5, 213, 229
    in *Papillons*, 139
Reynolds, C. A., 175, 190, 271
Richards, A., 20, 221, 271
Ritter, J. W., 30
Rochlitz, J. F., 16, 192
Rodgers, S., 156, 271
Roesner, L. C., 123, 205, 272
rondo form, 96, 102, 123, 197, 203, 204, 209, 219, 220, 229
Rosen, Charles, 3, 4, 26, 46, 51, 94, 130, 131, 135, 154, 160, 166, 168, 170, 172, 182, 184, 187, 231, 235, 237, 272
Rousseau, J. J., 181, 217
Rumph, S., 87, 272
Russian Formalists, 229

Sais (Temple of Isis), 148, 149
Sanskrit, 59, 126, 187, 191, 242
Schelling, Dorothea, 11

Schelling, F., 11, 53, 58, 59, 82, 200, 229
schemata in music, 6, 18, 20, 31, 72, 78–80, 89, 90, 123, 138, 201, 223, 246, 251, *see also* programmes in music
Schenker, H., 226, 231
Schiller, F., 17, 36, 72, 75, 77, 181, 182, 190, 192
Schlegel, A. W., 10, 11, 75, 227
Schlegel, F., 11, 12, 13, 53, 84, 228, 229, 234
Schleiermacher, F., 11
Schmalfeldt, J., 236, 272
Schoenberg, Arnold, 25, 272
Schroeder, S., 184, 272
Schubart, C. F. D., 234
Schubert, F., 14, 21, 31, 60, 74, 79, 87, 88, 125, 134, 136, 174, 183
    'Der Schmetterling', 53
    German Dances, 40
    'Great' C major Symphony, 228, 250
    Impromptu, op. 90.3, 174
Schubring, Adolf, 2, 238
Schumann, Clara *see* Wieck, Clara
Schumann, Eduard, 195, 196, 201, 217
Schumann, Emilie, 52, 258
Schumann, Robert
    acquaintance with philosophy, 11–13, 244
    agitated depression, 34, 110, 147, 217
    on the 'art-historical ball', 40, 53
        Ambrosia, 112
        Beda, 40, 53, 54
        de Knapp, 40, 60
    and the 'butterfly' metaphor, 19, 34, 53, 125
    and 'Davidsbund', 17
    and the 'eagle' metaphor, 105, 125, 177
    and Eusebius, 17, 40, 52, 138, 226
    'Faschingsschwänke', 41
    features of his music. *See under* allusion, dissonance, expressiveness, form and structure, genre, gesture, irony, key relationships, linear complexity, metre and rhythm, phrase structure, sonority, texture, tonality, use of titles, use of words
    and Florestan, 17, 34, 39, 40, 51–2, 53, 61, 114, 138, 146, 226
    on Lebenszustände, 75
    loneliness, 147
    music criticism. *See Neue Zeitschrift für Musik*
    plans for a novel, 9, 15, 16, 39, 61, 122
        Caecilia, 15, 16, 123
        Eusebius, 15
        Florestan, 15, 16, 122

Schumann, Robert (cont.)
   Hummel, 15, 16, 123
   Paganini, 61
   Raro, 15, 16, 123
   Seraphine, 16, 123
   Zilia, 15, 61, 123
  and Raro, 17, 226
  reading, 9–16
  on Seelenzustände, 75, 181
  stylistic evolution, 7, 20–5, 124, 125–40, 194, 223
  works
   Albumblätter, op. 124, 72, 202
   Arabesque, op. 18, 194
   Blumenstück, op. 19, 194
   Brautbuch, 194
   Bunte Blätter, op. 99, 72
   Carnaval, op. 9, 1, 2, 3, 4, 6, 26, 33, 34–69, 78, 91, 123, 124, 125, 129–40, 175, 178, 179, 180, 186, 194, 223, 227, 229
   Davidsbündlertänze, op. 6, 123, 128, 129, 131–3, 139, 175, 205, 224, 230, 235
   Dichtergarten, 12, 14, 104, 126, 213, 248
   Dichterliebe, op. 48, 121, 202
   Drei Romanzen, op. 28, 194
   'Eichendorff' *Liederkreis* op. 39, 173
   Fantasiestücke, op. 12, 1, 2, 4, 6, 79, 80, 90, 91–124, 125, 128–30, 131, 138, 148, 175, 177, 178, 179, 223, 224, 230, 231, 251
   'In der Nacht', 1, 4, 79, 89–90, 91, 92, 105–12, 113, 118, 121, 123, 129, 225
   Fantasy, op. 17, 5, 128, 130, 131, 136, 175, 176, 177, 224, 230, 235
   Faschingsschwank aus Wien, op. 26, 3, 194, 196
   Four Pieces, op. 32, 22, 107, 136, 170, 194
   'Hoffmann works', 1, 2, 7, 27, 33, 70, 71, 72, 79, 83, 174, 184, 192, 223, 230, 236
   Humoreske, op. 20, 65, 129, 135, 163, 194–5, 224
   Impromptus, op. 5, 26
   Intermezzi, op. 4, 7, 22–6, 79, 136
   Kinderszenen, op. 15, 128, 138, 157, 160, 194, 251
   Kreisleriana, op. 16, 1, 3, 4, 6, 26, 72, 89, 124, 128–40, 141–73, 174, 177, 178, 192, 193, 197, 223, 224, 227, 230, 231, 235
   'Leides Ahnung', 202
   Mottosammlung, 12, 53, 105, 178
   Myrthen, op. 25, 103
   Nachtstücke, op. 23, 1, 2, 4, 5, 6, 26, 80, 124, 130, 136, 139, 140, 193, 194–222, 223, 225, 227, 229, 231, 233
   Novelletten, op. 21, 128, 129, 172–3
   Papillons, op. 2, 1, 2, 7, 17–20, 25, 39, 53, 70, 79, 80, 90, 124, 129, 130, 135, 139, 140, 175, 178, 223
   Piano Sonata in F minor, 128
   Piano Sonata in G minor, op. 22, 128
   Variations on the Name Abegg, op. 1, 9
Schumann, Therese, 17, 147, 196
Schunke, L., 48
Schütze, Stephan, 73
Scruton, R., 33, 78, 272
Seyfried, Ignaz von, 3, 89
Shakespeare, W., 5, 10, 11, 16, 17, 20, 31, 77, 146, 246
  Comedy of Errors, 57
  Hamlet, 10, 82, 127, 217, 235
  Much Ado About Nothing, 185
  The Tempest, 10, 114
  Twelfth Night, 10, 57, 114
Shelley, P. B., 186
Simonett, H. P., 3, 50, 53, 272
Sire, Simonin de, 65, 125, 141, 148
Smith, P., 134, 272
Solidist physiology, 185
Solomon, M., 22, 272
sonata form, 92, 100, 127, 135
sonority in the 'Hoffmann works', 8, 51, 92–6, 112, 118, 123, 178, 179, 223, 224, 231, 232
Sphinxes in *Carnaval*, 34, 35, 38, 46–9, 51, 53, 55, 59, 61, 62, 63, 67, 125, 180
Spohr, L., 79
Steinberg, M. P., 210, 269, 272
Sterndale Bennett, W., 32
Struck, M., 1, 272
Sublime, the, 20, 73
Summer, A., 3, 272
Swales, M., 15, 273
symbolism in aesthetics and music, 30, 107, 139, 179, 182, 184, 190, 195, 199, 238, 239, *see also* Goethe on symbolism
  in *Kreisleriana*, 143, 144, 149, 150, 151, 152, 155, 157, 171, 172
sympathetic vibration, 27, 60, 185, 186
Synofzik, T., 18, 34, 257, 258, 273

Tadday, U., 1, 4, 9, 12, 29, 84, 86, 90, 109, 182, 226, 273
Taylor, R., 73, 273
texture
  in Beethoven, 127
  in C. P. E. Bach, 20

in Schumann's works, 8, 24, 135, 136, 139, 231
   in *Carnaval*, 56
   in *Davidsbündlertänze*, 132
   in *Fantasiestücke*, 92, 94, 96, 101, 103, 113
   in *Humoreske*, 194
   in *Kreisleriana*, 159, 162, 163
   in *Nachtstücke*, 202, 210, 219
theory and theoretical models, 6, 8, 27, 81, 183, 184, 230–4, 236
Thibaut, A. F. J., 146
thought in music, 181–2
threads in music, 4, 7, 19, 28, 77, 83, 89, 91, 122, 138, 139, 159, 177, 180, 194, 225, 235, 238
Thym, J., 90, 273
Tieck, Ludwig, 11–12, 15, 20, 34, 37, 65, 67, 77, 104, 142, 182, 187, 229, 237
   'Der blonde Eckbert', 11, 209
   Der gestiefelte Kater, 39, 41
   Der Phantasus, 11, 227
   'Der Pokal', 11, 200, 222
   'Der Runenberg', 93, 147, 200
   'Die Töne', 182, 185, 187, 192, 234
   Franz Sternbalds Wanderungen, 11, 15
   'Liebeszauber', 200
   Novalis, Schriften. See Novalis: Tieck's edition
   William Lovell, 147
Tiepolo, G. D., 36, 37
Todd, R. Larry, 2, 136, 264, 267, 271, 272, 273
Tolstoy, L., 229
tonality in Schumann's works, 8, 73, 130–5, 195, 224, 230–1, 235, 238, 263, 265, *see also* key relationships
   in *Carnaval*, 3, 38, 41, 42, 43, 48, 51, 52, 55, 138, 139
   in *Fantasiestücke*, 91, 92, 123, 223
   in *Humoreske*, 194
   in *Kreisleriana*, 6, 152–3, 160–2, 179, 223
   in *Nachtstücke*, 199, 202, 215, 219
'translate' *see* music as translation of content; music as transmutation of content
transubstantiation, 85, *see also* music as transmutation of content
trauma, 208, 229
Treitler, L., 231, 232, 273
Tudor, J. M., 181, 273
Tunbridge, L., 128, 136, 167, 171, 173, 267, 268, 273, 274

Uhlig, Theodor, 90
uncanny, the, 205–10, 212, 213–15, 218

Unendlich, 70, 191, 238
   in Brendel, 250, 251
   in Goethe, 189
   in Hoffmann, 85, 86, 248, 249
   in Jean Paul, 85, 191
   in music, 192
   in Novalis, 57, 191
   in Schiller, 192
Ursatz, 230
use of titles in music, 1, 28, 30, 65, 78, 90, 131, 137, 139, 177, 180, 183, 184
   in the 'Hoffmann works', 1, 224
   in *Carnaval*, 3, 175
   in *Fantasiestücke*, 4, 91, 94, 100, 114, 119, 122, 123, 129, 138
   in *Kreisleriana*, 4, 142, 178
   in *Nachtstücke*, 5, 196, 200, 201, 210, 213, 215, 218, 220
use of words in scores, 136–9

variation sets, 6, 150, 151, 154
Virgil, 238
Voigt, Henriette, 2, 48, 148, 206
Voltaire, 66

Wackenroder, W., 11, 58, 76, 86, 182, 185, 237
   'Die Wunder der Tonkunst', 54, 104, 234
   Herzensergießungen, 15, 96, 98, 104, 142, 143, 146
Wadsworth, B. K., 52, 134, 235, 273
Warner, M., 40, 273
Watkins, H., 1, 2, 5, 22, 29, 30, 84, 146, 180, 185, 187, 189, 190, 199, 203, 227, 273
Webster, J., 100, 233, 264
Weill, Kurt, 229
Wendt, M., 15, 273
Whistling, F., 142
Wieck, Clara, 15, 39, 48, 123
   and Chopin, 54
   as commenting on Schumann's music, 171, 194, 196, 219
   as composer, 61, 91, 136, 174
   'Nocturne', op. 6, 55, 172–3
   and Paganini, 61
   as pianist, 65
   as Schumann's beloved, 9, 34, 50, 55, 109–12, 123, 131, 147, 205, 206, 214, 217
   as Schumann's correspondent, 4, 28, 71, 79, 120, 121, 125, 141, 147, 148, 195, 225
   as Schumann's editor, 164

Wieck, Clara (cont.)
    Soirées Musicales, op. 6, 54
    Valses Romantiques, op. 4, 60
Wieck, Friedrich, 9, 14, 64, 78, 217
Williamson, G. S., 114, 273

Youens, S., 190, 274

Zeitung für die elegante Welt, 2, 51
Zelter, C. F., 77, 126, 146, 170, 190
Ziolkowski, T., 15, 93, 146, 147, 227, 274
Žižek, S., 229, 274
Zumsteeg, J. R., 120–1, 174, 175